S0-GXL-432

# CRITICAL RESPONSES TO JOSIAH ROYCE, 1885–1916

## Volume 2

Edited and Introduced by
Randall E. Auxier
Southern Illinois University, Carbondale

**History of American Thought**

# Critical Responses to Josiah Royce, 1885–1916

Edited and Introduced by **Randall E. Auxier**
*Southern Illinois University, Carbondale*



Printed in England by Antony Rowe Ltd, Chippenham

# REVIEWS AND ARTICLES

With an Introduction by
Randall E. Auxier

THOEMMES PRESS

Published by Thoemmes Press, 2000

Thoemmes Press
11 Great George Street
Bristol BS1 5RR, England

Thoemmes Press US Office
22883 Quicksilver Drive
Sterling, Virginia 20166, USA

http://www.thoemmes.com

Critical Responses to Josiah Royce, 1885–1916
3 Volumes : ISBN 1 85506 833 8

Selection and Introduction © Randall E. Auxier, 2000

*British Library Cataloguing-in-Publication Data*
A CIP record of this title is available from the British Library

All rights reserved. No part of this publication may be reproduced, stored in a retrieval system, or transmitted in any way or by any means, electronic, mechanical, photocopying, recording or otherwise, without the written permission of the copyright holder. Enquiries should be addressed to the Publisher.

This book is printed on acid-free paper, sewn, and cased in a durable buckram cloth.

# CONTENTS

# INTRODUCTION

In 1902, a twenty-two-year-old college junior named Helen Keller wrote: "This year is the happiest because I am studying subjects that especially interest me, economics, Elizabethan literature, Shakespeare under Professor George L. Kittredge, and the History of Philosophy under Professor Josiah Royce. Through philosophy one enters with sympathy of comprehension into the traditions of remote ages and other modes of thought, which erewhile seemed alien and without reason." It is a valuable exercise, perhaps, to follow one's imagination to Royce's classroom at Radcliffe, a smallish group of young women variously listening, scribbling down phrases and sentences from the lecture, their eyes occasionally glazing over at the avalanche of abstractions being variously linked and torn asunder before them. And in the corner, one very different pupil who could neither hear nor see what Professor Royce was saying, an assistant spelling out his words on her hand as quickly as he said them. Helen Keller's access to Royce, the living teacher, is somewhat analogous to the access we have to him today. He is neither seen nor heard in the present, but the words remain. Yet the words alone cannot convey the man. To the extent he is present to us, it is because we learn to imagine him, just as Helen Keller was obliged to do. She learned from Royce that what seemed alien and distant can be made familiar by the power of "sympathy of comprehension." And it is sympathy of comprehension the reader of the present volume needs to bring Royce back to life. If the reader will allow, I would seek to evoke that sympathy here at the outset. But perhaps it is not an everyday sympathy we require.

Keller's "response to Royce" included also the following general observation:

> College is not the universal Athens I thought it was. There one does not meet the great and the wise face to face; one does not even feel their living touch. They are there, it is true; but they seem mummified. We must extract them from the crannied wall of learning and dissect and analyze them before we can be sure we have a Milton or an Isaiah, and not merely a clever imitation. Many scholars forget, it seems to me, that our enjoyment of great works of literature depends

> more upon the depth of our sympathy than upon our understanding... . Again and again I ask impatiently: "Why concern myself with these explanations and hypotheses?" They fly hither and thither in my thought like blind birds beating the air with ineffectual wings. I do not mean to object to a thorough knowledge of the famous works we read. I object only to the interminable comments and bewildering criticisms that teach but one thing: there are as many opinions as there are men. (*The Story of My Life*, ch. XX)

One wonders if Keller had just finished Royce's lecture on Kant when she wrote this, a true test of nearly anyone's sympathy and patience. But if this is Keller's final view of the matter, I think we would have to conclude Royce failed her as a teacher. The present volume is precisely a collection of the sort of writing Keller found so exasperating – comments and bewildering criticisms, sometimes seeming to lack a fully developed sympathy for Royce, and *apparently* offering even less mercy to the reader's need to develop such sympathy.

But is Keller right to claim that our sympathies need to be activated first? What kind of sympathy? Why not engage our critical abilities first, saving our sympathies for whatever may withstand our criticism? There is an important difference between the sympathy of intellectual good will, which is generated out of a shared love of truth, and sympathy that comes from an ability to share humanely a common viewpoint. Perhaps Royce did not communicate to Keller Aristotle's valuable insight, who, finding himself obliged to disagree with a fundamental aspect of his teacher's doctrine, said:

> We had perhaps better consider the universal good and discuss thoroughly what is meant by it, although such an inquiry is made an uphill one by the fact that the Forms have been introduced by friends of our own. Yet, it would perhaps be thought to be better, indeed to be our duty, for the sake of maintaining the truth even to destroy what touches us closely, especially as we are philosophers or lovers of wisdom; for, while both are dear, piety requires us to honor truth above our friends. (NE 1096a10–16)

Here Aristotle considers the importance of the sort of humane sympathy of which Keller speaks, and on the whole decides that serving truth is the higher calling. There is no question that Royce's life is a testament to this higher calling. Much published criticism and commentary is indeed the ineffectual beating of wings, but none of that is to be found in this volume. Royce's best "friends" were also his keenest critics, achieving a different kind of sympathy, a sort that only an unswerving servant of truth can ever grasp. Whether Keller later grasped this I cannot say (we must not be overly quick to judge someone twenty-two years old), but what I can state with some confidence is that Royce's presentation of Kant, or whomever, was not a blind and ineffectual beating of his wings, and that Kant would have called Royce a "philosopher" for having held truth above friendship.

The selections in this volume are chosen on this very criterion. Royce was challenged to his very soul by the comments and criticism contained herein, but he understood from the outset that the cost of placing truth above friendship, emotionally and spiritually, can be quite dear. Contrast, however, Keller's impression with the assessment of George Herbert Mead, in a piece from this volume, as he reflected upon his own youthful response to Royce:

> To youths of such minds and attitudes Professor Royce opened up the realm of romantic idealism. What had been barriers of thought became but hazards in the game. Contradictions, instead of marking the no thoroughfares of reflection, became the guide posts toward higher levels of reality... . The predominant impression he left upon me was of clear ideas and luminous vistas, of subtle athleticism of thought, and an inexhaustible universe of explication and illustrations.

It seems that blind birds to one can be luminous vistas to another. What seem mere opinions to one can be moments of dialectic to another. As Mead put it, "to have achieved dialectic was to have won a liberty" worth defending. And in that "challenging forth," Mead seems to have found the higher sympathy I mentioned earlier: "...I received an impression from him of freedom of mind, and of dominance of thought in the universe, of a clear, unclouded landscape of spiritual reality where we sat like gods together – but not careless of mankind – and it was a vision that followed me for many years." But Mead was a great philosopher; Keller a great humanitarian. One seeks what is most divine; the other what is most humane. Both are dear, but as Aristotle says, piety requires us to honor truth above our friends. I hope these selections, critical as they often are, may be deemed the offerings of pious philosophers.

Randall E. Auxier

# REVIEW OF *THE RELIGIOUS ASPECT OF PHILOSOPHY*

Samuel Alexander, Review of *The Religious Aspect of Philosophy*, *Mind*, vol. 10, old series (1885).

*The Religious Aspect of Philosophy: A Critique of the Bases of Conduct and of Faith.* By Josiah Royce, Ph.D., Instructor in Philosophy in Harvard College. Boston: Houghton, Mifflin, 1885. Pp. xix., 484.

Dr. Royce's book may be described as an essay on the Limits of Doubt. It is concerned principally with the limits of doubt in respect of religion, though necessarily, as the preface tells us, it sketches the basis of a whole system of philosophy. Dr. Royce's attitude towards his own and other people's thoughts and theories is that of a thorough sceptic; but what he claims to prove is that, if you only doubt honestly and as far as doubting can go, you arrive at a positive truth, scanty if it be. A great deal of doubting takes us away from God, but a little more brings us near to him again. For have we not a final question to put: What is the meaning of there being such a thing as doubt at all? And the answer to this question is that doubt can exist only in relation to something which is above all doubt, so that scepticism if pushed to an extremity is seen to be limited by idealism.

Of what nature this idealism is, and how the ultimate truth is related to the doubts and errors which lead up to it, remains to be seen. The above is merely an indication of the method pursued. The thought implied in this metaphysic of doubt or error is, of course, a very simple one: it is the positive form of the old negative saying that a thorough-going scepticism contradicts itself. But the problem of philosophy receives a new light from being put in this connexion, and the thought is worked out with a freshness and independence of mind which make it original in the best sense. Dr. Royce gets at his own results in his own way, and this gives his book a real interest and stimulus. His manner has merits corresponding: he writes a vigorous and clear style, quite unencumbered with technicalities; but its most striking quality is its imaginativeness (which, however, now and then betrays him into melodrama). He prefers to take his illustrations from poets rather than from philosophers, and there are some admirable philosophical essays on literature in the course of the work, especially the account of Romanticism (pp. 110 ff.) and of *Faust*.

The book falls into two parts, which are applications of the method described to Ethics and Speculative Philosophy respectively. These problems arise out of two of the three elements involved in religion, the moral, the theoretic and the emotional. "A religion must teach some moral code, must in some way inspire a strong feeling of devotion to that code, and in so doing must show something in the nature of things that answers to the code or serves to reinforce the feeling" (p. 4). Its question is: "Is there, then, anywhere in the universe, any real thing of Infinite worth?" and the answer must supply an object of theoretic belief, which shall also be an ideal of action and thereby inspire with feeling; or, following the order which is of most importance to religion, it must supply an ideal, which shall be verified by a theory of things.

Beginning then with the moral element, Dr. Royce passes in review all the ideals of action that men have proposed to themselves. All these fail to satisfy him because they depend ultimately on a "physical fact" and have no guarantee besides this "fact of human nature." Thus Plato's ideal, in spite of its "deeper significance, is not complete nor consistent." It can offer no inducement to be just except the pains that accompany injustice and the misery which the wicked soul must suffer. Who knows whether the tyrant may not be the happier? And, in any case, is not ideal justice, founded on the constitution of the soul, a bare physical fact which might have been different? It is the same with Christianity: for the morality of Jesus, considered as morality, is founded on a peculiar insight that each man is to have into the duty of returning the divine love (p. 45). Why should this unearned love be gratefully returned? The only reason is "the physical fact that man often feels gratitude." Or again, if the ideal of action is to act by conscience, "why is conscience right?" (p. 57). Conscience or the moral sense as such, only happens to be what it is; often it prompts to wrong, and it might for all we know have been different. It is plain that ideals founded on sympathy and pity are open to the same criticism: we may and we may not feel sympathy or pity. And still more with ideals of pleasure, whether egoistic or altruistic: we want to know why it is right to be unselfish, not whether it will assure happiness. Thus all the ideals require a judge to decide between them, and failing that they are in a state of warfare with each other. It is the scepticism which this warfare produces which reappears as pessimism, the ground of which is "not so much in the hopelessness of our efforts to reach our ideals once chosen, as in our perpetual hesitation in the choice of ideals" (p. 108). We feel indecision only because we sympathise with two opposing wills, both of which are united at one moment in our will (p. 133). Hence this very scepticism about our ideals implies a higher ideal than all, namely, the harmony of all conflicting aims. Complete ethical scepticism ends therefore with a principle which Dr. Royce expresses thus: "Act always in the light of the completest insight into all the aims that thy act is to effect" (p. 141); or again (p. 148), "In so far as in thee lies, act as if thou wert at once thy neighbour and thyself." This is the "moral insight," or full realisation of the wills of others, in contradistinction to the merely formal and external way in which we ordinarily realise them. On this principle may be founded two precepts for the guidance of life: the first a formal one, "Extend the moral insight among men and in thy own life"; or, "So act as to increase the number of those who possess the insight": the other concrete (p. 211), "Organise all life," in the service of the ideal required by the moral insight. This ideal is a Will which is the absolute unity of life and will include activities, such as those now devoted to Beauty, Knowledge and the State, that claim from those who own them freedom from selfishness. Such an ideal is even now partially realised in scientific activities.

In judging moral ideals by the test whether they are merely capricious or affairs of the individual, which "are" but contain no "ought," Dr. Royce is undoubtedly right. It amounts to the claim that the law of morality should be objective and independent of the particular person, and all moral ideals founded upon sentiment fail to satisfy this test. Dr. Martineau, by including in conscience an objective reference, has in part met the charge in this case; though it is very questionable whether even this objective conscience is more than the representative in sentiment of something which is not a matter of feeling at all. But Dr. Royce's criticisms of Plato and Christianity are more difficult. As to the latter, it seems difficult to separate the ethical from the theological view, and if the ethical belief of Jesus is to be stated as a theory and as a matter of "religious insight," it should at least receive the benefit of its metaphysical basis; and, so understood, to do God's will from love of him is hardly the same as following the instinct of gratitude. As to the former, it is true that Plato's theory is based on an analysis of human nature as it is; but then the problem to be solved – the nature of the good – is different with him from our problem – "what is there which is binding?" – and at any rate Plato's ideal is not a physical fact in the sense that it is the satisfaction of a caprice. These distinctions needed stating.

But the chief difficulty is in the final conclusion. It is true that the indecision as to which of several ends is the true one implies that there is an end, but is this end therefore "the harmony of all the conflicting aims"? The true ideal must indeed harmonise all ideals in the sense that it includes them: that is, given the former it becomes apparent how the latter can be entertained. But this is a conception which Dr. Royce disapproves in the case of Mill and Herbert Spencer when they seek to find confirmation for their own theories in those of others; though, when on p. 176 Dr. Royce himself says that Hedonism is the product of an imperfect understanding of the moral insight, he seems to be winning assent for his view by the same means. If, on the other hand, the ideal contains all other ideals in the same way as, according to Dr. Royce's belief (to be described later), the absolute consciousness contains error included in truth, this is true; but it does not follow from the warfare of the ideals. Or we may put the difficulty thus: all of us aim at different ends, but does this prove that each of us aims at an end which harmonises the ends of all? And if Dr. Royce replies that the extreme sceptic himself realises all ends, is not that merely a physical fact also? For, not even for the very best ends need you be so very sceptical. If it is to be otherwise, or if we are to conclude from what different people desire to the common aim of each, it must be because we already assume that each person is a self and is communicable with all other selves. We are only stating the difficulty in yet another form when we question the principle of the moral insight. What are the aims of all whom an act is to affect? Are they simply desires or wants of individuals? or are they already moral aims? If the former, then the theory would be only a reassertion of the natural fact that our conduct does imply a compromise of inclinations, and that is not what Dr. Royce means. If the latter, then the individuals are already credited with the moral insight, and the standard prescribed is open justly to the old charge of tautology. For there is no account of how these individual ideals can be the basis of a moral ideal, except the assumption from common sense (an assumption acknowledged on p. 154) that my neighbour is a self like myself, with a will and consciousness like mine: and how is that known?

These objections may seem to be academical, but they are meant to suggest that Dr. Royce's results, so far as they are true, are obtained by a method not different from that of the theories he rejects, namely, by an analysis of certain facts, which a true theory will explain adequately, an untrue one inadequately. Some of these facts are physical, and some not physical, and we have to discover the nature and relation of these two sets of facts. If so, then the most important fact of all would be the nature of the self or the will, and an analysis of this shows that it includes a reference to an outward order in which other selves are the elements: that the self is, in other words, a moral agent only because it at once attracts and repels others. The moral law does then "harmonise" the aims of all, because a moral action is one which is compatible with and advances the claims of others; but those claims are *just* claims, which are settled by the very same moral judgment as prescribes his conduct to the individual whom we suppose to observe them. Such an analysis will also show that there is a reason in the nature of moral action for all possible ideals yet proposed or to come.

The second and larger half of the book is much more technical in character than the first. It deals with the question of what there may be in the real world to support the ideal position already attained, and the result is more satisfactory. It begins with the "World of Doubt": this is the world regarded "as a theatre for the display of Power, physical or metaphysical" (p. 238). We do not mean to follow Dr. Royce in all his doubts about such conceptions. His view of the Monistic theory, very common now-a-days as the theory of mind-stuff, was set forth in MIND XXIII. His treatment of Panlogism does at least point out a real difficulty in the notion that the Logos needs to perfect itself through a process. The problems raised by the existence of evil are discussed in an important section (pp. 264–71). All these conceptions, whether the popular scientific conception or Monism or the ordinary Theism with its notion of creation, seem to him to afford no ground for a religion; yet that we can mistrust all theories of reality in turn does at any rate admit the possibility of error, and thus arises the final problem of scepticism. How is error itself possible? The great merit of Dr. Royce's book is to have put this question in this definite form. His answer seems to us perfectly true: that error is possible only in virtue of an actual consciousness to which both the truth and the error are present (p. 377). This result follows from a very careful statement of the nature of judgment and the difficulties contained in different kinds of error. Take the error that one person makes about another: A is in error about B, means that if B could know A's idea of him, and compare it with his own idea of himself, he would know it to be error. Again, if I make a mistake about fact, it is because what is true and my apprehension of it are present together and compared in one consciousness. Thus error is possible only to a single all-seeing consciousness which contains all truth and knows too all judgments which, by comparison with the truth, it sees to be errors. Or, to quote Dr. Royce's words, "an error is an incomplete thought, that to a higher thought, which includes it and its intended object, is known as having failed in the purpose that it more or less clearly had, and that is fully realised in this higher thought" (p. 425). The preceding chapter on Idealism had sketched by way of anticipation the relation of such an infinite consciousness to the individual, and we may give Dr. Royce's hypothesis as he gives it himself "in a nutshell." "Take as a final case Professor Clifford's well-known example of the man looking at the candle. In time world-consciousness there is the group of states, *c*, *c*1, c2... . That is the real candle. In the world-consciousness there is also the group of states, *h*, *h*1, *h*2... . That is the 'cerebral image' of the candle, a physiological fact. Finally, according to the laws of reality, the existence in the world-consciousness of the facts, *h*, *h*1, *h*2... grouped as they are, has co-existent with it, the group of ideas C in the man's mind. This group C corresponds more or less completely to the group *c*, *c*1, *c*2... as that group exists beyond the man's mind in the world-consciousness. The group C is the man's idea of the candle" (p. 353).

Thus "all truth is known to One Infinite Thought" (p. 437), which, therefore, includes also a knowledge of all wills and of their conflict (p. 433). This thought is, therefore, the Ideal Judge of all good and evil (p. 436). Here the moral joins the speculative theory, and the end is seen to be the "progressive realisation by men of the eternal life of an Infinite Spirit," which is Truth, and "Truth is God." In the Divine Thought is realised the moral insight and the universal will. And in this conception the problem of evil is solved; for evil we regard no longer as merely a set-off against good or a means to it, but the evil enters as a conquered element into the organic total that constitutes the good will. Even so God's life includes, in the organic total of one conscious eternal instant, all life, and so all goodness and evil; or God is good only because "he includes the evil will in the structure of his good will."

Dr. Royce does not reach his end so directly as we have represented. There are two chapters (ix. and x.) called respectively "The World of Postulates" and "Idealism" which prepare his reader for the final result. He assumes or postulates that the world has a religious meaning, and then he goes on to confirm this postulate by showing how completely ordinary and scientific knowledge of the world depend on similar postulates. There is a faith in science that the world is rational, and that the truth of it is the simplest possible adequate description ("Postulate of Parsimony"); and this faith is like the religious faith that that description of the world is the truest which arouses the highest moral interest and satisfies the highest needs (p. 330). The chapter on Idealism forecasts what this highest postulate might be, and the subsequent chapters, which we have described, turn it from a postulate into a matter of knowledge. This part is by far the most difficult in the book: some of it has appeared in *MIND* XXV. It is full of good criticism: but when Dr. Royce says (p. 355) that causal sequence cannot be placed first (that is, before external reality) but second, as enabling us to develop in detail the idea that reality is like our own states of consciousness, we feel inclined to say: After all, external reality is not like our states of consciousness. And is not the final problem this: How can reality being present, as it surely is, in the Infinite mind, yet be unlike our consciousness? or conversely, What need is there for the Infinite thought so to reproduce itself in our finite thoughts as to appear in part unspiritual?

Undoubtedly, Dr. Royce's discussion of evil throws a great deal of light upon this question. It is quite true that in God the evil will is conquered or, if you will, transcended: and we may illustrate this belief that the good exists as a process, and is yet different in kind from the process, by the familiar doctrine of Aristotle that God is ἐνέργεια ἄνευ ὕλης. According to this we are not made for the glory of God, but in the consummation of our conquest of evil the glory of God is made visible. But it is strange that Dr. Royce should not have seen that there is here exactly the same difficulty as he found in the belief of a World-Logos. What need of this process of gradual realisation of the Logos by finite beings, and still more what need of this merely physical evil we cannot help, to which we can only take up the attitude of "stoical indifference" (p. 451)? For if moral progress takes place through gradually impressing a spiritual character upon what is ultimately physical fact, then are we not face to face with the problem: What then is this nature, these physical facts; and how can God appear in the form of nature? This is not the question 'Why should God have made the world?' which, as Lotze has shown, is an unphilosophical question, but the question, What is implied in there being a world of nature as opposed to spirit? or, How can spirit so divest itself of its spirituality as to appear as nature? This is the question which is shirked by theories that the atoms have souls, or that the ultimate reality is mind-stuff: but it is the question which it will be the immediate business of philosophy to answer. Until it is so put and answered, Absolute Idealism will always seem to say something which is very true, but which goes such a little way. And this is likely enough to be the impression which Dr. Royce's book may produce. But the central truth of idealism is so easy to forget that we cannot be too grateful to anybody who reminds us of it in a way that puts it in fresh lights and connexions.

There is one more difficulty which needs to be suggested. It is not clear how the Ideal Will of the first half of the book is identical with the Ideal Thought of the second half. That the Infinite Thought knows also all good and evil, follows from the conception of the world-consciousness; but how is the transition made from its knowledge of goodness to its being absolute good? It can only be made by showing that, in the nature of God, Will as it takes in him its ultimate shape is one with the ultimate nature of Thought. Now the moral insight does not help us here, for there too we need to be shown how knowledge of what our neighbour really is, is equivalent to the will to set on foot such activities as that knowledge demands. A similar objection has been urged against Green's ethical doctrine, and the transition certainly ought to be explicitly shown. But here again success depends, we think, upon the solution of the problem already stated.

# REVIEW OF *THE RELIGIOUS ASPECT OF PHILOSOPHY*

William James, Review of *The Religious Aspect of Philosophy*, *Atlantic Monthly*, vol. 55 (1885).

*The Religious Aspect of Philosophy: A Critique of the Bases of Conduct and of Faith*. By Josiah Royce, Ph. D., Instructor in Philosophy in Harvard College. Boston: Houghton, Mifflin & Co. 1885.

It is certain that we live in a philosophic age. Mrs. Partington's mop, as she plied it against the Atlantic Ocean, was a potent engine compared with the command to "halt" with which Positivism tried, and tries, to bring the heaving tides of man's inquisitiveness to rest. The worst of it is that we are getting deeper and deeper in. Every new book thickens the fray, and is one more thing with which to settle accounts; and any bit of scientific research becomes an angle and place of vantage from which arguments are brought to bear. When a branch of human activity is fermenting like this, it happens that individual sharers in the movement profit by the common level being raised, and do easily what, perhaps, in an isolated way they never could have done at all. We doubt if, at the dawn of our present philosophic movement, say in Sir William Hamilton's time, a writer with Dr. Royce's ideas could possibly have expressed them in so easy and unencumbered and effectual a form. A familiar catchword replaces a tedious setting forth; a reference to a popular writer serves instead of the heavy construction of an imaginary opponent; and above all, important objections are not likely to be overlooked or forgot.

But although the age is philosophical, it is not so after the fashion of Hegel's age in Germany, or Cousin's age in France. We have no Emperor of Philosophy in any country to-day, but a headless host of princes, with their alliances and feuds. This seems at first anarchic, and is apt to give comfort to the scoffers at metaphysical inquiry, and to all who believe that only the study of "facts" can lead to definitive results. The addition to the combatants of Dr. Royce, with his book, can only increase this first impression of confusion; for, like Descartes and Fichte and many another hero of belief, he begins by laying about him ruthlessly, and establishing a philosophic desert of doubt on which his own impregnable structure is to be reared. And yet a closer survey shows that to a great extent all these quarrels and recriminations of the modern thinkers are over matters of detail, and that, although they obey no common leader, they for the most part obey a common drift, – the drift, namely, towards a phenomelistic or idealistic creed. To this conclusion Dr. Royce also sweeps, with a momentum that carries him beyond Ferrier and Mill and Bain, beyond Hodgson, Renouvier, and Bowne, beyond the disciples of Schopenhauer and the disciples of Fichte and Hegel, wherever found, and beyond a number of contemporary German idealists whose names need not be cited here. Such thinkers all agree that there can be no other kind of Reality than reality-forthought. They differ only in the arguments they use to prove this thesis, and in deciding *whose* thought and what *kind* of thought that thought which is the reality of realities may be.

Dr. Royce's new and original proof of Idealism is, so far as we know, the most positive and radical proof yet proposed. It is short and simple, when once seen, and yet so subtle that it is no wonder it was never seen before. These short and simple suggestions that philosophers make from time to time – Locke's question about essence, for example, Berkeley's about matter, Hume's about cause, and Kant's about necessary judgments, – have an intolerable way with them of *sticking*, in spite of all one can do. To scholastic minds, who have made their bed, and wish for nothing further than to snore dogmatically and comfortably on, these questions must seem like very vermin, not to be conquered by any logical insect powder or philosophic comb.

The particular gadfly which Dr. Royce adds to the list is this: "how *can* a thought refer to, intend, or signify any particular reality outside of itself?" Suppose the reality there, and the thought there; suppose the thought to resemble just that reality, and thought besides in the world: still, asks our author, what is meant by saying that the thought *stands for* or *represents* that reality, or indeed any reality at all? Why isn't it just like the case of two eggs, or two toothaches, which may, it is true, resemble and duplicate each other exactly, but which are not held to mean or intend each other the least in the world? If the eggs and the toothaches are, each one of them, a separate substantive fact, shut up in its own skin and knowing nothing of the world outside, why are not one's thought, for example, of the Moon and the real Moon in exactly the same predicament? The Moon in our thought is our thought's Moon. Whatever we may think of her is true of her, for she is but the creature of our thinking. If we say "her hidden hemisphere is inhabited," it *is* inhabited, *for us*; and otherwise than for us *that* moon, the moon in our mind, has no existence. A critic cannot prove us wrong by bringing in a "real" moon with an uninhabited back hemisphere; he cannot, by comparing that moon with ours and showing the want of resemblance, make our moon "false." To do that, he would first have to establish that the thought in our mind was a thought *of* just that external moon, and *intended* to be true of it. But neither he nor we could establish that: it would be worse than a gratuitous, it would be a senseless, proposition. Our Moon has nothing to do with the real moon; she is a totally additional fact, pursuing her subjective destiny all alone, and only accidentally perceived by an outside critic to agree or disagree with another moon, which he knows and chooses to call real, but which is really out of all relation to the one in our mind's eye. At most, the critic might say he was reminded or not reminded of that other moon by our Moon; but he could not say that ours gave either a true or a false account of the other, simply because ours never pretended to give any account, or to refer to the other moon, at all. Nor can we ourselves *make* it refer to that other moon, by "proposing" or "supposing" that it does so refer; all we can propose or suppose is some altogether new moon in our own mind, and refer the old one there to that one. Over all such moons we have complete control, but over nothing else under heaven. At least, thinks Dr. Royce, such ought to be our inference, if the notion of common sense be true, that our thought and the reality are two wholly disconnected things.

The more one thinks, the more one feels that there is a real puzzle here. Turn and twist as we will, we are caught in a tight trap. Although we cannot help believing that our thoughts *do* mean realities and are true or false of them, we cannot for the life of us ascertain how they *can* mean them. If thought be one thing and reality another, by what pincers, from out of all the realities, does the thought pick out the special one it intends to know? And if the thought knows the reality *falsely*, the difficulty of answering the question becomes indeed extreme.

Our author calls the question insoluble on these terms; and we are inclined to think him right, and to suspect that his idealistic escape from the quandary may be the best one for us all to take. We supposed, just now, a critic comparing the real moon and our mental moon. Let him now help us forward. We saw that even *he* could not make it out that our mental moon should refer to just that individual real moon, and to nothing else. *We* could not make it out either, and certainly the real moon itself could not make it out. We saw, however, that we *could* make anything in our own mind refer to anything else *there*, – provided, of course, the two things were objects of a single act of thought; and the reason why our moon could not refer to the real moon was that the two moons were not facts in a common mind. But now imagine our "critic," instead of being the mere dissevered third thing he was, to be a common mind. Imagine his thought of our thought to *be* our thought, and his thought of the real moon to *be* the real moon. Both it and we have now become consubstantial; we are reduced to a common denominator. Both of us are members of the one total Thought, and any relation which that Thought draws between its members is as real as the members themselves. If that Thought intend one of its members to "represent" the other, and represent it either falsely or truly, "it is but thinking, and it is done." There is no other way in which one thing can "represent" another; and no possibility of either truth or falsehood unless the function of *representation* be genuinely there. An "Over-Soul," of whose enveloping thought our thought and the things we think of are alike fractions, – such is the only hypothesis that can form a basis for the reality of truth and of error in the world.

The reality of truth and error are, then, Dr. Royce's novel reason for believing that all that is has the foundations of its being laid in an infinite all-inclusive Mind. Upon the highest heights of dogmatism and in the deepest depths of skepticism, alike the argument blooms, saying, "Whatever things be false, and whatever things be true, *one* thing stands forever true, and that is that the Enveloping Mind must be there to make them either false or true."

To the lay-reader, this absolute Idealism doubtless seems insubstantial and unreal enough. But it is astonishing to learn how many paths lead up to it. Dr. Royce's path is only one. The others are of various kinds and degrees, and may be found in all sorts of books, few of them together. But taken altogether, they end by making about as formidable a convergence of testimony as the history of opinion affords. The persons most pleased by Dr. Royce's book will no doubt be the Hegelians here and in Great Britain; for it seems to us that he has reached a religious result hardly distinguishable from their own, by a method entirely free from that identification of contradictories which is the great stumbling-block in the Hegelian system of thought. The result is that all truth is known to one Thought, that is infinite, in which the world lives and moves and has its being, which abides and waxes not old, and in which there is neither variableness nor shadow of turning. The ordinary objection to a pantheistic monism like this is the ethical one, that it makes *all* that happens a portion of the eternal reason, and so must nourish a fatalistic mood, and a willingness to accept and consecrate whatever *is*, no matter what its moral quality may be. Dr. Royce is not as disdainful of this difficulty as the Hegelians are. We are not sure he has got over it, but he has bravely and beautifully attacked it; and his section on the problem of evil, in his last chapter, is as original and fresh a treatment of the subject as we know.

Unfortunately, we have no space to do more than recommend it to the reader's attention. And now that we find ourselves at the end of our tether, we wonder whether a notice entirely made up of quotations would not have been a better thing than this attempt of ours to set forth the most fundamental, it is true, but still the driest, portion of the book. Never was a philosophic work less dry; never one more suggestive of springtime, or, as we may say, more redolent of the smell of the earth. Never was a gentler, easier irony shown in discussion; and never did a more subtle analytic movement keep constantly at such close quarters with the cubical and concrete facts of human life as shown in individuals. In the entire ethical portion of the work its author shows himself to be a first-rate moralist, in the old-fashioned sense of the word, as one who knows delightfully how to describe the lights and shadows of special moral types and tendencies. In his discussions of the ethics of "sympathy" and of the ethics of "progress" are passages which are masterpieces in this line. And here again, from the very depths of the desert of skepticism, the flower of moral faith is found to bloom. Everything in Dr. Royce is radical. There is nothing to remind one of that dreary fighting of each step of a slow retreat to which the theistic philosophers of the ordinary common-sense school have accustomed us. For this reason the work must carry a true *sursum corda* into the minds of those whofeel in their bones that man's religious interests must be able to swallow and digest and grow fat upon all the facts and theories of modern science, but who yet have not the capacity to see with their own eyes how it may be done. There is plenty of leveling in Dr. Royce's book, but it all ends by being a leveling-up. The Thought of which our thought is part is lord of all, and, to use the author's own phrase, he does not see why we should clip our own wings to keep ourselves from flying out of our own coop over our own fence into our own garden. California may feel proud that a son of hers should at a stroke have scored so many points in a game not yet exceedingly familiar on the Pacific slope.

# REVIEW OF *THE SPIRIT OF MODERN PHILOSOPHY*

J.E. Creighton, Review of *The Spirit of Modern Philosophy*, *Philosophical Review*, vol. 1 (1892).

*The Spirit of Modern Philosophy: An Essay in the Form of Lectures.* By Josiah Royce, Ph.D., Assistant Professor of Philosophy in Harvard University. Boston and New York, Houghton, Mifflin, & Co., 1892. pp. xv, 519.

The nucleus of this book was a number of non-technical lectures, in which the author attempted to describe to a circle of friends something in regard to the chief names and problems of modern philosophy. After being enlarged several times, and delivered before public audiences in Harvard University and elsewhere, the author now presents them to the public in book form, under the above title. The work has two main divisions. The first part is devoted to an historical account of the most prominent philosophical thinkers and their problems, from the seventeenth century to the present time. In the second part we have the author's own confession of philosophical faith, which, he claims, is not without originality. His doctrine however he tells us, is no new gospel, but a reconstruction, a synthesis of truths discovered through a study of the history of thought.

The book is written in a simple and non-technical fashion, the style is easy and unconventional, and the treatment of problems, though sometimes diffuse, is always interesting. The artistic biographical sketches, the wealth of illustration and happy quotations, all combine to render it a most attractive work.

Professor Royce frankly confesses, and one feels throughout the entire book, that he is most concerned with those problems of philosophy which deal more immediately with the spiritual interests of mankind. "There is, after all," he writes, "no beauty in a metaphysical system which does not spring from its value as a record of spiritual experience" (p. 23). It is no doubt true that these practical questions regarding our "permanent spiritual possessions" must remain problems to which human reason can never be indifferent. Yet the uncharitable strictures which the author places upon writings where this interest does not appear, sound to me suspiciously like cant, and certainly have no justification. A writer's human interests may be not less true and deep because for the time he resolutely keeps them out of sight.

The author's purpose, in the historical section of his work, is to select certain aspects in the systems of the more prominent thinkers which seem to him to be significant and of permanent value. Each philosopher becomes in his hands "a character in a story, an attitude towards the spiritual concerns of humanity." He carries out this purpose in a manner which leaves scarcely anything to be desired, and one cannot help regretting that the plan of his work did not allow him to include Leibniz. The whole history of modern thought is illuminated and vivified by Professor Royce's brilliant and masterly exposition, from which professional teachers of philosophy may obtain many useful hints. It seems to me, however, that Berkeley has hardly received justice in this sketch. Grandly simple as was his thought, it was yet so deep that it was misunderstood by all the philosophers of his time. And although his system may appear one-sided and incomplete when compared with later expressions of idealism, we have still to remember that they are but fuller developments of that principle which he was the first to emphasize. Two points are dwelt upon in dealing with Kant. First, what we may perhaps call his heroic attitude towards life and the demands of the moral law. Secondly, a truth, the consequences of which Kant perceived himself only dimly; *viz.* that experience implies a relation to a universal or transcendental ego. The problem of philosophy after Kant is to understand the nature of this Universal Self. In the chapter which deals with "The Rise of the Doctrine of Evolution," the author traces the origin of this theory to that historical movement which the thinkers of the Romantic School were led to undertake through their interest in the affairs of the human spirit. The connection is a very obvious one, although it is one that has not often been pointed out. In the same chapter he has also very justly called attention to the fact that the "return to reality" in our century has not been a return to the outer world of the seventeenth century, but "a return to a world pervaded with the spirit of idealism." Our age has given up the attempt to deduce reality, and has devoted itself to science, yet we must carry with us what we have learned from idealism. The business of science, like that of philosophy, is to discover the laws, the ideas, or rationality of things.

With the tenth lecture begins the constructive part of the work. The author adopts the realistic position of natural science, and seeks to show that its explanations, when pressed to the limit, become involved in paradoxes and contradictions. The theory which he examines is that of the nebular hypothesis, which represents the world as undergoing a continuous process of aggregation, and, as a consequence, constantly suffering loss of energy. To explain how we may conceive this process as without a beginning, Clifford has suggested that going backward from the present condition of the world, at an indefinite past time the molecules which now compose matter were at an infinite distance from each other. This would imply that the world could only exist in its present condition if the molecules of which it is composed *were once actually an infinite distance* apart. But this lands us in an absurdity. It is therefore impossible the author concludes, to conceive of a continuous process in the same direction going on through infinite time. Therefore the physical world, the world in space and time where such paradoxes are inevitable, is not the truth of things. Although I agree with the conclusion, it does not seem to follow in this case. The author has shown that Clifford's postulate is untenable, but it is yet quite possible that the process of the world may be "cyclical;" that what appears to us as a straight line, because we see so small a portion of it, may in reality be a segment of a circle.

The eleventh lecture is a reaffirmation of a position which Professor Royce reached some years ago in his *Religious Aspects of Philosophy.* The conclusion of the first half of the chapter is, "the real world must be a mind or else a group of minds" (p. 368). That there is only one world of ideas, that of the Universal Self, which is inclusive of all finite beings, Professor Royce finds implied in the relation of "meaning" anything beyond our present consciousness. "When what is meant is outside of the moment which means, only a Self inclusive of the moment and its object could complete and so confirm or refute the opinion that the moment contains" (p. 377). If we suppose that there exists some reality beyond our consciousness, say, "a world of spirits," then the truth of any thought of mine will consist in its agreement with this reality. That there must be *some* relation between the knowing mind and the thing known, that both must somehow form parts of one cosmos, is beyond dispute, but I cannot see that this necessarily implies that they are included in a Universal *Consciousness,* or even that such a consciousness exists. Such a reflective consciousness is not necessary to constitute truth. The twelfth lecture is the most important and original part of the book. He here applies his idealistic theory to the problems of cosmology and freedom, and the treatment is highly suggestive. Facts which belong to the world in space and time, and to which we apply the categories, he calls the "World of Description." The world of spiritual facts on the other hand which is not subject to the categories of the external world, he denominates the "World of Appreciation." "What I see and describe is simply the physical, the phenomenal aspect of the inner and appreciative life." The mind does not influence the body, but the body is only a translation of the mind into the describable language of space. It is to be hoped that the author will work out the results which are only indicated here with more fulness. His solution of the problem of Freedom is, in the condensed form in which it is here presented, very difficult to understand. "As parts of an eternal order we do not indeed choose this thing or that in time, but help to choose out and out what world this fatal temporal world shall eternally be and have been." These seem like words without meaning, but it is doubtless unfair to criticise such a general indication of position. The last chapter of the book is a discussion of the moral order of the universe, and the rational attitude towards life. Professor Royce is no shallow or sentimental optimist, who shuts his eyes to the real evil of the world. The only optimism worthy of a brave man is that which recognizes sin and evil as a part of the real world, and yet *wills* that these shall be overcome, with a faith that the Infinite Spirit upon whom the world depends is rational. In conclusion, I would like to call attention to the excellent workmanship and attractive form of this book, which add not a little to its charm.

# TWO CRITICAL POINTS IN PROFESSOR ROYCE'S PAPER ON "SELF-CONSCIOUSNESS, SOCIAL CONSCIOUSNESS, AND NATURE."

John E. Russell, "Discussion of Prof. Royce's Papers on 'Self-Consciousness, Social Consciousness, and Nature,'" *Philosophical Review*, vol. 5 (1896).

In the very able and suggestive paper of Professor Royce, published in this REVIEW of September and November, 1895, there are two points which especially drew my attention, and upon which I venture some criticisms of the author's position. I refer to the proof that there is other human experience than my own, and that Nature is other reality than human experience.

The proof which Professor Royce offers in support of his thesis, that there are finite beings like myself, other human experience than my own experience, is the following. "A man becomes self-conscious only in the most intimate connection with the growth of his social consciousness. These two forms of consciousness are not separable and opposed regions of a man's life; they are thoroughly interdependent. Take away the conscious *Alter*, and the conscious *Ego*, so far as in this world we know it, languishes, and languishing dies... . Hence I am not first self-conscious and then secondarily conscious of my fellows. On the contrary, I am conscious of myself, on the whole, as in relation to some real or ideal fellow; and apart from my consciousness of my fellows I have only secondary and derived states and habits of self-consciousness" (p. 468). "In us men there is no self-consciousness apart from some more or less derived form of social consciousness. I am I in relation to some sort of a *non-Ego*" (p. 470). "It is by virtue of this very contrast (*i.e.*, that between our own inner life and what we regard as the inner life of our fellows) that we become self-conscious" (p. 471). "A man is conscious of himself as this finite being only in so far as he contrasts himself with what he takes to be the life and, in fact, the conscious life of some other finite being – unless, indeed, he modifies his natural self-consciousness by contrasting his own life with the conceived fulness of the life of God. But except by virtue of some such contrast one cannot become self-conscious, and the result is that, as a matter of simple and necessary meaning, if any metaphysical argument is to prove that I am I, viz., this finite being, then, at the same time this argument will prove that there is other conscious life besides mine. For otherwise my own finite life cannot be defined or conceived" (pp. 471–72). "Without knowledge that the other experience is, there can be no meaning in saying that the presented experience itself is" (p. 481). "That there is some experience not individually mine, is an assertion precisely as sure as the assertion that my own experience is; for neither assertion has meaning apart from the other" (p. 483). Hence one ought not to say, as Descartes does, "*Cogito, ergo sum*"; but, "I think; therefore other beings like myself exist also."

The argument is to this effect. The existence of other human experience is so connected with my own existence both in its genesis and its meaning, so far as it is known and definable to myself, that whatever reasons there are for affirming that I am, are equally valid for affirming that other human beings are. Looking at my self-consciousness psychogenetically, I must say that, in its origin and development, my consciousness of self is so bound up with my social consciousness that, but for that social consciousness, there is no reason to suppose that I should possess any self at all. At all events I could not have the self-consciousness I now have, were there not other selves with whom I have been in communication from the beginning of my conscious life. I have "rounded to the separate mind" I now am, and my "isolation has grown defined," only in consequence of that social environment in which my experience has been set from the beginning.

Again, looking at my self-consciousness epistemologically, the knowledge of myself, the meaning of my experience, is possible, is explicable, only if there are other experiences not mine. "My actual inner life is then always contrasted with experience other than is now mine" (p. 479). "Whichever way I turn, I am definable to myself only in terms of a contrast with other experiences" (p. 480). Another characteristic of my experience demands the same explanation, viz., systematic continuity and persistency. For instance, the existence for me of such an object as the valley of the Upper Nile is explicable only if there are other beings, other experience than mine. "When I conceive the Upper Nile Valley, there are presented to my inner life words, images, map-experience, and the like; and these I know as meaning something to me, in so far as I contrast these relatively immediate data with the conceived contents of the experience of other men who more directly verify what I only conceive as to that region" (p. 479).

To the objection that the other experience than mine need not be an actual one, but only a conceived one or a possible one, the sufficient reply is that any such conceived other experience, whether rightly conceived or not, must have "relation to a real experience which is other than my presentation" (pp. 482, 483); and any possible experience for me, if that is to mean anything, must presuppose some actual experience not mine. "Possibilities need actualities to give them meaning." "Bare possibilities to which no actualities correspond are meaningless" (p. 483).

But now is this reasoning really to the point, and is it conclusive? We do not think so. And first, in reference to the genesis and development of self-consciousness, admitting the correctness of Professor Royce's view, we can hardly suppose that he would make the psychological history of my experience a proof that there is other experience than mine, unless it is to be assumed that genesis carries with it validity. All that this account of self-consciousness proves that I have always believed in the reality of other experience than own. But, from the standpoint of epistemology, the question is a legitimate one: Is that belief true or well founded? My self-consciousness might conceivably have had such a genesis, if in reality there were no social fellows and my belief in their existence were an illusion. It is only upon epistemological grounds that the fundamental question which Professor Royce raises can be answered, namely, What warrant have I, philosophically speaking, for assuming that there is any other experience than mine at all (p. 481)?

And, in fact, the argument upon which Professor Royce relies is the argument from knowledge, or rather from my own experience as known and definable to myself. The epistemological argument which have reproduced, does, we think, prove the proposition that there must be other reality of some sort than my own existence, – other experience of some kind than my own experience; but what the content of that experience is, whether it is or embraces other finite experiences like my own – my social fellows – or is the "conceived fulness of the life of God" as the absolute experience, the reasoning so far does not determine.

Up to this point the existence of other human minds has not been proved. The only proof on this point which Professor Royce offers, in the passage on page 484, where he undertakes to explain how "we get information about the contents of experience not our own." This information we get "when we communicate socially with our fellows, and the essence of social communication is this. My fellow does something in a certain situation, – deals with his environment so and so. He uses tools, utters words, makes gestures." These expressive acts of my fellow "get a meaning to me as the suggestion of his concrete inner life, just in so far as I am able to imitate these deeds of his by bodily acts of my own, brought to pass under conditions like those in which he, my fellow, acts. For, when I definitely repeat a bodily act that expresses any human meaning, the act, as I repeat it under definite conditions, gets for me an inner meaning, which I could never grasp so long as I merely observed such an act from without, as an event in my perceived phenomenal world. But this inner meaning which the act gets when I repeat it, becomes for me the objective meaning of the act as my fellow performs it. And thus the meaning of the imitated act, interpreted for me at the moment of my imitation, gets conceived as the real meaning, the inner experience of my fellow, at the moment when he performs the act which is my model."

The argument contained in this passage is really the argument from analogy; and it presupposes, as something already known or established, the objective reality of my body. It is only as I first know that I have a body which sustains certain definite and constant relations to my inner experience, that I can know that there are any other inner experiences like my own; and my inference to the reality of such inner experiences is based solely upon an assumed identity of relations, viz., the relations I know to exist between my body and my inner experience, and the relations between what I take to be the like body of my fellow and his inner experience. I reach, then, the minds of my social fellows only through the medium of a body common to us both. I reach an inner human experience, not mine, only through a something which is not human experience; and this must mean, not the mere fact that I get more definite information about the content of my fellow's inner experience which I have already proved exists in reality, but the fact of *there being* such inner experience other than mine.

Now, unless it is first established that there is common to me and my assumed fellows such a reality as I mean by my body, it has not, we think, been proved that there is a world of human experience other than my own. But my body is a physical object, a part of nature; it is a nature-object; and the order of proof which Professor Royce follows is from human beings to non-human beings. He teaches that, both in the order of psychological growth and logical proof, the existence of nature is dependent upon self and social consciousness.

Turning now to the proof that there is non-human experience which he calls nature, or nature-objects, we find this proof is based upon the fact of social communication – the social consciousness. The fact of communication between human experiences proves there is body, my body and the bodies of my fellows, which are the necessary media of our communicable experiences; and, since body is indissolubly connected with the totality of those phenomena we call Nature, the argument from continuity establishes the reality, of nature-objects whose content is non-human experience.

We think, however, this argument is open to two rather serious criticisms. In the first place, unless it assumes without proof that there are social fellows, in communication with each other, the proof that there are other human experiences than my own presupposes the existence of just those nature-objects which it is the aim of this argument to establish. In a word, the argument either rests upon an unproved assumption, or the proof moves in a circle. Our position is that, without the previous assumption that body exists common to me and my fellows, Professor Royce has not proved that we have social fellows; and without the assumption of such human experiences in communication with each other, there is no proof that bodies as extra-human experiences exist. But even supposing it had been established that other human minds than mine exist, this argument does not prove what it undertakes to prove, viz., that there must be some non-human experience, or that nature is such experience.

There are, as Professor Royce says, two possible hypotheses respecting nature. According to the one view, nature is "the sum-total of those facts of our various experiences concerning which our conceptual experiences seem most easily to agree" (p. 581); that is, nature-objects are merely agreeing human experiences. The other conception is that, while the content of nature is experience, that experience is other than human, *i.e.*, nature-objects are non-human experiences.

Now Professor Royce rejects the first hypothesis and maintains the second; for "there is," he says, "one class of nature-objects in case of which just this negative and sceptical hypothesis cannot be carried out without destroying the very basis of our social consciousness itself" (p. 581). This class of objects is our bodies, phenomena which are "definable as the expressive movements, the gestures, words, deeds of our fellows." The argument here is, that the fact of communication between human minds is inexplicable, if nature-objects are only agreeing experiences; such a fact can be explained only if there is an experience not human and of identical meaning for all minds in communication. The fact of communication between our inner experiences is therefore an exception, fatal to the hypothesis which makes nature a merely human experience, and it is to be explained only by the hypothesis that our bodies at least are nature-objects, whose contents are extra-human experience. Professor Royce takes the concrete case of a desk in the lecture-room and myself communicating with my fellows. In reference to the desk, he asserts: "You could say that if this desk were here alone, you could indeed so far talk sceptically of phenomenal experiences in various observers, which only seemed to be experiences relating to the same object, but which as a fact do not demand the real sameness of their object. But it is no longer so if, in terms of the social consciousness, you consider not the desk but me as your nature-object; for I am to you not only nature-phenomenon represented in you by comparable and merely similar perceptual experiences of your various private worlds; but I am, as communicating fellow-man, the same outer object for all of you" (p. 582).

Now we maintain that this proof is not cogent. All that the argument proves is, that there must be some content in our human experiences, which is so far common to them all, that it can be a medium of communication between them. The argument does not prove that this common or identical element must be something which transcends our experiences; or, if some extra-human reality is established, that reality certainly need not be what Professor Royce maintains, viz., our bodies as he conceives them.

Why not in reference to our bodies, as well as other nature-objects, keep within our human experience, and explain this fact of communication by a supposition of this sort: Within my experience there is a certain group of elements or events, relatively stable, uniform, and persistent, which I call my body; this content possesses the peculiarity of being regularly connected with those more internal experiences I call ideas, feelings, emotions, volitions; and what is true of myself, I assume to be the case with my social fellows.

Now, if I find on certain occasions, that events or phenomena occur within my experience, which closely resemble those I know as my body, though of course not identical with them, I shall interpret them to mean the existence at that time of experiences in my fellows, which correspond to my own more internal experiences, and which are of like character. Now, if this supposition is inadmissible, and we must transcend our human experiences, why not set up the Berkelyan hypothesis of an Infinite Spirit operative in our finite spirits, and the actual medium of communication between them?

Our conclusion is that Professor Royce has not established the two most important theses in his paper. He has not proved that other finite minds like my own must exist, nor has he proved that nature-objects must be finite, non-human experiences.

# THE REAL ISSUE IN *THE CONCEPTION OF GOD*

George Holmes Howison, "The Real Issue in *The Conception of God*," *Philosophical Review*, vol. 7 (1898).

The very full and careful notice of the book bearing the above-quoted title, in the May number of the REVIEW, repeats an omission which, singularly enough, has been made in every important account thus far given of the work. This omission, unfortunately, is of the very kernel of my own contribution to the discussion recorded in the volume. I can hardly avoid the suspicion that its happening must be due, at least in part, to some serious defect in my method of statement; for the omission has been made in common by such capable writers as President Schurman, Professor Charles Carroll Everett, Professor James Seth, and the pungent if not judicial reviewer in the New York *Nation*. It is therefore with satisfaction, as well as with thanks, that I avail myself of the space here kindly granted me by the editors of the REVIEW, to make a restatement of the matter omitted.

The omission amounts to a complete misstatement of the case really at issue between Professor Royce and me. It results in leaving the impression that I do nothing more than confront his acutely-argued theory of Monistic Idealism with the inertia of traditional prejudices, bedded in moral common-sense. In his *Supplementary Essay*, Professor Royce himself represents the case in this light. He says (p. 136) "The antithesis *between Monistic Idealism and Ethical Individualism* [italics mine] upon which Professor Howison...has laid such stress, reveals...a very deep and instructive antinomy of Reason." Still more explicitly (p. 220): "The antinomy...has appeared thus far as [italics again mine] *an antinomy between the claims of theory and the presuppositions of ethics*." Finally, in his *Replies to Criticisms*, he recurs to this 'antinomy,' and (p. 329) states it with technical formality as follows:

| "THESIS. | "ANTITHESIS. |
| --- | --- |
| "The entire world of truth, natural and ethical, must be present in the unity of a single Absolute Consciousness. | "The...moral world demands a real Variety of Individuals – such as cannot be present in the unity of any single consciousness. |

"The world of truth, for the reasons developed in Part First of this paper, must constitute an Organic Whole of Fact, realizing ideas. Otherwise, there would be relations of ideas and facts which were real relations, and which yet transcended all consciousness. Such real relations, as transcendent 'things in themselves,' prove to be meaningless. Hence the Thesis is established."

"Moral relations are relations of individuals; who are free as to their will, and independent both of one another and of any whole of reality to which they belong. Such independence implies...separateness, and forbids the...individuals to be the mere fulfillment...of ideas of any one being. Hence the individuals cannot be contained in any single unity of consciousness; and the Antithesis is proved."

With the thesis and antithesis formulated in just this fashion, it is made to appear as if I only deny the thesis so far as it concerns the *ethical* world. It seems to be implied that I must perforce admit the argument in proof of the thesis, and therefore must admit the thesis too, so far as it concerns the 'natural' world (by which I presume the *theoretical* is meant). The implication is, in any case, that if I do not outright admit the thesis in its theoretical bearing, I have at any rate neglected to call it in question or to challenge its proof.

It would not surprise me if this piece of dialectical technics should turn out to have been quite as much responsible for the general overlooking of my central contention as any defect in my former method of statement. A presentation could hardly be more misleading, as to the main matter really in dispute. Yet in the published volume I have taken special pains to forestall, if possible, this misleading impression. In the "Introduction" it is said (p. xxxv): "Professor Howison's point is not at all to set the moral consciousness, simply as a 'categorical imperative,' at odds with the theoretical, and merely have the 'heart' breathe defiance to the 'intellect'... . His position is by no means correctly apprehended as one side of 'an antinomy between the claims of theory and the presuppositions of ethics.' Ethics for him, as for Professor Royce, can have no valid presuppositions except such as find their place in a totally coherent, totally embracing *theoretical* view. His position is that of a side in a controversy between two schemes of *theory*." But the same thing had already been set forth in the body of my part of the discussion. On page 106, reliance on, the "warnings of moral commonsense," as a basis for philosophizing, is expressly repudiated. Speaking of our instinctive moral sense as indicating the reality of many independent self-active minds, I there say: "By spontaneous moral sense we doubtless believe, indeed, that we are each entirely real, and a seat of inalienable right...this feeling of rights, though it be no more than a resentment at intrusion, points directly to our belief that there are other beings as unreservedly real as we, with rights alike inalienable, who lay us under *duty*. Still, [the italics here are new] *this uncomprehended instinct, ethical though it be, is not philosophy. Until we shall have learned how to give it in some way the authority of rational insight, we have no right to its effects when we are proceeding as thinkers; so far as we merely accept them, we do not* THINK, *we only feel.*" In short, as I remind the reader in a footnote to p. 181, the soul's *instinctive* allegiance to its membership in the "City of God" I use only as "a stubborn Warning that any logical system which fails to satisfy it is defective, and requires revision." At the critical juncture of my discussion, I say (p. 123): "The religious reason firmly avers there must be some flaw in such philosophizing, and, in the name of *all* reason, protests against the claim that this [monistic] conception of God is 'the inevitable outcome of a reflective philosophy.'" And thereupon I proceed at once to point out precisely what the flaw in the argument for Monistic Idealism is; precisely where in the argumentative process it is found; and precisely what its causes were in Kant's misconstruction of his own principles of "critical" Idealism.

So far, then, from my difference with Professor Royce being simply a dissent from his *results*, backed up merely by an appeal against them to our moral sense – so far from its being merely the obstinate assumption of an "ethical" standpoint antagonistic to his "philosophical" or "theoretical" position – it is, rather, expressly a dissent from his *argument*, from his whole scheme and method of proof. In brief, it is a *philosophical*, a *theoretical* difference. It begins, to be sure, by calling attention to his *results*, and to the offense these give to moral ideals, the profoundest religious feelings developed in the ascending course of human history thus far; but, this once done, it proceeds directly to a critical examination and valuation, both positive and negative, of his *argument*. My real difference with him thus comes out of a rigorous analysis of that argument, resolving it (p. 120) into its two main premises: (1) "That no conception of God can have any philosophical value unless it can be proved real, or, in other words, unless it is the conception that of itself proves God to exist; and (2) that the conception [offered by Professor Royce and other monists] is the only conception that can thus prove its reality." It is precisely in denying the validity of this second premise that the vital point of my dissent consists. Thus (p. 120): The first...nobody with a proper training in philosophy would deny. The second has a very different standing, and I take but little risk, I am sure, when I question its truth entirely."

The remainder of my discussion (pp. 120–27) is spent in bringing out the philosophical warrant for the denial of this premise. I point out the fact that any apparent force the premise may have comes from the Kantian and post-Kantian tenet that every object of *knowledge* must fall within the compass of the knower's "possible experience"; or, as the technical expression is, must remain "immanent" within the subject's being, and can by no means ever be "transcendent" of this. I then proceed to attack this now time-honored assumption, and to indicate wherein it is destitute of warrant. I suggest the steps for showing that the proofs of it supposed to be furnished in the course of Kant's *Æsthetic* and *Analytic* (chiefly in the famous *Deduction and Schematization of the Categories*) are unmistakably fallacious.

Finally, I go on (pp. 125–27) to indicate the several steps, mentioning each specifically, by which having gone "back to Kant" out of the crooked bye-paths wandered into under the misguidance of Fichte, Schelling and Hegel, we may still, now at last, advance "beyond Kant" in the "main highway" to which he really introduced human thinking; a highway genuinely "critical," and genuinely continuative (by a *theoretical* fulfilment) of the moral philosophy which he did so much to establish, – genuinely continuative, because it will abide in maintaining the reality of that "Kingdom of Ends," that Divine republic of autonomous Persons, which is at once the spring and the goal of Kant's philosophy, and yet will vindicate this, not simply by showing that our consciousness of duty *commits* us to it irretrievably, but by bringing to light the truth that this "City of God" is itself the only sufficient condition of *knowledge*; that the certainty of it is just as strictly presupposed in every cognition that surmounts the suspicion of subjective illusion, as the certainty of the union of time and space with the categories is presupposed in the formation of any "object" of subjective experience and any judgment *a priori* concerning the order of such objects; in fine, that the unweakened word "objective," and the equivalent word "true," can have no valid meaning except as marking the *a priori* collective consensus of an absolutely total society of minds, independent and yet disinterested and harmonizing.

Let us look at the proclaimed "antinomy" as my view now explained would present it. It would run:

| THESIS. | ANTITHESIS. |
|---|---|
| The world of Truth, including truths of fact and law as well as truths of value and conduct, springs, as a whole and in every part, from the world of self-active intelligences; presupposes, and in its wholeness *is*, a Plurality of such strictly free minds, and cannot be contained in the unity of any Single Consciousness. | The world of Truth, including truths of value and conduct as well as truths of fact and law, cannot spring, either as a whole or in any part, from a world of many self-active intelligences, but prohibits a Plurality of such strictly free minds, and cannot be contained in the unity of a single Absolute Consciousness. |

The thesis is my position, the antithesis is Professor Royce's. The antinomy is now genuine, – exact and whole. I solve it by pointing out the illusion – a case of Kant's "*transscendentaler Schein*" – at the bottom of the supposed proof of the antithesis. The required unity in the world of the surviving thesis is found in the rational nature characteristic of each conscious Self. It is the *Unity of Harmony* demanded by the problem, not the fatal *Unit of Experience* which the survival of the antithesis would give, and which would make the solution of the problem impossible – the reconciliation of God, Freedom, and Immortality.

# REVIEW OF *STUDIES OF GOOD AND EVIL*

J.W. Chadwick, Review of *Studies of Good and Evil*, *The Nation*, vol. 67 (1898).

*Studies of Good and Evil; A Series of Essays upon Problems of Philosophy and Life*. By Josiah Royce, Professor of the History of Philosophy in Harvard University. D. Appleton & Co. 1898.

As if fearing that his "indolent reviewers" would not read all his essays in this volume, Prof. Royce has written an elaborate introduction, and possibly those will be most successful in reviewing him who stick closely to that, which gives an admirable account of each separate article, and endeavors (with some waste of ingenuity) to relate them all to the main title of his book. They are, in fact, of diverse character. Four of them, all in the vanguard, are "Studies of Good and Evil," clearly enough, while the ninth article, "An Episode of Early California Life: The Squatter Riot of 1850 in Sacramento," is a study of evil only within certain narrow limits. The tenth and twelfth articles are biographical and critical studies of Meister Eckhart, the scholastic mystic, and Jean Marie Guyau, the young French philosopher whose early death so touched his brilliant life with pity and regret.

The ninth article, "Originality and Consciousness," is much less abstract and difficult than Prof. Royce's account of it in his introduction, and those who are scared away from it by that account will lose what is certainly the pleasantest chapter in the book, and the one that comes most clearly within the range of practical ethics, albeit the ethics of the intellect. Written for the *Harvard Monthly*, it is possible that this article makes some concession to the weakness of the undergraduate mind; but in general Prof. Royce will be found as clear as anybody when he is writing of simple matters, and only difficult when he is penetrating mysteries for the expression of which language is too dull an instrument. The thesis in this article is that the conscious wish and intent to be original is one of the most powerful enemies of effective originality in art or life of any kind. "It is Life, and not Consciousness, that, in us men, is the originator." But there are happy moments in the thinker's and the artist's life, in the man-of-action's, too, and, when they come, to bid them stay is to achieve the originality which no deliberate volition can effect.

"I have supposed," says Prof. Royce, "that the essays from the fifth to the ninth in the present volume might serve to contribute in a genuine way to the issues suggested by my title," but he confesses that these essays lead us into "very theoretical regions, where the ethical problems are, for the time being, in the background." They are very far in the background, and the only ethical implication of these articles, except the fifth and ninth, is through the fact that "consciousness is the basis of all the good and evil that we human beings know." They are all studies of self-consciousness in one aspect or another, and are as stiffly metaphysical as Prof. Royce can be in his most characteristic mood. If one wants a good intellectual gymnastic he will find it here if anywhere in contemporary philosophy, but not a few will find these exercises somewhat dizzying in the intricacy of their involutions. The first of the three essays which are exclusively metaphysical, is Prof. Royce's contribution to the discussion which was excited by Huxley's "Romanes Lecture." Its subject is "Natural Law, Ethics, and Evolution." Huxley could find no ethics in the cosmical process; he declared the cosmic process to be anti-ethical, and for much of the way in his essay Prof. Royce keeps Huxley company. Conceive the cosmical process as one of describably rigid law, and then, he says, the ethical process can form no part of it. It is utterly opposed to the cosmical process so conceived. But (and here Prof. Royce parts company with Huxley and combats his general position) the opposition resides entirely in the ethical point of view which desires novelty, progress, the unattained ideal; and "against such things there is no law" in the cosmical process. Merely to state this is not to make it plain, but that it is so to Prof. Royce those who read his essay carefully will generally agree.

The sixth, seventh, and eighth essays are even more remote, if possible, from practical ethics than the fifth, and more profoundly metaphysical. They are entitled "The Implications of Self-Consciousness," "The Anomalies of Self-Consciousness," and "Self-Consciousness, Social Consciousness, and Nature." They are intimately related, and have for their common note the Hegelian interpretation of man as an essentially social being. "It is not the goal but the course that makes us happy," said Jean Paul, and not a few, we imagine, will find an illustration of the proverb in these fine-spun disquisitions. The doctrine of the first essay of this series is that "there is and can be only one complete Self, and that all finite selves and their objects are organically related to this Self, are moments of its completeness, thoughts in its thought, wills in its will, individual elements in the life of the absolute individual." The same doctrine has been urged in Prof. Royce's

*Religious Aspect of Philosophy* and his *Spirit of Modern Philosophy*, and, with much more elaboration, in his part of *The Conception of God*, a discussion in which he took part with Professors Howison, Le Conte, and Mezes, endeavoring to show that human personality is not an illusive bubble on the surface of the Infinite Reality. He did not succeed to the satisfaction of Prof. Howison, with whom many of their readers will agree. But the discussion there, as here, was proof how strong was Prof. Royce's (possibly illusory) sense of his own "life in himself"; and of his sense in general of the reality of human personality, we have abundant proof here in these essays, and much more in the closing sections of *Spirit of Modern Philosophy*.

The argument of the article on the anomalies of self-consciousness is that self-conscious functions are all of them in their finite, human; and primary aspect social functions, due to the habits of human intercourse. In the next following essay we hark back to the one immediately preceding for much of the way, and there are some delightful paradoxes to the effect that we cannot be egoistic without being altruistic. "I can aim, for instance, to be a political 'boss.' That appears to be a very egoistic aim. But the political 'boss' exists by the suffrages of interested people, and must aim at their conscious, even if illusory sense of advantage in so far as he wills them to be sincerely interested." But this essay goes beyond the preceding, first as showing that, except through our social relations, we can get no idea of the non-Ego which we call nature, and then in arguing for a Self of which nature is to us the visible experience. "No evidence can indicate nature's inner reality without also indicating that this reality is, like that of our own experience, conscious, organic, full of clear contrasts, definite." On the way from the social ego to this inner Self of things we have a doctrine which suggests the mind-stuff theory of Kingdon Clifford, but which Prof. Royce carefully distinguishes from that: "Natural objects, if they are real to us at all, are prima facie simply other finite beings, who are, so to speak, not in our social set, and who communicate to us, not their minds, but their presence." So stated, this doctrine appears fanciful, but it appears less so when Prof. Royce's skilful dialectic is brought to bear upon it. This essay concludes with considerations that really constitute a separate essay, which has a kind of cousinship with the doctrine of Prof. Cope and Mr. Charles Peirce that the laws of Nature are fixed habits which she has gradually acquired. Prof. Royce is not so sure that they are fixed; imagining that our conviction that they are so is possibly an illusion of our contracted "apperceptive span," while in reality the world is one of mingled permanence and novelty. Whereupon, will not the miracle-mongers cry, "He has become as one of us"?

Turning now to those essays which most clearly justify the title of the book, the first of these – first in the book also – "The Problem of Job" – is an attempt to solve that problem by identifying the sufferings of mankind with the sufferings of God: "When you suffer, *your sufferings are* God's *sufferings*, not his external work, not his external penalty, not the fruit of his neglect, but identically his own personal woe. In you God himself suffers, precisely as you do, and has all your concern in overcoming this grief." This is less doubtful consolation when it is urged that God is God in virtue of his triumph over evil, and we most God-like through our coöperation with him on this line. All this is worked out much more effectively than here in the concluding sections of Prof. Royce's *Spirit of Modern Philosophy*. And however elsewhere he may seem to merge our human personality in God's, his sense of it here, and wherever the same thought is prominent, is as rigorous and strenuous as we could wish. Strangely enough we breathe the same moral atmosphere as in Prof. William James' *Will to Believe*; we have the same conviction that we have there that it is a real fight in which we are engaged; we are in the procession, not mere lookers-on.

Prof. Royce has a very stout abhorrence of what he calls "pseudo-idealism, "the idealism which explains away the sin and evil of the world as illusions of our subjectivity. He wrestles with them, like Jacob with the angel in the dark. He will not let them go unless they bless him. He is happier in his pessimism than are the optimists in their optimism. His third essay, on "Tennyson and Pessimism," compares the "Locksley Hall Sixty Years After" with the first "Locksley Hall," and finds the pessimism of the second poem healthier than the optimism of the first, because the evil is recognized as something we can master and control, and the good is something that will come because we will to have it come. This paper also was written for the *Harvard Monthly*, and the young men who read it must have felt their hearts knocking against their ribs in no unmanly fashion. In the Job article various solutions of the problem of evil are reviewed and set aside. Some that are extremely popular in the pulpit are subjected to satirical analysis and hilariously laughed to scorn. Prof. Royce makes no pretence that his solution is any of those offered in the book of Job, where we have three at least.

"The Case of John Bunyan" is an essay in cerebral pathology, an account of Bunyan's spiritual miseries which hardly seems to justify the labor spent upon it. "The Knowledge of Good and Evil" pleads in the true Hegelian spirit for knowledge as in itself an unmixed good. How the knowledge of evil can be made subservient to virtue, while yet we may not continue in sin that grace may abound, is shown in a very pretty piece of exposition. But Prof. Royce is not equally satisfactory in his making all virtue identical with struggle and victory. In his despite we must believe that the best man is the man who is good with the least effort.

It is a long way from these abstract considerations to such an essay as that on the Sacramento riots of 1850. The essay is an expansion of certain parts of the concluding chapter of Prof. Royce's *California* in the series of State histories. It was written for that and proved disproportionately long. Even as printed here it is too long for the importance of the matter. It is interesting to find Dr. Charles Robinson, of Kansas fame, the leading rioter. Prof. Royce praises him and damns with amusing incongruity. But his account of him makes it easier to understand how at one time Robinson could praise John Brown to the skies, and years afterward execrate his memory. Evidently Robinson had no ethical "wholeness of tissue." Prof. Royce's concluding essay, "Jean Marie Guyau," is more than an extremely sympathetic appreciation of a brilliant young philosopher. It contains some general reflections on the operation of the French as compared with the German and English mind that are extremely pertinent, praising it for its superior fearlessness. Guyau's *L'Irreligion de l'Avenir*, a translation of which has recently been published in America, is highly commended, while the title is criticised as misleading. Prof. Royce tells us that he should unhesitatingly call Guyau's opinions religious if they were his own, for the reason that he should himself see in them what Guyau saw, the fulfilment in reasonable form of what the religious instinct of humanity has been seeking. But in these days, when so many are using the old names to obscure the new thought, it is refreshing to find a writer loving frankness so much that he exaggerates his difference from the conventional type.

# REVIEW OF *STUDIES OF GOOD AND EVIL*

J.E. Creighton, Review of *Studies of Good and Evil*, *Philosophical Review*, vol. 8 (1899).

*Studies of Good and Evil: A Series of Essays upon Problems of Philosophy and of Life*. By Josiah Royce, Professor of the History of Philosophy in Harvard University. New York, D. Appleton *&* Company, 1898. – pp. xvii, 384.

Professor Royce has in former books presented, in more or less detail, the arguments for philosophical idealism. In the present volume, he is mainly concerned, as he himself tells us, with the application of this doctrine to concrete and practical problems of life. Idealism "is not, as many have falsely supposed, a theory of the world founded merely upon *a priori* speculation, and developed solely in the closet. It is, and in its best historical representatives always has been, an effort to interpret the facts of life" (pp. iii, iv). By employing his idealist doctrine to throw light upon various complex problems of man's psychological and moral nature, Professor Royce not only furnishes the best test of its truth in its power of explaining facts, but this contact with actual experience seems to react upon the theory itself, and to render it more many-sided and richer, even from a speculative point of view.

The essays of which the volume is composed have the following titles: "The Problem of Job"; "The Case of John Bunyan"; "Tennyson and Pessimism"; "The Knowledge of Good and Evil"; "Natural Law, Ethics, and Evolution"; "The Implications of Self-Consciousness"; "Self-Consciousness, Social Consciousness, and Nature"; "Originality and Consciousness"; "Meister Eckhart"; "An Episode of Early California Life"; "The Squatter Riot of 1850 in Sacramento"; "Jean Marie Guyau." All of these, except the one on "Meister Eckhart" and that on "Guyau," which now appear for the first time, have been printed in journals during the last four or five years, and are now reissued without any material changes. The paper on "Self-Consciousness, Social Consciousness, and Nature," is a reprint of the author's articles in this REVIEW (Vol. IV, Nos. 5 and 6), and gives, together with the essay on "The Implications of Consciousness," a theoretical statement and expansion of the author's previously-published views on ultimate philosophical questions. The former paper seems to the present writer one of the most important pieces of speculation which has appeared in recent years. As, however, the readers of the REVIEW are familiar with the position there advanced, and, as it has already been discussed to some extent in this journal, we may turn to notice some of the applications which Professor Royce makes of his idealistic doctrines.

In discussing "The Problem of Job," the author shows by an instructive analysis of various aspects of experience that we must not be led by "the abstract meaning of the words good and evil into thinking that these two opponents exist merely as mutually exclusive facts side by side in experience." "When we go back to the fact of life, we perceive that all relatively higher good, in the trivial as well as in the more truly spiritual realm, is known only in so far as we accept as good the thwarting of an existent interest, which is thereby declared to be a relative evil, and love a tension of opposing impulses which is thereby declared to be good." To simply destroy and obliterate moral evil would be to destroy all knowledge of moral good. "What is needed, then, for the definition of a divine knowledge of a world that in its wholeness is perfect, is not a divine knowledge that shall ignore, wipe out, and utterly make naught the existence of any ill...but a divine knowledge to which shall be present that love of the world as a whole which is fulfilled in the endurance of physical ill, in the subordination of moral ill...and in the discovery that the endless tension of the finite world is included in the contemplative consciousness of the repose and harmony of eternity. To view God's nature thus is to view Him as the whole idealistic theory views Him, not as the Infinite One beyond the finite imperfections, but as the being whose unity determines the very constitution, the lack, the tension, and relative disharmony of the finite world" (pp. 24, 25). Moreover, Job's difficulty came from the thought that God is a far-off sovereign, and that for his pleasure man has to suffer. But Idealism, which regards God as the complete Self within whose experience all things fall, and in which alone they have meaning and reality, teaches that God suffers and sympathizes with us. But we cannot say that God wills evil. The function of evil in the Divine life, as in that of the finite individual, is to be endlessly triumphed over and suppressed (p. 28).

The essay on "The Knowledge of Good and Evil" (pp. 89–122), is directed against an article by Dr. Georg Simmel, of Berlin, which appeared in the *International Journal of Ethics* (Vol. IV, pp. 48–80), in which the author attempted to show that moral deficiencies, to a certain degree at least, favor intellectual development. Against this view Professor Royce argues that morality does not consist in simple innocence, that moral life, as well as physical and intellectual life is a unity of opposites. In all moral excellence there are always present tendencies which *if they were alone* would be the very destruction of any such excellence. "And this must be the case, not because of the weakness of man, but because of the organic dignity and consequent complexity of virtue; and not because the moral world is a mere maze of perplexing confusions, but because the very principles of every organic life is the combination in harmony of opposing tendencies" (p. 98). Virtue then is the choice of the good and the consequent inhibition of opposing tendencies. And "the chances are largely in favor of the greater knowledge of the virtuous chooser, since in general strong temptations are comparatively elemental, while the reasons in favor of goodness are in nature usually complex and abstract" (p. 103). Nor does moral progress, the formation of virtuous habits, involve a loss of knowledge, but progress here is exactly parallel to progress in the intellectual field. But it may be said that it is only from an experience of comparative immorality that one can understand the elemental passions of the soul. To this the answer is that such an experience in itself is not a sin. The fault of a man is not that he has elementary passions, but that he does not order and subordinate them. Moreover, one does not better understand these passions because one has yielded to their chaotic rule. The moralist should be a man of experience in a wide range of elementary life. But this does not imply that he should be a sinner in order to be wise (p. 116).

It will be noticed that Professor Royce solves the paradox which Dr. Simmel has advanced by insisting that 'good' and 'evil' are *not mere* verbal opposites, but are constituted by the relations of concrete impulses and tendencies; and this concrete tendency which refuses to rest in abstract opposites, characterizes all his discussions. Indeed, throughout the whole book, a reader cannot but be impressed with the wealth of the author's empirical knowledge, his eye for the facts, as well as by the skillful use which he makes of analogy and generalization in interpreting facts from the point of view of idealism. The style, as in Professor Royce's earlier works, is often provokingly diffuse, but there are fewer carefully prepared paradoxes than in some of his former writings, and the discussions perhaps gain as a consequence in seriousness of tone, without losing at all in logical clearness and acumen.

# REVIEW OF *STUDIES OF GOOD AND EVIL*

G.F. Stout, Review of *Studies of Good and Evil*, *Mind*, vol. 8, new series (1899).

*Studies of* Good *and Evil: A Series of Essays upon Problems of Philosophy and of Life*. By Josiah Royce, Professor of the History of Philosophy in Harvard University. New York: D. Appleton & Co., 1898. Pp. xv., 384.

"I have called these papers *Studies of Good and Evil*. The title is in its nature wide. It commits the essays contained in this volume merely to one character. They are all, directly or indirectly, contributions to the comprehension of the ethical aspects of the universe. The papers are of very various relations to technical philosophical issues. Four of them are essays in literary and philosophical criticism. One is directly concerned with the effect of the 'Knowledge of Good and Evil' upon the character of the individual man. One is a contribution to the metaphysical 'Problem of Evil' in its most general sense. Five, while dealing with metaphysical and psychological problems connected with the nature and relationships of our human type of consciousness, are somewhat more indirect contributions to the ethical interpretation of our place in the universe. One is an historical study of a concrete conflict between good and evil tendencies in early California life" (Introduction, p. v.).

The first Essay, entitled "The Problem of Job," deals with the existence of evil in the world in relation to the Divine Being. Prof. Royce's solution of this problem is by him identified with the solution given to Job himself. The answer to Job is: "When you suffer, *your sufferings are God's sufferings*, not his external work, not his external penalty, not the fruit of his neglect, but identically his own personal woe... . The true question then is: Why does God suffer? The sole possible, necessary and sufficient answer is: Because without suffering, without ill, without woe, evil, tragedy, God's life could not be perfected" (p. 14). All moral development involves the sacrifice of a lower to a higher interest, and with the necessity for this sacrifice suffering and evil are essentially connected. The same thesis is developed from the purely human point of view in the fourth Essay, on "The Knowledge of Good and Evil."

The second Essay, on "The Case of John Bunyan," is a most interesting piece of psychological analysis, executed with masterly ability and sympathetic insight. The third, "Tennyson and Pessimism, treats of the contrast between Tennyson's earlier and later *Locksley Hall*. Prof. Royce points out that the optimism of the first poem is the sort of day-dreaming which leads to disillusion and melancholy. In the later poem, Tennyson has become alive to the reality of things, and to the necessary conditions and limitations imposed by this reality. His later mood is relatively the saner and truer and, in a sense, the more optimistic, because it forms a transition to an optimism which will stand wear and tear. In the fifth Essay, the ethical despair of Huxley in face of the dominance of non-ethical natural laws is shown to be founded, not in the nature of things, but in an opposition between two subjective points of view, the naturalistic and the ethical. In the sixth Essay, "The Implications of Self-Consciousness," Prof. Royce takes up the old Cartesian argument, and tries to show, successfully, as we think, that the limitations of our finite self-consciousness imply an all-embracing consciousness, which in some sense is all that we aspire after. Perhaps this argument has never before been developed with so much force and lucidity.

The following Essay treats of "Anomalies of Self-Consciousness." It is well known that perversions of the concept of Self are produced by disturbing organic changes. Prof. Royce most ingeniously suggests that the strange organic sensations have this effect because they are characteristic of certain emotions involving specific attitudes towards the social environment.

The eighth Essay, on "Consciousness and Nature," is of special importance. It treats of the nature of our consciousness of the external world. According to Prof. Royce, those experiences have the stamp of external reality, which are an intersubjective possession. "What you can experience as well as I, is as such a physical fact... . If ten stones lie on the highway, and you and I count them, common-sense supposes that though your counting of ten is not my counting of ten, though your perception of the stones is not mine, though your inner life is in no fashion, here noteworthy, identical with mine, still the real stones that I count are identically the same as the real stones that you count." Prof. Royce argues that this common-sense notion of nature is not illusory. We cannot maintain that in truth each human being is aware of a separate fact presented only to himself, though it may resemble the objects severally presented to others. Such an assumption would destroy the basis of social consciousness; for it would imply that when many persons suppose themselves to be thinking about the same person each of them is thinking about a different person. This, according to Prof. Royce, is a *reductio ad absurdum*. This discussion of the nature of external reality is valuable; but in our opinion it does not go far enough back. The germ of the distinction between Self and Not-Self lies in the perceptual consciousness, and precedes the stage of ideal construction and inter-communication. The external reality of the bird to the cat which hunts it does not consist in the bird being a common possession of the social consciousness of cats or other beings.

The book concludes with four Essays, on "Originality and Consciousness," "Meister Eckhart," "An Episode of Early California Life," and "Jean Marie Guyau." These are very interesting, but not of the same far-reaching philosophical importance as those which precede them.

In conclusion, we may say that *Studies of Good and Evil* is a book which imperatively demands to be read, and that reading it is a keen pleasure. It is to be commended not only to philosophers by profession, but to all who are interested in the ultimate problems of life.

# REVIEW OF *THE WORLD AND THE INDIVIDUAL*, FIRST SERIES

J. Ellis McTaggart, Review of *The World and the Individual*, First Series, *Mind*, vol. 9, new series (1900).

*The World and the Individual*. First Series. "The Four Historical Conceptions of Being." By Josiah Royce, Ph.D., Professor of the History of Philosophy in Harvard University (Aberdeen Gifford Lectures). New York: Macmillan, 1900. Pp. xiv., 588.

Dr. Royce has given us a treatise of the greatest value and interest. His lectures form one of the most thoughtful and original presentations of an Idealistic Philosophy that have appeared since the tide of opinion began to flow again towards Idealism. His system may be considered as based on Hegel, and as profoundly influenced by Mr. Bradley, but there is much in it which is distinctively his own, and which cannot fail to profit an attentive reader.

Dr. Royce has the courage of his great master. "The central problem of our discussion," he announces in the first lecture, "will be the question: What is reality?" (p. 6). "Philosophy," he remarks, not only in Hegel's spirit, but very much in his manner, "necessarily involves a good deal of courage; but so does life in general" (p. 7). "As for the fine-drawn distinctions and airy abstractions, no distinction is ever too subtle for you, at the moment when it occurs to you to make that distinction for yourself, and not merely to hear that somebody else has made it. And no abstraction seems to you too airy in the hour when you rise upon your own wings to the region where just that abstraction happens to be an element in the concrete fulness of your intellectual life" (p. 8). With these words we get the key-note of the book.

"I am one of those," the author proceeds "who hold that when you ask the question: What is an Idea? and: How can Ideas stand in any true relation to Reality? you attack the world-knot in the way that promises most for the untying of its meshes" (p. 16). Now ideas have two aspects. "An idea is any state of mind or complex of states, that, when present, is consciously viewed as the relatively completed embodiment, and therefore already as the partial fulfilment of a purpose" (p. 24). This purpose Dr. Royce calls the Internal Meaning of the Idea. But ideas "at least appear to have that other sort of meaning, that reference beyond themselves to objects, that cognitive relation to outer facts, that attempted correspondence with outer facts, which many accounts of our ideas regard as their primary, inexplicable, and ultimate character. I call this second, and, for me, still problematic and derived aspect of the nature of ideas, their apparently External Meaning" (p. 26).

The problem of the nature of Being will then take this form, "How is the internal meaning of ideas consistent with their apparently external meaning?" The solution of this may be found, we are told, "in the consideration that unless ideas first voluntarily bind themselves to a given task, and so, by their internal purpose, already commit themselves to a certain selection of its object, they are neither true nor false...that despite the seemingly hopeless contrast between internal and external meaning, ideas really possess truth or falsity only by virtue of their own selection of their own task as ideas" (p. 32).

In the second lecture, we are told that there are four fundamental conceptions of Reality. The first is the Realist conception. For it, "that is real which is simply *Independent* of the mere ideas that relate or that may relate to it." "For the second" or Mystical "conception, that is real which is absolutely and finally *Immediate,* so that when it is found, *i.e.*, felt, it altogether ends any effort at ideal definition, and in this sense *satisfies* ideas as well as constitutes the fact." The third is the typical view of modern Critical Rationalism, for which "that is real which is purely and simply Valid or True." "But for the fourth conception, that is real which finally presents in a completed experience the whole meaning of a System of Ideas." This is called the Synthetic conception (p. 61).

The remainder of the second lecture is taken up with an exposition of Realism and Mysticism which is admirable both as metaphysics and as literature. The contrast, as Dr. Royce draws it, is decidedly to the disadvantage of Realism, which, we are told, "has never been held wholly clear and apart from other conceptions of reality by any first-rate thinker" (p. 70). Space permits only of one quotation, "The realist loves to talk of 'wholesome' belief in reality and to hurl pathological epithets at opponents. It is thus often amusing to find the same thinker who declares that reality is quite independent of all merely human or mental interests, in the next breath offering as proof of his thesis the practical and interesting 'wholesomeness' of this very conviction" (p. 75).

Mysticism gets much more favourable treatment. Its essence is defined as follows: "The true historical importance of Mysticism lies not in the subject to which it applied the predicate real, but in the view it holds of the fundamental nature of that very ontological predicate itself. No matter what subject the mystic seems to call real. That might be from your point of view any subject you please; yourself, or God, or the wall. The interest of Mysticism lies wholly in the predicate. Mysticism consists in asserting that to be means, simply and wholly, to be *immediate*, as what we call pure colour, pure sound, pure emotion, are already in us partly and imperfectly immediate... . That...the mystic is a very abstract sort of person, I will admit. But he is usually a keen thinker. Only he uses his thinking sceptically, to make naught of other thinkers. He gets his reality not by thinking, but by consulting the data of experience. He is not stupid. And he is trying very skilfully to be a pure empiricist. Indeed, I should maintain that the mystics are the only thorough-going empiricists in the history of philosophy" (pp. 80, 81).

In the third lecture Dr. Royce discusses Realism, and rejects it on grounds not substantially different from those which have been put forward by other idealists. In the fourth lecture Mysticism is further discussed. The example selected for illustration of the principle is the Mysticism of the Upanisheds. Dr. Royce also quotes Browning's "Last Ride Together," in which he finds an "ontology in essence one with" that of the mediæval and Hindoo mystics. This seems scarcely fair. Browning's ideal here, as elsewhere, is no doubt something that transcends finite experience. In this respect he is a mystic, in the company of Hegel, and also, I imagine, of Dr. Royce. But his ideal is never in a merely negative relation to the finite.

And it is in this merely negative relation to the finite that Dr. Royce finds the fatal defect of the Mysticism which he discusses here. Both Realism and Mysticism he says "define in the end nothing whatever. Only the realist does not intend this result, while the mystic often seems to glory in it. He thus glories, as we have seen, because in fact he is defining a very fascinating and a highly conscious contrast-effect – a contrast-effect that, far from being itself anything absolute, or actually unknown and ineffable, is a constantly present character of our human type of finite consciousness. As a fact, our thinking is a search for a goal that is conceived at once as rationally satisfying and as theoretically true. And this goal we conceive as real precisely in so far as we consciously pursue it, and mean something by the pursuit. But now this goal, since it is not present to us, in our finite form of consciousness, is first conceived by contrast with the process of this pursuit. So far indeed we conceive it negatively" (p. 180). "But when the mystic, defining his goal wholly in negative terms, lays stress upon the contrast as simply absolute, he finds that so far his Absolute is defined as nothing but the absence of finitude, and so as apparently equivalent to nothing at all, since all definite contents are for us so far finite, and since the absence of finitude is for us the absence of contents" (p. 181).

Mysticism then must be amended by a recognition that our finite life is no more mere illusion than it is absolute reality. It is too unreal to do more than lead us to something beyond itself, but if it can do even this, it cannot be absolutely unreal.

The fifth lecture gives us the transition to the Third Conception of Reality. If Realism, while giving up the hopeless task of defining the Real as absolutely independent of knowledge, wishes still to emphasise the fact that it is outside my particular knowledge, and that my ideas must conform to it, it is led to the view that the Real is that "which, if known, is found giving to ideas their validity, that to which ideas ought to correspond" (p. 201). And, again, the mystic only reached his conception of the Absolute by setting aside our finite experiences as contradictory, and not conforming to the ideal of knowledge. It would seem to follow then that true Being resides in the Validity of Ideas.

The next lecture begins by tracing the conception of Being as Validity in the philosophies of Aristotle, Aquinas and Kant. The question then arises: "What is a valid or a determinately possible experience at the moment when it is supposed to be only possible? What is a valid truth at the moment when no one verifies its validity?" (p. 260). Actual experience is always individual. But *merely* valid truths appear as mere universals. Can this Third Conception recognise and accept this difference?

The seventh lecture considers "the Internal and External meaning of Ideas," and in it Dr. Royce's own views begin to come to the front. To begin with, he takes the definition of Truth as "that about which we judge." All judgments, he holds, assert something about a real world. The assertion of hypothetical judgments is a negative one. "In general, the judgment, 'If A is B, C is D,' can be interpreted as meaning that there are, in the world of valid objects, no real cases where, at once, A is B, while at the same time C is nevertheless not D." (p. 274). It follows from this that universal judgments can never fully attain the end with which they set out. Taken by themselves, they can only tell us "what external Reality is not." Now what we want to know is what external Reality *is*. But our negative judgments could only give us this if they exhausted all possible alternatives. And this is a task which is "not only endless, but hopeless" (p. 279).

In particular judgments, indeed, we get positive assertions about Reality. But then no particular judgments will ever enable us to determine an individual as individual. We can never, by means of them, know an object so that we can know it to be absolutely unique in the universe. That is, we cannot determine it completely. But "the Other that we seek is that which, if found, would *determine our ideas to their final truth*. Now only what is finally determinate can, in its turn, determine... . Whoever should try, as, in fact, our Third Conception of Being seems to try, to define the world of Being in terms exclusive of individuality, seems forced to say, 'The final fact is that there is no individual fact, or, in other words, that there is no unique Being at all, but only a type; so that the Being with which our thoughts are to correspond does not determine the "mere ideas" to any single and unique correspondence with itself, but leaves them finally indeterminate.' But is the *Veritas* that is thus left us any *Veritas* at all? Is not the very expression used self-contradictory? Can the absence of finality be the only final fact?" (pp. 295, 296).

The point raised in the questions with which this extract concludes would have repaid, I venture to suggest, further treatment. It has been held, by thinkers who cannot lightly be passed over, that universal and particular judgments, in all their relative indefiniteness, are, nevertheless, the ultimate truth. A refutation of this view seems necessary, if Dr. Royce's position is to be maintained – and no one is better qualified than Dr. Royce to give one.

We now pass to consider Truth as the Correspondence between any Idea and its Object. This correspondence, as the author points out with admirable clearness, depends on the purpose which we entertain in using the idea. "The idea is true if it possesses the sort of correspondence to its object that the idea itself wants to possess. Unless that kind of identity in inner structure between idea and object can be found which the specific purpose embodied in a given idea demands the idea is false" (p. 306). Again "the idea intends to attain this correspondence to some particular object – not to any object you please, not to whatever happens to correspond to the ideal construction in question, but to a determined object. The determination of what object is meant, is, therefore, certainly again due, in one aspect, to the internal meaning of the idea. No one else can determine for me what object I mean by my idea.

"But hereupon we seem to face, indeed, a fatal difficulty... . And this is that, if the idea predetermines what object it selects as the one that it means, just as it predetermines what sort of correspondence it intends to have to this object, the idea, nevertheless, does not predetermine whether its object is such that the idea, if finite, shall succeed in attaining entire agreement with the object. Otherwise truth would be mere tautology, error would be excluded in advance, and it would be useless even to talk of an object external in any sense as the idea" (pp. 319, 320).

What is the solution? Dr. Royce gives the following, which is in harmony with the result attained from the first definition. "The idea so selects the object, that, if the idea has a perfectly definite meaning and truth at all, this object is to be a precisely determinate object, *such that no other object could take its place as the* object *of this idea*. And in spite of the fact that the object is such solely by the will of the idea, the idea undertakes submissively to be either true or false when compared with that object" (p. 327). But with this we have reached the fourth and final Conception of Being, "that What is, or what is real, is as such the complete embodiment, in individual form and in final fulfilment, of the internal meaning of finite ideas" (p. 339).

This Fourth Conception is then developed, and defended against various misconceptions. After this, in the ninth lecture, we pass to the discussion of Universality and Unity. This begins, if I understand it rightly, with an attempt to identify the ultimately true and the ultimately desirable, which does not seem to follow logically from what has preceded it. In every case in which our ideas are not expressed, we are told, "the reality, which shall positively refuse it expression, is *ipso facto* the reality to which the idea itself appeals, and is not independent of this appeal. For you are not put in the wrong by a reality to which you have made no reference; and error is possible only concerning objects that we actually mean as our own objects. The object that is to defeat my partial and fragmentary will is then *ipso facto* my whole will, my final purpose, my total meaning determinately and definitely expressed" (p. 389). And again, "My will, as it is now transiently embodied, can fail in any partial way of realisation, but only because I now fail to be wholly aware of my own will... . However far I wander in the wildernesses of my temporal experience, the eternal fulfilment of my own life encompasses me. I escape not from the meshes of the net of my own will" (p. 390).

This seems too short a road to a final harmony. No doubt every act of knowledge is a fulfilment of the will, for we cannot know, as Dr. Royce points out, without willing to know. And every volition is an experience of reality, for, when we will, our volition is part of the real. Thus nothing real could be absolutely alien to our will, and no ideal could be absolutely void of reality. But, after all, the will to know is only an element in the whole system of volition. And it is conceivable that this element might be satisfied without the others. We might know the universe, *e.g.*, and know it to refuse satisfaction to our demands for beauty, or for love. In that case it would give us something we had willed – namely, knowledge – but not everything, nor, perhaps, what we regarded as highest. In such a case as this "the eternal fulfilment of my own life" would not be realised.

Such a contingency could be disproved by a system which worked out in comparative detail the ultimate nature of the real and of the good, and which would then show, of these independently attained results, that in fact they coincided. I do not mean to assert that the identity, if attained, would be a mere brute conjunction. On the contrary, it would consciousness has some unique character, and when we have asserted, as we have also done, that in our rational life our momentary will and its finite expression belong to this very unique aspect of our finite life, we have indeed found, in our finite will, an aspect which *no* causation could even by any possibility explain. For whatever else causality may be, it implies the explanation of facts by their general character, and by their connexion with other facts. Whatever is unique, is as such not causally explicable. The individual as such is never the mere result of law. In consequence, the causal explanation of an object never defines the individual and unique characters as such, but always its general characters. Consequently, *if* the will and the expression of that will in any moment of our finite life possess characters, namely, precisely those individual and uniquely significant characters which no causal explanation can predetermine, then such acts of will, as significant expressions of purpose in our life, constitute precisely what ethical common sense has always meant by free acts" (p. 467). This view is one of great importance. It may be doubted whether "ethical common sense" would accept a life as free which was "a stage or case of the expression of the divine purpose at a given point of time" (p. 464). But then it might also be doubted if it has a coherent conception of freedom at all.

The lectures are followed by a Supplementary Essay on The One, The Many, and the Infinite, which is mainly a criticism of Mr. Bradley. Dr. Royce admits that Mr. Bradley "has shown that every effort to bring to unity the manifoldness of our world involves us in what he himself often calls an 'infinite process'" (p. 474). But does this involve that all our efforts must be considered to have failed, and that the way in which the manifold is really unified is, for us, a mystery? Is a real infinite process an impossibility?

At any rate, we come across such processes in mathematics, where they "lie at the basis of highly and very positively significant researches" (p. 499). And, outside the reach of mathematics, there are important cases where "a single purpose, definable as One, demands for its realisation a multitude of particulars which could not be a limited multitude without involving the direct defeat of the purpose itself" (p. 501). For example if, on part of the surface of England, an absolutely accurate map of England was constructed, such a map would contain a map of itself, since it *is* part of the surface of England, and it represents all of the surface of England, itself included. But this second map would also have to contain a map of itself, and so on in an infinite series (p. 505). Now, whether we believe such a map to be possible, or whether we follow Mr. Bradley in rejecting it as impossible, "our faith, or a doubt, would equally involve seeing that the *one* plan of mapping in question necessarily implies just this infinite *variety* of internal constitution. We doubtless be a supreme unity compared to which both reality and goodness would be mere abstractions. But it remains true that the good and the real can only be united through a third term. It is impossible to prove that the ultimately real is *as such* the ultimately good, or that the ultimately good is *as such* the ultimately real.

Dr. Royce now passes on to the personality of the Absolute. "In the world as we define it, there can exist no fact except as a known fact, as a fact present in some consciousness, namely, precisely to the consciousness that fulfils the whole meaning of whoever asserts that this fact is real. In view of this essential feature of our finite situation as thinkers, it follows at once that the whole world of truth and being must exist only as present, in all its variety, its wealth, its relationships, its entire constitution, to the unity of a single consciousness, which includes both our own and all finite conscious meanings in one final eternally present insight" (p. 397).

It may, perhaps, be granted that we cannot conceive reality except as conscious experience, and that there is much which we call real of which it is in the highest degree improbable that any finite being is at present conscious. It is by no means as certain, however, that there is anything which we should at present call real of which no finite being ever was or ever will be conscious. Of course a consciousness which has been or will be is, so far, a consciousness which now is not. And if the existence of finite selves was merely temporal, we should have to postulate the infinite consciousness which is perpetually conscious of all reality. But Dr. Royce would not, I suppose, deny that a finite self had an eternal significance. And surely this leaves another alternative open – that we call Being real of which no finite self is at present conscious because we find in its future or past consciousness of it *sub specie temporis*, the sign of a timeless consciousness of it *sub specie æternitatis*.

Of the rest of the lecture it is only possible to mention in passing the well-balanced exposition which is given of the extent to which we are justified in interpreting the universe in terms of our own consciousness. Dr. Royce steers a middle course between Mr. Bradley on the one hand, and Hegel's practice on the other. (Hegel's theory might not impossibly be found in the middle with Dr. Royce.) The result – not to be either limited to humanity nor alien to it – is brought out with great clearness.

The last lecture is entitled "Individuality and Freedom." That Individuality does not suffer in such a system is plain. The whole aim of knowledge, it tells us, is to find the individual. And the close unity of the whole, so far from destroying the individuality of the parts, is essential to it. With regard to freedom, the author points out that causal determination can never be the last word about anything individual. "When we have assumed, as we have now done, that every moment of every finite should, moreover, see how and why the one and the infinitely many are here, at least within thought's reach, conceptually linked" (p. 507).

Now such a system, says Dr. Royce, quoting Dedekind, is found in my own realm of thoughts (p. 511). For whenever I have a thought, I can also think that I have it. And then I can also think that I have this second reflective thought, and so on without end. And any theory which holds the Absolute to be self-representative involves such an infinite series. For the representation falls within the Absolute, and must be represented. And so must this second representation, and so on *ad infinitum*.

The Essay ends with a consideration of the arguments for holding that such an infinite series could not be real. It is maintained that an infinite series which is involved in the unity of a single purpose, can be a true individual, and may therefore be real.

It would be impossible within the limits of a review to adequately criticise this theory, or to raise a further question – on which the practical importance of the theory depends. Granted that the Absolute is a harmony, is it ultimately a harmony of self-representation, or is there some more adequate form? Something would have to be said on this point, but here I must content myself with closing my account of a most valuable and interesting book.

The second series of lectures is promised within a year. It is to contain the more detailed application of the results here reached to problems that directly concern religion.

# REVIEW OF *THE WORLD AND THE INDIVIDUAL*, SECOND SERIES

J. Ellis McTaggart, Review of *The World and the Individual*, Second Series, *Mind*, vol. 11, new series (1902).

*The World and the Individual.* Second Series. "Nature, Man, and the Moral Order." By Josiah Royce. Ph.D., LL.D., Professor of the History of Philosophy in Harvard University. (Aberdeen Gifford Lectures.) New York: Macmillan, 1901. Pp. xvii., 480.

This volume, the author tells us, is more practical in its aim than its predecessor. "The previous discussion dealt with the Theory of Being: the aim of what is to come shall be a doctrine about Life" (p. 4). The first Lecture, "The Recognition of Facts," after some admirable remarks on the relation of philosophy to life, recapitulates the view taken in the First Series, that "what we experience is, in one aspect, always our own will to be compelled by facts" (p. 30). It is no doubt the case, as Dr. Royce points out, that we can never be out of harmony with facts except in so far as our own nature leads us to postulate something inconsistent with them. But it appears from the fuller statement previously given (*cf.* First Series, pp. 389, 390) that Dr. Royce finds in this a ground for a belief in an ultimate and supreme harmony between our will and reality. And this does not seem a legitimate inference. If my will had no relation to the facts before me, I could not be dissatisfied. But it does not follow from this that my will will ever be in that special relation to the facts which produces satisfaction.

The second Lecture is entitled "The Linkage of Facts." Here we deal with the distinction between the World of Description and the World of Appreciation. The World of Description is that which we form when we view facts "as if the only purpose which they could fulfill was the purpose of being discriminable" (p. 98). This world also is "anybody's world." From whatever individual standpoint we may start, we shall come to the same result (p. 99). And it is therefore "abstract and inadequate" (p. 101).

"The true world," on the other hand, "the World of Values or of Appreciation, as rightly viewed by an absolute insight, would be a world of Selves, forming in the unity of their systems One Self" (p. 106). And its unity "determines not merely what is the same from many points of view, but what is uniquely present, once for all, from the divine point of view, as the one true Order of things" (p. 102).

The distinction here indicated is, no doubt, of great importance. But Dr. Royce's terminology tends to suggest an absolute gulf where, as it seems to me, there is in reality a continuous development. Between the abstract universality of mathematics and the full individuality recognised, if not completely expounded, by such a philosophy as Dr. Royce's, or Hegel's, there surely lie many stages which give gradually increasing recognition to individuality. And "the one true Order of things," while it is certainly more than "what is the same from many points of view," is not so much a fresh conception as a higher form of the same conception.

The rest of the lecture is largely occupied by the development or the view that the "best single word for expressing what is essential to a lawful order in the world of facts is the term Series" (p. 72). In the World of Appreciation the series are such that "every fact has its next-following fact." In the World of Description, on the other hand, a fresh fact can always be inserted between any two facts – or when this is not empirically possible, we postulate the intermediaries we cannot observe (pp. 98, 107).

All order may no doubt be expressed as a Series. But is it worth while to do so? Everything which makes a conception of order adequate or inadequate as an expression of reality is left untouched by such an expression. If reality is conceived as a mechanical aggregate, or as an organism, or as the *Civitas Dei*, it could be said to form a series. But the important point is to know what relations are predicated, in each case, between the points forming the series, and it is just this which the conception of series ignores – as is natural with a conception taken originally from mathematics.

The third Lecture deals with the Temporal and the Eternal. Dr. Royce first expounds the conception of the Specious Present, as applied to the consciousness of finite individuals. The lives of finite beings, he tells us, must be considered as being in a temporal order, because every finite being is striving towards an Other, which involves time (p. 134). Nevertheless, the Other towards which such a being strives is the whole of which the striving being is a part, and this leads on to the assertion that "this same temporal whole is, when regarded in its wholeness, an Eternal order. And I mean by this assertion nothing whatever, but that the whole real content of this temporal order, whether it is viewed from any one temporal instant as past or as present or as future, is at once known, *i.e.*, is consciously experienced as a whole by the Absolute. And

I use this expression *at once* in the very sense in which we before used it when we pointed out that to your own consciousness, the whole musical phrase may be and often is known at once, despite the fact that each member of the musical succession, when taken as the temporally present one, excludes from its own temporal instant the other members of the sequence, so that they are either no longer or not yet, at the instant when this element is temporally the present one" (p. 138).

An adequate discussion of this most interesting theory is impossible here. I wish only to make two comments. The first is that the Specious Present of the Absolute contains the future as well as the past, in opposition to the view held by Mr. Bradley, by which "the 'now' contains merely the process of present into past" (*Appearance and Reality*, p. 41).

The second point is that this view really asserts the absolute validity of Time, and leaves no place for Eternity at all. If I understood Dr. Royce rightly, he holds that even for the Absolute the distinction of past, present, and future really exists. Even from the standard of the Absolute, therefore, some events are no longer, and others not yet. It is true that the Absolute is directly conscious of what is no longer and what is not yet. But that does not make them real at the moment at which the Absolute is conscious of them – for then they would respectively still be, and already be, which Dr. Royce has denied to be the case. What then is eternal? Nothing but events, apparently, since Dr. Royce speaks of nothing else. But not the events of which the Absolute is conscious, for the reasons I have just given. Not, finally, the event of the Absolute's consciousness. For that must change every moment, since every moment it regards as present something which it had previously regarded as future, and regards as past something which it had, in the previous moment, regarded as present.

Lecture IV. ("Physical and Social Reality") contains a very interesting study of the social element in our view of nature, which is summed up in the assertion that "the so-called axiom of the unvarying character of the laws of nature is no self-evident truth, is not even at once an empirically established and a universal generalisation, and possesses its present authority because of the emphasis that our social interests give to the discovery of uniform laws where we can discover them" (p. 195).

If among our "social interests" be included our interest in understanding the universe, it is no doubt true that, in so far as we do not attempt to understand the universe, we do not need the axiom of the uniformity of nature. But this would also be the case with every other truth, including the law of contradiction, and Dr. Royce certainly does not hold that all truth depends on our social interests in the way in which the uniformity of nature depends on them.

If "social interests" is taken in a narrower sense, I do not think the proposition can be maintained. No doubt the world would be inconvenient if there were no uniform laws to be found in it. But would that be all. Would it not also be contradictory? And then the uniformity of nature can scarcely be said to be a merely social interest. That uniformity is not the whole truth, and is therefore not quite true. But an approximation to the truth is not quite the same as a merely practical expedient.

Lecture V. deals with the Interpretation of Nature. Dr. Royce points out that the laws of reversible processes are valid only for Matter as such. "But the other laws, the laws of the irreversible processes, are, in their most general type, common to Matter and Mind, to the physical and the moral world" (p. 218). To these latter much greater importance is to be attached. "We know that Nature, as it were, *tolerates* our mathematical formulas. We do not know that she would not equally well tolerate many other such formulas instead of these. But we do know, meanwhile, that the processes called by us growth and decay are facts as genuinely real as any natural facts whatever" (p. 225).

This is followed by the development of a theory which seems to me to be of great novelty and importance. Those systems which hold that all centres of reality must be conscious beings have generally considerable difficulty in explaining the finite centres of reality behind that inorganic nature which behaves so differently from our bodies. Dr. Royce suggests that "the actually fluent inner experience, which our hypothesis attributes to inorganic Nature would be a finite experience of an extremely august temporal span, so that a material region of the inorganic world would be to us the phenomenal sign of the presence of at least one fellow creature who took, perhaps, a billion years to complete a moment of his consciousness, so that where we saw, in the signs given us of his presence, only monotonous permanence of fact, he, in his inner life, found momentarily significant change (p. 228). "If...personal individuality is an essentially ethical category, then a new person exists whenever, within a conscious process of a given time-span, intercommunication with the rest of Nature results in the appearance of processes significant enough to express themselves in new ideals, and in a new unification of experience in terms of these ideals" (p. 229).

"Meanwhile, our hypothesis supposes that, in the case of the animals, we may well be dealing not with beings who are rational in our own time-span, nor yet with beings who are irrational. The rational being with whom you deal when you observe an animal's dimmer hints of rationality, may be phenomenally represented rather by the race as a whole than by any one individual. In that case, this individual animal is no rational person, but he may well be, so to speak, a temporally brief section of a person, whose time-span of consciousness is far longer than ours" (p. 232).

The next two lectures are devoted to the doctrine of the Self. Dr. Royce reminds us of the distinction drawn in the previous volume between Internal and External meaning, and declares that primarily "the contrast of Self and not-Self comes to us as the contrast between the Internal and the External meaning of this present moment's purpose" (p. 272). The significance of the Self is teleological. "By this meaning of my life-plan, by this possession of an ideal, by this Intent always to remain another than my fellows despite my divinely planned unity with them – by this, and not by the possession of any Soul-Substance, I am defined and created a Self" (p. 276). And again, "in our present form of human consciousness, the true Self of any individual man is not a datum, but an ideal" (p. 287).

This is followed by an attempt to show how a part of a Self may, in time, assume a separate Selfhood, which it did not previously possess. It would seem that the new Self may remain a part of the original larger Self , or (if I understand the theory rightly) may become independent of that original Self. I must confess that I entirely fail in attaching any meaning to the inclusion of one Self in another, or to the transformation into a Self of something which previously was not one. Nor do I see how Dr. Royce can be so confident as he apparently is that the genesis of the Self in time is not inconsistent with its immortality when produced. Even if, as he says, all facts have teleological relations with the Absolute (p. 322) how are we, on such a theory, to be convinced that the end of each finite Self is not to efface itself and vanish as a means to something else?

Lecture VIII. deals with the Moral Order. The following sentences seem to give the fundamental aspects of the doctrine put forward. "To seek anything but the Absolute itself is, indeed, even for the most perverse Self, simply impossible. All life is looking for God, however base the forms of idolatry beneath which the false love of the world may ignorantly hide its own meaning, at any one temporal instant" (p. 347). "The Self may seek its self-expression explicitly in the form of rebellion. Nor is such a rebellious attitude by any means wholly evil. Conscious choice of a total evil is, indeed, impossible. For the Self, at its worst, seeks finality of self- expression, and seeks this self-expression through a life that is at once Other than its present Internal meaning, and perfected in its form and content… . As a fact I can only assert my finite Self by transforming myself; so that I actually obey, in some measure, even while I rebel. For the finite Self cannot seek its own, without passing over into new life. And there is self-sacrifice involved in even the most stubborn rebellion; and courage and endurance are exercised, unwillingly, even by the most cowardly of pleasure-seekers" (pp. 349, 350).

"Now once considering the individual as acting in time, what you have a right to say to him is, that, if he intends evil results...then, just in so far as he succeeds in carrying out his end, he produces what, at just that point of time, is indeed an actual evil" (p. 362). "Every evil deed must somewhere and at some time be atoned for, by some other than the agent, if not by the agent himself" (p. 368).

I take the position to be this – moral evil has an eternal significance, but in its eternal significance it is so transcended that it is no longer evil. But, *sub specie temporis*, it is evil, as opposed to good, and must be atoned for before it is left behind. By such a view we combine the assertion that the universe is fundamentally good with a recognition of the phenomenal reality of evil which is quite sufficient for practical purposes – the only purposes for which we need be anxious to assert its reality. The theory and its exposition both seem to me to be admirable. My only doubt is as to the adequacy of Dr. Royce's conception of Eternity for such a purpose. Would not something more mystical and less temporal than an all-embracing Specious Present be required before the evilness of evil could be transcended?

"The Struggle with Evil" forms the subject of the ninth Lecture. "Every ill of human fortune is, presumably, either directly due to the magnitude and ideality of our finite plans, or else is more or less directly the expression of the morally defective intent of some human or extra-human moral agent, or of the inadequacy of such an agent to his own ideals" (pp. 387, 388). I would suggest that these are not so much alternatives as joint factors, both of which must be present in all cases. The evil fortune of any being must imply both an ideal which the facts hinder him from carrying out, and the facts which hinder him from carrying out the ideal.

This is followed by an admirable criticism of the forensic view of morals, which asserts that a man is only corrupted by his own sin, and ought only to suffer for his own sin. "In a sense the sin of every evil-doer among us taints all of us" (p. 389). And, again, the denial that any real evil falls on any man, except on account of the sins he has freely committed, reduces all attempts to help others to an absurdity (*cf.* pp. 402, 404).

The Lecture closes with an assertion that "our sorrows are identically God's own sorrows" (p. 408), and that "unless God knows sorrow, he knows not the highest good, which consists in the overcoming of sorrow" (p. 410). This supports my doubt as to the sufficiency of the Eternity ascribed to God by Dr. Royce for the purpose of completely transcending evil. And yet we have been told that the Absolute "transcends" evil (p. 396). Again God's Eternity is an all-embracing Specious Present. Therefore the evil, like everything else, is eternally present to him. If it is present *as* evil, and not as transcended and transmuted into what is not evil, how can he be said to have overcome it, or how can reality be held to be, *sub specie æternitatis*, completely good?

The Union of God and Man forms the subject of the last lecture. The most important part of this lecture deals with Immortality. "The same considerations," we are told, "which imply the intimate union of every temporal instant's passing striving with the whole life of God, equally imply that an individual task which is ideal, which is unique, and which means the service of God in a series of deeds such as can never end without an essential failure of the task, can only be linked with God's life, and can only find its completion in this union with God, in an individual life which is the life of a conscious Self, and which is a deathless life" (p. 430).

This seems to me to be more than Dr. Royce is, on his own principles, entitled to assert. Every finite Self is included within the infinite Self, in a manner which apparently is analogous to the way in which different conscious moments are included within each finite Self. What guarantee have we that the different finite Selves are not transitory episodes in the infinite Self in the sense in which a particular mood, or a particular effort are transitory episodes in my finite Self? Each finite Self is, no doubt, unique. But the "passing striving" of each temporal instant is also unique, and yet it passes. It is true, also – at least on Dr. Royce's principles – that every moral task, when completed, gives birth to a fresh task. But I do not see that Dr. Royce has proved that the new task is a task for the same Self as the one who performed the previous task. And without this, the endless succession of tasks would be compatible with the transitoriness of all finite Selves.

This volume will satisfy even the high expectations which were raised by the First Series. If Idealists in general can combine the old courage with new caution so admirably as Dr. Royce does, they will have learnt a lesson which will be of great value to themselves and the world.

# REVIEW OF *THE WORLD AND THE INDIVIDUAL*, FIRST SERIES

John Dewey, Review of *The World and the Individual*, First Series, *Philosophical Review*, vol. 9 (1900).

*The World and the Individual.* Gifford Lectures, First Series: The Four Historical Conceptions of Being, by Josiah Royce, Ph.D., Professor of the History of Philosophy in Harvard University. New York, The Macmillan Co., 1900, pp. xiv, 588.

If the book before us lacked other noteworthy characteristics, it would be remarkable for the simplicity and force with which it grasps a single conception and follows it through its various forms, using it as an instrument of both criticism and construction. Natural religion, the topic *ex officio* of a Gifford lecture, is interpreted from the standpoint of the "nature of things" or ontology. The aim is so to define Being as to arrive at some conception of what is meant by the reality of God, and of the world and the human individual in relation to God. The originality of which I have spoken does not consist in this fact, nor yet in just taking the epistemological road towards Being. These things, as Professor Royce recognizes, are familiar enough. It is the special way in which the nature of the cognitive idea and its relation to Being are handled, the attempt to center the whole discussion about the nature of the idea as such, that give the book force and freshness, and that challenge the reader to raise the problems anew for himself, to reëxamine his own conceptions, and modify his own method, even if at the end he, like the present writer, finds himself forced to dissent.

We are to start with the world as idea and not as fact. If we start from the world as fact, we are "sunk deep in an ocean of mysteries"; for it is a "defiant mystery." It bewilders, angers, and baffles us in its contrast of order and chaos, its combination of goodness and cruelty. Because this world of fact is persistently baffling, we turn to the world of idea to get the key to unlock it. We find that the defect of the world of fact "is due at bottom simply to the fault of our human type of consciousness" (p. 18). So we must devote ourselves to a criticism of the latter. By this criticism we may purify it; we may raise it to a higher level and thus win insight into reality. This mode of approach at once compels the definition of an idea, and at least a preliminary conception of its relation to reality.

In defining idea, Mr. Royce starts from the familiar conception of recent psychology which views the ideational life from the standpoint of organism and environment, and thus connects it with the motor or behavior side of experience. An idea of a thing "always involves a consciousness of how you propose to act towards the thing of which you have an idea." Mr. Stout's remark that an idea is a plan of action, or way of constructing an object, is quoted with approval. The idea thus represents a sort of will or active meaning. It is an intention. Or, in the more technical definition, it is "any state of consciousness, whether simple or complex, which, when present, is then and there viewed as at least the partial expression or embodiment of a single conscious purpose" (p. 22). For example, in singing a melody we are conscious that this act partially fulfils and embodies a purpose; as such it constitutes a musical idea. The purpose, so far as embodied, constitutes the internal meaning of the idea.

But finite ideas always appear to have a meaning not exhausted in what is present as internal meaning, or fulfilment of purpose. They at least seem to refer beyond themselves, to objects. This secondary and problematic aspect we may call their apparent *external* meaning. The melody, for example, may be regarded not simply as the fulfilment of the musical purpose, but as meaning, attempting to copy or corresponding to, a certain theme of Beethoven. Indeed, in all our cognitive experience this external meaning *appears* to be fundamental. In knowing, "our ideas seem destined to perform a task which is externally set for them by the real world" (p. 28). Common sense would say that this reference of ideas to facts wholly apart from themselves, and the necessity of correspondence to these external facts in order to secure truth for ideas, is the important thing; and that the mere inner meaning, uncontrolled by such reference, is either just fancy or else a positive source of error. Yet there are reasons for doubting whether the contrast is as ultimate as it seems. In a certain sense the idea must have the primacy. Unless the idea has a meaning, a purpose of its own in relation to the object, unless it assigns its own special task of correspondence, there can be no question of the supposedly external object which is to serve as standard or model; there will be no telling what fact is to be used as basis for judging successful correspondence. The truth, for example, of the meaning that I put into my idea of a cow (so we may paraphrase Professor Royce), cannot be told by sheer reference to *any* object – to object as such; we must first find what object the idea itself means; what is the task of reference and correspondence that it sets for itself – what itself *means* or *intends*. Admitting then, that we must go to an object, it is to an object selected and determined by the idea itself.

It is this conception that gives unity and characteristic originality to Professor Royce's discussion. It leads him in the end to declare that the whole external meaning, the reference to objects, must be interpreted in terms of the inner purpose of the idea itself. It leads to the interpretation of the apparent external meaning – the dependence upon external things – as in truth only an instrument of the adequate expression and development of a meaning partially fulfilled in the idea itself. It leads, that is, to the proposition that the whole distinction between inner and outer meaning, between the significance that an idea has as an idea, and that which it has as dependent upon an external object, is due to the difference between a partial and a complete embodiment of a purpose. The defect of our "present human form of momentary consciousness, lies in the fact that we just now do not know precisely what we mean" (p. 39). Our ideas, in other words, express our purposes only vaguely, abstractly, without determination – or, as it is afterwards put – they are mere universals. Hence our discontent with our ideas; hence our search for an "Other," for the object which, though appearing to be external to the idea, in reality is just the supplementation necessary to give complete fulfilment to the purpose only partially presented in the idea. This completeness of determination of meaning is the individual. Complete will, complete meaning, complete individuality (p. 40), are thus the "limits" of the development of all ideas. Here we get, in outline, the answer to the question, What is reality? "To be, means simply to express, to embody the complete internal meaning of a certain absolute system of ideas – a system moreover which is genuinely implied in the true internal meaning or purpose of every finite idea, however fragmentary" (p. 36; see also p. 341).

This far the discrepancy of external meaning from internal has been treated as problematic only, as due to the abstract reflection of the critic, (*e.g.*, p. 33). In discussing the root ideas that differentiate the various systems of ontology, Professor Royce appears however to indicate that, *for the finite consciousness as finite*, the discrepancy is inherent and necessary. "Experience comes to us, in part, as brute fact...merely immediate experience...apart from definition, articulation, and in general from any insight into its relationships." But experience "in addition to its mere presence possesses meaning" (pp. 55–56). On this side, we have ideas. These two aspects are at war with each other. The brute, immediate facts are obstacles obdurate to our ideas. There is "endless finite conflict of mere experience and mere idea." So far as the ideas attempt to comprehend, to master the data in terms of themselves, there is thought. This is the collection of ideas contrasted with fact and yet trying to possess fact. So far as successful, we get an immediate experience luminous with meaning.

Four fundamental ontological conceptions arise as typically different modes of interpreting the relative significance of these two factors, fact and idea, immediacy and thought. The first, technically speaking, is realism, it emphasizes the external independence of the object, and defines reality from this point of view. Mysticism dwells upon that which is actually present in experience, the immediate, and hence defines reality as that in which all otherness is lost in immediacy, and all diversity is at an end. According to the third view, that of critical rationalism, the real is the object which gives truth or validity to our ideas: neither the idea nor the independent object is real, but an object of possible experience which would verify our idea (p. 61). The criticism of realism shows the necessity of defining Being as in essential relation to ideas; that of mysticism, the necessity of conceiving it as fulfilling, and not merely cancelling, the meaning of our fragmentary, finite experiences; while that of the "Possibility of Experience" theory shows the necessity of conceiving validity and truth to be actually and individually experienced, not merely universally and abstractly possible. The development of these three necessities of interpreting Being, leads inevitably to the fourth, Professor Royce's own conception: viz., that Being is the eternal, exhaustive, determinate, and individual presentation in immediate experiences of the really possible meanings of all ideas – a *totum simul* in a living experience of immediate appreciation of all valid significances, the absolute consciousness. And since, in its individuality, it fulfils the real purpose and strength of all finite consciousnesses, it preserves and validates within itself finite wills and individualities.

Limits of space prevent an adequate exposition of Mr. Royce's statement and criticism of realism and mysticism. Mr. Royce's position, however, is so coherent, so sequential, that if I have been at all successful in reporting it above, even a brief summary will not be wholly meaningless. Strictly consistent or extreme realism asserts the entire independence of the object as regards ideas; it is totally unaffected by them; it is "whether or no" they are. Hence the theory has really no way of defining Being except as that which is thus independent of ideas – *any* nature or content may be ascribed, and historically has been ascribed to it, provided only it remains wholly other than ideas. But, clearly, if its sole definition is to be independent of no ideas, ideas cannot refer to it, cannot have connection, relation or community as regards it; certainly cannot correspond with it. Hence it is, for us, a realm of nothing at all; moreover, since by the realistic hypothesis this Being was to furnish the standard for truth and falsity of ideas, there is no longer any possibility of discriminating true from false. All ideas equally exist, are "existent entities" on the same footing – the "forgotten thesis" of realism (p. 134). Realism thus contradicts itself in the most thoroughgoing way.[1]

Mysticism realizes that the discrepancy of idea and fact, immediacy and object, is the source of all struggle, failure, and disquietude. It sees the utter impossibility of ending this conflict in terms of the mere "other," the independent Being of realism, since it sees not only the contradictory character of such a Being, but also that its apparent or illusory presence is the source of all our woe, intellectual and moral. Hence it seeks Being in the escape from, or destruction of such external being, in the selfhood of sheer immediate distinctionless feeling. Hence the self-contradiction of mysticism; since it can define Being only as the goal of our struggle, only as a "contrast-effect," and if the struggle, the finite ideas, are absolutely illusory, Being itself remains absolutely without content. It is a "zero which is contrasted with nothing...and thus remains a genuine and absolute nothing" (p. 181).[2]

In the statement and criticism of the "Possibility of Experience" theory we enter, in effect, upon the exposition of Mr. Royce's own position, for he accepts it as true "as far as it goes," but holds that in order to retain the amount of truth which it possesses, it must be further developed. The transformation resulting from the required development gives his own conception of Being.

Even common sense is quite familiar with objects which obviously have Being only in relation to our ideas: it makes no difficulty, however, in ascribing objective reality to them. In this case objective reality clearly means *truth, validity*. Instances of such beings are the constitution of a

[1] It is only fair to say that in this condensation I have omitted reference to the nominally most characteristic feature of Professor Royce's discussion, namely, the consideration of Being as many or one. But, if I understand his argument, the above gives its *real* force; indeed, to be frank, the other phase of his argument seems to me to be either tautology, an elaborate reiteration of the fact that realism has no definition for its real except mere and complete independence of ideas, or else to be fallacious.

[2] Personally I have found the discussion of mysticism one of the most interesting and enlightening portions of the book. But doubts arise as to the logical conclusiveness of the criticism. Can it be said that mysticism defines Being in terms of *total* contrast with our "finite" experience? Does it not rather define it exclusively in terms of *one phase* of our present experience – namely, the immediate phase – and insist, *not* upon the illusoriness of the whole "finite" experience, but upon that of objects "other than" this immediacy and consequently upon the need of withdrawal from or negation of these externalities?

state, social status, the commercial realm of credits and debts. Again, mathematical truths, the value of π, the fact that a function continuous within certain intervals need have no differential coefficients within those intervals; and, again, the moral order. In considering cases such as the reality of mathematical truths we come upon a most instructive characteristic. In one sense we seem here to be dealing merely with ideas or meanings, arbitrary constructions of our own definitions, having no necessity except to remain consistent with the intentions we ourselves embody in the definitions. But none the less it is a problem with the mathematician whether within his realm certain new (mathematical) objects may be found; he is liable to error in his assertions about such objects – as is illustrated in the case of the differential coefficient just alluded to, and, in general, he has to experiment, to produce, to wait and observe results, much as does the chemist or astronomer. Moreover, mathematical laws and results, originally quite independent of one another, finally often come together and reveal, in a fertile way, further quite new and I unexpected truths – thus again simulating what happens in our knowledge of the physical world.

Philosophically it was Kant who first brought to consciousness the significance of reality as equivalent to validity, and generalized this conception as giving the clue to all Being – save, of course, to the things-in-themselves. He insisted that when we deal with objects other than our present ideas, we mean not objects independent of any knowledge, but *possible objects of experience*. Accordingly, the worth of ideas, the correspondence which they must possess, is decided, not by reference to Being independent of ideas, but by the determinate possibility of objects of experience which would make the ideas valid, true – such questions as arise with reference to the liquid or solid condition of the interior of the earth, the state of parts of the moon beyond direct observation, etc. The whole problem of Being is then one of the validity of ideas, not of the existence or nature of objects just other than ideas.

Mr. Royce, as already intimated, attributes worth to this conception "as far as it goes" (p. 251). He holds, however, that validity as such, or *mere* validity, is not valid; an idea must be immediately fulfilled to be completely or determinately true; it must be actually experienced, in order to be really "*possible.*" The problem develops as follows: Validity, alter all, is an ambiguous term (pp. 261 and 268). On one side, there is always some actual, present experience. Even in mathematics, one does not rely upon *mere* reasoning; one insists upon ability empirically to realize, in inner constructions, in observable symbols, diagrams, etc., the actual course of a certain development; and this, *a fortiori*, is true in what we would term physical truths. But, on the other hand, "the range of valid possible experience is viewed by me as infinitely more extended than my actual human experience" (p. 259). The mathematician goes straight on to assertions about an infinity of objects not actually present, but regarded as valid. Even empirically there are infinite valid possibilities about the commercial world which one does not immediately realize, which, indeed, one deliberately chooses not to realize, such as bankruptcy, bad investments.[3]

And so in the case of knowing a ship, unless it has for you, even as a merely valid object in the content of possible experience, more Being than you have ever directly verified, you would call it a figment of the imagination (p. 258 ). The second meaning of validity is, thus, that the realm of nature, of social life, of mathematical truth, has a character *not* tested, not exhaustively presented. To sum up: on one side is validity living, present in individual experience; on the other side, merely universal, formal, a mere general law. The first sense has the advantage of being given in experience, but the disadvantage of being only the "creature of the instant," a limited, fragmentary case. The second sense has the advantage of being eternal, infinite, exhaustive; but it is merely and only possible, not actual. What is the solution of the ambiguity? Clearly, a conception of Being is indicated in which the meaning of validity shall lose this ambiguity, in which the relative advantages of these one-sided conceptions shall be combined in a harmonious, exhaustive whole.

Since for reasons that will appear later, I cannot, without taking too much space, give an exposition apart from criticism of the method by which Mr. Royce moves on from "Possibility of Experience" to an "individual life, present as a whole...at once a system of facts, and the fulfilment of whatever purpose any finite idea, in so far as it is true to its own meaning, fragmentarily embodies...a life, which is the completed will, as well as the completed experience, corresponding to the will and experience of any one finite idea" (p. 341): I shall, at present, assume this step to be taken, and note the further characteristics of such Being.

In the first place, it solves for us the whole problem of the relation of inner and outer meaning. On one side, the object can have no essential character which is not predetermined by the purpose or meaning of the idea itself. The idea must *mean* the object; and it must also mean, must decide, the *kind* of correspondence that is required between itself and its

3 It is not irrelevant to say that in such cases we prefer the solid gains for ourselves, and prefer to leave the experiences of bankruptcy, etc., to God. Since they are "valid possibilities," the very point of Mr. Royce's argument is that they shall not remain *mere* possibilities, but be fulfilled. To deny their fulfilment in God would be to cut the nerve of the argument by which we pass from the third to the fourth conception.

object; for correspondence varies with the purpose in question, and if at times it demands copying or resemblance, at other times it does not; and even when it does, this is only because the idea itself set out to be just that kind of a copying idea. But since, on the other side, knowing requires effort, and since error is possible, the internal meaning *cannot* precisely predetermine the object, and external meaning is also necessary. The solution is in recognizing that our ideas are finite, fragmentary fulfilments of purpose. As *fulfilments* they predetermine their own objects; but, in so far as the idea is itself vague, abstract, indeterminate, it does not fully understand its own purpose, and to acquire completeness of meaning, individuality of purpose or will, has to hunt for its "other." But this is now seen to be no mere external "other"; it is just that which is required to make an idea truly valid, that is, adequate, determinate (pp. 300–11, 320–35). Thus, real Being is just that being in which idea, inner meaning, and object, external meaning, no longer stand apart, but idea is an exhaustive individual, and object is meaningful.

In the second place, such Being is Unity. Any valid idea must be a consciously experienced fact. Therefore, even if we assume that finite forms of consciousness are sundered, this, as true, valid idea, implies that they are all present in a single consciousness which realizes them all, and the fact of their mutual exclusiveness. "What is, is present to the insight of a single Self-conscious Knower" (p. 400). This abstract logical statement is reënforced by considerations of the material and psychological unity of experience – the unity of the world as known, and of its empirical knower.

In the third place, this unity is not subversive of the multiplicity of finite consciousnesses. Every idea or meaning is a purpose; as such it is a will, or act of will; for, so far as rational, it already embodies, however fragmentarily, a purpose. The complete or perfect reality can only be an exhaustive, an individualized, realization of these same meanings or wills. Every idea means or wills its own specific unique realization; and this is its individuality – its experience in such form that there can be no substitute for it.[4] Nothing can take its place. How then can the Absolute, which is precisely the complete realization of all purposes only partially fulfilled in us, do other than conserve and present all such wills, or individuals? The meaning of every life is unique, and uniquely maintained in the Absolute. This is just what ethical common sense means by *activity*. You alone mean just this purpose: that is activity.

[4] Lack of space compels me to omit the interesting discussion of individuality, even in an object, as dependent upon purpose or will.

You are yourself, that unique individual, in your meaning, your purpose: that is freedom (pp. 468, 469). Such, then, is in outline the final conception of Being.

I have said that to save time it would be found expedient to combine exposition and criticism as regards the exact steps by which Mr. Royce, through his criticism of "the possible-experience" theory, passes on to his own. I now return to that point. So far as I can make out, the ambiguity which Mr. Royce attributes to the conception of validity, the contrast between actual, partial experience, and infinite, but merely possible experience, is not inherent in the theory criticised, but results from the fact that Mr. Royce himself gives two different, and quite inconsistent statements of it. If this ambiguity of his own be eliminated, his own theory may conceivably, of course, still be true, but so far as dependent upon the method by which it is arrived at, it falls to the ground.

What are these two differing statements? On the one hand, it is asserted that the theory is committed to "mere possibilities," "empirically valid general truths." It "consciously attempts to define the Real as explicitly and only the Universal" (pp. 240 and 241). Its realities are "merely more or less valid and permanent ideas" (p. 243). In defining possibilities of experience, it "tells you only of mere abstract universals" (p. 269). If we identify, as we must, the inner meaning with the universal, and the empirically experienced objects with the external meaning, then we can say that this theory regards "the antithesis of internal and of external as finally valid" (p. 288). It "leaves Reality too much a bare abstract universal" (p. 290). "All that is thus defined about the object is its mere *what*" (p. 357).

But upon other occasions we have it clearly enough stated that the validity of an idea is dependent upon an experience in which that idea shall be empirically verified – in other words, that an idea, *qua* mere idea, cannot be valid. A valid idea, and a possible experience are not synonymous; but the possibility of sense-experience is the test by which the validity of an idea is determined. And, moreover, this possibility is so far from being a *mere* possibility that it must be *necessarily* connected with what is actually experienced, it must, indeed, be necessary to the true, integral meaning of the present experience. The whole point of the argument of Kant is that you cannot draw a line and say this is merely actual, and that merely possible. If the idea of the liquidity of the earth is valid, it is because there is somewhat, which is directly present to us as real, which demands this idea as a part of its *own* meaning. It is only a construction of the present; *and the present apart from such construction* is, in turn, meaningless. That such is the case is brought out in Mr. Royce's quotation from Kant (p. 237) when the test of the validity of an idea is its connection with "our *perceptions according to the principle of the empirical synthesis of phenomena*" (italics mine). And, again, when Professor Royce says (p. 245) that the only basis for the assertion of an unexperienced Being is that an experience of facts sends us beyond themselves, and to further possible experience for their own interpretation. Again, it is a matter of recognizing that our *present experience is interwoven* with the whole context of the realm of valid or of possible experience (p. 248, italics mine. See also bottom of p. 242 and top of p. 243; – on pp. 254–56, it is shown that even mathematical ideas to be valid require immediate presentation).

There can be no question which of these two views comes nearer to representing the true spirit of Kant. Indeed, one rubs one's eyes when one finds the "attempt to define the Real as explicitly and only the universal" associated with the name of Kant. That this view is the rationalism against which the Kant of *critical* rationalism asserted that thought in itself is empty, and can give only consistency, never validity, is of course obvious. Professor Royce confounds in his exposition three notions which Kant carefully distinguishes – and then uses this confusion not only to condemn the theory in question, but to furnish the terms of his own solution. These three notions are: (1) 'The real' (in its phenomenal sense, of course, which alone is considered by Mr. Royce). This is immediate sense determined by thought, by mediate conceptions: – so far is Kant, from defining the real as merely universal, merely possible. (2) 'The valid or true idea.' Here, of course, his entire point is that the true idea is not a mere idea, any more than it is the real. It differs from the real in not being directly experienced; it differs from mere thought in that we have reason for assuming that there is a *possible* experience in which it would be directly presented in sense. (3) And thus there is 'possible experience' – that which tests the validity of an idea. It is neither, *qua* possible, the same as the real, nor is it the same as the valid idea. It is not definable in terms of ideas as such, because of its necessary connection with the content of immediate experience. (On p. 247 it is correctly stated: "Experience furnishes the ground for truth.") Mr. Royce, however, assumes that these three notions are synonymous.[5] Except in so far as he does this, he has no basis for

[5] Thus on p. 248 "experience as a whole" is identified with the "realm of truth," and both have a "valid constitution." The realms of valid' and of "possible" experience are identified. On p. 259 we are told of "valid possible experience." In the first paragraph of p. 236 we deal with "objects of possible experience" (3) above; in the next paragraph with "experience as having a necessary constitution" (1) above; on the first paragraph of p. 239, it is a world of "valid empirical truth" (2) above. On p. 241,

contrasting validity as immediate but fragmentary, with validity as universal, ideal but infinite;[6] and no basis for his own positive conception of the really valid idea as itself a living experience. So far as he does this, it is not surprising that he concludes that "all validity, as an incomplete universal conception needs another to give it final meaning" (p. 341).

I am forced to conclude, then, that Mr. Royce's own theory, so far as developed as affording the needed completion of the "validity" theory, rests upon an elaborate misinterpretation. Barely stated in this way the criticism is merely destructive. But what is enlightening is that precisely this oscillation is required *in order to give Mr. Royce's own conception its meaning*. From one point of view, our starting point is no idea, nor universal: it is actual, immediate experience. But this has to be contrasted with universals, possibilities, in order to be condemned as finite and fragmentary, in order to suggest the contrast of an infinite or exhaustive. Now the other side comes into play; if these possibilities are merely universals, merely possibilities, while the conception of them would convict our present experience of a certain limitation, it would give no basis for the reality of an *infinite experience*. So the scene shifts. It is now our experience, which as such, is *only* universal, only abstract, only indeterminate; and, hence, what it is contrasted with (previously only possibilities, abstractions) becomes the actual, immediate, individual experience.

Professor Royce's argument is in this predicament. Unless he can find something good to say of ideas, and of our experience, there is no

"substances," "causes," are instanced as cases of Kant's "empirical objects" (1), and these again are "empirically valid general truths!"

6 There is no space to make the point good here, but I would ask the reader to go carefully over the discussion of the "universal and particular judgments" (pp. 274–90) and see if there is not exactly the same ambiguity in the treatment of these ideas. Sometimes the universal appears as the abstract, the possibility, the ideal construction, as reasoning which while not real, *i.e.*, presented in experience, is valuable as an instrument for reducing indeterminateness by eliminating possibilities (*e.g.*, pp. 277–79); while at other times it appears as our actual present immediate experience of ideas, so far as this is finite, incomplete, and, therefore, *itself* indeterminate, (*e.g.*, pp. 292, 295, and whenever the universal is identified with the "inner meaning" which is really experienced, but which as "finite," "fragmentary" needs an "other"). And, of course, the particular goes through similar transformations. At one time the particular judgments are what "*positively assert Being* in the object viewed as external;" hence, of course, they come in to give concreteness to the mere abstract universal, or ideal construction. But so far as the "universal" is our present but incomplete, inner meaning, the particulars appear as the ideal possibilities which, *if realized, would* give exhaustiveness or infinitude to our limited present meaning.

ground for defining the Absolute in terms of ideals, or as experience. Hence, at times he insists in that, even with us, the truly valid idea is that which is presented in our immediate experience. This point of view comes out in its essential meaning on p. 422, when he says that it is "the wholeness and not the mere fragmentariness, the presence and not the mere absence of unity in our consciousness...which guides us towards a positive view of how the unity of Being is...attained." It finds expression again on p. 424, when we are told that as to the "general form of the absolute unity, our guide is inevitably the type of empirical unity present in our own passing consciousness." When this necessary homogeneity or community is in mind (required in order intelligibly to describe the Absolute as experience or consciousness at all), validity means present actual experience. *It must mean this for us, or it cannot mean it for Absolute.* So we have the emphasis on the genuinely Kantian interpretation of reality. But, on the other hand, pretty radical discredit must be cast on our ideas, on our experience; for otherwise there is no ground for making the radical distinction between ourselves as fragmentary, finite, etc., and the infinite or completed' consciousness; otherwise we should end as well as begin with Kantianism, with experience as an organized system. Hence the necessity of conceiving our experiences, our ideas, which previously were defined as immediate realities or *presented* purposes, as mere meanings, indeterminate universals at large, and therefore requiring the infinite experience to fulfil them. The dialectic is this: (1) Our experiences are meanings, purposes fulfilled. Then, since reality cannot be conceived apart from experience, *the* reality – absolute reality – is meaning fulfilled. (2) But our purposes are only partially, inadequately, merely universally or indeterminately, fulfilled. But since absolute reality is meaning fulfilled in experience, it must be exhaustively, eternally fulfilled. The Absolute experiences all at once, adequately and completely, that which we try to experience in pieces, in series and in distorted fashion. The gist of my criticism is that the argument depends upon taking propositions (1) and (2) alternately. They cannot be taken together without destroying each other. Insist upon (1) alone, and you get the system of experience as the Absolute; insist upon (2) alone, and you cannot get anywhere. Mr. Royce, I say it in no flippant spirit, blows hot and cold upon our "finite" experience. When he wishes to establish the experienced, the significant character of his Absolute, it is good enough. But when he wishes to give an all embracing, single, exhaustive, *totum simul* character to his Absolute, our finite consciousness appears in a condition which logically would justify no conclusion, and which, practically, would not amount to enough even to suggest the problem of its own nature – mere vague universals, indeterminate possibilities and the like!

To put the matter somewhat more positively: If our experience justifies us in entertaining the idea of the Infinite, the Perfect, as valid, then we are not mere fragments or parts in that Infinite; it is in and through us, and in such an organic and pervasive way that the contrast between us and it, as the "finite" over against the "infinite," the fragmentary over against the complete, the serial over against the *totum simul* is contradicted. If such be the case, we do not need a definition of the Absolute which makes it the realization of everything we intend but cannot effect; everything we mean, but cannot express. What we need is a reconsideration of the facts of struggle, disappointment, change, consciousness of limitation, which will show *them*, as they actually are experienced *by us* (not by something called Absolute) to be significant, worthy, and helpful. On the contrary, if we are fragmentary and finite in such a way that our meanings and realizations are not presented in and to us, but only to and in the Absolute, what boots either the Absolute, or the struggle! Let us eat, drink and be merry – let us glean the satisfactions of our passing life, for as to serious meanings, only the Absolute knows what they mean; as to serious efforts, only the Absolute experiences their realization – and since he is Absolute, we cannot rob him of that in any case, nor will he grudge us such pleasures as we can snatch as we hurry along. Omar Khayyam knew such philosophy long ago.

Professor Royce has shown his capacity to be sceptical. He has declared that only through doubting does the truth appear. But the category of the "finite," the "fragmentary," the "flying moment," he seems never to have questioned. It is the one positive, fixed datum. Upon it he builds his whole conception of real or absolute Being – and yet to build upon it at all, he has to combine with it qualities such as meaning, purpose, fulfilment, which contradict this rigid finitude and require its reinterpretation.

I need hardly say in closing that it is quite possible to disagree pretty fundamentally with an author's conclusions, because one is not convinced as to his method, and yet recognize the scope and power of his work, and admire, to the point of envy, his skill in managing the course of his ideas and in presenting them to the reader. The book before us, together with its author's *Conception of God*, can be compared only with Mr. Bradley's *Appearance and Reality* in recent metaphysical thought. I should regret, even more than I do, the limitations which have confined me to the bare skeleton of Mr. Royce's argument, were it not that its many admirable traits are so obvious that they cannot fail to secure recognition from any competent reader.

Meantime the serious effort critically to face Mr. Royce's method is the tribute – the highest of all tributes, it seems to me – which the importance of his work exacts.

# REVIEW OF *THE WORLD AND THE INDIVIDUAL*, FIRST SERIES

Charles Sanders Peirce, Review of *The World and the Individual*, First Series, *The Nation*, vol. 70 (1900).

*The World and the Individual*: Gifford Lectures delivered before the University of Aberdeen. First Series: The Four Historical Conceptions of Being. By Josiah Royce. Macmillan. 1900. 8vo, pp. 588.

We can do no more than explain in untechnical language what this important book is about. Its purpose is to say what it is that we aim at when we make any inquiry or investigation – not what our ulterior purpose may be, nor yet what our special effort is in any particular case, but what the direct and common aim of all search for knowledge is. This is a question of fact. Prof. Royce has clothed the matter in such academical guise that a reader untrained in philosophy might suppose it was a mere dispute about a definition, and therefore a profitless discussion; but, stripping off technicalities, we find this question of fact beneath them.

The only opinion on this subject generally held at this day that Prof. Royce considers to be essentially different from his own, is one which may be attributed to Bishop Berkeley more justly than to any other individual. It is the opinion of Possible Experience. Though this has taken slightly different shapes with different thinkers, it will suffice, in order to explain the purport of Prof. Royce's book, to state it in one of its forms. The answer, then, generally given, or virtually given, to the question what any inquiry is instituted for, is approximately that it is intended to settle doubt on the subject. Did Sir Philip Francis write the Junius letters? I can imagine, as the handwriting experts say, that he did. I can imagine, as most of the recent inquirers say, that he did not. I feel no compulsion to attach either idea to my mental representation of the historic world. There are some images which I am forced, whether I would or no, to attach to mental objects – such as a dark skin and jealousy to Othello. The course of life has developed certain compulsions of thought which we speak of collectively as Experience. Moreover, the inquirer more or less vaguely identifies himself in sentiment with a Community of which he is a member, and which includes, for example, besides his momentary self, his self of ten years hence; and he speaks of the resultant cognitive compulsions of the course of life of that community as Our Experience. He says "we" find that terrestrial bodies have a component acceleration towards the earth of 980 centimetres per second, though neither he nor many of his acquaintances have ever made the experiment.

Now, such being his state of mind, two hopes motive his inquiry: the first is, that the course of "our" experience may ultimately compel the attachment of a settled idea to the mental subject of the inquiry; and the second is, that the inquiry itself may compel him to think that he anticipates what that destined ultimate idea is to be.

Such, approximately, is the ordinary opinion of Possible Experience, in one of its modes of statement. According to it every inquiry is directed toward the resultant of certain compulsions; and, therefore, so far as a sense of compulsion is an immediate knowledge of something outside of self, exerting a brute force on self, this opinion is that every inquiry relates to a brute something without the mind. It was substantially on this ground that Kant opposed the anti-materialism of Berkeley. But, regarded from another side, this opinion is that the only object to which inquiry seeks to make our opinion conform is itself something of the nature of thought; namely, it is the predestined ultimate idea, which is independent of what you, I, or any number of men may persist, for however long, in thinking, yet which remains thought, after all. The whole course of life within which the experiential compulsions appear is a purely psychical development. For the gist of the opinion is that the flow of time consists in a continual assimilation into "our" inwardness, the Past, of a non-ego that is nothing but the ego that is to be – the Future. The Past acts upon the Future intelligibly, logically. But those blind compulsions are glimpses of an unknown object. Now, the unknown, according to this theory, is nothing but what is bound, as our hope is, to emerge in the future. Those blind compulsions, then, can be regarded as actions of the future on the past. From that point of view, it is seen that they can but be brute and blind, and, further, that in the course of time they must be seen to rationalize themselves and fall into place as the cognition develops.

To Prof. Royce's thinking, this opinion is unsatisfactory. He finds four faults with it, and sets them before us with his own argumentative lucidity and admirable mastery of the subject. Of the nature of three of them – that the opinion under examination makes the object of knowledge to be no more than a "would-be"; that its "experience" is no experience for an inquirer; that it seats an abstraction on a throne of reality – we can here find room for no clearer hint than those phrases may convey. Whatever solid skeleton the three objections may clothe is pretty much the same as that of the fourth and strongest, that if the non-ego to which the inquirer seeks to make his ideas conform is merely an idea in the future, that future idea must have for its object an idea future to it, and so on ad *infinitum*. There is no escaping the admission that the ultimate end of inquiry – the essential, not ulterior end – the mould to which we endeavor to shape our opinions, cannot itself be of the nature of an opinion. Could it be realized, it would rather be like an insistent image, not referring to anything else, and in that sense concrete. Passing from the consideration of a single inquiry to that of the aggregate of all possible inquiries, the phantom ultimate issue of them all would be the real universe. To be that, however, it must include the mental world as well as the physical, and must set forth to itself all laws and modes of conception. It must, above all, exhibit to itself the whole course of time, with that process of complete rationalization of ideas upon the assumption of which the very hypothesis of a fated ultimate destination of opinion is based. It must, therefore, be conceived as a perfect rational consciousness. In short, it is such a conception of Deity (necessarily a one-sided one) as considerations limited to the Theory of Cognition could reasonably be expected to yield.

This inevitable outcome of the doctrine of Possible Experience is the very same goal, roughly speaking, to which Prof. Royce's explorations have brought him, too, by a path nearly parallel to that for which we have set up a sign-post for whoever may care to follow it out, though the hedgerows of thought may prevent the traveller over the one from being aware how close he is to the other. Prof. Royce reaches his conclusion by analyzing the nature of the purpose of an idea. Now this same conception of the purpose of an idea ought equally to be seized as the guiding thread to the doctrine of Possible Experience, although Prof. Royce believes his position to be quite foreign, even hostile, to that. One divergence is, that where another thinker might speak of a hope, as we have done above, Prof. Royce would substitute a *reductio ad absurdum* of the contrary opinion – a diminution of man's natural sublime attitude to a sorry "A is A." Fortunately the logic of those arguments is never impeccable, so that the hopes retain their matter and are not reduced to mere formulæ.

Two other views are examined. One is that of cognitive Dualism, which Professor Royce calls by the objectionable name Realism (as if the Dualists alone admitted outward realities). The other is that of Mysticism, which is less an opinion than an attitude of mind, of which Professor Royce gives an exceedingly penetrating analysis. There is a long and technical supplementary essay on the One, the Many, and the Infinite, which is very important.

The dress of the book is as charming as that of one so sure of being long and often perused ought to be.

# ROYCE'S WORLD AND THE INDIVIDUAL

## Review of *The World and the Individual*, Second Series

Charles Sanders Peirce, *Review of The World and the Individual*, Second Series, *The Nation*, vol. 75 (1902).

*The World and the Individual.* Gifford Lectures [on Natural Religion], Delivered before the University of Aberdeen. Second Series: Nature, Man, and the Moral Order. By Josiah Royce. The Macmillan Co. 1901. 8vol, pp. 480.

Professor Royce's second and concluding volume discusses questions of intimate interest to everybody. It is more persuasive than the first, of which it enhances the significance. The design of the whole now comes out – to introduce into the Hegelian philosophy of religion such rectifications as must result from recognition of scientific conceptions worked out during the century now completing itself since that philosophy first appeared. Of these new conceptions, some are psychological, some logical; but the chief of them are the new mathematical ideas which cluster about that of an infinite multitude. Mathematicians, perhaps, still linger on the stage, who, in their best days, used to be quite positive that one cannot reason mathematically about infinity, and used to feel, like the old lady about her total depravity, that, this cherished inability being taken away, the bottom would fall out of the calculus. Such notions are obsolete. Various degrees of infinity are today conceived with perfect definiteness; and the utter misapprehension of the metaphysicians about it, above all of Hegel, glares. As a first serious attempt to apply to philosophical subjects the exactitude of thought that reigns in the mathematical sciences, and this, not on the part of some obscure recluse whose results do not become known to the public, but on that of an eminent professor in a great university, to whom the world is disposed to listen with attention, Royce's *The World and the Individual* will stand a prominent milestone upon the highway of philosophy.

Our space will permit only the most salient features of Professor Royce's theory to be roughly sketched. "An Idea is any state of mind that has a conscious meaning." In reference to meaning, logicians have never failed to recognize "quod fere in omnium ore celebre eat, aliud scilicet esse quod appellativa [*i.e.*, adjectives] *significant*, et aliud esse quod *nominant*. Nominantur singularia, sed universalia significantur." So John of Salisbury, Abelard's pupil, expresses the distinction. That for the most important signs the signification is intrinsic, the denotation *(quod nominant)* extrinsic, is generally recognized. Professor Royce marks the distinction by the terms Internal Meaning and External Meaning. He conceives of the internal meaning in a special way. Another writer, a quarter of a century ago, proposed this maxim: "Consider what effects that might conceivably have practical bearings we conceive the object of our conception to have. Then our conception of those effects is the *whole* of our conception of the object." Carrying this pragmatistic spirit a trifle further, Professor Royce holds that the internal meaning of an idea is a Purpose, instead of regarding it, with his predecessor, as a germinal purpose. This purpose – obscurely recognized, since not all to which it will lead is foreseen; partially fulfilled in being recognized, since a purpose strives first of all to understand itself; but mainly unfulfilled, since it would not remain a purpose after fulfilment – is the internal meaning, or signification, or depth, of the idea. The purpose is vague – anything that refers to the future is more or less vague; and a sincere purpose to do a thing "right now" actually does it. The purpose is to do a thing under certain circumstances. Completely to define these circumstances, it would be necessary to give a biography of the purposer from birth, without any omission. The purpose is to do something in order to produce certain results. Completely to define the result accomplished must involve a complete representation of the agent's future life. In short, the complete fulfilment of any purpose, which alone is the external meaning of the idea, is no less than the entire life of the thinker. The reviewer will say, for clearness, that neither these nor the majority of the author's positions have been satisfactorily shown to be true (in the reviewer's opinion, but the author holds them to be perfectly demonstrated). The principal of them may rank as verifiable hypotheses possessed of the plausibility and other qualifications that render them eminently worthy of further examination, even if an engine of rare usefulness must be drawn away from other work for the purpose.

That the object of an idea, then, its external meaning, is of the nature of a sign could hardly be gainsaid. But Professor Royce finds it not only a sign but an idea; not only one idea but a "concrete" idea in the Hegelian sense, and that, not relatively, but perfectly, and so of the nature of life; and not only life, but an entire life. "The Being of the real object of which you now think, means a life that expresses the fulfilment of just your present plan."

But suppose the reader to ask, How can an idea, so microscopic a piece of a life, contain within its implication a distinct feature corresponding to every feature of the entire life of which it is only a part? This difficulty is happily removed by the author in a way which ought to be instructive to those metaphysicians whose horizon is limited by the walls of a theological seminary. He resorts to Gauss's conception of an *Abbild,* which has played a great rôle in mathematics. That is to say, he likens the idea representing the entire life to a map of a country lying upon the territory of that country. Imagine a map of England, absolutely perfect in its minutest details, to lie upon the soil of England, without covering the entire country it maps. Upon this map would be shown the very ground where the map lies, and the map itself, in all its minutest details. In this map of the map, the map will he shown again; and so on endlessly. Here, then, will be a part fully representing its whole, just as the implicit meaning of the idea is supposed to represent the entire life. It is to be noticed that, each successive map lying well inside the one which it immediately represents, unless there be a hole in the country which a ring-shaped map encloses, the endless series of maps will converge to a single point, which represents itself throughout each and every map of the series. In the case of the idea, that point would be the self-consciousness of the idea. An idea, being a state of mind with a conscious purpose, must evidently be self-conscious.

There, then, would seem to be a beautiful and a needed (though not a complete) confirmation of the aptness of the metaphor. Yet here the author recoils, and refuses to admit the continuity, or even the analytic continuity, of the map. He insists that no representation represents itself; a hard saying, which exact logic appears directly to refute. "The world of Self," he says, "whatever continuity of internal structure it may, in some aspects, possess, is, in its principal form of expression, embodied in a discrete series of...individual expression... . Experience at any moment shows how I am conscious of my...approaches to selfhood in any way in the form of a discrete series in which one stage...is followed by the next." The argument which supports this assertion is not assented to upon all hands. If it be true, there are but two alternatives: either, notwithstanding this, in the respects in which an idea represents an entire life there is continuity, or, at least, a higher infinity than that of the simple endless series; or else the doctrine that to an idea a reality must in some shape correspond must fall to the ground.

According to Professor Royce, an idea fails of being a Self only because it is general and not perfectly determined; which the reader may deem a dark saying unless the sword of Hegel is invoked to cut the knot.

Its implicit or germinal inward meaning would, then, be a little Self, representing the entire life as its external meaning. In a similar way, the Self of the man is perhaps included within a larger Self of the community. On the other hand, the man's Self encloses intermediate selves – the domestic Self, the business Self, the better Self, the evil spirit that sometimes usurps his sovereignty. Of course, the system of delineation for the larger and for the enclosed selves will be different. Here the author draws support from the psychological doctrine of what he calls the "time-span," a doctrine which, so far as it has really been placed beyond important doubt, amounts to little more than that our image of the events of the few seconds last past is, or is very like, a direct perception, while our representation of what happened a minute or so ago is relatively of a far more mediate character. This phenomenon had already been seized upon by several idealistic writers as affording a refutation of dualism; but there is no better way of appreciating the large calibre of Royce's thought than by comparing their styles of putting this idea to the service of metaphysics with his. He imagines that the greater selves will naturally have vastly longer time-spans than the lesser selves. Now a consciousness whose time-span, or "specious present," or "empirical present," as it is variously called, was a thousandth of a second or a thousand years would not ordinarily be recognized as a consciousness at all by a human observer of its external manifestations. The time-span of the All-enclosing Self must cover all time; and this gives a sort of support to the imagination if we wish to reconcile foreknowledge and free will after the manner of Boëthius, St. Augustine, and others.

Every reality, then, is a Self, and the selves are intimately connected, as if they formed a continuum. Each one is, so to say, a delineation; with mathematical truth we may say, incongruous though the metaphor is, that each is a quasi-map of the entire field of all the selves, which organic aggregate is itself a Self, the Absolute Idea of Hegel. So far as a philosophical conception can be identified with God it is God.

All reasoning goes upon the assumption that there is a true answer to whatever question may be under discussion, which answer cannot be rendered false by anything that the disputants may say or think about it; and further, that the denial of that true answer is false. This makes an apparent difficulty for idealism. For if all reality is of the nature of an actual idea, there seems to be no room for possibility or any lower mode than actuality, among the categories of being. (Hegel includes modality only in his Subjective Logic.) But what, then, can be the mode of being of a representation or meaning unequivocally false? For Hegel, the false is the bad, that which is out of harmony with its own essence; and since, in his view, contradiction is the great form of activity of the world, he has no difficulty in admitting that an idea may be out of harmony with itself. Prof. Royce, however, seems almost to resent the idea that anybody could suppose that he denied the validity of the distinction of truth and falsehood. He is fairly outspoken in pronouncing sundry doctrines false (a word Hegel hardly uses), even if we do not quite hear his foot come down; and nothing does he hold more false than the usual form of stating the distinction now in question, namely, that a true proposition corresponds to a *real matter of fact,* by which is meant a state of things, definite and individual, which *does not* consist *merely in being represented (in any particular representation) to be as it is.* For example, if I dream that I find I can float in the air, this matter of dream is not matter of fact, for the reason that the only sense in which I can float in the air is that so my dream represented the matter. Now Prof. Royce offers to demonstrate by necessary reasoning that the statement – or, as he expresses it, that "to be real means to be independent of ideas which relate to that being" – is false. His argument to this effect will serve as a sufficiently characteristic, but rather favorable sample of his general style of argumentation.

Having given us to understand that he is going to disprove the proposition, he opens his argumentation by declaring that he does not know what the proposition means. Thereupon, he proceeds to propound a general maxim of procedure for all cases in which one has to refute a proposition without knowing what it means. It is to begin by assigning to it its "most extreme form." This certainly does not signify the most extremely defensible meaning, but rather the most extremely indefensible meaning that the language will bear. The proposition having been refuted in this extreme sense, it will only be necessary afterwards to argue that other interpretations make no essential difference. This maxim, one would suppose, would prove very serviceable to anybody who should have any large amount of that sort of refutation to perform. In accordance with this maxim, Prof. Royce begins by assuming that realists hold that no idea in the slightest degree determines the real object of it, whether causally or in any other manner. Whether this does not overstep the limits of admissible interpretation, seeing that a realist who meant this would deny that any promise can really be kept, or that any purpose can influence the real result, the reader must say. At any rate, It would not seem to be a difficult position to refute.

Now in order that he may get the realist where he wants him, there are two acknowledgments which Professor Royce endeavors to extort from him. To bring him to the first, the author assumes the principle that all causal action is reciprocal, or of the nature of reaction. This is evidently contrary to popular opinion, which holds that while the past has exerted some efficient causality upon the future, the future cannot have any *effect,* in the strict sense of that word, upon the past; and that while the future may have influenced the past by final, or ideal, causation, the past cannot possibly influence the future as the aim of the future. The reader may judge whether a realist of so extreme a type as that which Professor Royce has set up would or would not admit that the real object of an idea cannot have influenced the idea, in the absence of any attempt on the part of Professor Royce to prove his general principle of reciprocity. If he would not, old-fashioned logic (which Hegelians, it is true, hold in high contempt) would pronounce the attempted demonstration to be a bald *petitio principii.*

In order to extract the second acknowledgment from the realist, Professor Royce produces an argument which would seem to have as much force for one kind of realist as for another. He supposes two objects, B and R, to be related to one another as the realist supposes the Being, or the real object of an idea, and the Representation, in the form of an idea of that object, to be related; and he undertakes to define the relation between them. "The definition in question," he says, "is, as a mere abstract statement, easy." One would think so. The realist simply says that B is not constituted by its being represented in R; that is, he says that the fact that B is as it is, would be logically consistent with R's representing it to be otherwise. But in place of this easily comprehensible relation, what fantastic attempt do we find at the definition that was pronounced to be so easy! Professor Royce will have it that the realist holds that the relation is such that no matter how R may be metamorphosed, it is logically possible for B to remain unchanged. In such a sense, what two things in the world are independent? Change the problematic madness of Hamlet into the pacification of the Philippines, and it will become logically inconsistent with the continuance of great disturbances there. But change the doubtful *representation* by Shak[e]spe[a]re that the fictitious Hamlet was unhinged into the *representation* that the Philippines were pacificated in 1901, and it will not have the slightest logical consequence for the real state of things. The truth is, that Professor Royce is blind to a fact which all ordinary people will see plainly enough; that the essence of the realist's opinion is that it is one thing to *be* and another thing to *be represented;* and the cause of this cecity is that the Professor is completely immersed in his absolute idealism, which precisely consists in denying that distinction. It is his element, and there is total reflection at its surface, That, however, is what Professor Royce asks the realist to admit as a premise. The conclusion which he deduces from it is that if B is linked as cause to any determination of R, there must he a *tertium quid* by the mediation of which the causation takes place. Now the premise is absurd; and the formal rule is that from an absurd premise every conclusion must he allowed to be logical; that is to say, it is needless to dispute its logicality, the premise being false. The argument, therefore, cannot be called formally bad; nor can we object that a few lines below, in a restatement of the conclusion, B's being linked as cause gets changed into B's having any causal *or other* linkage.

Professor Royce, armed with his wrong definition of realism, goes on to a dilemma to show that, whether the realist says that real things are one or are many, he equally involves himself in contradiction. But, although the characteristics of his style of argumentation become even more prominent in that dilemma, the exigencies of space forbid our following him further. But we should like to say one word to this powerful and accurate thinker who has been so completely led astray in his argumentation by his Hegelian logic: Absolute Idealism depends, as Hegel saw that it did, upon assuming that position at the outset. If your refutation of realism is addressed to students who are already absolute idealists at heart, we will not undertake to say whether it will be serviceable for the development of that doctrine, or not. But if it is addressed to realists themselves, it must conform to the logical principles recognized by realists, or be nugatory. Now you know very well that realists do not admit that matter of fact can be apodeictically demonstrated. You ought to know, and surely you do know, that if you drive them into a corner, they will simply modify their admissions so far as may be necessary to avoid self-contradiction, and that from the very nature of apodeictic proof it is absolutely impossible to close off such escape in arguing about matter of fact. The history of the doctrine of parallels illustrates what logic shows to be necessarily the state of the case. But the question of realism is a question of hard fact, if ever there was a hard fact; and therefore your method must be revolutionized if you are ever to convince any master of logic.

# REVIEW OF *THE WORLD AND THE INDIVIDUAL*, FIRST SERIES

Charles M. Bakewell, Review of *The World and the Individual*, First Series, *International Journal of Ethics*, vol. 12 (1901–2).

*The World and the Individual.* Gifford Lectures delivered before the University of Aberdeen. First Series. *The Four Historical Conceptions of Being.* By Josiah Royce. York: The Macmillan Company, 1900. Pp. xvi, 588.

*The World and the Individual.* Second Series. *Nature, Man and the Moral Order.* 1901. Pp. xvii, 480.

The volumes before us offer nothing less than a complete system of philosophy. In them Professor Royce has gathered up the threads of all his previous philosophical discussions and woven them into a single complete and, in many respects, decidedly novel system of absolute idealism. This is the most elaborate, sustained and closely knit effort in philosophical construction that has appeared in many a year. It is a work of scholastic subtlety and exhaustiveness, and, we must also add, not wholly free from scholastic prolixity.

The first volume is concerned mainly with the World, the second mainly with the Individual; the first with pure theory – the meaning of reality in general, the second with the application of that theory to the interpretation of the facts of nature and of man. More specifically, the first volume contains an exhaustive discussion of the concept of Being; the scope of the second "includes a sketch of an idealistic Theory of Human Knowledge, an outline of a Philosophy of Nature, a doctrine about the Self, a discussion of the origin and destiny of the Human Individual, a summary consideration of the world as a Moral Order, a study of the Problem of Evil, and, finally, an estimate of all these views in the light of what seem (to the author) to be the interests of Natural Religion" (II., p. vi).

Naturally it is impossible to condense into review-length a summary of the contents of a work conceived on such a generous plan, and equally impossible to present any adequate criticism of steps in the argument that seem to provoke further discussion. Besides, there is a baffling serenity and self-confidence in the author's manner that make one pause before urging his objections. One feels that his difficulties cannot have been ignored, that his is a point of view that he must find subsumed and transcended somewhere in the course of the discussion if he only search hard enough. When he comes like Indra in the Indian tale to the wise Prajapati with a difficulty, saying, "Master, I see no good in this," he hears ever the same bland reply: "Abide with me yet another thirty years." One feels, in short, that the doubts which remain after a fourth reading a fortieth might dispel. This feeling is intensified by our author's persistent and conscientious endeavor to scrutinize his own doctrine from all conceivable points of view that differ from his own. The "objector" is always given the courtesy of the house. Whatever his trouble he is pretty sure to find himself at some time occupying the floor, and stating his own case with exceptionally convincing power. Whether or not one finds the author's replies equally convincing, it is apparent that the view set forth gains much, perhaps too much commanding force from the discovery that no serious obstacles in the way of its acceptance have been coolly and deliberately ignored.

It is a very old and very familiar criticism of Absolute Idealism, of whatever type, that it leaves no room for the reality of the individual, and, therefore, no room for a genuinely ethical order; that, furthermore, precisely in so far as it fails to provide for the reality of the individual as independent and free at least in his capacity as judge of truth, in just so far does it leave its own conclusions without force, and so, as theoretical philosophy also, defeat its own end. Many and subtle are the defenses that idealists have brought forward, until the question appears well-nigh threadbare. Professor Royce, however, considers the criticism still a respectable one. He had already faced the issue in his interesting discussion in the California Controversy (The Conception of God) and in some of the papers in his "Studies in Good and Evil." In the present work he has given us an independent and exhaustive treatment of the whole question, in which he undertakes "to define God, the World, and the finite Individual, and the most fundamental relations that link them together." The problem concerning the nature of the individual, and the kind of reality to be ascribed to the individual, is held to be involved in the deeper problem: what is the exact meaning of reality in general. The fundamental question then is, what is the real *qua* real? Professor Royce's answer is given in the first volume. It takes the form of a constructive criticism of three historically important ontological positions that have been maintained by philosophers: that of Realism, that of Mysticism and that of "modern Critical Rationalism" – under which last rubric fall alike the critical idealism of Kant and the

Empiricism of later English writers. The author undertakes to show that each of these three positions recognizes a permanently valid aspect of the truth while denying other aspects no less permanently valid; that, taken together, they prepare the way for the fourth – the author's own – conception of reality, which is called "the synthetic or the constructively idealistic conception of what it is to be."

The common mark of all realistic systems is the assertion that "to be real means to be independent of ideas, which, while other than a given real being, still relate to that being" (p. 92). Realism asserts that objects are real "whether or no" you, or anyone else, may be aware of them; that being is entirely independent of ideas, and also that ideas, as mere ideas, *i.e.*, apart from their truth or falsity, are independent of being. Taking the realistic thesis, as thus characterized, strictly, Professor Royce has no difficulty in showing that it introduces in its notion of entire independence a fatal chasm which it can neither destroy nor bridge; that, in consequence, the would-be real world itself vanishes, and leaves behind a "meaningless wilderness of absolute nothingness." To put the difficulty otherwise, Realism makes hard and fast the distinction between the *what* and the *that* of things. Now this distinction while important and real is, none the less, an abstraction, and, if taken absolutely, leaves us with neither a *what* nor a *that* remaining.

The position of the Mystic is described with a fine fairness that evidently issues from a fond appreciation of its value. Our author seems almost reluctant to point out the fatal defect of inner contradiction which this view contains. The Mystic holds that "*to be* means *to fulfill the inner purpose of ideas*. What is, is as such the perfect, the absolute, the finality" (I., p. 386). To be real means to be in such wise immediate that, in the presence of this immediacy, all thought and all ideas, absolutely satisfied, are quenched so that the finite search ceases, and the Other is no longer another, but is absolutely found. In all finitude is dissatisfaction, unrest. The real in so far as found brings rest and satisfaction; the absolutely real would bring final rest and satisfaction – the finite would be quenched in the immediacy of the ineffable experience. Now the Mystic indeed holds that this experience is just the opposite of nothingness, "for it is fulfilment, attainment, peace, the goal of life – in a word, all Truth." And yet, inasmuch as he always defines his absolute in negative terms the contrast between the finite life of struggle and the goal is an absolute one. The real, conceived simply as goal, gets its meaning in the contrast with finitude, and if it is to be in reality different from nothing, it must be shown to stand in real contrast with our own *real though finite* life.

The Critical Idealist sees that "our ideas of Being and the Being of which we have ideas must occupy essentially the same ontological position" (I., p. 260) – a truth denied by both the Realist and the Mystic. He sees, moreover, that the assertion that the world is "involves a judgment that (his) present experience is interwoven in the whole context of the realm of valid or of possible experience" (I., p. 248). Knowing the truth consists in reading off the structure of an actually presented experience and thereby discovering a realm of abstractly possible experience (I., p. 257 *ff.).* In asserting the reality of any fact of experience one simply asserts the validity of a certain idea about further possible experience. But this view fails to tell us "what is a valid or determinately possible experience at the moment when it is supposed to be only possible;" fails to tell us what a valid truth is "at the moment when nobody verifies its validity" (I., p. 260). The validity of an idea that is tested gets an individual life and meaning by appearing in an individual experience; but what of the "realm of valid truth in general," of the world of nature not presented, and perhaps never to be exhaustively presented in our human experience? (I., p. 261).

Thus by a consideration of these partially true views and their specific defects, Professor Royce leads up to the synoptic view of constructive idealism. The apparently external meaning of an idea, its reference to another, is obviously very largely determined by the selective purpose of the idea itself. Facts are stubborn controllers of ideas only with the ideas' own connivance. Professor Royce, however, undertakes to show that the real to which ideas refer is not only in part but wholly determined by the internal meaning of the ideas. The idea is always a will, a plan of action; and the object, the real, to which it refers is always just the idea's own conscious purpose embodied in some more determinate form than it now consciously possesses. No finite embodiment is, however, finally adequate. The true internal meaning of any finite idea is a certain absolute system of ideas.

We have not the space to give in any detail the steps whereby this position is independently reached. So far as we now have the conception before us it does not seem to differ very essentially from the view which students of philosophy are familiar with from the writings of Kant and his immediate followers. And, for my part, I must confess that I find the discussion of the Third Conception far from satisfactory. What is there described as the position of Critical Idealism is perhaps a fair account of the attitude of John Stuart Mill, but hardly of the Kantians. Reality for them is not left hanging in the void in company with a lot of abstractly possible but never to be realized alternatives, until the definite experience comes that fixes it in the concrete. It is only in so far as future events may be regarded as at the present moment not completely determined (and for Professor Royce also there are such real alternatives) that real occurrences are left suspended in the limbo of possibilities. In all other respects the real is just the completely elaborated implications of any present fact. But our author's view does differ from Critical Rationalism in two important respects: (1) in the persistent emphasis of the active aspect of ideas, and the consequent conception of reality as the purpose accomplished, the plan fulfilled; and (2) in holding that the complete meaning of every finite idea is once for all individuated, completely determined, embodied in a wholly adequate empirical content. In a word, whatever your idea, you mean the Absolute, you mean God. And God sees at a glance, *totum simul*, "the one plan fulfilled through all the manifold lives, the single consciousness winning its purpose by virtue of all the ideas, of all the individual selves, and of all the lives" (I., p. 427, *cf.* Ib., pp. 36, 327, 339, 359, etc.).

This latter aspect of the doctrine, however, whereby our author would preserve the not yet verified facts by giving them a local habitation and a name in the eternally verified, *totum simul*, experience of the Absolute, seems to have been reached by an all too easy transition from the consciousness of just this individual seeker after truth to a supposed single and all-inclusive consciousness. What our argument has shown is that every idea is a partially fulfilled purpose; that, further, just this individual seeker after truth can know when experience gives the larger, more complete embodiment of his purpose; he thus knows relative reality, and he applies the standard which shows that he, as this individual experiencer, possesses the finally complete measure of truth. In other words, it is just this individual life that is his, and while it remains his, that expands to the fullness of the complete life. So we are not entitled to infer from this that the empirical world is "*a* life fulfilling the purpose of *our* ideas" (I., p. 368). Nor should we say: "As really one with its object, my idea in seeking its Other seeks only the expression of its own will in *an* empirical and conscious life" (I., p. 387). Clearly, we should here write "its" for "an." Now it is just by such apparently insignificant substitutions as this that we reach our one omniverous Absolute. Where we need to be particularly on our guard is precisely at this point when we come to view the relation of the individual conscious life conceived in its totality to other individual lives, similarly conceived, and to the Absolute. I am not unmindful of the arguments whereby Professor Royce would exhibit the individual as the object of exclusive interest. But, in spite of his interesting discussion of the individuality of the beloved to the lover, it remains clear that all the deeper human relations show that we have in this notion but a partial and inadequate account of the principle of individuation. Nor do I overlook the arguments by which he proves that for me the Other which I am incessantly seeking both in the natural world and in the world of social relations is always the larger and inclusive self, the complete embodiment of my present purpose. But from another point of view, my own purpose fails of its fulfillment, at least in the case of the social relations, unless I and my fellows are contrasted, distinct and independent. This our author explicitly states (*cf.* II., p. 271). Now must not the same thing be true when we speak of the relation of this individual self to the absolute self? In which case we could not speak of the Absolute as expressing his purpose in my life, except in the sense in which I could speak of expressing my purpose in the lives of my fellow-men. Professor Royce would save his absolute from the fate of the mystics' real by making it include in its own being all the infinite wealth of finite expressions, precisely as they are in our finite human lives. Only, he adds, God sees each finite expression in its relations to all others, sees them all *totum simul*, as the complete expression of his single purpose. Now in this last assertion we over-emphasize the Unity of the Absolute to such an extent that, in spite of our repeated assertions to the contrary, we introduce an element of illusoriness into the finite world. Our Absolute is supposed actually to live in the finite, to seek with the seeker, to be baffled when the seeker is baffled, to know not the future at this present moment when for him who lives in this moment the future is unknown. Then, however, we turn around and say: But, from another point of view, all time, with all its contents, for the Absolute simultaneously now is, is the one complete definitive embodiment of the one divine plan (*cf.* II., p. 148). (I can only in passing refer to the interesting, subtle and illuminating discussion of Time and Eternity as contained in this chapter and regret the lack of space to analyze the argument with special reference to this problem of the human individual). Is not this to make God win his way after all by playing a very subtly elaborated game of hide-and-seek with himself?

This is the crucial point in this philosophy – the application of the theory to the human individual and to the determination of the place of the self in Being; the point specifically discussed in the seventh and eighth chapters of the second series – the key chapters to both volumes. I must here enter a protest against the summary fashion in which our author throughout the work lumps together all types of pluralists and forces them to keep company with the most crude and naïve realists and share their hard lot. Surely the subtler thinkers of this type, including even Leibniz (spite of the "windowless monads"), have seen that their independent reals could not be "chopped off with a hatchet." With regard to the dependence, independence and interdependence of their many real beings they have more or less clearly seen that one must pass beyond the *entweder-oder* level of thinking where they believe the strict realist is stranded. The pluralistic idealist does not maintain that his real beings are absolutely independent, in the sense that they are out of all relation to one another, or indifferent to such relation; but he does maintain that relations are intelligible which are in no wise limitations of the members related, that strictly voluntary association is real, and that furthermore we are not by reason forced to carry our formal logic-machine into the heavens to get a bird's eye view which will make all these members moments, of however long "time-span," in the life of a single race selfhood, and give them their whole reality as such. Or, at any rate, if we are forced to take this flight to make our meaning clear, we must ever be mindful of the fact that in so doing we are really entering the world of abstraction, and that, to use the language of our author, to make this abstraction the real world is precisely to defeat the very purpose of the idea that inspired the flight. To make our meaning finally clear we must continually return to the concrete experience of the actual unity in actual independence of self with self. Our author's own epistemology, in its recognition of the part played by the "acknowledgment" of the ethically controlled will in the determination of the facts of the individual's world, has decidedly pluralistic implications when we remember that the will in question is not that of a race selfhood, but that of this individual human self.

Professor Royce shows in a very striking manner the confusing ambiguities attaching to the notion of the self and then points out that the "nobler self," the self of eternal worth that strenuous morality affirms, is not found in some underlying soul-substance, but in the unity of one's life purpose, in the uniqueness of one's task. The self is properly defined in ethical terms (II., pp. 267 *ff.*, 276). Such a self cannot be regarded as caused or teleologically determined by another, for that would be to make this my life the expression of a purpose "in some sense *not* my private or individual purpose" (II., p. 329). Thus I the individual exist in one aspect as the expression of nobody's will but my own. Yet I am also an expression of the one divine will. The apparent contradiction here our author thinks is removed by the discovery that it is my will, just as my individual will, that has its place in the Absolute (II., p. 330). It is this view of the human individual, he holds, that furnishes the basis for our belief that man is free and the world a moral order. But then we find our author going on to give us a theory to account for the genesis and temporal origin of the self. The argument here rests upon the analogy with the rise of a new sort of self-hood in the development of the empirical ego within the range of our human experience and seems to me to suffer from the defects usually incident to this type of argument. With that, however, I am not here concerned, but rather with the contradiction involved in holding to the origin empirical or logical of that which is, we are told, neither causally nor teleologically determined, of the ethical self whose conscious purpose is an eternal mission.

In brief, my difficulty is this: I fail to see how we can save ourselves from the mystic's fate unless we can keep God and persons on the same ontological plane, and this we do not accomplish unless the many selves are also eternally real and underived.

Moreover, our author, in his Supplementary Essay, has developed a view that not merely meets Bradley's objections to the possibility of putting positive content into the notion of the Absolute, but also prepares the way for the formulation of his own doctrine in a more pluralistic, more concrete and valid way than he seems willing to employ. In this essay, drawing upon the recent mathematical discussions of the concept of the infinite, Professor Royce has shown how the Absolute may be conceived as a self-representative system, and as such an infinite series may be regarded as given at a stroke, in the very purpose that defines the system, although, serially regarded, there will and can be no "last term." But such an infinite series he further shows to be one of many infinite series within the same system. Here we have in these many infinite series the analogue, but only a rough analogue, of the ethical selves. But then we cannot speak of such selves as having a temporal origin.

There are many important and novel features of this philosophy which we have had to pass over in silence. Particularly noteworthy are: the deduction of the categories, the discussion of the logical origin of the contrast between the "world of description" and the "world of appreciation" and the illustration of these two points of view by the mathematical doctrine of the two forms of serial order, and the whole section on the philosophy of nature.

Where so much is given perhaps it is hardly fair that more should be required, but I regret that our author did not find time to bring into sharper contrast with his own doctrine the views which it most closely resembles, as for example the views of Hegel and Fichte and Plato. Very considerable portions of the work might be read as a commentary on Plato's idea of the good as the object of knowledge. We might well place historically one important phase of this view by saying that Professor Royce has read his Fichte with the eyes of Plato, and his Plato with the eyes of Fichte, and then recast the result in the light of recent mathematical discussions of the concept of the infinite.

The author's answer to all such doubts as we have been raising has been given in advance: They "are founded upon a failure to grasp our doctrine of Being in its wholeness," they arise from "persistently dwelling now too exclusively upon this and now too abstractly upon that aspect of our theory, and neglecting to regard the meaning of all its aspects together" (II., p. 337). I am not sure that the answer would not be fair. One must have a large thought-span, must be, in short, in our author's sense, a godlike person to be able to hold before his consciousness *totum simul* all the phases of this subtle and intricate philosophy.

# PROFESSOR ROYCE'S GIFFORD LECTURES

## Review of *The World and the Individual*, First Series

Richard C. Cabot, Review of *The World and the Individual*, First Series, *Harvard Graduate Magazine*, vol. 8 (1900).

*The World and the Individual.* By Josiah Royce. Gifford Lectures, first series, delivered in 1899. Macmillan: New York.

Professor Royce is a man intimate beyond any that I know with the many-sided life of our time, – not merely with academic life, but with that expressed in newspapers and novels, in the politics of various nations, in scientific research, in music, and in mathematics. His historical and technical knowledge of philosophy is unsurpassed, but the unique and most characteristic thing about him is the closeness of his thought to the life around him. Indeed, I think it is his mission and effort to express in terms of reflection the essential spirit of modern democracy.

We "deem nothing human foreign to us," *and nothing extra-human either*. That nothing is too high nor too low for study, that to criticise a writer means to interpret him and so to give him his place, that every sentient being deserves our best consideration – in short, that there is no rubbish anywhere in the world – this truth is the inspiration of constructive idealism. This spirit which is alive and at work in modern science, modern philosophy, modern criticism, modern educational programs, and modern methods of writing history, Professor Royce describes and makes explicit in his writings.

In the talk of any representative group of educated people one finds characteristic tendencies or attitudes towards life, certain of which recur with especial frequency. These points of view come out very clearly when a distinction is made between what is sham and what is genuine, what is solid fact and what is rumor or illusion.

Professor Royce studies these points of view as a piece of natural history and endeavors to interpret and express the presuppositions which they imply. He transcribes four answers to the question, "How do you tell the genuine from the sham?"

I. The Realist's answer.
II. The Mystic's answer.
III. The Critical Rationalist's answer.
IV. The Idealist's answer.

I. The Realist is the man who insists on the stubbornness of fact, its crushing, compelling character when compared to our theories or desires. You cannot escape from fact; it is what you find when you get yourself out of the way as much as possible, and allow the truth to record itself without additions from you. This reverence for things as one finds them, makes the Realist politically a conservative and a stanch supporter of whatever keeps people in order. Law is for him a command enforced by a penalty. His pet examples of what is *genuine* or real are money, land, tools, property in general. "If you doubt the stone's reality, kick it." The *real* is the opposite of ideas. The farther you get from ideas, the nearer to facts.

The weak side of this point of view comes out when it begins to develop its negative aspects. If fact is what compels assent, what one finds when one simply looks about him, and if it is *only* this, then anything that does not force itself on my notice is to be considered unreal, and to be unreal is to be nothing at all – mere rubbish, figments of fancy. This in fact is the weak side of the conservative or aristocratic mind. It makes him in parts of his life narrow towards research or reform, cruel as a Spaniard to people who do not happen to impress him, intolerant towards those who differ from him.

II. The Mystic's view of Reality is treated by Professor Royce most sympathetically, though it represents to him but one aspect of the truth. It is, he says, the ancient historic foe of Realism, as is expressed in the line, "Good-by, proud world, I'm going home." The outer material world on which the Realist insists so exclusively is to the Mystic infinitely unsatisfying, unrestful, cold, purposeless – in fact unreal. "The world of realities – the kingdom of heaven – is within you. There only are peace and unity to be found; without, lie strife and discord." We recognize here, of course, the spirit that pervades most devotional writings, much of the most impressive poetry, and the lives of many great religious teachers.

We may test the range of its application by observing its treatment of the negative. What is the unreal? Apparently everything that goes on around us, and all mental activity that develops plans and purposes for expression in this unreal outer world. The deeper, the more inexpressible. Pushed to its logical extreme, Mysticism gives us the inner absorption of the Buddhistic trance, or the unworldliness of the

Christian anchorite. In our own time it appears in much of the teaching of Christian Science.

But since thought has no meaning save as expressed, and since expression must mean taking part in the strife and disorder of the outer material world, even thought must be abjured by the Mystic, and he is left with utter vacancy for his kingdom.

III. The Critical Rationalist's solution of the problem, "What is genuine in this world?" will be recognized in history, says Professor Royce, as especially characteristic of the 19th century. The Realist has no satisfactory answer to the question, "What makes us think things or people real even when they *don't* impress us, as a color, a sound, or a kick does?"

Our century's answer is, "We know that they *might* impress us. The opinions we differ from, the condition of the centre of the earth, the family affections of the Mormons, are facts, although we can't now realize or verify them – because we *might* do so." They are "permanent possibilities" of knowledge for us. Typical examples of such are the laws and forces of nature. We never have any direct experience of such laws or forces, but they are what we have to suppose to account for the experiences we have. Energy, or the moral law, cannot be experienced in sensation, but they must be assumed in order to account for experience and make it rational.

"If there were no God we should have to invent one." What is, is never what ought to be. The "ought," therefore, has strictly no existence, but it must be postulated. The ultimate realities, then, are hypotheses, postulates, ideals, possibilities.

IV. The Idealistic solution of the problem claims to be one which includes and harmonizes the others. How else could it be? If nothing human is foreign, opinions that differ from ours must supplement them; and if nothing extra-human is foreign, the "crushing, brute facts" of the Realist must dovetail into the inexpressible inner peace of the Mystic as well as into the "permanent possibilities " on which, for the Critical Rationalist, hang all the Law and the Prophets.

To show how this dovetailing or organization takes place needs two hundred pages in Professor Royce's book, and cannot here be compressed into a paragraph. The Idealist challenges you as a Realist to show him any reality that is not saturated by ideas, and challenges you as a Mystic to show him any inner light that does not refer to sense facts. Facts *are* stubborn and unexpected, as the Realist says; but so are ideas or ideal facts, like custom and law, which compel and crush as earthquakes do. When facts are worked up, understood, controlled, they get more reality and influence, and not less. To maintain the reality of his facts, the Realist must get them infected through and through with that inner ferment of meaning-for-consciousness which the Mystic so exclusively loves. On the other hand, the Mystic's ineffable glory shrinks away into a state of dreamless sleep the instant he ceases to think about the same sort of objects which the Realist insists upon. Neither theory can go a step without the other.

But if the deepest reality cannot be expressed either as something foreign to us, nor as inner peace – if we always *can* grasp it, provided we are rational, while yet we obviously *do* not, as our errors and sins attest – it seems as if we might define it as an ideal possibility – something which we may reach, ought to reach, in future or under more favorable conditions. "Certainly," says Idealism, "this is true, but not the whole truth, for this is defining our ignorance, and not that of which we are ignorant. To be real is to have meaning for consciousness, and all that is real (including the centre of the earth and the future of which we are ignorant) must therefore be more than Ideal possibilities. They must be so related to a total consciousness, inclusive of ours, as our experience is related to us. They must express a life of the Whole, of which we are parts."

In fact, the Idealist conceives the world to be organized as a *Committee of the Whole*, in which the contrasting elements need each other and could not exist apart.

Show me an utterly "wild," meaningless fragment, and in every word or thought which you use to point it out you will be asserting its tameness and membership in the Whole, which everybody's ideas mean if carried out, and which everybody's activities express piecemeal. No item can be recognized without being organized. To say, "There is no Whole," or "I doubt whether there is any," is to use a phrase ("there is") which necessarily implies knowledge of the Whole which we are trying to doubt.

Professor Royce has in this book undertaken his first systematic and thoroughgoing inquiry into first principles. Compared to his earlier works, *The World and the Individual* must seem technical. But I believe that no one can read it through with care without finding that his understanding of his work, his companions, and his future has been deepened.

# PROFESSOR ROYCE'S REFUTATION OF REALISM AND PLURALISM

Ralph Barton Perry, "Professor Royce's Refutation of Realism and Pluralism," *The Monist* (1902).

Professor Royce's recent book, *The World and the Individual (First Series)*, is without doubt one of the most substantial of contemporary contributions to philosophy. The work is avowedly devoted to a systematic consideration of the central problems of metaphysics and epistemology. It proposes, moreover, not only to be comprehensive and fundamental, but irresistible in its logical force. The author's claim for the "absolute logical necessity" of his conception of being (*The World and the Individual*, p. 349) will naturally be accepted as a challenge by any one who ventures to dissent. I undertake in this discussion to evade this same logical necessity by proposing certain miscellaneous criticisms, first of Professor Royce's general method, and secondly of his systematic refutation of realism and pluralism.

A critic approaches Professor Royce's dialectic with some timidity in view of his preparedness for a very aggressive sort of defence. There are three doors which invite the entrance of the dissenter; No. 1, labelled "Realism"; No. 2, labelled "Mysticism"; No. 3, labelled "Critical Rationalism." If you enter any one of the three, "Absolute Logical Necessity" is there waiting for you; and, after being vigorously assaulted, you are led in a dazed condition directly into No. 4, which is the proper abiding place of this monster, and is called "Constructive Idealism." The critic's only hope of safety is to linger outside, and bombard the whole fortification with masked batteries.

Professor Royce's treatment of ultimate problems is essentially epistemological. His classification and criticism of metaphysical theories, as well as his own constructive argument, are based upon a consideration of the ways in which reality presents itself as an object of thought. He is "one of those who hold that when you ask the question: What is an Idea? and: How can Ideas stand in any true relation to Reality? you attack the world-knot in the way that promises most for the untying of its meshes" (*ibid.*, pp. 16, 17). Realism he finds to be a metaphysical theory defining the real as that which is independent of ideas. Mysticism is a definition of the real as that which satisfies ideas by substituting an irrational immediacy. For "Critical Rationalism," the real is empirically verifiable truth. Finally, the author himself finds that to be real which "presents in a completed experience the whole meaning of a System of Ideas" (*ibid.*, p. 61). These definitions show not only that Professor Royce's method is that of reflection upon thought, philosophy's self-criticism, but that the real end of the discussion is a logical one. Although he announces as his central problem, "What is Reality?" (*ibid.*, p. 6), it soon becomes evident that he is not seeking to discover what is real, so much as what it is to be real. In short, it is the conception of being that he is concerned with first and last. The object of study is the intension rather than the extension of that term. This it seems to me is an essentially fruitless metaphysical method, which found its *reductio ad absurdum* as long ago as the time of Parmenides. Its essential fruitlessness follows from the fact that it is untrue to the original philosophical consciousness. Philosophy is begotten by the desire to know more about a certain definite world that is already evident in part. The philosopher is desirous not of creating but of enlarging knowledge. He would never seek after reality if he had not already found it. The proper philosophical motive is not the self-conscious pursuit after the inner meaning of unconscious utterances, but the desire to know more and better the world that is continuous with the thinker's practical life. The philosophical spirit does not direct a man from the study of real things to the study of the adjective "real," but to a study of more real things in the hope that he may compass all things in some thoughtful belief. He has no need of defining the predicate of existence, nor is this a part of his search; for he is already familiar with that predicate before he can conceive the philosophical problem. I believe that it is only by being true to the original healthy philosophical impulse, that our results will be sane and enduring.

But the fallacy of making the idea of being the object of our reflection, is more directly evident in the fact that such reflection can never reach a definition of its object. A definition that contains the term to be defined, is, of course, no definition at all; and every definition must contain the existential predicate. As Professor Royce himself assures us, every universal proposition cancels certain particular beings; and in so doing it must employ the idea of being. The existential predicate cannot, therefore, be defined; and it very properly does not occur to the ordinary mind to attempt to define it. The man who first enters upon philosophical reflection is already familiar with a great many real things of various kinds. Some of these fulfill his desires, others thwart them; some appear to be independent of his will, some dependent; for some he has appropriate ideas and meanings, others appear only in immediacy, and can be represented only symbolically. But he calls them all "things," or "facts," and they already have about them one common aspect which he recognises implicitly in the crudest activities of his consciousness. As our human being proceeds with his reflection he continues to assume this predicate. His aim is to enlarge, and possibly to unify his experience; that is, to find more real things, or to find certain latent similarities in those he has already observed. His problem is best expressed by the question: What is all reality *like*? Is it composed of many ingredients after the manner of his present experience? Is it reducible to some one of those ingredients? Or is it all composed of some neutral element analogous to certain of those ingredients? He is interested in the composition of the real, and not in reality as an hypostasised aspect of his experience. The true classification of philosophical theory will be that which states the different answers to this objective inquiry. Realism, Mysticism, Critical Rationalism, even Constructive Idealism may be so defined, and made to assume the form of hypotheses about the composition of this world – a world whose reality is accepted in the beginning as an aspect of the preliminary experience of maintained that, *e.g.*, *A*'s selfhood was indifferent to *B*'s thought about it. Professor Royce now explains his definition as follows: "You, for instance, as a conscious mind, might be viewed by a realist as a being that he would call real in his sense. That assertion, if made by a typical realist, would simply mean that the contents of your mind, although present within your own consciousness, are real without regard to whether anybody else knows of your existence or not." (*Ibid*., p. 96.) Realism now means that it is of the essence of reality to be independent of such representative ideas as may be referred to it. The entity may be an object of experience. If so, there is a primary order of experience in which it is real, and which is to be contrasted with a secondary order of ideas, having a purely symbolic and representative value. The real may be essentially irrational, or accidentally irrational, *i.e.*, capable of being rationalised; but its being is in no sense derived from ideas.

This conception of realism corresponds more nearly with common sense, in so far as there can be said to be any utterance of that authority in this particular matter. Common people are not epistemologists, and realism is an epistemological theory. Hence it is doubtful whether there is any such thing as the "naïve realism" so commonly referred to. But there are certain general practical postulates which are capable of a realistic interpretation. The common man assumes that things, for the most part, "stay put," *i.e.*, may be depended upon to endure for some period of time. At any rate they are regardless of his will, unless he can bring other things to bear upon them. He must reconcile himself to them, even if he is to change them. They are what they are, for better or for worse. He is liable to respect the independent reality of other human beings in proportion as they exhibit a similar indifference to his will. This same presumption applies in the case of his *thought* about things. He imagines what they may be, names them, defines them, asks about them, constantly taking for granted that if any discrepancy between them and his thoughts is revealed, *he* must give way. The facts are stolidly indifferent to his gropings, and unsympathetically "stare him in the face," when he finds them. The term "fact" signifies more of reality for the common mind than any other popular quasi-epistemological expression, and as ordinarily employed it stands for the givenness of the real. We have it "on our hands." Possibly the tacit realism of everyday life might be summed up by the saying: "It is a *situation* and not a theory that confronts us." Or, as Professor Royce well says in another connection, "Necessity comes home to us men through the medium of a given fact" (*ibid*., p. 257).

We may now state a definition of realism that seems to me to be representative of both philosophical realism and common sense; and to be the most consistent statement possible of what Professor Royce has named realism in his account. The realist believes reality to be a *datum, a somewhat that is given independently of whatever ideas may be formed about it*. According to the realist, the real has a *locus*, a *habitat*, whether or no within some individual experience. Here the real primarily *is*, and is, regardless of whatever secondary meanings, symbols, names, relations, or ideas of any kind may be referred to it. The realist conceives of a *thing*, and *thought about that thing*. They are two orders, not necessarily two kinds; for the thing may be a thought. But in every case the thing of the first order is indifferent, as far as its being is concerned, to the thought of the second order; which may reveal, but does not constitute or create its object. Realism being so defined, has Professor Royce succeeded in overthrowing it?

The first step in his argument is to inoculate realism with pluralism. It should be evident from what has been said, that the realist has in mind a very definite relation between the idea and its object. The real may be found or interpreted by ideas, which are nevertheless adventitious as respects its being. The idea, on the other hand, is strictly dependent upon the reality, being derived therefrom, pointing thereto, and tested thereby. This relation may present difficulties, but the realist means it, and would never recognise as descriptive of himself, Professor Royce's statement of the *absolute mutual separateness* of idea and object. Nevertheless our author argues that this mutual independence is the logical outcome of the realist's position as stated above. Let us examine the argument.

In the first place, as we have seen, realism defines the real object *o* so as to be independent of the idea of *o*. One may suppose the idea of *o* to vary or to vanish; and there is no relation between the two such as to compel a corresponding change in *o*. But the idea of *o* is itself a real object, and upon the realistic basis must therefore be similarly independent of – what? Professor Royce says, of *o* (*ibid*., pp. 265, 266); but this is obviously fallacious. The realist would contend that the *idea of o*, as a psychological entity, was independent, not of *o*, but of another idea, the idea of *idea of o*. So this proves no reciprocal independence.

But in another connection, we are told that, "The idea will have to be, in its own separate essence, independent of the object. Otherwise, by merely examining the idea, taken by itself, you could prove something about the existence of its object" (*ibid*., p. 119). The contention is, supposedly, that if the idea were in every case in some way related to an object, the presence of the idea would be a sure indication of the reality of the object; and the being of the object would be logically dependent upon the existence of its idea, which, according to our author, would contradict the realistic hypothesis. Now how far is this argument really cogent? Let us suppose the idea to be in every case dependent upon an object. Consider any cognitive idea, *e.g*., the idea *o*, where by hypothesis the idea is derived from *o*. The idea has a certain content, *o*′, and a certain objective reference. *o*′ may be attributed to reality in general, or in particular. If to reality in general, then its object, *reality in general*, is, it is true, deducible from it; *i.e*., finding the idea of *o*, you may he sure of reality in general. Or the idea of *o* may attribute *o*′ to reality in particular. In this case reality in some particular is deducible from the presence of the idea of *o*; *i.e*., the specific locus to which *o* is attributed, may be assumed to exist. That locus is defined by its context, and the experienced self of the moment is a part of that context. But has the realist's original position meanwhile been abandoned? Has reality become dependent upon idea, when reality in general, or a certain direction from the experienced self of the moment, is made a certainty by the presence of an idea? We may apply Professor Royce's own test. Under the circumstances described, no change in *o* need follow from a change or the disappearance of the idea of *o*. Two kinds of change may be considered, (1) eternal, and (2) temporal. (1) Omit the idea of *o* from the universe, and only my deduction of *o* is impaired, since, by hypothesis, the idea of *o* was originally derived from *o*, and not *o* from its idea. (2) Cause the idea of *o* to vary or disappear in time, and *o* does not necessarily change; for *o* need not be sensitive thereto any more than a body to its shadow. On the other hand the annihilation of *o* will inevitably affect its object. (1) Omit *o* from the universe, and you destroy the idea, since the idea was by hypothesis derived therefrom. (2) Cause *o* to disappear in time, and you destroy the idea, since you destroy the self, from which *o* was defined as a direction. *o* may, however, *change* without a concomitant variation of the idea of *o*; or the idea may have inaccurately represented *o* from the beginning. These will be the cases of erroneous ideas, to which our author refers. Such have an objective point of reference, to which they ascribe a content that does not correspond to the actual experienced content. Thus it is possible to state the realistic hypothesis in such a way as to involve the relation of an idea to its object without vitiating the independence of the object; or, so as to specify that the object shall be independent of its idea, without implying a similar independence on the part of the idea. The importance of this analysis consists in its defense of realism against Professor Royce's imputation of abstract pluralism. The realist means a certain definite kind of relation between idea and object. The most important step in Professor Royce's dialectic is the reduction of that relation to absolute mutual aloofness. The writer finds no other proof to warrant this step than that which has been examined above. For the sake of clarifying the issue let us formulate as representative examples as possible, to express the realistic position at this stage of the discussion:

1. An idea of the State House in Boston. My idea has a content derived from actual experience, and consisting mainly in visual memories. I attribute this content to a certain locus in human experience. That locus is defined by spatial and temporal direction from my present moment of experience, and by contiguity with other remembered and imagined moments of experience. My idea may refer to the past state of its object, in which case I judge that were I to retrace my own experience back from the present moment, I should meet with a definite fulfilled expectation. In this case my idea is incorrect in so far as such expectation would be thwarted. The degree of surprise would indicate the degree of error. On the other hand, my idea may refer to the present condition of the State House. In this case, I judge that were I now standing in a certain place in Boston, I would not be at a loss, but would recognise my surroundings. Meanwhile the State House may have been burned to the ground, in which case my error would consist in the hypothetical defeat of expectation, the failure of my present mental content to be such as to prepare me for the actual experience to which I refer. My idea, it is seen, has been derived from the actually experienced object, and is not possible in a universe without the individual State House in Boston. Were the object to become in time absolutely nothing, my self and my idea must disappear with it. For the object as referred to is a direction from the self; and one direction cannot be lost without the loss of all direction, or that orientation upon which self-conscious existence depends. Nevertheless the State House may have burned down without my ever knowing it; *i.e.*, a relative change of content may have

taken place, and have falsified my idea without at the same time changing it. On the other hand, the main realistic contention holds, since the waxing and waning of my idea has no effect upon the Boston State House, and a universe without my idea might still be a universe containing the Boston State House.

2. The realist's idea of the world. Professor Royce has used this same illustration in connection with the specious argument cited above. He maintains that since the realistic ideas of the world are real objects, they must be as regardless of the real world as the real world is of them (*ibid.*, pp. 135, 136). But it is perfectly possible for the realist to hold that his philosophy, though as content of his conscious life it is independent of what ideas others may form about it, is nevertheless as idea entirely derived from the actual world of experience. The realist's philosophy will consist in a set of ideas referred by him to the totality of experience. Their truth will mean their power to prepare their thinker for an experience indefinitely enlarged or prolonged. They will be erroneous in so far as they are baffled when confronted by experience, or in so far as such a perplexity is possible.

In such terms as these the realistic position may be stated without involving it in an absurd and self-contradictory statement of the absolute mutual independence of idea and object. Such a mutual independence once admitted, it is very easy, as Professor Royce does, to show that it prevents the idea from being an idea at all, since it could not refer to an object, or to the standards of truth and error.

Though we decline to assent to Professor Royce's reduction of realism to abstract pluralism, the next stage in the argument must be examined in the interests of pluralism itself. Assuming that he has reduced realism to a statement of the absolute mutual separation of idea and object, he considers such independence of many beings as representative of pluralism, and proceeds to attack that general thesis. At the outset let me enter a general demurrer to the way in which our author conducts his case. In the main he takes for granted that the burden of proof lies with the pluralist, and demands of him that he shall *prove* the existence of many absolutely separate beings. Now the pluralist, having empirical predilections, very properly refuses to make any such effort. He is concerned neither with abstract separateness, as the monist defines it for him, nor with proof, as the rationalist defines it for him. He has found the world to be many. He has encountered, *e.g.*, other selves, many of whom think quite differently, and all of whom feel quite differently, from himself. Such selves are not absolutely separate; on the contrary their community is the very source of their mutual discovery. He alleges that there is in the world just so much unity, and so much difference, as there seems to be. His proof of it is the seeing of it. Professor Royce, on the other hand, admits by the whole character of his discussion, that he is undertaking to demonstrate; and that he is undertaking to demonstrate the necessary reality of a transcendental unity. The burden of proof lies fairly and squarely with the transcendentalist. The importance of this demurrer is twofold. In the first place, it makes plain the futility of setting up for controversial purposes an absolute pluralism, which no other than a transcendentalist could ever have conceived, and the destruction of which injures nothing so much as the prestige of his own method. In the second place this general objection will very largely destroy the cogency of our author's specific arguments, of which we may consider three.

1. Applying first the empirical test, Professor Royce challenges the pluralist to find in the world any cases of objects that are mutually independent. For some reason he weakens his defiance by limiting such objects to "any two physically real objects which are so independent of each other that no change in one of them need correspond to any change of the other" (*ibid.*, p. 125). As respects "physically real objects," one will readily admit that in defining them so, Professor Royce has already precluded the sort of independence he assigns to pluralism. It is ridiculous to demand of the pluralist that he find two objects so independent, that he cannot imagine one to influence the other; and it is more ridiculous to posit that such objects shall be assumed to be "physical," *i.e.*, already defined as in space together. The pluralist would naturally reply that, as Professor Royce allows, he is not concerned in this particular argument with hypothetical possibilities, but with what he *finds* to be the case. He finds physical objects that, so far as he knows, do not influence one another. The actual variations of the one, as far as experience informs him, effect no concomitant variations in the other. More notable for their indifference to one another are the feelings and ideas of different subjects. In innumerable cases, *A's* idea *x* has been correct or incorrect, has come into existence or ceased to be, with no effect upon *B's* idea *y*; at least such is the testimony of experience. And we can conceive that in our world such objects should be eternally independent of one another, so that the changes of one should never in any way affect the other.

To be sure, we cannot conceive two objects to be so related that we cannot *conceive* them not to be so related. In the case of the independent objects that we experience or imagine, there will always be for our knowledge the possibility of a change to a relation of dependence. I can imagine *a* and *b* to be so sundered that no variation of one as a matter of fact ever effects the other. But I cannot describe that independence so as to preclude for my imagination the possibility of some event that may bring *a* and *b* into a relation of dependence. And here Professor Royce would contend that this theoretical possibility of interaction, is itself a bond of union. Given *a* and *b*, admit that though at present variations of one do not affect the other, they may conceivably come into such a relation of mutual affectibility; and you have already destroyed their independence. But why so? On the contrary, you have merely expressed your inability to state that *a* and *b* may not at some time change their relation. That possibility, which Professor Royce holds to be a part of the being of *a* and *b*, is merely a confession of one's ignorance as respects what the future, or the entire universe, may contain; and by the realistic hypothesis, this does not necessarily concern the objects.

There is great danger of confusing the contention just stated with what is distinctly another logical issue. "Possibility of definition," and "definition of a possibility," are obviously very different propositions. To be unable to define *a* and *b* so as to prevent their theoretical modification to a relation of dependence, is not the same as to define *a* and *b* as actually capable of entering into such a relation. So we have not yet raised the question as to whether *a* and *b* could be actually independent, and at the same time potentially dependent. This question of the possibility of change from independence to dependence is specifically discussed in the next stage of Professor Royce's argument. But up to this point the pluralist may insist that he finds objects which do not actually affect one another in their present observed changes, and that he can conceive the possibility of the permanent or eternal separateness of such. The burden of proof surely lies with those who deny the actuality or the possibility of such objects. For experience, though it testifies to the connectedness of much of reality, testifies to no ultimate all-comprehensive unity.

2. "Assuming the real world...to contain many mutually independent beings," says Professor Royce, "I will prove" that "the many different real beings once thus defined can never come to acquire or later to be conceived as possessing any possible real linkages or connections, binding these different beings together; and so these beings will remain forever wholly sundered, as if in different worlds" (*ibid.*, p. 127). Assume *a* and *b*, so defined that one might remain unchanged if the other vanished. Could they ever become so related as to be in any way dependent upon one another? Such a change would involve the entrance into the world of a new fact, *e.g.*, *a influencing b*. Can this fact come to be, and yet be purely adventitious as respects *a* and *b*? Professor Royce argues that if the new fact were purely adventitious it could not constitute a link. The argument is much clearer if we reverse the order. Suppose *a* to be influencing *b*; then *a* and *b* could never have been indifferent to one another's existence. For had *a* at any previous time disappeared, the event, *influenced by a*, would have been eliminated from the

future of *b*. In other words, if you define an object *b* so as to affirm that it sometime will be changed by another object *a*, you have already defined *b* as affectible by *a*, and so not independent of it. In this sense, once dependent, always dependent.

So far I admit the cogency of the argument. But the real value of the conclusion is determined by other considerations. In the first place, as has been remarked, the pluralist is not necessarily concerned with the reality of objects that are not in any way subject to alteration by one another. There may still be such independence of origin and such independence of being as refuses to be embraced in any closer unity. Again, the pluralist is not necessarily concerned that the absolutely independent objects, if there be such, should ever become dependent. Finally, he will still deny the validity of the more extreme pretensions of our author's argument. For Professor Royce has undertaken to prove that such independent beings as make no difference to one another can never acquire *any sort of relation*, but must remain "wholly sundered, as if in different worlds." This conclusion would follow from the above argument only in case we assumed that all relations involve dependence; and such is by no means either proven or self-evident so far in our discussion.

Let us suppose, *e.g.*, that *a* and *b* are thought together by a finite consciousness *M*, so as to give rise to the new psychical fact, the idea *a'b'*. They might still have been once so independent of one another that the vanishing of one would not affect the other. The non-being of *a* would have made *a'b'* impossible, but that would make no necessary difference to *b*. For by the realistic presupposition, *b* is indifferent to *a'b'*, *i.e.*, to thought about it. What *b* is and what *b* becomes, is by no means necessarily altered by what may be imputed to it of relation to other objects. To one who objects that we have not linked *a* and *b* but only their ideas, it is sufficient to reply that they are at any rate in the same world of thought and possible experience, and that they have obtained some sort of connection that they did not originally have. But Professor Royce might still reply that *a* and *b* defined as independent, could possess no such resemblance as that which would be necessary in order to make their comprehension in one thought possible. This is the substance of his third criticism of the "independent beings."

3. "The many real beings thus defined can have no common characters; they are wholly different from one another" (*ibid.*, p. 127). Suppose two objects *a* and *b* to possess a common quality *Q*. Could they at the same time be defined as independent in the sense that one could vanish without affecting the other? Professor Royce replies in the negative, alleging that if *a* were to vanish with *Q* in its possession, *b* would necessarily lose *Q*, and so change. Or, to state it differently, if *a*

were to vanish with *Q*, and *b* were to persist with *Q′*, *Q* and *Q′* could not be the same. The proposition is simple enough upon the supposition that for the realist similarity involves identity. Common sense would without hesitation attribute any quality such as *Q* to quite separate objects such as *a* and *b*. But even common sense would not conceive of *Q* as an identical entity leading a double life. On the contrary, similarity is commonly regarded as dependent upon the judgment of synthetic consciousness. One *finds a* resembling *b* in some particular, *Q*. In turning from *a* to *b* one experiences recognition as respects one part of the content of *b*. Now cannot *a* and *b* be independent, and yet similar in this sense? As has already been maintained, togetherness in consciousness may be adventitious as respects the being of the objects so experienced. Then it is no part necessarily of the being of *a* that it should be found to be like *b*, or different from the indefinite number of other objects with which conceivably it might be compared.

But would not the very possibility of such comparison indicate some sameness or community of character as already present? If *a* and *b* can be thought together must they not already be alike in that they are members of the same spiritual universe? Or, supposing finite consciousness *M* to compare *a* and *b*, were *a* and *b* not previously alike in that each was capable of becoming a part of *M*? We must reply in the affirmative, and would seem to be compelled to resort to some other comparing consciousness, which if it were not an eternal and all-embracing consciousness, would refer us in turn to another and so on *ad infinitum*. It must be admitted, then, that Professor Royce is upon us with his Absolute unless we can define similarity apart from actual joint presence in consciousness. And this issue is of the greatest strategic importance, because it involves the fundamental epistemological argument which is elaborated in the later portions of the book. It is there maintained that an idea can have an object, and be true or false, only when the intention of the idea is noted by a consciousness that embraces the totality of the world, and can observe the degree to which the idea attains its end. Must the fact of truth or error, or the fact of similarity, be contained in one individual synthetic consciousness?

The pluralist will reply finally, that it is perfectly legitimate to define sameness in terms of possible experience. Suppose *a* and *b* to be alike in the particular $Q_1$ when compared in the consciousness *M*. Before this observed relation there was that which made it possible; *a* in itself possessed a definite character; and *b* in itself a definite character. Whoever experienced *a*, experienced $Q_1$; whoever experienced *b*, experienced $Q_2$. The sameness of $Q_1$ and $Q_2$ consisted in the fact that should *a* and *b* be compared, just this likeness *Q*, might be noted.

Moreover this fact of sameness was not a *mere* possibility of experience, but existed in the experienced content of *a* and *b* severally. When *a* and *b* are actually compared, there is, to be sure, in *Q* a new fact of *observed* sameness. But such new facts cannot he explained away on any hypothesis. That finite individual *M* should come to see the resemblance between *a* and *b* denotes a new fact in the universe; a fact previously contained potentially in the separate elements here synthesised.

Similarly, one may contend that the truth or falsity of an idea can be construed as the hypothetical fulfilment or defeat of expectation. Subject *M*, holding idea *x* of reality, is mentally so constituted that were he to experience the content of that locus which his judgment designates as direction from himself, he would experience some degree of surprise or recognition.

A far more careful examination of the query, "What is truth?" as well as an examination of the problem of individuality, would be necessary before Professor Royce's challenge could be adequately answered. We have considered his refutation of realism and pluralism, in so far as it is nominally concerned with these theories. Thus considered, the argument is a fragment, since, according to our author's plan of campaign, realism and pluralism are to appear again as "almost persuaded," under the title of "Critical Rationalism." But it must suffice to express the belief that the general line of defence here projected could be maintained to the end.

I hope that these arguments may remind some who are of an empirical turn of mind that the great critical epistemology of *a priori* idealism is as yet unanswered; and at the same time suggest that it is not unanswerable. The writer of them arrogates to himself no little virtue for having turned from the tempting ethical and metaphysical quarry contained in this volume of transcendentalism, to an attentive examination of its proof.

# PROFESSOR ROYCE'S REFUTATION OF REALISM

William Pepperell Montague, "Royce's Refutation of Realism," *Philosophical Review*, vol. 11 (1902).

Professor Royce's recently published volume of Gifford Lectures contains a refutation of realism that is particularly account of the author's novel methods of treating that well-worn topic. To examine this refutation is the object of the present paper.

Professor Royce classifies ontological systems according to the attitude towards the epistemological question of the relation of an idea to its object. He shows that from this point of view all of the divergent systems of realism agree in asserting that it is the essence of a real object to be independent of its idea. The author's method of criticism is to develop the logical implications of this attitude, and by showing them to be self-contradictory and absurd, to discredit the premise from which they follow. The steps in his argument may, I think, be stated as follows:

Realism, in asserting the independence of object and idea, asserts the existence of a world of independent beings. The first implication of such a world is what we may call the externality of all the relations subsisting between its members. The very fact that things are independent in the realist's sense makes it incumbent on him to assume that any relations in which they may stand to one another (such, for example, as causality or correspondence) are external to the terms related. The significance of this implication will be seen later. The second is that the independence, if it is to answer to the demands of the realist, must be an absolute independence. The real object is to be regarded as so completely independent of all "mere ideas" which are held about it, that never at any period of its history, nor under any conceivable circumstances, can we suppose it to be influenced by these ideas. Nor may the realist stop here, for the third of the alleged implications of his thesis is that the independence of object and idea is a mutual independence. The object is of no more consequence to the idea than the idea to the object; either member of the pair could be altered to any extent, could in fact be annihilated without producing the slightest change in the other member. The author then proceeds to the last portion of his argument, which consists in the application of the realistic theory to the dilemma of monism and pluralism. The pluralistic horn of the dilemma is first considered, and two theses concerning it are laid down and proved. First, a world of many independent beings could never by any process whatever evolve into the actual world which we experience. For that world is one whose constituents are to a greater or less extent related to and mutually dependent on one another, while in the realistic world all beings are absolutely independent, and the relations in which they stand are external facts, and as such will be quite unable to bridge the chasm which divides the real beings from one another. As for the second thesis, it is nothing less than the proof that the real beings can only preserve their independence by being not merely entirely discontinuous spatially, temporally, and causally, but also by being utterly dissimilar – having not a single quality in common. "[T]hey are sundered from one another by absolutely impassible chasms; they can never come to get either ties or community of nature; they are not in the same space, nor in the same time, nor in the same natural or spiritual order."[1] In order to escape the consequences of pluralism the realist naturally turns to monism – reality is not many real facts but one real fact, a single unity, independent of all external to it, but internally a complex system of mutually dependent and mutually related elements. But this refuge is at once seen to be forbidden the realist, for "there are already at least Two genuinely and absolutely independent real Beings in the realistic world."[2] These two are the object and the idea of the object, and "ideas, even the most false ones, are facts in the mental world," and as such can never be joined or related, or made to correspond in any way whatsoever. Hence the dialectic which has just proved so deadly in the pluralistic world applies with equal force to realistic monism. No world at all is possible for the realist, and as a parting shot the critic grimly applies the consequences of the general theory to the special case of the realist's own idea of his real world, that idea being shown to be intrinsically unrepresentative of its intended object.

So much by way of brief general exposition of what I understand to be Professor Royce's line of argument; let us turn now to the examination of that argument.

Passing over the question of the propriety of the author's classifying the systems of ontology simply with regard to their attitudes towards a single problem in the theory of knowledge, what are we to say of his definition of realism? "According to this conception," says Professor Royce, "to be real means to be independent of an idea or experience

[1] *The World and the Individual*, Vol. I, pp. 131, 132.

[2] Ibid., p. 133.

through which the real being is from without, felt, or thought, or known. And this...is the view which, recognizing independent beings as real, lays explicit stress upon their independence as the very essence of their reality."[3] Now this definition seems to me to commit the more or less serious error of confusing the ratio cognoscendi with the ratio essendi. The independence of an object is not what makes it real, it is what makes us aware that it is real. The realist has, let us say, a visual perception of a chair; he wishes to find out whether the chair and its idea are merely two aspects of one fact, as the idealist believes, or whether they are two numerically separate facts, as he himself believes. Casting about for some means to test the question, he chances perhaps to turn away his head or to close his eyes; his visual perception of the chair at once begins to fade. He has various reasons for believing that what he calls the real chair is not fading, and as he cannot conceive how what is numerically identical can both fade and not fade at the same time, he is forced to believe that the chair and its idea are not "one fact in two different contexts," but two numerically different facts. The chair has remained independent of the variations in the idea of the chair, and this independence is evidence for regarding the two as separate. The method of procedure for determining whether idea and object are numerically separate, is, in fact, just the same as that for determining whether any two things are numerically separate. Suppose we wish to find whether a brass rod consists of one piece or of two pieces cleverly laid together so as to resemble one piece. Our natural impulse is of course to vary the position of what we suppose to be one of the pieces. If the other piece remains quite independent of these variations, we know that that independence results from the numerical separateness of the two things. Independence of an object in the face of the numerous variations in its idea is thus an effect of its reality, and not a cause of it – a sign by which we recognize the separateness of object and idea, and not a ground of that separateness. And I have dwelt upon what appears to me to be the obvious hysteron proteron involved in Professor Royce's definition because many of the dire consequences which are supposed to befall the realist depend solely upon that definition. This difficulty, however, need not prevent us from following Professor Royce's main argument, for even though 'independence' is not itself the essence of the realistic theory, it is in an inevitable consequence of it, and the realist is accountable for its implications.

The first of the alleged implications of the independence of the real object is what I have called "externality of relations." Professor Royce puts the matter thus: "this realistic definition seems to imply...that even

[3] Op. cit., p. 62.

if your knowledge and its object are facts which when examined, say by a psychologist, appear to him to be causally related, or which when externally observed seem to agree, still any such linkage where it exists is no part of the essential nature, i.e., of the mere definition either of your object in so far as it is real, or of your knowledge in so far as it consists of mere ideas... . Realism asserts that existent causal or other linkage between any knower and what he knows is no part of the definition of the object known, or of its real being, or of the essence of the knowing idea, if viewed in itself alone, as a 'mere idea.'"[4]

Before inquiring into the justice of this argument, let us consider the meaning of "a relation external to the terms related." A relation apart from the terms which it relates, would seem to be in much the same position as a fraction that was external to or independent of its own numerator and denominator, and however many subtle paradoxes the concept of relation may contain, it seems clear that it lies in the essence of that concept to exist only as relative to its terms. A relation without terms, then, is as good as no relation; and to say, for example, that the only kind of causality that is consistent with the realist's definition is a causality that has nothing to do with either cause or effect, is equivalent to saying that the relation of causality is not consistent with that definition. Let us then interpret Professor Royce's "first implication" as the statement that relations of causality and correspondence are impossible between an idea and its object, if they are dependent in the realistic sense. (That this is the true interpretation will become still more apparent when we consider the other alleged implications.) One naturally asks what there is in the realist's notion of an object's independence of its idea that would compel him to give up the thought of their being related. The independence posited by the realist is the independence that, following from numerical separateness, is a sign to us that that separateness exists. And any relation that is consistent with numerical separateness will be consistent with whatever independence is implied by that separateness. Now because two peas are numerically separate, and to that extent independent, they are not thereby precluded from causing changes in one another, nor from corresponding to one another. In fact, the only reason, so far as I can see, that could have led the author to assert the incompatibility of realistic independence and the existence of relations is what I have already referred to as the apparent failure to see that realistic independence is simply the result of numerical separateness, and that as such it is limited in its degree, and is by no means as absolute as to make all relations "external" or non-existent.

This brings us, however, to the second of the alleged implications of

4 Op. cit., pp. 115–17.

the realistic definition. Professor Royce here tells us explicitly that realistic independence must be absolute. He says: "In the second place, however, realism taken in its unmodified form, asserts that the independence here in question...is indeed in its own realm absolute. For it is the whole Being of the object, spatial, temporal, inner, and outer, that is independent of the fact that anybody knows this truth."[5]

The author then goes on to explain that when he says that the object must be conceived by the realist as absolutely independent of the idea, he means that independence at one moment logically implies independence for all time, and under all conceivable circumstances. Because we believe that a real object, such as a chair, is not always dependent upon every fluctuation of the ideas or states of consciousness by which we are aware of it, our critic would have us admit that the chair can never be changed in any way by our ideas concerning it. Of course the realist's answer to such an argument is to point to any two objects, which, though possessing the independence due to numerical separateness, are none the less capable of influencing one another. A mine and a fuse, for instance, have all the independence demanded by the realist for his idea and object, and yet we feel no difficulty in admitting that their independent existence or separateness is no bar to their complete interaction under appropriate conditions. Indeed, the lack of connection between a "state of separateness" (with the degree and kind of independence therein implied), and a "state of perpetual inability to interact," is so glaringly obvious that one might be pardoned for failing altogether to comprehend the author's idea in identifying them.

But let us turn to the "third implication" of the realist's definition of the relation of object and idea. "Moreover, the essential independence of object and 'mere idea,' in so far as each is first viewed by itself alone, will have to be a mutual independence. The idea will have to be in its own separate essence independent of the object."[6] Now there are two considerations which appear to lend color to Professor Royce's thesis of mutuality or reciprocality. In the first place, numerical difference is in itself a reciprocal relation, and the idea and its object stand in this relation. In the second place, the independence which each enjoys can only be overcome by the medium of self. Here, however, the reciprocity ends. The manner in which the self's ideas influence their objects and the degree of that influence, is different from the manner and degree of the objects' influence upon their ideas. As evidence of this non-mutuality, consider the case of an idea or belief existing in a mind which from blindness or inability refuses to put its judgments to an objective test.

[5] Op. cit., p. 117.

[6] Ibid., p. 119.

Under these conditions it is indeed true that the idea is as independent of its object as its object is of it. But this continued independence is not due to the numerical separateness of the idea, nor to an intrinsic power of resisting change at the hands of its object; it is due simply and solely to the artificial protection which it receives from a truth-hating self, or from the inaccessibility of its object. Once let these barriers be removed so that the object can confront its idea in the bright light of immediate experience – then indeed the naturally dependent and derivative nature of the 'mere idea' no longer remains in doubt. If false, it is at once extinguished – pushed out of existence by the true perception; if true, it continues to exist, but only on suffrance, subservient to the slightest observable change in its object. The inverse of this relation is however, quite different. The object, as we have seen, is independent of the idea qua idea which any one may have of it, such dependence as there is being due only to the active power of the self to express its ideas in the world. In short, a self or other artificial aid is needed to restrain the object from influencing its idea, while on the other hand the same help is required to enable the idea to influence its object. And although the idea is not always directly caused by its object (more often being caused by other ideas which are the effects of something connected with, or similar to, the object), yet the relation of object and idea, so far as absence of reciprocity is concerned, is practically that of causality. And an effect is only indirectly independent of its cause when removed from its spatial or temporal environment, or when protected by some counteracting cause, while the cause is only dependent upon its effect when reacted upon by the object in which, as its "state," the effect was produced.

As for the additional consideration adduced by Professor Royce in support of "mutuality of independence," I have not mentioned before because it seemed to me to weaken rather than strengthen his case. Probably, however, I have misunderstood it, hence I give it now in full. "The idea will have to be in its own separate essence independent of the object. Otherwise by merely examining the idea taken by itself, you could prove something about the existence of its object. But if so then the that would follow from the what, and the independent existence of a thing from the presence of some mere idea of the thing. That, however, is forbidden by the whole spirit of realism."[7]

I say that I feel that I have probably misunderstood the meaning of this passage, for as I read it, it appears to me to be a second and far more aggravated case of the confusion of the "reason of knowing" with the "reason of being." To say that you cannot infer the existence of a cause from the perception of its effect without thereby making the

[7] Op. cit., p. 119.

existence of a thing follow from the presence of its mere idea, is tantamount to saying that if you see a man in the distance with a peculiar kind of hat worn only by Smith, you cannot thereupon draw the inference that the man is Smith unless you are willing to admit that your perception of Smith's hat is the cause of Smith's existence. Is there any one at all, be he realist or synthetic idealist, who would seriously maintain in some similar concrete case that an inference from the perception of an effect to a belief in the existence of its cause, would be impossible except under the monstrous condition that we believed that our perception or idea of the effect had created the cause? But it is surely not necessary to say that when inferences are drawn in a realistic world (or, so far as I can see, in any conceivable world), it is not the that which follows from the what, or the cause from the effect, but the knowledge of the cause that follows from the knowledge of the effect – the conception of or belief in the that which follows from the perception of the what.

"But the definition is now complete. Let us at once set it to work. It has defined a world, let us enter that world and see what is there."[8] With these words Professor Royce passes from the first part of his argument to the second. From a consideration of the implications of the realistic definition, he proceeds to a study of the consequences of applying that definition to the world of facts. And we are first to ask the formal question: "In the realistic world whose Being is thus defined, could there exist Many different beings? And if they existed, in what relation would they stand? Or again, could a realistic world contain One sole Being to the exclusion of many beings?"[9]

The realist is supposed, for the sake of argument, to begin by taking the pluralistic horn of the dilemma. His world is composed of many real beings. Moreover, he is not to be compelled to say whether his real beings are simple, as were the 'reals' of Herbart, or complex as were the 'monads' of Leibniz. Realistic pluralism in general, and not any particular type of realistic pluralism, is all he need be concerned to defend. Naturally the realist turns first to the world of experience to find examples of his independent beings. He takes the drops of water in the ocean, and the wood of his writing desk, or Laplanders and Bostonians, or any pair of things that seem at first sight to be mutually independent. And then he goes on to show how experience, in addition to furnishing instances of independent objects, also gives examples of the manner in which those objects can enter into very intimate relationship. How, in short, his independent metaphysical realities can give rise to the interde-

[8] Ibid., p. 120.

[9] Op. cit., p. 121.

pendent world of phenomenal appearance, thereby demonstrating of his pluralistic hypothesis to explain things. But Professor Royce has no sooner stated this argument in behalf of the realist than he rejects it. He reminds us that the facts cited in support of his theory are themselves inconsistent with that theory. For the Bostonians and Laplanders could not become future business correspondents, ocean water could not in the future, when transmuted into rain, warp the wood of the desk, unless they had been in the past dependent upon, and not, as the realist would hold, independent of one another. To put the matter in general terms, we may say that no two objects could exist in the same world of time and space without thereby being mutually dependent in a sense that is barred out by the realistic theory. Thus it is that the realist in his search for "many independent beings" is driven out of the world of actually experienced objects into the world of the supersensuous.

Now the force of our author's refutation of the realist's claim to take his independent beings from the world of experience depends solely and confessedly on the thesis advanced in connection with the "second implication," the thesis, namely, that the independence asserted by realism is an absolute independence, applying not merely to any one period of time but to the entire past and future possible and actual history of the object and its idea. And, in discussing that second implication, we saw that it was only a "temporary" independence, i.e., only such independence as would be the inevitable accompaniment of the numerical non-identity of an object and its idea, that is asserted by the realist. In fact, if we call this illegitimate type of independence which applies to any possible past and future history – "hyper-independence," we may fairly say that Professor Royce's entire refutation of realism is based on his theory that there can be no independence in a realist's world except hyper-independence. No realist would admit this theory as true – no realist would deny that a view which accepted hyper-independence would be self-contradictory.

But to return; we had left the realist at the point where his failure to find hyper-independence in the world of experience had condemned him to abandon that world and with it his hope of a comfortable empiricism. "Unhampered, therefore, by empirical guidance we turn back to the chill realm of the hypothetical many beings of our realist's hypothesis... . And hereupon, assuming the real world now before us to contain many mutually independent beings, I will prove at once two theses: (1) The many different real beings once thus defined can never come to acquire or later to be conceived as possessing any possible real linkages or connections binding these different beings together, and so these different beings will remain forever wholly sundered as if in different worlds. (2) The many real beings thus defined can have no common character; they are wholly different from one another. Only nominally can any common characters be asserted of them."[10]

Now the first of these theses is contained in Professor Royce's definition of independence; and its proof consists practically in a repetition of that definition, and of the grounds for assuming it. If the independence of two objects means a hyper-independence that precludes all future connections between them, then it will certainly be easy to prove that future connections are precluded. And as new reasons, so far as I can see, are advanced to show that the realist's temporary independence logically implies hyper-independence, I pass at once to the second thesis.

The many real beings can have no common characters. "For suppose that they are first said to possess in common a quality Q. Then let one of the two beings be destroyed... . Q, then, the quality supposed to be the same in both beings survives unchanged in the being that does not vanish." (Certainly, for a universal quality is not as a quality affected in the slightest by the fact that there is one less particular object that exemplifies it.) "But now if one man survived a shipwreck in which another was drowned, could you then call the survivor the same as the drowned man? But by hypothesis the quality Q, together with all relationships essential unto its reality survives unchanged in the being that remains, while what is called the same quality in the other being has passed away."[11] But not at all! There was no question of the quality "passing away," it was the object that "had" the quality that passed away. No quality has ever been shipwrecked and drowned. A quality could not be drowned any more than it could be chopped. It is not so constituted. Nor has the realist any need of the loop-hole from which he is warned in the next lines by Professor Royce as follows: "But our realist, unwilling to concede this last consequence, may hereupon say that what he meant was that the quality Q in the two beings was partly the same and partly not the same." The realist did not mean this, however; he meant just what Professor Royce would have him mean, viz., that the two objects had exactly the same quality, and that this qualitative similarity had absolutely nothing to do with the dynamical independence (or lack of independence) in the two bodies. To confuse qualitative similarity or dissimilarity with numerical identity or non-identity is sufficient to destroy all thinking. Professor Royce certainly would not neglect this distinction himself. Why does he make the poor realist neglect it? What is there in the realist's theory of independent beings, even if that independence were extended to the past and future, that justifies our author in inflicting upon him the burdens of Mediaeval

[10] Op. cit., p. 127.

[11] Op. cit., p. 130.

nominalism? The realist, by Professor Royce's own account, asserts "numerical" or "quantitative" or "substantial" non-identity, and the independence therein implied, between the object, and the idea of the object. That is his thesis. Now I ask again, What is the nature of the step from the numerical separateness of object and idea to the qualitative dissimilarity of object and idea? Indeed it is not a step, it is a sheer leap. Professor Royce does not think that two peas are any nearer to being one pea if both are green than if one were green and one red. Neither does the realist. Why should he?

Of course this assertion of the total qualitative dissimilarity of the realist's many real beings is the finishing stroke that is necessary to destroy what little plausibility they might have retained after their complete independence in space and time had been assumed. And the realist now turns in desperation from the pluralistic world to the world of monism. "There are indeed not many real beings, but only One Being indefinitely rich in its own nature." But here the realist, just as he is entering this port of refuge, is debarred by the fact that in this single interdependent system there are at least two absolutely independent real beings, viz., the object and its idea, for at least this much of plurality is postulated by the mere definition of realism. But plurality of any sort in connection with beings of the realistic type has already proved to be fatal. Hence this last consequence completes the refutation of realism.

And now by way of conclusion let us note again the essentially defensive attitude of the realist. The idealist has discovered a difficulty in the ordinary view of the nature of knowledge – the difficulty of imagining how the mind can conceive of things which are not inside it. A sort of "action at a distance" would seem to be involved in the common-sense dualism, and hence the idealist proposes as a substitute for that dualism the theory that all so-called real objects are, in so far as they are objects of knowledge, inside the mind of the knower; the common-sense notion of a numerical difference of object and "mere idea" being thus replaced by a difference of relational context. The realist on his side fully admits the genuineness of the difficulty discovered by the idealist, but he cannot bring himself to accept the latter's solution – the remedy seems worse than the disease. In short, he prefers to admit his ignorance of the nature of the relation between idea and object, and the manner in which two such disparate things can interact and correspond, rather than to admit that they are but the same thing seen under two different aspects. When asked to justify his rejection of idealism he replies by an appeal that is given in experience, to the fact, namely, that the variations of object and idea are seen to be independent of one another under certain conditions. If the object and idea were numerically identical, this independence of variation would be an all but impossible consequence; if they were numerically separate, it would be all but necessary. Hence he concludes that they, the object and its idea, are two numerically separate facts. This is, I take it, the theory of realism. Independence of behavior is not the realistic doctrine; it is the experiential basis for the doctrine. And in spite of the novelty and interest that attaches to Professor Royce's argument, it appears to me to be lacking in finality, just because the author, mistaking this experiential evidence of realism for realism itself, attempts to force upon the realist the strange conclusion that such independence as is implied by and indicative of the numerical separateness of object and idea carries with it a total inability of these two to interact, or to correspond, or to be in any way related.

# REVIEW OF *OUTLINES OF PSYCHOLOGY*

J.H. Muirhead, Review of *Outlines of Psychology*, *Mind*, vol. 12 (1903).

*Outlines of Psychology: an Elementary Treatise with some Practical Applications.* By Josiah Royce, Ph.D., LL.D.. Professor of the History of Philosophy in Harvard University.

Prof. Royce's Book is he tells us an expansion of a formerly published Essay on the elementary principles and practical applications of psychology, with a view to its inclusion in the Teachers' Professional Library, edited by Mr. Butler. Besides its value as the contribution of so distinguished a philosopher to the starving Science of Education, it has a special interest for readers of *MIND* as the most systematic exposition of the writer's psychology which he has as yet given us. The Introductory chapters deal with definitions, the physical signs, nervous conditions and general features of conscious life, including one of the clearest and ablest criticisms of the "mind stuff" theory that we remember to have seen. The second and main portion of the book (chaps. v.–xiii.) rejects the usual division of modes of consciousness as the basis of discussion, substituting for it a classification of mental factors into Sensitiveness, Docility, Initiative and bringing the different phases of mental life under one or other of these heads: Sensation, Imagery, Feeling appearing as forms of Sensitiveness; Perception, Thought and Action of Docility. The last of these three factors is connected with the recent investigations of Prof. Loeb and others into the tropisms or general orientising reactions of plants and animals, effective use of which is further made in the author's account of the origin of our spatial perceptions. A further departure from orthodox text-book treatment is the recognition of a second series of feelings besides that of pleasure and pain, *viz.*, restlessness and quiescence taking the place of Wundt's two additional series of excitement and depression, tension and relief. The third part of the book (chaps. xiv., xv.) is a suggestive and practically useful review of the varieties and "abnormities" of emotion, intellect and volition.

Prof. Royce's psychology, which is here presented in condensed form, will doubtless give rise to considerable discussion. We have only space to mention one or two points which seem open to criticism. The emphasis upon tropism as a principle of psychological explanation is a happy thought, but it is doubtful whether the opposition between docility and initiative is not pressed beyond the point where it is an instructive distinction. Docility is defined as control by our past. But such control is what we commonly mean by self-restraint or independence of the present stimulus and so far falls on the side of initiative. Mere restlessness, on the other hand, as opposed to such control is the lowest form of subjection to present impulse and might with equal propriety be taken as the type of docility. But passing this over it is still more doubtful whether anything is gained, at any rate for the class of students for whom the book is primarily designed, by the above inversion of current methods of treatment. We may grant that, as Prof. Royce claims, his classification is more fundamental than the ordinary distinction into elements of consciousness in the sense that the mind's general attitude to stimulus is more fundamental than the features of the resulting experience. But just on that account it might be contended it is less suitable as a basis for the discussion of specific forms of consciousness, as seems to be proved by the paradoxical attempt to treat social opposition and with it conception and inference as forms (though "higher forms") of Docility and the obscurity in which "restlessness" is finally left after having been treated at one time as a form of feeling, at another (surely the true doctrine) as a more general forum of instinct or conation.

But a still more fundamental point than either of these is the reproduction of a doctrine of mental development in its main outlines identical with Prof. Baldwin's well-known account based upon imitation. Prof. Royce's recent philosophical writings had led us to expect a more thorough-going criticism of the conception of Imitation than it had yet received, and we confess to a certain disappointment in finding it here employed in the older uncritical sense. Briefly, is imitation simply reproduction? If so, it is not only doubtful whether it plays any large part in mental development, but whether it plays any part at all. We may say if we like that the child reproduces in its imitative play the actions of others, but even here the important thing is not the reproduction but the modification of the actions of others to suit the particular environment and the reactions expected from it. *A fortiori* the important thing to notice in our ordinary practice is not that we repeat but that we co-operate under the general pressure of the social structure. The centre of psychological interest is not the impression which the actions of others make upon us, but the consciousness (clear or obscure) of the whole to which we and others belong as co-operative members. If it be said that what the term Imitation is intended to express is merely one aspect of a complex fact, the term, we submit, is unfortunate, and nowhere more so than when used of the process of thought. The exaggerated emphasis it leads Prof. Royce to lay upon the self-conscious element in the thought process ("one who thinks makes it part of his ideal to be conscious of how he behaves in the presence of things," p. 284) is perhaps a minor point. But the seal it seems to put on the ordinary dualistic interpretation of thought ("All science is an effort to describe facts, to set over against the real world an imitation of it," p. 292) must appeal, we think, to the Author of *The World and the Individual* as more serious. Psychology he may tell us is not philosophy, but he would probably agree that it ought at least to be a preparation for it, and that it scarcely serves this purpose by lending itself, even by implication, to the consecration of one of the principal stumbling-blocks to a philosophical interpretation of experience.

# REVIEW OF *HERBERT SPENCER*

Edward H. Griffin, Review of *Herbert Spencer*, *Psychological Bulletin*, vol. 2 (1905).

*Herbert Spencer*. Josiah Royce. New York, Fox, Duffield & Co., 1904. Pp. 233.

This volume – for which the "Autobiography" furnishes the occasion – contains a discussion of Mr. Spencer's contribution to the concept of evolution, a criticism of his theories of education, and a chapter of personal reminiscences by James Collier, for nine years the secretary and for ten years the amanuensis of Spencer. The reminiscences are interesting, but add nothing of moment to what is given in the 'Autobiography.' Mr. Spencer's opinions regarding education are so well known that there is little need of discussing them, except for the purpose of showing – as is very clearly done in this review – that their singular onesidedness is due to the fact that they reflect his own individuality, and are a generalization from the method of training to which he was himself subjected.

The most important content of the book is the first paper. Professor Royce points out that Spencer's view of his own work was somewhat provincial, and that he was ignorant of the historical relationships of his doctrines. He did not understand that "the great historical enemy of the evolutionary interest in philosophy has been not 'supernaturalism,' nor yet the doctrine of 'special creation,' but *the tendency to conceive the universe as an eternal, and so, temporally viewed, as an essentially permanent order*." The proof that an alternative view has always, quite aside from Christian theology, existed along side of the evolutionary hypothesis is not presented in detail; it might be worth while, for the benefit of uninstructed readers, to show more specifically how large a part the conception of the eternity of the 'forms' of things has played, both in ancient and in modern thought.

Professor Royce would exempt the synthetic philosophy from some of the controversial tests which its opponents have sought to apply to it. He would not, for example, judge it on the basis of the theory of knowledge with which it is implicated. These discussions of knowledge and being expressed their author's "limitation to certain very simple intuitions – the wholesome, straightforward intuition of an English Radical, who, having early seen that we *can* know about natural causation, but cannot know anything about theology, and that we *can* know our rights and our duties, but cannot make out what it is that interests some people in Plato, and in Kant, and in all such speculators – henceforth reflects upon ultimate problems only for the sake of bringing to sharp expression the beliefs that he never learned to question or to analyze." In other words, the system should be treated, not as a philosophy, but as a systematization of science. Another exemption, which many would not be so ready to concede, is from responsibility for the application of formulas derived from material phenomena to the description of mental and moral process. "Spencer's formula was intended to hold true of phenomena only." His "business, as a student of phenomena, was with 'mechanism,' in the general sense, rather than with 'teleology.'" "He ought not therefore, to be condemned merely because he undertook to conceive evolution in mechanical terms. He would have been false to his philosophical purpose if he had conceived it otherwise." Yet the question may be asked whether this restriction of view may not have led to the misinterpretation of some of the phenomena involved.

In his restatement of the Spencerian formula, Professor Royce exhibits its inadequacy to the task assigned to it. As an empirical description of changes observed to take place in every process of development, its accuracy and ingenuity must be admitted. But is it a principle of explanation, which can be applied, like the law of gravitation, deductively, in individual cases? It is safe to assume that the ultimate verdict will coincide with that here rendered. "Spencer's theory of evolution does not determine the relations of the essential processes of evolution to one another, does not define their inner unity, and does not enable us to conceive a series of types of evolutionary processes in orderly relations to one another."

One need hardly ask better help toward a just estimate of the great career so lately closed than is afforded by this little book in which historical, biographical and critical insights are happily blended.

# THE THIRTEEN PRAGMATISMS

Arthur O. Lovejoy, "The Thirteen Pragmatisms," *Journal of Philosophy*, vol. 5 (1908).

The purpose of this paper, as indicated at the beginning of the former instalment, is to discriminate all the more important doctrines going under the name of pragmatism which can be shown to be not only distinct, but also logically independent *inter se*. Three such divergent pragmatist contentions have thus far been noted. "Pragmatism" was primarily a theory concerning the "meaning" of propositions; but this theory, because of a latent ambiguity in its terms, breaks up into two: (1) The meaning of a proposition consists in the future consequences in experience which it (directly or indirectly) predicts as about to occur, no matter whether it be believed or not; (2) The meaning of a proposition consists in the future consequences of believing it. The first of these was seen to suggest (though it by no means necessarily implies) the third variant of pragmatism, namely, a doctrine concerning the nature of truth; viz., that the truth of a proposition is identical with the occurrence of the series of experiences which it predicts, and can be said to be known only after such series is completed. "Its truth *is* its verification." This contention, that judgments acquire truth only in the degree in which they lose predictive character and practical bearings, has been shown to be wholly barren and useless, since it affords no answer to the real epistemological question concerning the criterion of the truth of propositions whose specific predictive implications have not yet been experienced.

4. It is, however, not difficult to see through what associations of ideas some pragmatists have been led to emphasize this notion of the *ex post facto* character of all truth. Largely, it would appear, it derives its plausibility from its resemblance to the ordinary empirical doctrine that those general propositions are to be regarded as true which, so far as they have been applied, have been found to be realized in past experience. This latter doctrine, from which the former is often not clearly distinguished, may be set down as another of the things that pragmatism is frequently supposed to be. It is the doctrine sometimes sententiously expressed by the observation that those propositions are

true which "will work" or "which you can live by." What the evolutionary empiricists who are fond of this observation almost always really mean by it, is that those judgments are true which hitherto *have* worked; in other and more precise words, that I am, in advance of the actual realization or verification of the future experiences which may be predicted by a given judgment, entitled to regard it as true if it is *similar* to, or is a special application of, a general *class* of judgments which my memory tells me have thus far had their implied predictions realized. But this is by no means identical with the principle mentioned in the preceding instalment, and vigorously insisted upon by some pragmatists, that each *individual* judgment can *become* true only through, and contemporaneously with, the presentation in consciousness of those specific subsequent experiences which it points to and prognosticates.

5. If, now, we are to set down this evolutionary empiricist criterion of truth as one expression of pragmatism – at least as that is popularly understood – it is necessary to add that this formula, too, suffers from ambiguity, and therefore breaks up into two quite distinct criteria. The ambiguity is analogous to that already pointed out in the pragmatist's theory of meaning. A belief may "work" in two very different senses, either by having its actual predictions fulfilled, or by contributing to increase the energies or efficiency or chance of survival of those who believe it. The Jews, for example, believed persistently for many centuries that a national Messiah would come in the next generation to restore the independence and establish the supremacy of Israel. In one sense, this belief did not work; for the events which it predicted did not occur. But biologically considered it worked wonderfully well; for it assuredly did much to produce the extraordinary persistency of the Jewish racial character, and the exceptional energy, self-confidence, and tenacity of purpose of the individual Jew. Many beliefs involving false predictions are biologically unfavorable, namely, if they lead to physical conduct ill adapted to the conditions of the believer's physical environment. You can not "live by" the belief that fire will not burn. But, also, some false or never-realized predictions, and many beliefs having apparently no predictive character – and no capacity for empirical verification – have shown themselves to be excellent things to live by. And if we are to take the doctrine that the true is the "livable" in its second and more unquestionably pragmatistic sense – if we are to identify the validity of beliefs with their biological serviceableness – we should apparently have to classify as "true" many judgments which predict nothing, and many which confessedly predict what is not going to occur.

6. Partly, however, what I have called the theory of the *ex post facto* nature of truth is a somewhat blurred reflection of a certain

metaphysical doctrine, which, although not always very explicitly put forward, appears to me to have a rather fundamental place in the characteristic mode of thought of most representatives of pragmatism. This is the doctrine of the real futurity or "open-ness" of the future, and of the determinative or "creative" efficacy of each "present" moment in the ever-transient process of conscious judgment, choice, and action. The two parts of the doctrine obviously enough go together: if the process truly brings into being at each new moment a genuinely new and unique increment of reality, then, so long as any moment's increment has not yet been brought forth, it can not yet be called in any intelligible sense real; and if, similarly, the thing that is to be is a sheer nonentity until it enters into actual, temporal experience, the moment in which it becomes an experience must be credited with the creation *"ex nihilo"* of a new item of being. This doctrine of what M. Bergson calls a *devenir réel*, and of the creative function of consciousness, which is the pregnant ontological preconception from which a great variety of confused pragmatistic ideas have proceeded, unquestionably has certain epistemological implications. Such a metaphysics appears to imply the partial contingency and (from the standpoint of any "present" knowledge) indeterminateness of the future content of reality. But these implications are not synonymous with the *ex post facto* theory of truth in the generality with which that has usually been expressed. The future may be – and by the same pragmatists, when they adumbrate this sort of metaphysics, apparently is – regarded as presenting to our understanding only a narrow margin of the unpredictable; its general character, and the greater mass of its content, may be supposed, without departing from the conception in question, to be predetermined by the accumulated and crystallized results of reality up to date, of which any possible future and novel increment of being must be the child, and to which it must be capable of accommodation. And at all events, there is nothing in this sort of thoroughgoing metaphysical temporalism which justifies the denial of the possibility of the making of "true" judgments about contemporaneous or past (but not yet consciously verified) realities.

7. It is a frequently repeated observation of pragmatists, in moments when they are more mindful of the psychological than of the metaphysical antecedents of their diversely descended conceptions, that the true, in its most generalized character, is "the satisfactory"; it is, says James, that which "gives the maximal combination of satisfactions." Or, in Perry's careful formulation – with an amendment which we have recently been told, upon good authority, would make it entirely acceptable to a pragmatist – "the criterion of the truth of knowledge is the satisfying character of the practical transition from cognitive expec-

tation to fulfillment, or the resolution of doubt into practical immediacy."[1] Now this doctrine which identifies the truth with the satisfactoriness of a given judgment may mean any one of three things. It may, in the first place, be a simple psychological observation – from which, I fancy, few would dissent – indicating the *genus* of feelings of which the "emotion of conviction" is a species. To doubt, to inquire, to have before the mind certain potential material of judgment that is not yet accepted as true, is, of course, to experience dissatisfaction; a specific sense of discomfort and of non-fulfillment is the emotional concomitant of the doubting or the deliberative moment, and is doubtless the principal spring which prompts men's search for truth. And to believe, to hold true, whatever more it may be, is always at least to be satisfied in some degree with one's mental content of the moment, to find it good, or at all events not so bad as some contrary judgment which, for its sin of insufficient satisfyingness, has been shut away into the outer darkness of non-acceptance.

8. But this psychological truism, that to pass from doubt to belief is to pass from dissatisfaction to a relative satisfaction, is quite a different thing from the first of the pragmatist epistemological contentions that appear to be based upon it. This asserts that the way to determine whether a proposition is true is to apply the test of "satisfyingness"; and to apply it directly and *simpliciter*. There is, according to this version of the nature of truth, to be no attempt to determine the differentia which distinguishes the species "conviction" from the genus "satisfaction," or the subspecies "highest discoverable type of certitude" from "conviction" in general; and there is to be no arranging of satisfactions in a hierarchy and no pretension to define the conditions under which a maker of rational judgments *ought* to be satisfied. From many expressions of pragmatist writers it would appear that, while the term "satisfaction" is "many dimensional," one dimension is as good as another; and that the final and decisive warrant for belief – the mark of the valid judgment – is the capacity of the judgment to yield the maximum bulk of satisfaction, measured indifferently in any of its dimensions. But since the dimensions *are* many, it may manifestly turn out that the greatest total volume may not give the potential maximum of any given dimension taken singly. The liking for luminosity of meaning, or for conceptual consistency, or for completeness of empirical verification, may fail to get full satisfaction in a judgment; but the judgment may, it would seem, still be "true," if it compensates for these limitations by a preponderant satisfactoriness with reference to other desires or interests: by its congruency with our habitual ways of belief, or its charm for the

[1] A. W. Moore, *Journal of Philosophy, Psychology and Scientific Methods*, Vol. IV., p. 576.

imagination, or its tendency to beget a cheerful frame of mind in those who accept it.

I think it possible that some pragmatists may at this point protest that they know of no one who seriously holds this view; certainly, it appears to me to be a curious view to hold. But I think one is justified in calling upon all of the name who reject this doctrine to take (and faithfully observe) an oath to abstain from a fashion of language which they have much affected; to refrain from identifying the true with the satisfactory *simpliciter*, to cease speaking of satisfaction as a *"criterion"* of validity, and to confine their assimilation of the two concepts to the much more qualified and commonplace thesis which follows.

9. This is pragmatism number seven *plus* a more or less explicit admission that our "theoretic" satisfactions have a special character and special epistemological pretensions; that our "intellectual" demands – for clear meanings, for consistency, for evidence – are *not*, and can not be, satisfied, unless their peculiar claim to precedence in the determination of belief is recognized; and that this claim is a legitimate one, to which men should (though they often do not) subordinate their impulse to accept any conclusions that have any kind of satisfactoriness. According to this view, "satisfaction" is still insisted upon as an essential mark of the apprehension of "truth"; but it is precisely a satisfaction which is not to be had except upon condition that other possible satisfactions be ignored or, in many cases, flatly rejected. Between this and the preceding (eighth) doctrine some pragmatist writers seem to waver. James, for example, often uses expressions (some of which have been quoted in the two foregoing paragraphs) implying the doctrine of the commensurability and equivalence of all satisfactions. But he elsewhere (*e.g.*, in a controversy with Joseph in *Mind*, 1905) expressly distinguishes the "theoretic" from the "collateral" satisfactions connected with the processes of judging thought; and he does not appear to deny that the former may conflict with the latter, or that, in the event of such conflict, they ought to be preferred. To the objection, offered by his critic, that if such admissions be made the pragmatist's criterion of validity is not practically distinguishable from the intellectualist's, James opposes nothing more relevant than a sketch of the genesis and evolution of the demand of the human mind for consistency.[2] This sketch purports to show – if I understand it – that the desire (more characteristic of some minds than of others) to avoid self-contradiction is historically engendered through the crystallization of repeated experiences of uniformity in "things" into fixed subjective habits of expecting specific uniformities – habits so fixed that when such an expectation is

[2] *Mind*, N. S., Vol. XIV., p. 196.

disappointed "our mental machinery refuses to run smoothly." How the transition from the idea of uniformity to that of consistency is accomplished here, remains obscure to me; but even supposing the evolution of the one into the other to be completely and convincingly traced, these interesting historical speculations do not show, they do not even tend to suggest, that the demand for consistency in our judgments, as we now find it – playing its captious and domineering role among our mental cravings – is not quite distinct from all its fellows and their rightful, though their often flouted, overlord. In the present sense, then, the pragmatist's criterion of truth, whether right or wrong, seems entirely destitute of any distinctive character; it is simply the old, intellectualist criterion, supplemented by the psychologically undisputable, but the logically functionless, remark that, after all, a "theoretic" satisfaction is a kind of satisfaction.

10. Another pragmatism, and one that undoubtedly has real epistemological bearings, is the doctrine of radical empiricism conjoined with the doctrine of the necessity and legitimacy of postulation; the doctrine, in other words, that "axioms are postulates" and that postulates are as valid as any human judgment ever can be, provided they be the expression of a genuine "practical" need. This may look like our eighth kind of pragmatism over again, expressed in other terms; but in certain important particulars it is really a distinct theory. It contains, in the first place, a special negative contention: namely, that there are no strictly compulsive or "necessary" general truths, no universal propositions that can force themselves upon the mind's acceptance apart from an uncoerced act of voluntary choice. And on its positive side, it identifies the true not with those judgments which slip so easily into the mind that they afford a present emotional state of satisfaction, but with those that man's active nature requires as working presuppositions to be followed in its reaction upon present experience and its instinctive endeavor to shape future experience. This doctrine seems to me to be quite unequivocally expressed by Schiller in a well-known essay in "Personal Idealism." "The 'necessity' of a postulate," we are told, "is simply an indication of our need. We want it, and so must have it, as a means to our ends. Thus its necessity is that of intelligent, purposive volition, not of psychical, and still less of physical, mechanism." "Behind the 'can't' there always lurks a 'won't'; the mind can not stultify itself, because it will not renounce conceptions it needs to order its experiences. The feeling of necessity, therefore, is at bottom an emotional accompaniment of the purposive search for means to realize our ends."[3]

[3] Schiller, "Axioms as Postulates," § 11, in "Personal Idealism."

11. A kindred but a much less thoroughgoing doctrine seems to constitute one of the pragmatisms of James. The author of *The Will to Believe* would, I suppose, still vigorously deny the possibility of reaching "necessary" conclusions with respect to many issues, including some of the greatest importance in relation both to the purely utilitarian requirements of our living and to our higher interests; and he would, clearly, still maintain the propriety and the practical inevitableness of voluntary postulation in such cases. But that there are *some* truly coercive and indubitable truths, some items of *a priori* knowledge inhering in the native constitution of a rational mind, James pretty fully and frankly declares, in his recently published volume of lectures. "Our ready-made ideal framework for all sorts of possible objects follows from the very structure of our thinking. We can no more play fast and loose with these abstract relations than we can with our sense experiences. They coerce us; we must treat them consistently, whether or not we like the results."[4] This, obviously, is no doctrine that axioms are postulates, or that behind every "can't" there lies a "won't"; it is the doctrine that axioms are necessities and that the action of voluntary choice in belief is always limited by a permanent system of *a priori* principles of possibility and impossibility inhering in the nature of intellect, at least as intellect is now evolved. It is compatible, at most, with the opinion that there are not so numerous, nor so useful, axioms as some dogmatic philosophers have supposed, and that, when axioms fail us, postulates must in many cases be resorted to.

12. A point of pragmatist doctrine separable from (though not inconsistent with) either of the two last mentioned, is the assertion of the *equal* legitimacy of those postulates (such as the uniformity of causal connection, the general "reliability" of nature, and the like) which appear indispensable as presuppositions for effective dealing with the world of our physical experience, and of those which, though lacking this sort of "physical" necessity as completely as they do the logical sort, yet seem demanded in order to give meaning to, or encouragement in, men's moral strivings, or to satisfy the emotional or esthetic cravings of our complex nature. It is conceivable enough that some pragmatists should refuse to recognize the equal standing of these two classes of postulates, should accept the first while rejecting the second; and it is a fact that not all who find a place for both agree as to the number and range of the second sort. The more extremely liberal forms of the doctrine of the right to postulate freely and to treat postulates as truths, tend to lapse into identity with the eighth variety of pragmatism, which identifies the true with the "maximally satisfying"; but in its more

[4] James, "Pragmatism," p. 211.

cautious and critical forms, the argument from the practical inevitableness of certain scientific to the legitimacy of certain ethico-religious postulates must be regarded as a distinct type of pragmatist epistemology, and perhaps the one which – if pragmatism ought to have practical bearings – best deserves the name.

13. Lastly, there remains a second pragmatist theory of the *meaning* of concepts or judgments – which brings us back to the topic, though by no means to precisely the doctrine, with which our enumeration began. It may be expressed thus: an essential part of our idea of any object or fact consists in an apprehension of its relation to some purpose or subjective interest on our part; so that no object of *thought* whatever could be just what, for our thought, it *is*, except through the mediation of some idea of purpose or some plan of action. The language of some pragmatist writers might lead one to suppose that they consider the *whole* meaning to be reducible to this teleological reference; but such a view does not seem to me intelligible, and it does not appear certain that any one really intends to maintain it. But it is evident that there are several logicians who think it both true and important to declare that a relation to a purpose constitutes an intrinsic and a determinative element in the connotation of any notion. It is, I suppose, such a principle that Moore intended to illustrate in recently pointing out that, however objective the virtues of a given candidate for office may be, he could neither be "clean" nor a candidate were there not present in the mind of every one so representing him the idea of possible voting to be done. And I suppose the same view is, in part, at least, what Schiller has sought to enforce in these columns, in insisting that nobody can be "lost" except with the aid of the existence in the universe of some purpose in some mind, requiring the presence of the "lost" person (or of the persons from whom he is lost) in some place or relation from which he is (or they are) excluded by virtue of his "lostness."[5] Schiller appears to me to have entangled this theory of meaning in a confusing and illegitimate manner with questions about "truth" and "reality"; but to pursue this distinction would involve a somewhat long and complicated analysis, which may not here be undertaken.

These thirteen pragmatisms have been set down, not in a topical order, but according to the leading of those associations of ideas through which the ambiguities of the several doctrines, and the transitions from one to another, become relatively intelligible. But it may be useful to arrange them here in a more logical manner, while still retaining the original numbering. Those forms of theory, the separate

[5] *Journal of Philosophy, Psychology and Scientific Method*, Vol. IV., p. 42, and pp. 483, 488.

enumeration of which results from distinctions made by this paper, but overlooked by pragmatist writers themselves – in other words, the doctrines formulated by pragmatists in more or less equivocal terms – are indicated by the sign (*a*); each group of doctrines hitherto improperly treated as single and univocal has a common superior number:

I. *Pragmatist Theories of Meaning.*

1. The "meaning" of any judgment consists wholly in the future consequences predicted by it, whether it is believed or not ($a^1$).

2. The meaning of any judgment consists in the future consequences of believing it ($a^1$).

13. The meaning of any idea or judgment always consists in part in the apprehension of the relation of some object to a conscious purpose ($a^1$).

II. *Pragmatism as an Epistemologically Functionless Theory concerning the "Nature" of Truth.*

3. The truth of a judgment "consists in" the complete realization of the experience (or series of experiences) to which the judgment had antecedently pointed; propositions *are* not, but only *become*, true ($a^2$).

III. *Pragmatist Theories of Knowledge, i.e., of the Criterion of the Validity of a Judgment.*

4. Those general propositions are true which so far, in past experience, have had their implied predictions realized; and there is no other criterion of the truth of a judgment ($a^2$).

5. Those general propositions are true which have in past experience proven biologically serviceable to those who have lived by them; and this "livableness" is the ultimate criterion of the truth of a judgment ($a^2$).

7. All apprehension of truth is a species of "satisfaction"; the true judgment meets some need, and all transition from doubt to conviction is a passage from a state of at least partial dissatisfaction to a state of relative satisfaction and harmony ($a^3$). – This is strictly only a psychological observation, not an epistemological one; it becomes the latter by illicit interpretation into one of the two following.

8. The criterion of the truth of a judgment is its satisfactoriness, as such; satisfaction is "many dimensional," but all the dimensions are of commensurable, epistemological values, and the maximum bulk of satisfaction in a judgment is the mark of its validity ($a^3$).

9. The criterion of the truth of a judgment is the degree in which it meets the "theoretic" demands of our nature; these demands are special

and distinctive, but their realization is none the less a kind of "satisfaction" ($a^3$).

10. The sole criterion of the truth of a judgment is its practical serviceableness as a postulate; there is no general truth except postulated truth, resulting from some motivated determination of the will; "necessary" truths do not exist.

11. There are some necessary truths; but these are neither many nor practically adequate; and beyond them the resort to postulates is needful and legitimate.

12. Among the postulates which it is legitimate to take as the equivalent of truth, those which subserve the activities and enrich the content of the moral, esthetic, and religious life have a coordinate place with those which are presupposed by common sense and physical science as the basis of the activities of the physical life.

IV. *Pragmatism as an Ontological Theory.*

6. Temporal becoming is a fundamental character of reality; in this becoming the processes of consciousness have their essential and creative part. The future is strictly non-real and its character is partly indeterminate, dependent upon movements of consciousness the nature and direction of which can be wholly known only at the moments in which they become real in experience. (Sometimes more or less confused with 3.)[6]

Each pragmatism of the thirteen should manifestly be given a name of its own, if confusion in future discussions is to be avoided. The present writer has neither the necessary ingenuity nor the ambition to devise a nomenclature so extensive. But however the several theories be designated, the fact of their difference, and of the incompatibility of some of them with some others, can hardly, just now, be too much insisted upon – in the interest of pragmatism itself. What the movement commonly so named most needs is a clarification of its formulas and a discrimination of certain sound and important ideas lying behind it from certain other ideas that are sound but not important, and certain that would be important if only they were not unsound. The present attempt to list the chief varieties, and to clear up the hidden ambiguities, of a doctrine nominally one and indivisible, is accordingly offered as a species of *Prolegomena zu einem jeden künftigen Pragmatismus.*

6 It is impossible to bring out the nature, motives, and reciprocal relations of dependence or incompatibility of these theories in any such condensed formulas. I hope no reader will attempt to take the above recapitulation as a substitute for the analytical discussion contained in the preceding paragraphs.

# REVIEW OF *THE PHILOSOPHY OF LOYALTY*

Frank Thilly, Review of *The Philosophy of Loyalty*, *Philosophical Review*, vol. 17 (1908).

*The Philosophy of Loyalty*. By Josiah Royce. New York, The Macmillan Company, 1908, pp. xiii, 409.

This new book of Professor Royce's is, as he tells us, not a text-book, and does not mean to be an elaborately technical research. Nor is the author writing merely and mainly for philosophers, but for those who love ideals, for all those who love their country, – "a country so ripe at present for idealism, and so confused, nevertheless, by the vastness and the complication of its social and political problems. To simplify men's moral issues, to clear their vision for the sight of the eternal, to win hearts for loyalty, – this would be, in this land a peculiarly precious mission, if indeed, I could hope that this book could aid, however little, towards such an end" (Preface). The goal at which Professor Royce is aiming is the old one of finding the fundamental principle of morality; it is a *Grundlegung der Sitten*, with the accent, however, placed upon the practical application. Like Kant, he seeks to establish a supreme standard which shall serve as a guide even to the commonest reason and in all the relations of life, a criterion that will put an end to our moral doubts and give meaning and stability to human conduct, a concept from which all the other duties may be rationally deduced. This basal virtue is loyalty, "the heart of all the virtues, the central duty amongst all the duties" (p. viii). About a rational conception of loyalty, he thinks, you can truthfully centre your entire moral world. Justice, charity, industry, wisdom, spirituality, are all definable in terms of enlightened loyalty (p. 15).

What is this loyalty? Professor Royce devotes the largest part of his book to defining the term and showing all that it implies. Loyalty is the willing and practical and thoroughgoing devotion of a person to a cause. Your cause is something objective, it is not your private self. Moreover, it is wholly impersonal, it concerns other men; loyalty is social. Again, a cause is general and so tends to unite the many fellow-servants in one service. Whoever is loyal, whatever be his cause, is devoted, is active, surrenders his private self-will, controls himself, is in love with his cause, and believes in it. Loyalty tends to unify life, to give it centre, fixity, stability. Since no man can find a plan of life by merely looking within his own chaotic nature, he has to look without, to the world of social conventions, deeds, and causes. Now, a loyal man is one who has found, and who sees, neither mere individual fellow-men to be loved or hated, nor mere conventions, nor customs, nor laws to be obeyed, but some social cause, or some system of causes, so rich, so well knit, and, to him, so fascinating, and withal so kindly in its appeal to his natural self-will, that he says to his cause: 'Thy will is mine and mine is thine. In thee I do not lose but find myself, living intensely in proportion as I live for thee' (Lecture I). Loyalty is for the loyal man chief amongst all the moral goods of his life, because it furnishes to him a personal solution of the hardest of human practical problems, the problem: 'For what do I live? Why am I here? For what am I good? Why am I needed?' (p. 57).

But some causes are good, while some are evil. We therefore need a test of good and evil. A cause is good, not only for me, but for mankind, in so far as it is essentially a loyalty to loyalty, that is, an aid and a furtherance of loyalty in my fellows. Hence so choose your cause and so serve it, that, by reason of your choice and of your service, there shall be more loyalty in the world rather than less. All the common-place virtues, in so far as they are indeed definable effective, are special forms of loyalty to loyalty, and are to be justified, centralized, inspired, by the one supreme effort to do good, namely, the effort to make loyalty triumphant in the lives of all men. I shall serve causes such as my natural temperament and my social opportunities suggest to me. Nevertheless, whatever my cause, it ought to be such as to further, so far as in me lies, the cause of universal loyalty. My causes must form a system, they must constitute a single cause, a life of loyalty. Have I then duties to myself? Yes, my duty to myself is the duty to provide my cause with one who is strong enough and skilful enough to be effective according to his own natural powers. Have I private and personal rights, which I ought to assert? Yes, precisely in so far as my private powers and possessions are held in trust for the cause, and are, upon occasion, to be defended for the sake of the cause. And my duties to my neighbors, too, justice and benevolence, are mere aspects of our one principle. Justice means, in general, fidelity to human ties in so far as they are ties. If you are just, you are decisive in your choice of your personal cause, you are faithful to the loyal decision once made, you keep your promise, you speak the truth, you respect the loyal ties of other men, and you contend with other men only in so far as the defense of your own cause, in the interest of loyalty to the universal cause of loyalty, makes such contest against aggression unavoidable. Benevolence is that aspect of loyalty which directly concerns itself with your influence upon the inner life of human beings who enjoy, who suffer, and whose private good is to be effected by your deeds. Since no personal good that your fellow can possess is superior to his own loyalty, your own loyalty to loyalty is itself a supremely benevolent type of activity. And since your fellow-man is an instrument for the furtherance of the cause of universal loyalty, his welfare also concerns you, in so far as, if you help him to a more efficient life, you make him better able to be loyal (Lecture III).

But is the principle of loyalty to loyalty an actually general, safe, and sufficient test of what is right and wrong in the doubtful moral situations which may arise in daily life? Does our principle tell us what to do when loyalties seem to be in conflict with one another? It tells us: Decide, knowingly if you can, ignorantly if you must, but in any case decide, and have no fear. "As a fact, the conscience is the ideal of the self, coming to consciousness as a present command. It says, *Be loyal.* If one asks, *Loyal to what?* the conscience, awakened by our whole personal response to the need of mankind replies, *Be loyal to loyalty.* If, hereupon, various loyalties seem to conflict, the conscience says: *Decide.* If one asks, *How decide?* conscience further urges, *Decide as I, your conscience, the ideal expression of your whole personal nature, conscious and unconscious, find best.* If one persists, *But you and I may be wrong*, the last word of conscience is, *we are fallible, but we can be decisive and faithful; and this is loyalty*" (Lecture IV). That is, the way in which to show loyalty to loyalty varies endlessly with the individual and can never be precisely defined except by and through his personal consent. Provided the cause to which I am loyal involves the union of personal interests, provided I do not enter into any unnecessary destruction of the loyalty of others, provided I seek to further loyalty as a common good of all mankind, I must leave to the individual the choice of the cause or causes (pp. 200–203).

Now, what must be true about the universe if even loyalty itself is a genuine good, and not a merely human illusion? If loyalty has any truth, human lives can be linked in some genuine spiritual unity. Such a unity is a fact. Loyalty, therefore, has its metaphysical aspect. It is an effort to conceive human life in an essentially superhuman way, to view our social organizations as actual personal unities of consciousness, unities wherein there exists an actual experience of the good which, in our loyalty, we only partially apprehend. Whoever talks of any sort of truth whatsoever, be that truth moral or scientific, the truth of common-sense or the truth of a philosophy, inevitably implies that the world of truth of which he speaks is a world possessing a rational and spiritual unity, is a conscious world of experience, whose type of consciousness is higher in its level than is the type of our human minds, but whose life is such that our life belongs as part to this living whole. Against pragmatism Professor Royce declares that the loyal are not seeking *only* a mere collection of their private experiences of their personal thrills of fascination. You cannot express the value of your loyalty by pointing at the mere heap of the joyous thrills of the various loyal individuals. We need unity of life; in recognizing that need Professor Royce's own pragmatism consists. We never find unity present to our human experience in more than a fragmentary shape. We get hints of a higher unity. But only the fragmentary unity is won at any moment of our lives. We therefore form ideas, – very fallible ideas, – of some unity of experience, a unity such as our idea of any science or any art or any united people or of any community or of any other cause, any other union of many human experiences in one, defines. Now, if our ideas are in any case indeed true, then such unity is a fact successfully experienced upon some higher level than ours, and is experienced in some conspectus of life which wins what we need, which approves our loyalty, which fulfils our rational will, and which has in its wholeness what we seek. How do I know all this? I know simply that to try to deny the reality of this whole of truth is simply to reaffirm it. To deny that there is truth, or that there is a real world, is simply to say that the whole truth is that there is no whole truth, and that the real fact is that there is no fact real at all. Such assertions are plain self-contradictions (Lecture VII). "The thesis that the world is one whole and a significant whole of conscious life is, for these reasons, a thesis which can only be viewed as an error, by reinstating this very assertion under a new form. For any error of mine concerning the world is possible only in so far as I really mean to assert the truth about the world; and this real meaning of mine can exist only as a fact within the conspectus of consciousness for which the real whole world exists, and within which I myself live" (p. 372).

Our ethical theory has transformed itself into a general philosophical doctrine; and loyalty now appears to us not only as a guide of life, but as a revelation of our relation to a realm which we have been obliged to define as one of an eternal and all-embracing unity of spiritual life. This realm of reality is conscious, is united, is self-possessed, and is perfected through the very wealth of the ideal sacrifices and of the loyal devotion which are united so as to constitute its fulness of being. So we may now define loyalty as the will to manifest, so far as possible, the Eternal, that is, the conscious and superhuman unity of life, in the form of the acts of an individual self. Although one can be loyal without being consciously and explicitly religious, loyalty, if sincere, involves at least a latent belief in the superhuman reality of the cause, and means at least an unconscious devotion to the one and eternal cause. But such a belief is also a latent union of morality and religion, and such a service is an unconscious piety. However, whoever serves the universal cause inevitably loses his cause in our poor world of sense-experience, because his cause is too good for this present temporal world to express it. A lost cause, however, has two companions, grief and imagination, and these two are the parents of all the higher forms of genuinely ethical religion. Such religion interprets the superhuman in forms that our longing, our grief, and our imagination invent, but also in terms that are intended to meet the demands of our highest loyalty. For we are loyal to that unity of life which, as our truer moral consciousness learns to believe, owns the whole real world, and constitutes the cause of causes. In being loyal to universal loyalty, we are serving the unity of life.

We can know *that* we are linked to the eternal; *how* we are linked, our sciences do not make manifest to us. The symbolic portrayal of religion attempts to characterize, in its general outline, an absolute truth; this may be called the creed of the Absolute Religion, and consists in the following facts: First, the rational unity and goodness of the world-life; next, its true but invisible nearness to us, despite our ignorance; further, its fulness of meaning despite our barrenness of present experience; and yet more, its interest in our personal destiny as moral beings; and finally, the certainty that, through our actual human loyalty, we come, like Moses, face to face with the true will of the world, as a man speaks to his friend. All this seems to Professor Royce to be an inevitable corollary of his theory of truth (Lecture VIII).

It would be impossible, within the short compass of a review, to give an adequate criticism of this little volume, which evolves a complete philosophy of the universe and of life out of a single ethical principle. We might call this system a system of rationalistic and idealistic ethics. In method it resembles the system of Kant, for Kant, too, derives a whole host of truths from his supreme moral principle; in its results or content it betrays kinship with the school of thought which has been variously described as energism, perfectionism, ethical idealism, and which counts among its followers nearly all the great thinkers from Socrates and Plato down to Lotze, Green, Wundt, and Paulsen. It is not a new doctrine – only the terms employed are new; its fundamental teachings are as old as the history of ethics. Whatever criticism may be passed upon it by us will touch its form rather than its content, will bear on the rationalistic rather than on the idealistic side of it. As we said before, the author's aim is to find a basal principle of ethics, a standard which shall serve as a practical guide of life. This is a legitimate undertaking; human beings will never give up the search for principles that will bring meaning into their lives and conduct. Professor Royce finds such a principle in loyalty: "Be loyal to loyalty, do what you can to produce a maximum of the devoted service of causes, a maximum of fidelity, and of selves that serve and choose fitting objects of loyalty." This is a noble virtue, but unless we read into it all our virtues and our entire traditional morality, it cannot serve us as the basal principle of ethics; it will, like Kant's famous criterion, remain too general and empty to be of any great theoretical or practical value. 'Be loyal to loyalty,' – this is like commanding: Be just to justice; be good to goodness, be true to truth, or to thine own self be true; honor honor, etc. Professor Royce admits the impossibility of defining precisely how the individual shall show his loyalty to loyalty, and falls back upon the conscience, for better or for worse. But any one of the fundamental virtues would, if supported by a developed twentieth-century conscience, prove just as satisfactory as the loyalty principle as a general guide. In a certain sense it is true, as the old Stoics said, that he who has one virtue has them all, but in that sense loyalty has no advantage over the others. The fact is the different virtues describe different forms of moral behavior for us, and only by defining them to suit our purposes can we make any one of them stand for all. It may be wise in moral preaching, in order to reach practical ends, to emphasize a particular rule of conduct and group around it all the rest. But though this is part of Professor Royce's aim, his purpose goes deeper after all. "Our philosophy of loyalty," as he tells us, "must try to delve down to the roots of human conduct, the grounds of our moral standards." "And the lesson will be this: In loyalty, when loyalty is properly defined, is the fulfilment of the whole moral law" (p. 15, compare pp. 7–8).

The reason why Professor Royce is able to deduce from the concept of loyalty all the fundamental virtues and duties is that he reads them into it: he simply succeeds in getting out of his notion exactly what he has put in. He cannot therefore be said to have reached "the roots" of human conduct. He does not justify the virtues by a principle; he does not explain the moral laws; he simply defines his criterion in such a way as to embrace them all. Loyalty is not a principle; it a general label for all the virtues. Under it he embraces the forms of conduct which will, in his opinion, tend to realize the highest good; Have a cause or ideal; it will give plan and unity to your life, and make it worth living; let it be a social ideal, an ideal which will make it possible for your fellows to strive after the good. In order to realize the ideal, you must be loyal, devoted, truthful, trustworthy, faithful, etc.; you must care for yourself and others; you must be just and benevolent; you must follow the recognized rules of morality. All this appeals to us, and there is no particular harm in bringing all these excellent precepts under the term 'loyalty' – other terms would do equally well, – but that does not make loyalty the ground of our moral standards.

The real criterion which seems to me to lie in the background of Professor Royce's thought and by which he justifies all the loyalties, all the virtues and duties, is the social criterion, social unity, a kingdom of ends, a union of selves inspired by social ideals. This is the standard with which we are everywhere confronted in the book: Your cause is objective, not your private self, it is wholly impersonal, concerns other men, tends to unite many fellow-servants in one service, is an aid and a furtherance of loyalty in your fellows, that is, of universal loyalty. Thoroughgoing devotion to a social cause is the demand. Private rights and duties, the rights of neighbors and the duties to neighbors, all are to be justified by the effort to make loyalty triumphant in the lives of all men. Expressed in the language of the schools this would mean: The welfare or perfection of individuals in society, or social welfare, is the criterion of morality; such acts are good as tend to realize social welfare, the welfare of individuals in society.

But, as we have seen, Professor Royce deduces from the concept of loyalty not only the rules of conduct, but a system of metaphysics. It is a faith, a beautiful idealistic faith, a faith that has worked wonders in this world and will never cease to work wonders. We can even say that it is not an unreasonable faith, indeed, that it is a reasonable faith. Those who accept it have a basis for their ethics that will satisfy them. But it is not a logical deduction, an absolute truth, or even an inevitable corollary of Professor Royce's theory of truth. We wish it were. It is based on the longing for the eternal; it is the wish of the heart that the good may endure beyond the present, that there may be a spiritual kingdom in which all that is of highest value to us human beings may be preserved for evermore. Our moral life, however, would not be an illusion if we could not prove these things. Humanity could not exist and live the kind of life which the men we most revere have praised as the life of real worth, without obeying the rules which are the result of a long and hard-won experience. So long as we are what we are, we must value the higher life; and so long as we do that, we must value the means leading to it. So long as life exists on earth, it shall be a worthy life: that is our will; and it cannot be such a life unless it be a moral life, hence, that is our will too. We believe that men will hold it worthy as men have held it worthy, and we hope there is an Eternal Consciousness in which all that is true and beautiful and good may endure. But Critiques of Practical Reason, Prolegomena to Ethics, and Philosophies of Loyalty have not supplied the logical proofs.

These criticisms, however, do not affect the great practical value of the book; it gives beautiful and forceful expression to ethical idealism, and grandly fulfils its purpose "to simplify men's moral issues, to clear their vision for the sight of the eternal, to win hearts for loyalty." There is moral enthusiasm in it, there is patriotism in it, there is love of humanity in it. It comes from the heart of a man, from the big heart of a big man, from a fine loyal soul. Fichte never spoke with greater fervor and eloquence than does this idealist of Cambridge, and it is to be hoped that his words will sink deep into the hearts of the nation.

# REVIEW OF
# *THE PHILOSOPHY OF LOYALTY*

W.R. Sorley, Review of *The Philosophy of Loyalty*, *Hibbert Journal*, vol. 7 (1908).

*The Philosophy of Loyalty*. By Josiah Royce, Professor of the History of Philosophy in Harvard University. – New York: The Macmillan Company, 1908, pp. xiii, 409.

This book consists of eight lectures delivered before the Lowell Institute in Boston in 1907. The rather curious title was suggested by Steinmetz's book on the Philosophy of War; and it has been part of the author's task to break the "ancient and disastrous association" that makes loyalty subservient to the war-spirit. The warrior is not the only or the best representative of the spirit of rational loyalty: loyalty is of much wider significance; and the author attempts to show that "in loyalty, when loyalty is properly defined, is the fulfilment of the whole moral law." It is therefore with a philosophy of morals that we are here presented; and, although the title of the book may have been suggested by Steinmetz, a more important motive may perhaps be traced in the choice. Philosophers of Professor Royce's way of thinking have commonly expressed the moral ideal by some such conception as self-realisation, or the development or perfection of personal qualities; and this conception has often produced the impression of being only a form – though an idealist form – of egoism or individualism. The criticism does less than justice to the conception of personality as it is found either in Hegel or in T. H. Green. But it is obvious enough to affect the popular mind, and to make it worth while for an author who lays such stress as Professor Royce does on the social factor in life to avoid the suggestion from the outset, and to make it clear that morality does not lie in the self or its development as a mere individual, but in something that lifts it out of this mere individuality and unites it with the universe in which all selves are included. For this reason he seems to have chosen the conception of loyalty to describe his moral principle. For the loyal man devotes himself to a cause in which his mere individuality is lost; and he devotes himself to it willingly as finding in its success the fulfilment of his own life.

Loyalty is defined – at least preliminarily – as "the willing and practical and thoroughgoing devotion of a person to a cause." And a cause means "something that is conceived by its loyal servant as unifying the lives of various human beings into one life." And the whole law and the prophets can be summed up in the command "be loyal." There is a good deal of value in this way of putting the matter; and Professor Royce is no doubt right in pointing to many of the unhealthy conditions of modern, especially American, life as due to lack of loyalty to any worthy cause. For this reason the author's homiletics are to be welcomed. Loyalty is at least a primary and important factor in the moral life, if it is not the whole of it. From this point of view also the diffuseness of the author's style and his habit of constant repetition of the same idea in similar or identical phrase may be explained. Popular audiences can only be convinced by repetition. And the author unites all the accomplishments of the orator with the insight of the metaphysician. But it would be too much to assert that he has been able altogether to overcome the traditional opposition between the rhetorician and the philosopher. From the latter's point of view the book might have been better if it had been shorter. The reader is apt to be carried over the difficult places of the argument by the flow of the author's eloquence rather than by the force of his logical reasoning.

The fundamental difficulty of the whole position is that loyalty to a cause is, after all, a merely formal conception. Professor Royce is thus in the same difficulty as Kant was when he attempted to deduce a moral code from a formal principle. His method of solution is indeed different from Kant's, and consists in a certain modification, perhaps deepening, of the initial conception of loyalty. But the questions which arise are much the same. How are we to distinguish the good from the bad among the causes to which men may be loyal? And what canon of preference is there for choosing between competing causes, each of which by itself might be regarded as good?

For solving these and similar questions Professor Royce makes use of that modified or deepened conception which I have referred to, and which he expresses by the phrase "loyalty to loyalty." I am not sure that this phrase is always used with exactly the same meaning. In some cases it seems to mean much the same as what is commonly described by the term conscientiousness as applied to the man who is scrupulous in always observing and following the dictates of his conscience. The example given on pp. 135–37 seems to be a case of this sort, for in it the obvious loyalty of the official to his chief was superseded by the higher loyalty which the official's conscience told him he owed to truth. But the example is too long to quote or to discuss, and the explicit meaning given to the phrase "loyalty to loyalty" is simply the promotion of loyalty in self and others. "Be loyal to loyalty" means "do what you can to produce a maximum of the devoted service of causes, a maximum of fidelity, and of selves that choose and serve fitting objects of loyalty." The word "fitting" here might seem to beg the whole question of the distinction of good from bad causes. But this can hardly be intended, and "fitting" must be interpreted to mean simply fit to encourage or produce more loyalty. Maximum of loyalty, therefore, may be said to be the end for Professor Royce, just as maximum of pleasure is for the Hedonists. It is easy to show that the ordinary virtues of social life exhibit and encourage loyalty. In the same way the Hedonists had no difficulty in pointing out their felicific consequences. But can we use maximum of loyalty as a criterion for distinguishing between good causes and bad? The difficulties here are similar to those in the way of the Hedonist. If the example may be pardoned, we may say that loyalty to Tammany and organisations like to it is a prominent feature in American political life. This feature is not all bad. Yet this very spirit of loyalty so directed is a more serious danger to good government than would be the total selfishnesses of all Tammany's constituent members. Now, have we any calculus of loyalties capable of assuring us that if purity in politics were to triumph by the dissolution of Tammany and its fellows, there would be compensation in kind for the loyalties destroyed, and the maximum of loyalty throughout the American continent would be increased? I am far from saying that even in this way compensation would not be granted; but I do not know how the sum is to be worked, and I should not like to stake the cause of good government on the hazard of the calculation. And the author offers no suggestion of any such calculus of loyalties. The misfortune is that, apart from such a calculus or some substitute for it, his distinction of good from evil becomes a matter simply of common sense, not recognised as such.

The lack of any criterion – of any working principle – is most plainly disclosed when Professor Royce goes on to discuss the second question which I have put – a question which he states in the form, "How shall we decide as between two apparently conflicting loyalties, which one to follow?" Let it be granted that each loyalty contains promise of good – in his example, good to the community from trained fitness for a professional career in competition with good to a family which disaster had bereft of its head. In such a case the principle of loyalty "commands simply but imperatively that, since I must serve, and since, at this critical moment, my only service must take the form of a choice between loyalties, I shall choose, even in my ignorance, what form my service is henceforth to take." In other words, the principle of choice is – choose. Having chosen, I must of course be faithful to my cause. This is no caricature. What the principle "clearly says" is formulated with all the emphasis that italics can give in the words, "Decide, knowingly if you can, ignorantly if you must, but in any case decide, and have no fear." Nothing can better illustrate the bare formality of the principle than this statement. It is true that other ethical theories than Professor Royce's must allow that "my special choice of my personal cause is always fallible." But they usually point to some more or less definable end for their criterion: to happiness, or to well-being, or to the perfection of personal qualities – ends the way to which may be difficult or dubious, but which at least offer a concrete ideal for action. They do not rest content with the ineffectual advice that the principle of choice is to choose.

The two last lectures of the volume enter upon the metaphysics subject, and in them appears the author's final definition: "Loyalty is the will to manifest, so far as is possible, the Eternal, that is, the conscious and superhuman unity of life, in the form of the acts of an individual Self." There is value in this conception. But it adds nothing to the solution of those practical questions which occupy the greater portion of the volume. On the contrary, it increases the difficulties already pointed out. For the definition is so interpreted as to include all purposive activity of whatever kind. Evil, like good, becomes a will to manifest the Eternal, a "fragmentary form of the service of the cause of universal loyalty." Whatever be the truth of this view, it should be unnecessary to repeat that we are not helped to distinguish the evil cause from the good by being told that the distinction is merely a relative one.

The metaphysics of loyalty stated by the author is at the same time a theory of truth and of reality. And here he expounds his own views in connection and contrast with those of Professor James. His criticism of his Harvard colleague is so appreciative, and his references to their points of disagreement are so intimate and personal, that the reader feels as if he were the unwilling witness of a domestic dispute in which it would be indecent for an outsider to interfere. Such interference need not be required of the present reviewer, as he has already had an opportunity of commenting on Professor Royce's metaphysical theory in the pages of this journal. That theory remains substantially the same as it was. Only it seems to me as if his attitude were modified by an approach to the pragmatic method, as if he, too, chose his philosophic road by a voluntary preference – "knowingly if you can, ignorantly if you must" – and then found reasons to justify his course. There is another way of philosophising – a strait narrow way; and one would be glad to think that the author had not deserted it – in which logic leads instead of being made to follow, and in which no step is taken but under the direction of reason.

# REVIEW OF *THE PHILOSOPHY OF LOYALTY*

J.W. Scott, Review of *The Philosophy of Loyalty*, *Mind*, vol. 18 (1909).

*The Philosophy of Loyalty*. By Josiah Royce, Professor of the History of Philosophy in Harvard University. New York: The Macmillan Co., 1908. Pp. xii, 409.

It is somewhat equivocal praise of a brilliant writer to say of his book that it "gives new names to old ways of thinking." In this latest work of Prof. Royce's there is much to invite such a verdict. His task – that of presenting an ethical doctrine at once philosophically sound and practically applicable, within the limits of eight popular lectures – was indeed both a fresh and a hold one. And, we may say at once, from the "homiletic" point of view the enterprise succeeds. No reader of the type the Author means to address is likely to lay down the book without feeling that it has cast some light on the actual problems of life and duty. But to the philosophical section of his audience, Prof. Royce's "way of thinking" will not be new. His solution of the ethical problem is just what, in this country at least, would be understood as the ordinary idealistic solution. He claims indeed that the moral end is to be "loyal." But the fundamental assertion on which he bases the claim is the characteristic doctrine of idealism. Through Loyalty alone will a man be able to realise his own rational will in a good which yet transcends his private individuality. "If you want to know what is good for you," he says in Chapter I., "bring your own will to self-consciousness...this is a first principle, of all ethical inquiry"; but yet "I can never find what my own will is by merely brooding over my natural desires"; and the solution of this paradox – the realisation of my true will – can only lie "in some happy union between the inner and the outer, between my social world and myself." This happy union is what takes place wherever mere social conformity turns into exactly what in these lectures the Author calls "Loyalty."

Yet old and familiar as Prof. Royce's real standpoint is, his work is more than an idle shuffling of terms. The new form given to the old truth at once charges it with fresh power. It enables the philosopher to preach. It enables him to put to his reader, in a single, definite, terse statement, an applicable doctrine of the chief end of man. "*In Loyalty*," he prints in italics, "*when Loyalty is properly defined, lies the fulfilment of the whole moral Law.*" The simplicity of the conception transforms the philosophic doctrine into a kind of message. "Loyalty" is something men know – something, therefore, that they can be called to. There is more than a renaming, there is a genuine rejuvenation of idea in Prof. Royce's presentation of the idealistic doctrine of the moral end.

Now, to catch a popular word like this and proceed to find in it all the law and the prophets might have been quite a cheap and easy process. It is the characteristic device of the woolly-headed preacher everywhere. The danger to a thinker is that a term so serviceable as a moral rallying-cry may need some torturing before it can be taken to express the philosophic truth. It is the triumph of Prof. Royce's popular lecturing, however, that he can be faithful to his term. He has brought forward a conception – Loyalty, or "the willing and practical and thoroughgoing devotion of a person to a cause" – which, simple as it is, not only expresses the underlying idealistic truth that the moral end is the common good, but seems – at first sight at least – to meet the familiar difficulties which surround that doctrine in a remarkably adequate way.

For what is – at first sight – the standing difficulty of idealistic ethics in connexion with its theory of a common good? Is it not simply that of ensuring the double condition, first, that the good shall be really good, and, secondly, that it shall be really common? The difficulty with "Duty," *e.g.*, is that it is common without being clearly the doer's good; with "Self-realisation," that it may be good, but is not so obviously common. Now "Loyalty" seems to have the necessary double front. It is "common" – in at least this simple and obvious sense, that common people are capable of it. "It is no aristocratic gift of the few." It is a good, if good it be at all, equally open to the humblest and the highest. On the other hand, that Loyalty *is* a good, "viewed merely as a personal attitude" and "quite apart from all question as to its object," is the burden of three of the Author's most convincing chapters. By giving the individual a cause to which he can commit himself, Loyalty reconciles him to himself – gives him at once a will of his own and a field for its expression. Objections to Loyalty come mostly from the side of individualism, but they all presuppose the thing they object to. True it is that, in past history, the blind loyalty of men has been the food on which oppression and tyranny have thriven, but the alternative – freedom – is itself a cause which calls for loyalty. Narrow loyalties – to class honour and the like – may lead to conduct eccentric, preposterous and unjust: but when such action is condemned, it is condemned in the name of loyalty to some wider cause. Of the claim most characteristic of individualism – and echoed in so much of our modern literature – that we should before all things be autonomous individuals, the same is to be said. So far as its form goes we admit the demand. Autonomy is morally essential. "Only your own will brought to a knowledge of itself can determine for you what your duty is." But individualism errs by seeking it in the wrong place. Neither in personal pleasure, nor in personal might, nor in personal serenity of soul can that being be truly autonomous whose very nature is social, and who therefore craves for an extra-personal and super-personal to which he can be "freely loyal."

Loyalty, then, is an accessible good to all and a supreme good to each; and so far, Prof. Royce's conception is promising. But here it threatens to fall foul of the requirements of a real theory of the moral end. Is this which is said to he "accessible to all" really one good? Are all the actual loyalties of men genuine examples of one thing, or are they a mere collection of things utterly diverse, united only by the thin identity of a specious name? There are facts which seem to favour the latter view. Causes conflict. Loyalty to a clan at feud, for instance, or to a civilised nation in a state of war-fever directs all its force towards the death of the enemy's loyalty to his clan or nation. Loyalties seem to differ, indeed – and mortally. We assume that Loyalty is one when we call it the one supreme good. If so, we must call it self-destructive. And a self-destructive supreme good is simply supreme evil.

What is at stake is the identity of Loyalty; and Prof. Royce saves it by pointing out that its self-destructive character is accidental. The essential fact is that Loyalty is self-generating and self-supporting. Within the unity of a common cause its appearance in one member strengthens and promotes its manifestation in another. "Brother strengthens brother." This essentially unifying character of Loyalty makes an adjustment conceivable whereby all causes shall subserve one universal cause. To the crucial question, what shall be the universal aim? under what universal idea shall the adjustment be realised? the answer is at hand in the conception of Loyalty itself. If the loyalty of A is a supreme good for him and that of B a supreme good for him, the collision of the two means ultimate waste of good. Make it the ultimate aim, then, to prevent such collision. Make the promotion of Loyalty in all other men the ultimate cause, and in all your loyalty be loyal to that.

It would be petty criticism to dwell here on the fact that there is a circle involved – to object that the maxim "be loyal to Loyalty" could always be confronted by the question "loyal to loyalty to what?" After all, there must be a circle somewhere in human affairs, and in ethics if the circle be but big enough it is all that can fairly be demanded. That it is so in Prof. Royce's case is shown by the finely illuminating discussion in the central chapters of his book where he turns the light of his principle upon practical problems – problems of the individual conscience, of modern American social life, and of education.

A more serious criticism, however, lies just behind. Is this one good which is accessible to all, the same thing as that Loyalty which is said to be the good of each? or rather, has the Author shown it to be so? On the surface, he has not. His argument seems to be simply: "Loyalty is a good, hence the more of it the better; promote, therefore, the maximum of loyalty; choose your private cause with a view to that." The argument seems dangerously near to Mill's famous *iqnoratio elenchi*, "each person's loyalty is a good to that person, the loyalty of all therefore a good to the aggregate of all persons." Yet, though the Author has not raised this difficulty explicitly we venture to think he has implicitly met it, and in doing so, has met it in the only way compatible with the character of his book.

What is wanted is some proof that maximum loyalty in others is supreme good to that particular private being who finds his own good in his own loyalty. Now, it hardly needs to be proved that the virtues are loyalty. Further, it has been proved by Prof. Royce – it is a thesis central to his whole position – that the virtues are loyalty *to loyalty*; and that the way to be virtuous in highest degree – the way to define our duties and find our moral path in the most effective way – is to follow the maxim "be loyal to Loyalty." These two statements together, provided both are sound, seem to make the point. The more loyal I am to loyalty the more virtuous I become, for thereby I find my moral path better: which means, the more loyal I am to Loyalty, the more loyal I become as an individual, for to be virtuous is to be loyal. In other words: in proportion as I give myself away to the service of the universal good, in that proportion do I reap the "Loyalty," which is my individual good. Explicitly, Prof. Royce's popular statement has not gone further than to say that in Loyalty I *both* get *and* give good. His argument required more. It required that I get *in proportion as* I give. But his data really yield that conclusion, provided the latter of the two premises is right; that is, provided his principle furnishes the key to moral perplexity which he supposes it to furnish. This final question could only be answered by a critical examination, longer than can be undertaken here, of the cases to which Prof. Royce thinks his principle can be applied with success. It is important to note, however, that the issue all turns on the applicability of the principle – on the simple question whether the maxim "be loyal to loyalty" is good practical advice or no. In concentrating on this question the Author was giving the only "proof" of the idealistic conception of the moral end compatible with the popular character of his undertaking – ultimately, perhaps, the only proof it is possible to give.

Despite his able defence, throughout the first six chapters of his book, of the view that Loyalty contains all the private good that the individual can really want, the reader still feels that something more is needed before the ghost of individualism has been laid. Is it certain, after all, that the giving of oneself away in loyalty to a cause never means loss – that it never means curtailment of freedom or of power, or of any genuine individual good? These questions seem to demand some sort of religious philosophy to support the ethical structure. This is what the Author in the last two lectures tries to furnish. And his endeavour leads him into direct conflict with certain recent metaphysical tendencies represented preeminently by his friend and colleague Prof. James.

Prof. Royce would not come into conflict with Pragmatism unless it implied a truth for him. That the truth is no insignificant one becomes apparent from his problem. If Loyalty is to be the ultimate good, then loyalty to a cause however poor must never be sheer lost labour. Where are the grounds for such a belief? The Author finds them in the fact that there is one cause to serve which is to be ultimately successful, namely, Truth; and in the further fact implied therein, that all service, in so far as it is directed to a cause which is true, is similarly successful. Amid all causes have some truth. Now in order to see how Truth can be regarded as a cause at all, we must recall just such facts as Modern Pragmatism has brought into prominence. Truth, it has insisted, is an active attitude. There is no mere theoretic truth. The search for truth is an active seeking for practical congruity between our principles, and our attained empirical results. Principles are true if they "succeed" and they succeed if they are true. All this is a necessary part of Prof. Royce's own position. It remains for him only to push the last statement further, and ask what "success" means. To this he answers that success, in the sense in which truth is success, is not a merely private subjective experience. Neither is it any possible number of such experiences on the part of one individual or any number of individuals. "Success," in this application, is only where that state of facts towards which the individual's mind is directed – that which in the moments of his insight and devotion he becomes – is in itself verily and permanently real. This conception of an ultimately real, all-inclusive individual experience – the reality of that rational common spirit which appears wherever men try to think truly or serve loyally – is what the Author calls the "Eternal World." From it he derives his final definition of Loyalty. "Loyalty is the will to manifest, so far as is possible, the Eternal, that is, the conscious and superhuman unity of life, in the form of the acts of an individual self." This conception closes the system. In the universal Life the ultimate success of our loyal life is assured, for in it all our finitude and imperfection is completed.

Without these closing chapters the claim of Loyalty would not be stated in its most convincing form. The Author's metaphysic is no mere addendum to his Ethics. Until a philosophy of religion has shown where every imperfect effort comes to rest in "a conspectus of life which includes all temporal happenings and strivings in a single consciousness and fulfils all our actual purposes together and is all we seek to be," the fulness of the *good* of Loyalty is not disclosed. It is here, perhaps, that, to many readers, the greatest difficulties of the book will be found. It does not seem satisfying that even "in the end" our failures should cost us nothing – that a miraculous forgiveness should wipe out all error at a stroke and put saint and sinner together – and in the final "conspectus of life" such seems to be the result. If, in the Eternal, all our fragmentary efforts are to be caught up and fulfilled, where are we to find any ultimate distinction of result between the good among them and the bad? Still, it is perhaps hardly a blemish in a popular book, that it abstain from offering a solution of the problem of evil, if only it does not put obviously insurmountable barriers in the way of any possible solution. This reflection has the greater applicability to a writer who has worked out a theory of the evil will elsewhere, in view of which his present position is adopted. In seeking the missing distinction, it must not be overlooked that the will which finds ultimate fulfilment is "the will to manifest the Eternal." The will to thwart an Eternal which necessarily prevails – or any other will in so far as it cherishes this evil aim – must of necessity find its undoing.

The most serious difficulties, however, are likely to be found in that attempted union of voluntarism and realism – that mutual involution of will, thought and reality – which the conception of the eternal itself means to express. It is comparatively easy, with Pragmatism, to invest reality with the "dynamic" of living thought and purpose if we are willing to sacrifice everything to that. It is a different matter to try, as Prof. Royce does, to invest thought and purpose at the same time with the objectivity of reality. Yet the significance of the book as a statement of the idealistic view of life for a popular audience would seem to lie not a little in the fact that it has dared to put forward such a conception. There has been almost too much militant idealism in the air of recent years. For some reason, it has not rung sound. The very eagerness with which Pragmatic writers hasten to defend their claim to *make* our moral and religious postulates true, has tended to cast suspicion on their truth. There has been a lack of true philosophic humility, an absence of patient logic, an unseemly proneness on the part of many who deal with the ultimate nature of reality and life to report things not as they are but as they and we want to see them. Despite speculative difficulties, it will do something to restore the confidence of the educated mind in the spiritual view of the world, to meet for once a "recent idealist" who claims no subjective right over the reality he interprets, but dares avow from the outset that he believes in the Eternal and is in quest of it. Moreover, the very fact that his metaphysical speculations are so capable as they are of yielding the ethical system and the penetrating criticism of life which he has extracted from them, is itself no mean indication that the inherent difficulties they contain may in the end prove surmountable.

# REVIEW OF *THE PHILOSOPHY OF LOYALTY*

Frank Chapman Sharp, Review of *The Philosophy of Loyalty*, *Journal of Philosophy*, vol. 6 (1909).

*The Philosophy of Loyalty*. Josiah Royce. New York: The Macmillan Co. 1908, Pp. xii, 409.

Readers of *The World and the Individual* have been awaiting with eagerness the appearance of a work which should supplement the author's metaphysics by the presentation of his ethical creed, as held by him today. *The Philosophy of Loyalty*, in which this hope seems about to be realized, will, however, prove in some respects disappointing to the special student. For it is, as expressly announced in the preface, neither a text-book nor "an elaborately technical philosophical research," but rather a popular discussion of a single problem, which took its final form in a course of lectures delivered before the Lowell Institute. Nevertheless, the problem chosen is so fundamental and is treated with so much clearness that the essential features of the author's theory of ethics appear in unmistakable outlines, even though the reasons offered for its acceptance are not elaborated with anything approaching completeness.

The subject-matter of the book is, broadly speaking, the content of the moral ideal. This for Professor Royce, as for Hegel, consists in the identification of the individual will with the universal will. This universal is, of course, the organic whole of which each individual mind is a member. The creation of a harmony between myself and the world, in other words the setting before myself of ends the realization of which is at the same time the realization of the ends of my fellowmen, this is the task that the moral ideal lays upon mine. Such a prescription means, negatively, indifference to all satisfactions that are merely individual, except, as they may be incidental to the attainment of the ultimate end; with this will disappear all strife except that against the enemies of the ideal itself. Positively it means the giving up of one's life to the service – not of individuals as such, for there is no reason why I should supply others with what I do not allow myself, but of causes. For a cause is a tie binding a number of individuals into a unity through their struggle for or possession of a common object. What particular causes you and I are to work for must be determined mainly by our tastes, our abilities, and our circumstances. But whatever our cause may be, evidently we must so choose and serve it as to increase to the utmost of our power the amount of devotion to causes in the world. For only as society becomes thoroughly permeated by such a spirit can it become completely unified. If by narrowing somewhat the common signification of a word, we agree to call "the willing, practical, and thoroughgoing devotion of a person to a cause" loyalty, then it follows from the preceding that all virtue is loyalty of some sort, and the supreme virtue is loyalty to loyalty.

The evidence offered for the truth of this position is twofold. In the first place, it is maintained that this unity of the one and the many is the highest good of the individual himself, that, indeed, nothing is a good except as it is supported and made what it is by this consciousness of harmony. Whence by the convenient and (among philosophers) popular assumption that the right is always and everywhere identical with the agent's highest good, the equation, morality = loyalty, is obtained. In the second place, it is asserted that the ordinarily accepted virtues, as veracity, respect for property, and the rest, find their explanation and justification in terms of this conception.

But may not the conception itself rest upon a myth? Devotion to a cause may, indeed, be the individual's highest good, but he can find it such, as Professor Royce admits, or rather insists, only on condition that he supposes the cause to be worthy of his devotion. Now a cause, as we have seen, does not derive its ultimate value from the satisfaction its realization will afford to individuals. Is worth, or value, to be defined, then, in terms of something other than satisfaction? By no means; the good must represent the satisfaction of some conscious being. If, then, morality be not the worship of a fetish, the cause must be a super-personal being, an experience dwelling upon some higher level of consciousness than any human being ever reaches. And the cause of causes, the unity of the life of the race, can be nothing other than God. At this level of insight morality passes over into religion, and loyalty may be defined as "the will to manifest, so far as is possible, the Eternal, that is, the conscious and superhuman unity of life, in the form of the acts of an individual Self." The evidence for the existence of this super-personal consciousness occupies the two closing chapters of the book. In the seventh it is presented by means of a polemic against pragmatism, in the eighth by a more purely constructive argument. As these add nothing essentially new to the exposition in *The World and the Individual* and in the presidential address, "The Eternal and the Practical," they need not detain us here.

Such are the outlines of this simple impressive picture of the moral life. What, now, are we to say of the grounds upon which it is recommended for our acceptance? In attempting to estimate their adequacy we are confronted by the fact that the book is not a treatise, but a series of popular lectures. Now, if a lecturer wishes second invitation to address the same audience, even if it be an average "academic" audience, he must supply entertainment or edification, not evidence. If, then, the present reviewer finds himself compelled to say that (ignoring the metaphysical discussion as something already before the philosophical public) the arguments of the earlier chapters seem to him not merely unconvincing, but flimsy, he is not so much condemning this book as giving the author a hint as to how to deal with the difficulties of at least one reader when he comes to prepare a more thoroughgoing presentation.

Professor Royce, as we have seen, reaches his conclusion by two different paths, through a doctrine of the good and a doctrine of the right. The position that loyalty, as above defined, is the supreme good, by the side of which all other objects of desire are (as I understand it) worthless, is attained primarily by the author's favorite method of eliminating alternatives. The most important alternative attacked is hedonism. But his argument, if valid, will hold equally against a number of closely related theories such as Alexander's and Simmel's, which, for want of a better name, may be called voluntarism. Now the essence of both hedonism and voluntarism is catholicity and freedom. As far as the individual's own good is concerned, they assert that the satisfaction of no desire is as such worthless, and, provided that a harmony of desires has been attained which is both comprehensive, and stable, the individual's own judgment as to the relative position of his different desires is not to be condemned on any pretext, except as the interests of other persons are involved. The representatives of this position will accordingly maintain that he who picks out a single object of desire and holds it up as *alleinseligmachend*, must give definite and rigorously tested evidences to justify his contention. Unfortunately, this is precisely what we do not find. "Unless you can find some sort of loyalty," we are told, "you can not find unity and peace in your active living." The second of these two statements gets what measure of truth it possesses – not from the author's ethical, but from his metaphysical, position, according to which the universe is perfect. For the devotee of a lost cause, if he really believes it lost forever, will gain no peace from his devotion. The similar claim with regard to unity stands as a mere bold assertion. Unity with others in the pursuit of a common end undoubtedly enhances the value of that end for most of us. For some persons it is possible that no other kind of pursuit is capable of issuing in satisfaction. Such enhancement of value can as easily find a place in the hedonistic or voluntaristic account of the good as anywhere else. What is required, however, for Professor Royce's purposes, is a demonstration that it must occupy precisely the same place in every life; and, secondly, that everything else is worthless for every one. The very beginnings of such a demonstration are lacking.

With regard to the argument that all the commonly recognized virtues can be stated in terms of loyalty, it must be pointed out that all the virtues indispensable for the conservation of existence can he justified by any theory whatever which, in Nietzsche's phrase, affirms life. The real test comes when we apply our theory to the actions which aim at something more than the protection of the conditions of existence. No attempt is made to meet this test. Furthermore, since the theory claims to describe the moral life of common sense and not merely that of the philosopher, it assumes that the judgments of common sense never regard as moral the seeking for purely individual goods (whether for self or for another), and, further, that common sense looks upon the success of a cause as having a value independent of the good that may accrue to the individuals thereby affected. For the first of these assumptions no evidence whatever is offered. For the support of the second I suppose the author has in mind the peculiar enthusiasm which a cause is capable of evoking. Doubtless a million is a more impressive figure than one. But a million is, after all, made up of units, and whatever the source of its power over the imagination, it is in any event, not a product mysteriously generated by the fusion of zeros.

If, in conclusion, we turn to another aspect of Professor Royce's work, the pedagogical and homiletic, I believe all readers will agree in pronouncing it a masterpiece. The method of approach and the order and manner of treatment exhibit great skill. The style is transparently clear. Every sentence pulsates with life. And the whole glows with a warmth that can be infused only by a profound and generous nature that has seen a noble vision.

# REVIEW OF *RACE QUESTIONS AND OTHER AMERICAN PROBLEMS*

C.H. Rieber, Review of *Race Questions and Other American Problems*, *Journal of Philosophy*, vol. 6 (1909).

*Race Questions and other American Problems*. Josiah Royce. New York: The Macmillan Co. 1908. Pp. 287.

The five essays in this volume were delivered as popular addresses before various audiences. As the author states in the preface, this volume is part of an effort to apply, to some of our American problems, that general doctrine about life which he has expounded at length in his book entitled *The Philosophy of Loyalty*. He hopes that the various special opinions here expressed may be judged in the light of that philosophy. The present volume he regards as an auxiliary to its more systematic predecessor. This philosophy of loyalty is the practical aspect and expression of the author's idealistic philosophy. It is his answer to the pragmatist's protest that idealism is not a practical philosophy.

The closing essay of the present volume contains a summary of the theses upon which the philosophy of loyalty is based. The principle is stated thus: "*Be loyal, and be in such wise loyal that, whatever your own cause, you remain loyal to loyalty.* That is, so choose your cause, and so serve it, that, as a result of your activity, there shall be more of this common good of loyalty in the world than there would have been had you not lived and acted. Let your loyalty be such loyalty as helps your neighbor to be loyal. Despite the diversity of the individual causes – the families, countries, professions, friendships – to which you and your neighbor are loyal, so act that the devotion of each shall respect and aid the other's loyalty" (p. 248).

Everywhere that he has given an exposition of the new philosophy, both in this book and in his "Philosophy of Loyalty," Professor Royce is keenly aware of the fundamental criticism that will be offered to the doctrine of loyalty to loyalty. How is the first loyalty to which we are asked to be loyal determined? The author says: "But I freely admit that many men who have been enthusiastically and effectually loyal to various causes, and who in their personal lives have won as mature a notion of loyalty as they were capable of getting, have nevertheless often committed, in the name of loyalty, great crimes. And you may well ask how I explain this fact. You may well wonder how loyalty can be a central moral principle, when lives that were as loyal as the men in question knew how to make them have often been morally mischievous lives. My answer is that our loyalty leads us into moral error only in so far as we are indeed often blind to what the principle of loyalty actually means and requires. And such blindness is, as men go, human enough and common enough. The corrective to such errors, however, is not the introduction of some other moral principle than that of loyalty, but is just the discovery of the internal meaning, the true sense of the loyal principle itself. Whoever is loyal loves loyalty for its own sake" (p. 245).

The author makes the saving distinction for his doctrine between mere blind loyalty and enlightened loyalty. The former has done mischief in the past because it is pseudo-loyalty. It is turned into enlightened loyalty when it reaches the second dimension of loyalty, so to speak – the stage of loyalty to loyalty. The first commandment is: Be loyal. The second: Be loyal to loyalty. "That is, regard your neighbor's loyalty as something sacred. Do nothing to make him less loyal. Never despise him for his loyalty, however little you care for the cause he chooses. If your cause and his cause come into some inevitable conflict, so that you indeed have to contend with him, fight, if your loyalty requires you to do so; but in your bitterest warfare fight only against what the opponent does. Thwart his acts where he justly should be thwarted; but do all this in the very cause of loyalty itself, and never do anything to make your neighbor disloyal" (p. 253). From these consequences of his central principle follow all those propositions about the special duties of life which can be reasonably defined and defended. Justice, kindness, chivalry, charity – these are all of them forms of loyalty to loyalty.

In the first essay, on "Race Questions and Prejudices," Professor Royce finds the solution for our southern race problem by a study of the English solution of the once serious race question in Jamaica. The English have solved their problem by the simplest means in the world – by administration and reticence. "When once the sad period of emancipation and of subsequent occasional disorder was passed, the Englishman did in Jamaica what he has so often and so well done elsewhere. He organized his colony; he established good local courts, which gained by square treatment the confidence of the blacks. The judges of such courts were Englishmen. The English ruler also provided a good country constabulary, in which native blacks also found service, and in which they could exercise authority over other blacks. Black men, in other words, were trained, under English management, of course, to police black men" (p. 22). Therefore Professor Royce concludes that

"The southern race problem will never be relieved by speech or by practises such as increase irritation. It will be relieved when administration grows sufficiently effective, and when the negroes themselves get an increasingly responsible part in this administration in so far as it relates to their own race" (p. 29).

In the second essay, on "Provincialism," the author maintains that in "the present state of the world's civilization, and of the life of our own country, the time has come to emphasize, with new meaning and intensity, the positive value, the absolute necessity for our welfare, of a wholesome provincialism, the saving power to which the world in the near future will need more and more to appeal." The present state of civilization the world over is such as defines a new social mission which the province and not the nation as a whole can fulfill. "False sectionalism which disunites, will indeed always remain as great an evil as ever it was. But the modern world has reached a point where it needs, more than ever before, the vigorous development of a highly organized provincial life. Such a life, if wisely guided will not mean disloyalty to the nation; and it need not mean narrowness of spirit, nor yet the further development of jealousies between various communities... . But the two tendencies, the tendency toward national unity and that toward local independence of spirit, must henceforth grow together. They can not prosper apart. The national unity must not kill out, nor yet hinder, the provincial self-consciousness. The loyalty to the republic must not lessen the love and the local pride of the individual community. The man of the future must love his province more than he does today. His provincial customs and ideals must be more and not less highly developed, more and not less self-conscious, well established, and earnest" (pp. 64–66).

In the third essay, "On Certain Limitations of the Thoughtful Public in America," Professor Royce sees "mischief done by an unwise exaggeration of the tendency among Americans to reason, to argue, to trust to mere formulas, to seek for the all-solving word; in brief, to bring to consciousness what for a given individual ought to remain unconscious... . Thought, in any individual, must freely set limits to its own finite task. And when the thoughtful lovers of ideals forget this fact, they become mere wranglers, or doctrinaires, or pedants, or, on the other hand, in the end, through failure in thinking, they become cynics... . Now the human mind, in its present form of consciousness, is simply incapable of formulating all its practical devices under any one simple rule... . Restless search for the immediate presence of the ideal is often vain, like the pioneer idealism that burns the forests merely to see what they hide. Much of the best in human nature simply escapes our present definitions, is known only by its fruits, and prospers best in the forest shade of unconsciousness... . We are primarily creatures of instinct; and instinct is not merely the part of us that allies us with the lower animals. The highest in us is also based upon instinct, and only a portion of your instincts can ever be formulated. You will be able in this life to tell what they mean in only a few instances. But your life's best work will depend upon all of your good instincts together. Hence a great part of your life's work will never become a matter of your own personal and private consciousness at all. It is one of the duties of the thoughtful lover of ideals, then, to know that he can not turn into conscious thinking all of his ideal activities" (pp. 152–53).

The fourth essay. "The Pacific Coast," will hardly interest students of philosophy as much as the others, although it contains a very suggestive psychological study of the relations of climate and civilization. Professor Royce's estimate of the civilization of the Pacific Coast is, in the opinion of the reviewer, himself a native and a long-time resident of the state, an entirely just one. Californians are noted for their "independence of judgment," "their carelessness about what the outside world may think of them," "their apparent freedom in choosing what manner of men they should be," their "confident, and somewhat abrupt speech, particularly in speaking of the boundless future prosperity of their state." All these characteristics the author believes rest back, in large measure, on the peculiar climate and geographical isolation of the state.

# REVIEW OF *WILLIAM JAMES AND OTHER ESSAYS*

J.E. Creighton, Review of *William James and Other Essays*, *Philosophical Review*, vol. 21 (1912).

*William James and other Essays on the Philosophy of Life*. By Josiah Royce. New York, The Macmillan Company, 1911, pp. xi, 301.

This volume is made up of five essays, all of which were written by Professor Royce as public addresses. The leading essay on "William James and the Philosophy of Life" was given as the Phi Beta Kappa oration at Harvard University, while the paper on "The Problem of Truth in the Light of Recent Discussion" was read before the International Congress of Philosophy at Heidelberg. The other papers have the titles: "Loyalty and Insight," "What is Vital in Christianity," and "Immortality." In these essays Professor Royce undertakes to apply and illustrate the idealistic principles set forth in his more systematic writings by bringing them into relation to certain practical problems of life. While the positions maintained in this volume are familiar to readers of his other books, the form of statement is fresh and interesting. Indeed, the briefer and more direct form of presentation of these addresses gives sometimes a more definite form to his philosophical doctrines, while the applications and illustrations which are supplied should help to remove some misunderstandings of the bearings of the idealism which the author professes.

The opening essay is at once an eloquent tribute to Professor Royce's friend and distinguished colleague, and a fine appreciation and criticism of certain aspects of contemporary thought of which James was one of the foremost representatives. Whatever may be the verdict of the future regarding the special form of philosophical doctrine which James advocated, no one can doubt the propriety of linking his name, as Professor Royce does, with those of Jonathan Edwards and Ralph Waldo Emerson as the great representatives of American philosophy. The conclusion with which the address ends, that James's philosophy is something more than positivism, or pluralism; that it is an ethical idealism which recognizes a "Rule of Reason" in man and the universe –

may at first sight seem more questionable to some readers. But notwithstanding the length to which James was sometimes carried in his protest against abstract intellectualism, I think that Professor Royce's interpretation is correct. It was against the claims of an abstract or isolated reason that James protested unceasingly; against absolute principles that appeared to him to obscure or supplant the reality of the concrete variety and fluidity of experience. To preserve the latter he was willing, if need be, to repudiate logic and declare himself an irrationalist. But it seems to be a truer estimate of James's philosophy to recognize, as Professor Royce has done, that in spirit and in its best expression it is a demand for a more concrete rationality, a protest against the categories of the Understanding in the interest of the more distinctly vital and human point of view of the Reason.

The paper on the "Meaning of Truth" is more technical in character than the other parts of the book, being a criticism of current instrumentalism. This has lately been brought to the attention of readers of the *Review* by Professor Dewey's reply (Vol. XXI, pp. 69 ff.) which repudiates entirely the subjective or psychological view of experience which Professor Royce ascribes to the instrumentalist. It is to be hoped that the latter may be able to go on with a discussion which promises to yield significant results. For the points at issue between idealism and instrumentalism are now more exactly located and clearly defined than they were ten years ago, while during these years there has also been progress in mutual understanding, constituting something like a common platform upon which discussion can be profitably carried on. This of course implies that neither party has remained where it was. The instrumentalism which Professor Dewey advocates today requires a broader philosophical basis than the functionalism founded on the 'reflex arc concept.' And the whole emphasis of this volume of essays – the emphasis will, individual experience, and personal ideals, which is characteristic the present day, shows clearly that Professor Royce has not hesitated to gain instruction from his opponents.

# REVIEW OF *WILLIAM JAMES AND OTHER ESSAYS*

Horace M. Kallen, Review of *William James and Other Essays*, *Journal of Philosophy*, vol. 9 (1912).

*William James and other Essays in the Philosophy of Life*. Josiah Royce. New York: The Macmillan Company. 1911, pp. ix, 301.

What survives in any philosophic system is not so much its dialectic adequacy as its temperamental promptings. People do not embrace an *ism* for reason, but become reasonable by embracing an *ism*. A particular formula then becomes a genuine philosophers' stone, whose virtue it is to dissolve the dross of experience in the alembic of argument and to transmute its baser metal into the pure gold without alloy of canon or of system. These observations are commonplaces, I know. But no one can fail to feel keenly the deep and living truth of them who reads this book by Josiah Royce, with its familiar arguments so rejuvenated by the freshness of new contexts and new experience, its somewhat stern but not joyless piety so suffusing every evoking occasion, lifting it by the force of personality from the realm of utterance to the realm of worship, so wide the vistas caused to cluster about it, so deep the feeling that links them to the center. The book is made up of occasional pieces – an address before a learned society, a commencement audience, an undergraduate religious body, a congress of philosophers, a clerical assembly. The diversity of these groups is striking, but not less so than the unity of the lesson brought to them all, and the harmony and completeness with which occasion is assimilated to doctrine, so much so that the two are not to be separated, and one lives in the other as do the tones of a melody or the words of a sentence. Each piece is, in sum, a complete miniature of the great vision, a fully representative member of the self-representative system.

Admire as one must the esthetic excellence of such an interpenetration of vision with datum, the feeling is none the less inevitable that the admirable thing exists only by the rape of its individuality from the datum. In each instance the thing as it is is made over into the thing as it ought to be, and its intrinsic nature, "fragmentary," perhaps, but for all that something to be envisaged and appraised in and for itself, is absorbed in a "larger view," to be sure, lovely, but death to what enters it. To those who are interested in things as they are this is a defect, but it is a defect shared by all compensatory philosophies, and most philosophy is compensatory. It portrays a cosmos which is more loyal to desire than to perception. Perception shows a highly diversified world distinctly not made for man, inwardly discordant, a changeful flux, wherein life is a struggle to live, and human values are often lost, and when won, even at great cost. Philosophic "reality," on the contrary, from Plato to Royce is unified, harmonious, spiritual, eternally changeless, the very essence of human value, the ultimate and utter satisfaction of human desires. Such a "reality," which is biologically an ideational elaboration of the central goal of all that struggles to maintain itself – that vital equilibrium with a propitious environment which experience is always upsetting – thus designates the perennial excellences which the mind most desires, and becomes the transmuting formula of philosophic and religious reconstruction. So the world is to be thought, and the effort of most thinkers in the history of thought has been *to prove what is empirically not so* – that the world is one, of spiritual substance or spiritually regulated, and secures the eternal conservation of the being and freedom of the human mind. Systems offering such proof are compensatory: they pay to our desires, for the insolvencies of the actual, with promissory notes on the eternal. They respond to human wishes and either ignore the conditions which determine the satisfaction or disappointment of these wishes, or transmute and reconstruct them, designating these actualities as *appearance*, and reserving the eulogium of *reality* for that which is not, but is desired. This latter is then taken to be the secret and all-satisfying heart of existence.

This substitution is at once the pathos and the glory of the mind. It would be interesting, were there space, to trace the historic processes which culminate therein, to exhibit the causes of their persistence, to specify their effect on the progress of free thought. What is here to the purpose, however, is alone the mutative power which makes every act of thought on the part of a spirit whose force is their force a very miracle of transsubstantiation. Though he be just as justice and sympathetic as love, nothing that he touches retains its own contour or nature, nor can. Thus, pragmatism has never had, perhaps, a fairer, more sympathetic or learned critic than Royce. For him, if for anybody, criticism has always meant judgment, not destruction. No one has been more intent than he in conserving whole as much of pragmatic doctrine as might be. And yet – to me, at any rate, all that is distinctive of pragmatism seems to dissolve under his handling and when he is done quite another thing appears bearing its name.

It may be said that this is the general outcome of philosophic argument concerning an opposition, but surely analysis is not transmutation, and again, the same results appear in the papers where pragmatism is not in issue. Take first the discussion of "what is vital in Christianity." It appears that what is vital are the incarnation and the atonement. But the incarnation and the atonement as these are manifest in the mythology and history of Christianism? Not so: the incarnation and the atonement as poetic tropes for fundamental conceptions in the Roycean idealism. "First, God wins perfection through expressing himself in a finite life and triumphing over and through its very finitude. And secondly, our sorrow is God's sorrow. God means to express himself by winning through the very triumph over evil to unity with the perfect life; and therefore our fulfilment, like our existence, is due to the sorrow and triumph of God himself. These two theses express, I believe, what is vital in Christianity" (p. 183). The God here, be it observed, is not the God of the Christians, that is the Roycean absolute. His finite life is not the life of Jesus Christ, it is any and each empirical existence. The sorrow and evil are not those arising through freedom and original sin, they are the absolute inevitable "rule of the fame" of the far nobler Roycean "solution" of the "problem of evil." And the triumph and salvation are not the consequences of man's belief and God's free grace, they are involved inexorably in the absolute's nature. In sum, "what is vital in Christianity" turns out to be not Christian at all.

A still more striking example, because of the more radical inner difference of the mutatives, appears in the commencement address on "Loyalty and Insight." These two views of life are confronted – naturalism with loyalty, which designates anew and significantly Professor Royce's *lebensanschauung*. According to naturalism ideals are alien here on earth: "In no case...does the real world essentially care for or help or encourage [them]." The aim of life is to "be free from superstition, then; and next avoid false hopes" (p. 65). Loyalty, on the other hand, "is founded not upon a decision of nature's supposed mechanism, but upon a study of man's own inner and deeper needs. It is a doctrine about the plan and business of human life." It appears in the light thereof that "*the study of science is a very beautiful and human expression of a certain exalted form of loyalty*" (p. 83). But now; the study of science is and leads to most often just that decision upon nature's supposed mechanism which is the essence of naturalism, so radically contrasted with loyalty; its programme is exactly and supremely to be free from superstition and avoid false hopes. What difference, then, between naturalism and idealism? None. But the conclusion contradicts the premise? No. The premise has been altered. Naturalism has not really been meant to be taken as it is in itself. Its very statement has involved reservations and exceptions which, when considered, shall make it over into altogether an idealistic thing. These reservations and exceptions are the ideals of which naturalism is supposed to take no account, "man's own inner and deeper needs." Naturalism gets transmuted into their form and substance and becomes a thing not natural at all.

Of great importance, not more as an example of transmutation than for its bearing on the discussion of pragmatism, is Professor Royce's treatment of time in the present restatement of his well-known views on "immortality." Most of the experiences of life, he there asserts, "unite to show us that the reality of time is possessed especially by its past and future, over against which the present is indeed but vanishing" (p. 268). This is discovered in the act of willing. Therefore time is a function of volition. "In terms...of my attitude of will, and only in such terms can I define time, and its regions, distinctions, and reality." By analogy, since I discover hydrogen and oxygen by operating with water, I ought not to be able to define these gases in terms other than water. Such a definition would, however, invert the logical implications of whole with part, and where a complex used to imply its elements the elements would now imply the complex. This is logically inadmissible. And as empirically time is an element in the complex we call volition, and can itself be still further reduced to elements of which the most distinctive is duration, it becomes clear that time can be a function of volition only if the logic of implication is abrogated. The further question may yet be raised as to whether, empirically, the past and future do have superior reality. The experiences of life, I think, unite to deny that they do. But this point may be waived for the present, and inquiry made into the relation between the time in which past and future are more real than present, this "fragmentary" and relative time of actual experience, and that species of time which the absolute alone enjoys – a time in which future and past do not exist as such, but are present. It is to be noted that, though this time is the special privilege of the absolute, our own relative and fragmentary experience does contain prototypes of it. Musical progressions, at least, are experiences in which what had better be called actual duration is more prominent than elsewhere and which somewhat resemble the absolute's time. Why should this species of time be reserved for the absolute, the other attributed to men, and all identified with will, and ultimately with eternity? The answer is: compensation; but its elaboration must be postponed till the criticism of "truth."

Now if such inwardly oppugnant things as Christianism and absolute idealism, absolute idealism and naturalism, duration and eternity, can be thus transfused one into the other, so that all real distinctions get forgotten and lost, how much more facile, then, no matter how cautious and detached the investigator, a transsubstantiation of concepts that have a certain similarity of content – such as is denoted, for example, by "action," "deed," "purpose" – as do pragmatism and Royceian voluntarism. When, moreover, discourse is suffused by deep and commemorative emotion, and the address on "William James and the Philosophy of Life" is so suffused, it is well-nigh inevitable that feeling shall bring together and hold firmly in one glowing vision all things dear and cherished, without respect to how great be their oppugnance otherwise. The thought of William James may thus become indistinguishable from that of Josiah Royce, and I must confess that this is what seems here to have occurred, and that the address appears to me much more effective as history than as interpretation. The alignment of James with Edwards and Emerson, the exposition of his relation to his times, even the somewhat supererogatory defense of James against those who unjustly "confound pragmatism with the cruder worship of efficiency" seem rightly borne out by the facts. But as interpreted, the *Will to Believe* and the whole of James's philosophy of life gets, as with Boutroux, a very definite twist that makes it over as Royce would have it be, but as it is not. Here are characteristic passages: "Your deeper ideals always depend upon viewing life *in the light of the larger unities that now appear*, upon viewing yourself as a *coworker with the universe* for the attainment of *what no present game of human action can now reveal*" (pp. 38–39). "Moreover, these ethical maxims are here governed, in James's exposition, by the repeated *recognition of certain essentially absolute truths*, truths that, despite his natural horror of absolutism, he here expounds with a finished dialectic skill... . The need of faith in the unseen and the superhuman he founds upon these simple and yet absolutely true principles, principles of the true dialectic of life: First, every great decision of practical life requires faith and has irrevocable consequences, *consequences that belong to the whole great world*, and that therefore have *endless possible importance*. Secondly, since action and belief are thus inseparably bound together, our right to believe depends upon our right as active beings to make decisions. Thirdly, our duty to decide life's greater issues is determined by the *absolute truth* that, in critical cases, the will to be doubtful and not to decide is itself a decision, and is hence no escape from our responsible moral position. And thus our responsible moral position is *a position that gives us our place in and for all future life*" (pp. 41–42). I have italicized the transforming phrases. They turn the doctrines of James, who had tried absolutism and found it wanting, who was radically an empiricist, an indeterminist, a pluralist, impatient of *alls* and *wholes*, always asserting the externality of relations, into just that non-empirical absolutism he instinctively rejected upon trial and reflectively combatted. Only when these phrases are accepted can he be compared with the absolutists, Fichte and Hegel. Reject them, and you find that he resembles Fichte in those respects in which Fichte was most citizen and least philosopher; you find that what he has in common with Hegel is exactly not the Hegelian *spirit*, but what is characteristic of Hegel, as he himself points out,[1] "merely as a reporter of certain empirical aspects of the actual." Altogether, I can not overcome the impression that as this address progresses there is a gradual transmutation of the distinctive ideas of pragmatism into the characteristic conceptions of absolutism. In the end, I find attributed to William James the philosophy of life of Josiah Royce.

In this there is the undeniable appeal of a high pathos. The mind is so inevitably decking whom it loves, even though the beloved could not and will not wear them, with all its preferred supremacies and excellences. Such desire is the universal trait of lovers. Its execution gives recollection something of the flavor and glow of actuality, forges anew the chains which bind earth to eternal good. Though the naked fact were rougher, perhaps, yet nobler to utter, here compensation has a dual right – for to that which the mind inevitably craves is joined that for which the fact itself compels the yearning. In pure discourse, however, many would challenge compensation's place. Yet nowhere does it flourish more or win greater victories, for its nature is to grow by argument and to secure itself by dialectic. Compensatory philosophies, as a rule, play their game with loaded dice, and disingenuously: their answer, as Mr. Jacks boasts, exists prior to their problem: they bet on a sure thing. Now it is not one of the least splendid qualities of Royceian idealism that with respect to it the rule does not altogether hold. Its compensations are demanded with as much frankness as unconsciousness that they are compensation, and the essential begging of excellence and salvation, as well as of the question, appears as a right, not as a trespass.

Nowhere, I think, are the virtues and defects of the system so apparent as in the weighty and important address before the international congress of philosophy at Heidelberg, four years ago, on "The Problem of Truth in the Light of Recent Discussion," and here reprinted. The joining of the issues between pragmatism and absolutism is subtle as well as broad; just, as well as searching, and yet – what is true of the essays examined above is true also of this: the very presuppositions on which the issues are stated render them impossible as between

1 *A Pluralistic Universe*, p. 100.

absolutism and its opponent. Absolutism loves pragmatism, and with cannibalistic intensity; it swallows pragmatism whole and sublates in the "larger view."

Analysis – so the fable runs – lays bare three motives in the current descriptions of truth: that derived from biology, with its conception of the survival-value of ideas; that derived from "the longing to be self-possessed and inwardly free," and ramifying into individualism, personal idealism, and irrationalism; that derived from "modern logic" and identical with the Kantian motive "which leads us to seek for clear and exact self-consciousness regarding the principles both of our belief and of our conduct," a motive not altogether properly called intellectualism. These motives appear in realism like Russell's and voluntarism like Fichte's, as well as in the pragmatism of James and the instrumentalism of Dewey. Each and all of them leads to absolute idealism. "Individualism is right in saying, 'I will to credit this or that opinion.' But individualism is wrong in supposing that I can ever be content with my own will in so far as it is merely an individual will. The will to my mind is to all of us nothing but a thirst for complete and conscious self-possession, for fulness of life. And in terms of this its central motive the will defines the truth that it endlessly seeks as a truth that possesses completeness, totality, self-possession, and therefore absoluteness. The fact that, in our human experience, we never meet with any truths such as completely satisfy our longing for insight, this fact we therefore inevitably interpret, not as any defect in the truth, but as a defect in our present state of knowledge, a limitation due to our present type of individuality. Hence we acknowledge a truth which transcends our individual life" (pp. 235–36). "We can define the truth even of relativism only by asserting that relativism is absolutely true" (p. 237). The course of our daily life even as of dialectic must presuppose this absolutism. For it assumes the past, which transcends all individual experience, and it assumes the minds of other men, which transcend the individual experience of each man. If the truth of assertions about these two assumptions, which can not be verified, consists simply in the fact that such assertions are credited, truth-telling becomes indistinguishable from lying. For truth-telling *pre*-supposes, looks backward, to already existing facts which validate assertions by their mere existence. If not, the pragmatist shares the fate of Epimenides the Cretan, who called all Cretans liars (pp. 225–33), to say nothing of the Psalmist who extended this quality to all men. Withal, "instrumentalism in so far correctly defines the nature which truth possesses in so far as we ever actually verify truth" (p. 224).

The arguments here recapitulated are familiar to all readers of Royce: Pragmatism can not account for past time, other minds, and is self-contradictory. It happens, however, that the pragmatism which so fails is not pragmatism as it is, but pragmatism in the absolutistic version. This version derives from presuppositions which the pragmatist neither acknowledges nor entertains. Of absolutism, however, these are the critical center. They regard the nature of cognition or experience with respect to its volitional-durational character and with respect to its ego-centrality. In Professor Royce's version of absolutism, the analysis of time plays a leading rôle. He concludes, as is well known, that living time, the enduring present, is less real than past or dead time and unborn or future time. But this time itself is only a function of the will, whose operation is reality, and our own wills assume but never experience past and future as such. The result is that they are both real and unreal. This is a contradiction which is sublated by turning past and future into an actual present – the immediate experience of the absolute will, which alone thus possesses "completeness, totality, absoluteness." In it wish, need, and satisfaction are identical. In the finite mind they are different, and the difference is "a limitation due to my present type of individuality." Thirst is a guarantee thus of its own unreality. My thirst guarantees that what will assuage it exists and will assuage it, even though I die of it in the meantime. The upshot of this analysis of time is, then, that the past can never be present to us, but is together with the future present to the absolute, *in actu*. Absolutely, time hasn't a temporal nature at all. It collapses into "eternity," an ordinal simultaneity in space; when the absolute does experience it as such, he experiences it as duration (*vid. supra,* p. 551).

Now for pragmatism time is as central as for absolutism. But it finds no empirical ground for the superior reality of the past and future over the present. And as for "eternity," that is an empty, negative concept like "not-man." The real duration, which Professor Royce reserves for the absolute, pragmatism observes to be the substance of all experience. *This* it describes *as it flows*, and its flow, as Professor A. W. Moore has long ago shown, without rejoinder, consists of actual transitions from uneasiness and fragmentariness to "completeness, totality," satisfactions, the former leading durationally into the latter as one tone of a melody into another, and each in its turn supplying "conscious self-possession and fulness of life." For pragmatism, furthermore, each and every phase of this process is its own guarantee and is neither logically nor emotionally in need of aid and comfort from without. It is logically what it is, and no more, a matrix to be credited, at the creditor's own risk, as a starting-point for more experience which may or may not *grow* out of it, *indeterminately and freely*, but does not already preexist as its warranty in an absolute mind. Hence, our felt lack of a thing in idea is silent about that thing's existence or non-existence. As substance it is just that felt lack, and no more, capable of working generatively toward the making or the discovery of what is desired. It may fail to do so, and then becomes false; it may succeed, and becomes true, acquires through application or activity a new trait or function, is *verified.* We have Professor Royce's own word that this description of the nature of truth is correct "in so far as we ever actually verify truth." But what would be the "truth" of a *felt lack*, of a guiding idea which didn't guide, if it were *not* verified in some concrete way? Its truth would be *nil;* it would be mere *datum*, an existence having a logically real nature, but neither true nor false. Only if truth and existence be confused is it possible to speak of unverified truth. Such a confusion arises wherever a compensatory absolute experience is invoked to confirm natural experience. To that, since that is empirically generative, the dialectic of a block universe does not apply. Hence, the objection that not we, but the absolute only, can verify the past, falls beside the mark. A past event, even such an event as Newton's mind, may in so far as it perdures be presently known and is presently known. So we know the law of gravitation. Newton's body indeed and his lapsed emotions are, as such, irrecoverable. But they are none the less subjects of predicative propositions, are none the less terms we have *knowledge about*, that gets itself verified in acquaintance with such data as these have continued themselves into, not necessarily, but freely, determining in virtue of their inward nature our present experience of them. This consists in the books Newton wrote, the portraits that were made of him, and so forth. And so long as these are credited *forward*, and the crediting continually and prosperously enriches life, even as doctors' theses, can they be better, more truly known? Professor Royce himself agrees they can not, by us. But do they become any more immediate to us, is the truth *about* them changed for us into the fact *of* them, by declaring them to be the immediate possession of the absolute, who is still less immediate *to us?* Such a declaration is as reasonable as an attempt firmly to found a house of cards by building it on a quicksand.

What I have just said about Newton's mind as a past event applies equally to all other minds as presently active. This means, of course, that pragmatism regards minds as being as little private in their essential nature as things; propositions of which they are the subjects, hence, are amenable to verification. Absolutism regards other minds as something essentially private, therefore not amenable to verification and hence subjecting the thinker to the alternative between solipsism and the absolute. As the absolute's mind is *ex hypothesis* least of all subject to verification, the validating effect of that mind is, to say the least, highly questionable. But granting that I believe in the absolute, how am I thereby to be saved from solipsism? Does the alternative offer anything more than solipsism on a large scale as against solipsism on a small? Be this as it may, it can arise only if the purely, the "merely psychological" character of the individual mind be assumed. Pragmatism declares this assumption to involve a dialectical reconstruction of objective empirical data. It declares these data to be found in actual acquaintance with other minds themselves. It finds that a knower first discovers those minds, and only afterwards understands his own in the light of these discoveries. It finds those minds to be highly complicated objective organizations of terms and relations, not simple wills. And finally while it finds that empirically not all the elements in a mind are perceivable with equal facility, any more than are all the elements of the residual world, it exhibits the purely empirical fact that one mind *does* know another and demonstrates *how* this knowledge occurs. What, then, is to be gained by violating the principle of parsimony and invoking, *in addition* to actual verifications of propositions the subjects of which are objects of acquaintance, an utterly *unverifiable* and unknowable absolute mind to validate the knowledge of other minds admitted already to be valid so far as may be?

Altogether, pragmatism seems, thus far, to fall into the toils of absolutism only when it is transmuted into a thing absolutistic from the start. Is there not, however, one instance at least in which pragmatism falls of its own momentum into absolutism, like a meteorite into the sun? Does not pragmatism assert the absolute whenever it affirms a general proposition? Can the truth even of relativism be defined otherwise than absolutely? Impossible, says Professor Royce: and the impossibility arises by the use of the most dread weapon in his dialectical armory. "An absolute truth is one whose denial implies the reassertion of that same truth" (p. 251). We are facing the famous reflexive argument. In the essay it is incarnated in many and elaborate examples, from Epimenides the Cretan, Euclid and his theorem that there is no last prime number, to all the ramifications of the "new logic." Formally it has not, so far as I know, been met. Yet it is curious that so profound and sympathetic a student of symbolic logic as Professor Royce should not long ago have observed its formal impossibility. Logically the reflexive argument is coincident with the conception which Mr. Bertrand Russell designates as the "class of all classes" and this conception is, according to Mr. Russell's unquestioned analysis, self-contradictory. To choose one term of the contradiction and to call that the valid one is an act purely arbitrary, in no sense a solution of the contradiction. The solution of it, however, destroys the reflexive effect. When, for example, the Psalmist says, "all men are liars," all men formally become liars and not-liars at the same time. When the relativist declares, "There is no absolute truth," truth is thereby rendered both absolute and relative. Mr.

Russell's conclusion of his examination of the contradiction is that the *all* type of "formal truth" is not admissible; the *any* and *every* type is. Classes have to be taken as *many*, and when so taken can be logical subjects, but only in propositions *of a different kind* from those in which their terms are subjects. The proposition which applies to the Psalmist himself will be other than that which applies to the Psalmist as a member of the class *men*. As the latter, then, he may well be a liar. In and by himself he may be altogether veracious. So, also, the assertion, "there is no absolute truth," may be in itself "absolute," as a member of the class "truth" relative. The distinctions which lead to this particularism at once destroy the force of the reflexive argument and confirm the distinctly pragmatic reply to it.

This reply points to the fact that the *all* form of being is possible only in a block-universe in which time is unreal. Now empirically the universe is a collection of *eaches*, *i.e.*, of particulars, and time is real. The block-quality appears always in retrospect, for experience grows and *all* implies *more than all*. Reflexion is impossible under such conditions. The judgment in which it is said to occur is a *new fact* in the world, the latest in so far forth. What it regards and designates is not itself, but its predecessors. The *all* it makes use of becomes in this very use less than all. This is why, as Mr. Russell points out, it is subject to predicates *of a different kind* from those applying to its own members. Epistemologically, the reflexive argument rests on a confusion of kinds, namely, of *knowledge of acquaintance* with *knowledge about*, of existence with truth, of the perception of the *datum*, "all truth is relative" with the particular proposition "It is true that all truth is relative." The former is a fact, neither true nor false, but just so much brute being which may or may not perdure. It is the class as many. The latter is not designative, but predicative, it is *knowledge about*, and validates itself, in so far as it can validate itself at all, pragmatically. It may be added that only in the latter form can or does knowledge require validation. An illustration will clinch the argument: Suppose that on entering a room I formulate my perception thus, "There is no one here." According to the reflexive argument I contradict myself, for I deny that I am in the room while I am in it. Yet who, even among absolute idealists, would accuse me of self-stultification? Philosophers, none the less, in strictly similar logical situations make this accusation, and in good faith. Which exhibits again the attitude of pragmatism and of absolutism toward the actual processes of experience, one taking it as it comes, the other making it over.

The upshot is that the reflexive argument, no less than that from the knowledge of the past and the knowledge of one mind by another, is based on premises which pragmatism points to experience as denying.

The empirical data with which it starts must be dealt with alchemically before they can yield the desired results. Premises are made to conform to the wished-for conclusion rather than the conclusion to the premises. Unsatisfied interests must have their compensatory satisfactions. "Then what I have called the trivialities of mere instrumentalism will appear as what they are – fragmentary hints and transient expressions of the will whose life is universal, whose form is absolute and whose laws are at once those of logic, of ethics, of the unity of experience, and of whatever gives sense to life."

# REVIEW OF *WILLIAM JAMES AND OTHER ESSAYS*

R.F.M. Hoernle, Review of *William James and Other Essays*, *Mind*, vol. 22 (1913).

*William James and Other Essays on the Philosophy of Life*. By Josiah Royce, LL.D., Litt.D. New York: The Macmillan Company, 1911. Pp. xi, 301. Price 6s. 6d.

Among the many books and articles commemorating the life and work of William James, which appeared soon after his death in August, 1910, the essay which opens Prof. Royce's book strikes a distinctive note by its unusual standpoint. Whereas most other writers have spoken of James as a Psychologist and a Pragmatist, and have dwelt *e.g.*, on his protests against "Associationism" in the study of mental processes, and against "Intellectualism" in the theory of knowledge, Prof Royce dwells rather on the religious and ethical side of James's teaching. He ranks James as the third great typically American philosopher alongside of Jonathan Edwards and Ralph Waldo Emerson. Like these, James stands for and voices the ideas and ideals characteristic of a distinct phase of American national life. From this point of view the emphasis falls not so much on the *Principles of Psychology* or on *Pragmatism,* but on the *Varieties of Religious Experience,* on the *Will to Believe,* on the *Pluralistic Universe.* To us, in Europe, this is a less familiar side of James, notwithstanding what we all owe to the three books just mentioned. But it was, no doubt, a side very much more obvious to all who as pupils, colleagues, friends lived in daily contact with James and came directly under the influence of his rich and varied personality. It is interesting to learn that *Varieties* not merely ushered in a new era in religious psychology by teaching the psychologists "a new tolerance in their study of religion" (p. 21) and a more just appreciation of the genuineness of the individual's religious experience, but that it has actually quick-ended and invigorated religious life itself. "The new gospel, the glad tidings of the subconscious, began to be preached in many lands" (pp. 21–22). Prof. Royce makes it clear that he is unable to agree with a great deal in James's view of religion, but he puts it on record that *Varieties* "is full of the spirit, that in our country, has long been effective in the formation of new religious sects" (pp. 23–24). And his final verdict is "I am sure that only an American thinker could have written this survey, with all its unconventional ardor of appreciation, with all its democratic catholicity of sympathy, with all its freedom both from ecclesiastical formality and from barren free-thinking" (pp. 25–26).

In the sphere of Ethics Prof. Royce claims that the two ideals of "efficiency" and of "playing the game" represent the modern American's dominant attitude towards life. In the pursuit of these ideals there is much unrest, impatience, wilful caprice, but none the less "they characterise a people that is indeed earnestly determined to find itself, but that so far has not found itself" (p. 30). These ideals James deepened, purified and even, in a measure, "transcended." If he did propose to measure the truth of ideas by their "consequences," and to test them by their "working" in experience, yet he not only took experience in the deepest and most comprehensive sense, but he insisted in the *Will to Believe* above all on the necessity of high ideals and the faith which "plays the game" by living up to them strenuously and imposing them upon the world. Though he spoke, in his picturesque language, of the "cash-value" of ideas, the temper of his mind was essentially unworldly and spiritual. He was a kind of "American Carlyle" (p. 39), "a prophet of the nation that is to be" (p. 46). In drawing attention to this side of James's character and teaching – a side that is apt to be forgotten in the heat of controversy about Pragmatism – Prof. Royce has done a signal service to his memory.

The other essays in this volume require no detailed review here, for they mostly deal with topics like loyalty, the vital elements in Christianity, and immortality, on which Prof. Royce has written fully in his bigger works. One essay on "the problem of truth in the light of recent discussion" was read at the International Congress of philosophy at Heidelberg in 1908.

# REVIEW OF
# *THE SOURCES OF RELIGIOUS INSIGHT*

Jacob Loewenberg, Review of *The Sources of Religious Insight*, *International Journal of Ethics*, vol. 23 (1912).

*The Sources of Religious Insight: The Bross Lectures, 1911*. By Josiah Royce. New York: Charles Scribner's Sons, 1912, pp. xvi, 297.

This little volume is indeed Professor Royce's *Sonnenklarer Bericht* of his entire system. Shorn of its religious dress, – which the object and the occasion of these 1ectures demanded – the book contains a synthetic and popular (in the good sense) presentation of the sources of *spiritual* insight which a Voluntaristic Idealism affords.

Professor Royce, in applying his idealism to the problem of religion, uses old names for some new ways of feeling. The well-known religious categories, which in their original usage had a vital significance, but which later theology rendered abstract and threadbare, are reinvested by Royce with a concrete meaning. Such a category is Salvation. The higher religions are based on the postulate that man needs to be saved. For Royce, salvation is a universal need, a matter not of any one time or faith. It is a problem of life and experience. It arises whenever life is defined in terms of some highest good and whenever the danger of losing this highest good is realized.

An insight into the need and the way of salvation, an insight that man stands in danger of missing the goal of life, and that there is some means of escape from this danger, Royce calls a religious insight. There are several sources of such insight, with a study and criticism of which the whole volume deals.

A widely accepted source of insight is furnished, of course, by revelation. But whoever relies upon this source is involved in what Royce calls the "religious paradox" – the paradox of insisting that the individual, though unable to know the divine by his own light, is yet able to distinguish a divine revelation from any other report. "The paradox is that a being who is ignorant of his duty and of his destiny as to need guidance at every point, so weak as to need saving, should still hope, in his fallible experience, to get into touch with anything divine" (p. 25).

One way of solving this paradox seems to lie in the appeal to a personal religious experience defined by James as "the experience of individuals who regard themselves as 'alone with the divine'" (p. 27). It is an experience "which mysteriously wells up from the subliminal self, from the soundless depth of our subconsciousness" (p. 47). But valuable and necessary though such individual experience is, it does not solve the religious paradox. The paradox still remains: the individual in his isolation, "alone with the divine," finds salvation in which all other individuals shall share. Which of the many and the conflicting individual experiences reveals *the* divine? For an answer to this question one must appeal to social experience.

Social experience as a source of religious insight teaches "salvation through the fostering of human brotherhood" (p. 58). Such a doctrine insists upon the religious meaning of social service and upon the fact that men can only be saved together and not separately. But though the need of human companionship as a means to salvation is a universal need, yet mere companionship does not solve the religious paradox; for man and his fellow equally need salvation. Social experience, if it is to solve the paradox, must be viewed as a process "which is not only human but superhuman" (p. 74). "Human society as it now is...is a chaos of needs...the whole social order groans and travails together in pain...longing for salvation" (p. 75). How the social order as a whole may be saved, and through it the individual, reason must teach us.

Reason as a higher source of religious insight is indeed not the reason of "barren intellectualism" opposed to "intuition"; but it is a "broader intuition, the sort of seeing that grasps many views in one, that surveys life as it were from above" (p. 86). The office of reason is to get articulate insight – "insight into wholes rather than fragments" (p. 91). Now reason – conceived as a constructively synthetic process – shows that science and commonsense alike manifest what Royce calls the "religious paradox"; – they both involve the admission of human fallibility and ignorance and the confidence in a truth beyond the revelation of our momentary experience. It is a universal paradox which pervades all types of opinion – social, personal, and scientific. Commonsense, though incapable of being personally experienced or verified by any human individual, is yet a standard to which individual judgments appeal. And all expressions, such as the verdict of science, consensus opinion, human experience, are expressions which illustrate the universal paradox of appealing to standards which no man ever individually possesses and with which all individual opinions must agree. And upon such a reference to a super-individual standard depend the very ideas of truth and error; for truth and error can only mean agreement or disagreement with the "wider insight" of mankind which never belongs to any one individual.

This "wider insight" – of mankind, commonsense, science – must be universalized. To the synthetic insight of reason the universal paradox reveals the reality of a superhuman type of life which the religious need seeks. Royce's arguments for an Absolute are too well known to be summarized here. In this volume the arguments are not merely repeated, but sharply and lucidly restated.

The source of religious insight furnished by reason is not merely theoretical, but it has a vital relation to the Will. That the will and the reason have one logic in common; that the truth of an idea may be said to be constituted by its "workings," but that these workings must be conceived as "absolute workings" – all this is sufficiently familiar to the student of Royce's Voluntaristic Idealism or Absolute Pragmatism. Just as our ideas are true or false in so far as they agree or disagree with a "wider insight" of reality, just so our deeds have meaning only in so far as they are in conformity with the will of a larger life. And thus the will as well as the reason is a source of religious insight, for the meaning of any rational irrevocable deed implies an absolute view of reality.

How the individual can 'get religion,' so to speak, how the conclusions of a Voluntaristic Idealism may be practically applied in the life of every individual, Royce undertakes to show in the concluding chapters of the book. His philosophy of loyalty is here restated as the synthesis of all the sources of religious insight. The spirit of loyalty demands all the elements – individual experience, social coöperation, reasonable insight, voluntary choice – which the other sources have exemplified. Every individual who is loyal to his consciously chosen task is "loyal to loyalty" and has thus solved the religious paradox. "From the lonely and darkened depth of his personal finitude, from the chaos of his social promptings and of his worldly ambitious, amid all the storms of fortune, 'midst of hell's laughter and noises appalling,' he has heard the voice of the Spirit" (p. 210).

Loyalty, as the crowning source of religious insight, idealizes evil, for "there could not be loyalty in a world where the loyal being himself met no adversities that personally belonged to and entered his own inner life" (p. 253). Loyalty also define a kingdom of God, as it were, called by Royce the Invisible Church. All the loyal – whatever their cause, – constitute one genuine religious brotherhood. And thus the loyal co-workers in any field – in art, science, society – are, according to Royce, religious devotees and in communion with the Absolute Spirit; for they are loyal to super-individual causes whose meaning and rationality can only be understood in terms of one super-human Life.

Those who are repelled by Idealism on account of its alleged thin abstractions and remoteness from life should read this 'sun-clear' and 'life-intoxicated' book.

# A REPLY TO PROFESSOR ROYCE'S CRITIQUE OF INSTRUMENTALISM

John Dewey, "A Reply to Professor Royce's Critique of Instrumentalism," *Philosophical Review*, vol. 21 (1912).

The republication by Professor Royce of his important address at the International Congress of Philosophy at Heidelberg, upon the Problem of Truth,[1] will set many persons to reviewing the problem, and some, perhaps to considering it for the first time. Its criticisms of the instrumentalist position are so searching and its statements of that position so eminently fair – that is to say, intelligent – that, as one of those expounded and criticized, I should feel at once professionally stupid and personally unappreciative if I made no effort at response. I shall not attempt, however, to traverse the entire field but shall, in the main, confine myself to one point which Professor Royce has made peculiarly his own: The indispensableness to the instrumentalist theories of truth, even as working empirical theories, of a recognition of the social implications of ideas and beliefs. This indispensableness appears, to Professor Royce, fatal to the instrumental conception; to me it seems its essence.

In gist, Mr. Royce contends that if one admits the instrumental conception to be sound "as far as it goes," one is thereby bound go a good deal farther – all the way to absolutism. Or, in his own words: "Instrumentalism, consequently, expresses no motive which by itself alone is adequate to constitute any theory of truth. And yet, as I have pointed out, I doubt not that instrumentalism gives such a substantially true account of man's natural functions as a truth seeker. Only the sense in which instrumentalism is a true account of human life is opposed to the adequacy of its own definition of truth."[2] There is a sense in which – so Professor Royce repeatedly states – instrumentalism is (or better, "contains") a correct "report of the truth about our actual human life, and about the sense in which we all seek and test and strive for truth, precisely in so far as truth-seeking is indeed a part of our present organic activities."[3]

[1] *William James, and Other Essays*, Essay IV (New York, 1911).

[2] Ibid., p. 222.

[3] Ibid., p. 218.

It is obvious (is it not?) that when a criticism is made from the standpoint of the acceptance of a certain conception, and when the critical procedure tries to show that acceptance in logical good faith is quite incompatible with the version of the conception bruited abroad by those most actively engaged in circulating it, it is then obvious, I say, that everything depends upon *what* meaning is attributed to the conception that one accepts, upon *how* one conceives the conception that he announces himself as accepting. *If* the conception of instrumentalism that is 'accepted' is after all one's own conception rather than that of those who hold the definition of truth in question, what one has demonstrated at the end is that one's *own* conception of instrumentalism is logically compatible only with absolutism – a conclusion not entirely surprising at the hands of such an accomplished dialectian as Professor Royce.

My first task, accordingly, is a churlish one. I have to show that the logical success of Professor Royce consists in attributing to the instrumentalist certain ideas which are indeed Mr. Royce's own presuppositions, but which are quite foreign – in fact and in logic – to the instrumentalist's position. In short, Professor Royce has not, after all, adequately 'accepted' the instrumentalist account even as an empirical account of truth-seeking and truth-testing, for in accepting it he has read into it things so obvious, so self-evident to him that it has not occurred to him that the instrumentalist makes his way, for better or worse, precisely and only because he has rejected and eliminated them. I call this task churlish. And so it is. When one considers how often the pragmatist and instrumentalist have been refuted by denying to them any vestige of sense, to say nothing of truth, how often they have been refuted by attributing to them wilful perversity of facts evident to any sane apprehension, it would be a grateful task to acknowledge the sympathetic and just version – *in every point save one* only – of instrumentalism rendered by Professor Royce. But alas for one's natural piety; for present purposes it is just this one point that enters into the reckoning.

## I.

Let me quote at length a statement which an instrumentalist at once recognizes to be a sympathetic and just (if not complete) version of his own intention. "Human opinions, judgments, ideas, are part of the effort of a live creature to adapt himself to his natural world. Ideas and beliefs are, in a word, organic functions. And truth...is a certain value belonging to such ideas.[4] But this value itself is simply like the value

[4] The omitted words are, "in so far as we men can recognize truth at all." The phrase thrown into an exposition made professedly from the standpoint of the instrumentalist

which any natural organic function possesses. Ideas and opinions are instruments whose use lies in the fact that, if they are the right ones, they preserve life and render life stable. Their existence is due to the same natural causes that are represented in our whole organic evolution. Accordingly, assertions or ideas are true in proportion as they accomplish this biological and psychological function. This value of truth is itself a biological and psychological value. The true ideas are the ones which adapt us for life as human beings."[5]

Alas, for that little – or big – word 'psychological.' How great, indeed, are the oaks that little acorns start; what a cataract the little crack in the dam finally lets through – and like samples of proverbial philosophy! Surely the unprejudiced reader would infer from the above statement that, though the term psychological is undefined, the criterion for its definition lies in the conceptions of "life," of "organic functions," of "adaptation to [better *in*] a natural world." And the inference would correctly represent the point of view of the instrumentalist. But, as Professor Royce proceeds, "psychological" is employed to designate the merely private, the merely personal, and, at times, even the internal, transient "states of consciousness." Then the "psychological" swells and swells, till it swallows up the "live creature," the "natural world" and "biological functions." And if the instrumentalist wants them back (and he must get them back if he is to carry on his business) he must go to the Absolute to take out a license.

The instrumentalist "account of human organic and psychological functions may be – yes, is – as far as it goes true. But if it is true at all, then it is true as an account of the characters actually common to the experience of a vast number of men. It is true, if at all, as a report of the objective totality of facts which we call human experience. It is true, then, in a sense which no man can ever test by the empirical success of his own ideas as his means of controlling his own experiences... . If instrumentalism is true, it is true as a report of facts about the general course of history, of evolution, and of human experience – facts which transcend every individual man's experience, verification and successes."[6] The logic of this passage gives a narrow and exclusive sense to "individual man's experience," "his own ideas, his own experiences," a sense so narrow and exclusive as to throw between personal

is significant. Even Mr. Royce cannot wholly free himself from the notion that instrumentalism's account of truth is a statement of what truth is "for us" as distinct from some absolute truth or truth for itself. Of course, from its own standpoint, it is a statement about truth, about the sole intelligible meaning of the term truth.

[5] Ibid., pp. 193–94.

[6] Ibid., pp. 221–22.

experience and "objective human experience" or the historic experience of the race, a gulf so deep and wide that only the Absolute *ex machina* will bridge it and bring the objective human experience and the individual's experience together.

The contrast is explicit in such a passage as the following: "For no man experiences the success of any man but himself, or of any instruments but his own; and the truth, say, of Newton's theory consists, by hypothesis, in the perfectly objective fact that generations of men have really succeeded in guiding their experience by this theory. But that this is a fact no man, as an individual man, ever has experienced or will experience under human conditions."[7] Here we have the logic exposed. Men are individuals; therefore whatever is experienced is one's own individual experience; or, individuals experience only themselves, and their exclusive possessions, which are, in fact, parts of themselves. The ground I plow is my own ground; I plow it with my own instrument, my own plow; the harvest – the success – is my own. Therefore the ground was never anybody else's; it is impossible for me even to see from it any other person's land (unless I secure a transcendental telescope); it is impossible for my plow to plow other persons' land; and the harvest, being mine, must be mine only, and therefore unsharable by others.

To my mind there is just one interesting question about such a view as this of the "individual" and of "his own" – the historic question. What ever led intelligent human beings to such a conception of human individuality and of its acts and states? What led to the identification of the individual with the private, and of the private with the merely private, with the absolutely exclusive and isolated? We are not now concerned however with a question of fact, but with a question of logic. Only as he assumes that the instrumentalist does and must presuppose this monopolistic, all-swallowing octopus of an individual and "his own," does Professor Royce "accept" the instrumentalist account, and argue to its necessary implication of the Absolute. Speaking for myself, I may say that if I had any such nihilistic, anarchistically egoistic notion of the individual man, of his doings, states, tools and results, I should probably be willing to resort to an absolute to escape my "own" awful isolation and selfishness. For selfishness is agreeable only when it involves others. But even so, such atrophied logical sense as may be supposed to survive even in an instrumentalist would haunt me with a suspicion that this Absolute was but another of my purely personal belongings, the most precious of my private possessions in appearance, and, in fact, a huge joke that some peculiarly private part of my private being was working off on my more accessible private properties. For, to consider the matter

[7] Ibid., pp. 220–21. Yet Professor Royce, an individual man, knows this objective fact!

logically, it is passing strange that the private nature of my experience makes it impossible for me to be aware of such a prosaically limited matter as the existence of Sir Isaac Newton while it absolutely warrants the absolute truth of my belief in something which includes Sir Isaac Newton along with everything else past, present and future. Surely the proverb concerning straining at a gnat and swallowing a camel should be brought down to date.

But we are getting too far away from the instrumentalist's position as he himself "accepts" or conceives it. Let us try, with a more unbiased sympathy, to take that point of view from which "human opinions, judgments, ideas, *are part of the effort of a live creature to adapt himself to his natural world*," where beliefs are organic functions, and experiences are organic adaptations involving such functions; and where the issue – the success or failure – of these adaptations constitutes the *value* of the beliefs in question. Is there any conceivable way in which a person who had adopted (with however moderate an understanding of what he was about) such a position could still hold that the natural world was merely his own idea; that a live creature was just one of his own private entertainments or conceits, and that organic functions in their tools and results were confined to his own insides?

It is not necessary to enter into a definition of "psychological" upon the basis of the instrumental conception. But it must be conceived in accordance with the fundamental position of the live creature adapting itself to a natural world. And one of the most rudimentary traits of a live creature is its continuity with a racial organic life, just as that of an environment is its spatial diversity and its temporal perdurance. Without these features, adaptation and organic function are the most empty sort of term. Follow out the implications of *such* conceptions instead of the conception which Mr. Royce holds (and with great and fatal generosity lends to the instrumentalist) and the gulf between the objective human experience and the supposedly purely subjective individual experience disappears. Life individuates itself, and particular individuations appear and disappear. But the individuation is a trait of life; it is not the mystery of a private, isolated somewhat which destroys all the natural traits of life to replace them with its own quite opposite traits. We are not to interpret "life" in accord with some psychological preconception of the merely personal; we are to interpret the personal in accord with the functions of life.

A particular passage may serve to bring out the difference of conception. After stating what the truth of the Newtonian conception would consist in from the instrumental point of view, Professor Royce goes on to ask about the sense in which the statement of the historic episode of the formation and success of Newton's theory is itself true.

Unless the instrumentalist is quite stupid, he will, I take it, apply his own criterion. It is true by the same token; it enables predictions, it gives control, it facilitates intercourse, it clears the path of obscurities, it guides (instead of obstructing) new observations and reflections, it brings men together instead of dividing them – so far as it is acted upon and thus genuinely asserted. But this path seems to Professor Royce to be quite closed to the instrumentalist. "Newton is dead. As mortal man he succeeds no longer. His ideas, as psychological functions, died with him. His earthly experiences ceased when death shut his eyes. Wherein consists to-day, then, the historical truth that Newton ever existed at all, or that the countless other men whom his theories are said to have guided ever lived, or experienced, or succeeded?"

Such statements followed by such a question are well calculated to inspire one with a feeling of despair regarding the possibility of arriving at any philosophic understanding. Newton is dead; therefore how can I assert as truth that he ever lived? The obvious answer is so obvious and so easy that it cannot be relevant to what Mr. Royce has in mind: the answer, namely, that Newton cannot be dead unless he once lived, and that, organic life being what it is, if he lived in the seventeenth century, he is surely dead by this time. I cannot imagine any beliefs operating and succeeding as organic functions in the development of life unless such simple and ordinary beliefs as these are capable of working, and working with a reasonable degree of success. If the propositions were that Newton is dead, though he never lived; or that because he was living in the seventeenth century, he must be living now, I can see how the propositions would offer difficulties to a pragmatic theory; I confess I do not see how they could "work." Seriously, and not in levity, this seems to me the inevitable answer and the only answer that instrumental theory can make to the question just cited.

But equally I have no doubt this reply is quite irrelevant to what Professor Royce had in mind. And, accordingly, I shall have to make a guess as to what presuppositions underlie the question and address a reply also to them. There are a number of phrases in the discussion which lead me to infer that Professor Royce identifies truth with existence. Now if the truth about Sir Isaac Newton's existence is the same thing as that existence itself, it is quite sure that no possible present experience will yield truth. For the working in experience of a belief or conception for its control, guidance, clarification, for social intimacy and emancipation, will not operate to raise Sir Isaac Newton *in propia persona* from the grave; it will not in short constitute (or reconstitute) his *existence*. But instrumentalism never pretended to encroach on the idealistic privilege of creating natural existences by formulating truths about them. It is content with the humbler task of describing how men do as matter of fact recreate, transform, *some* natural existence by intellectual formulations about *some other* existence. (The successful transformation of some things by use of intellectual formulations about other things being what instrumentalism calls the truth of these formulations.)

I know of no *a priori* compulsion to formulate conceptions or beliefs regarding Sir Isaac Newton; it is a safe guess for instance, that many an Oriental potentate has gone to his grave about whom no belief will ever be entertained, just as the vast majority of natural happenings go by without being reflected upon. But when there is a specific need for thinking, and a specific hypothesis emerges in response to the need, it is needful that we should have some way of testing its value, of developing it to the point of being true or false. And acting upon the hypothesis to select and collate data, to predict, to guide new observations and reflections, to organize the seemingly discrepant and to illuminate the hitherto obscure is the way. The success of the hypothesis upon and along this way is its truth.

If, however, the death of Sir Isaac Newton, and the cessation of his experiences, carried with them the absolute interruption of organic life, of all experience, if his experience, in other words, operated in absolute discontinuity in matter and method from mine and mine from yours, I can well see that the instrumentalist would be put to it to frame any idea about Newton, to say nothing of verifying it. But the difficulty would not be confined to the instrumentalist. Even the absolutist would, in such a situation, be unhelped by the Absolute. And if instrumentalist and absolutist alike do make judgments about Newton and, within certain degrees of approximation, arrive at successful outcomes, it is because life, experience, has its own continuities and sociable relationships.

And this brings me to my second guess about the difficulty which Professor Royce feels his question to involve. He presupposes, again, the completely egoistic, exclusive nature of Newton's experience – his life, his acts – on one side, and of mine on the other. "His ideas, as psychological functions, died with him." But did they? And if they did, what are we going to do about it, even with the help of the conception of the Absolute? For so far as they "died with him," the problem is not that of some eventual verification of our ideas about his ideas, but of our having any idea about his ideas.

In short, we come again to our basic statements: one about the instrumentalist, the other about Professor Royce's position. (*a*) By calling Newton's idea, his theory, a *function*, instrumentalism means to emphasize precisely that it *was* a function – to insist upon the need of reinterpreting the adjective "psychological" from the standpoint of function – an organizing and organized act, public, objective, impersonal just as surely as private, individual, personal. Certain images, a certain emotional tone of inward landscape, may be said to have "died" when Newton died. But to say that his idea of gravitation, as a vital *function*, died with him is to traverse the facts. Newton acted through it, lived it out, so adequately, that it became an integral part of the activities of educated men and scientific inquirers throughout the civilized world. Since this transmissive operation is just one of the things that is included in the conception of "success" of a vital function, one is not accepting the standpoint of instrumentalism when one conceives the vital function as something which renders impossible this transmissive operation. That the idea was made true means precisely that as a *function* it did not die.

(*b*) As to the logic of Professor Royce's own conception. Professor Royce says of certain statements about Newton: "No doubt all these historical and socially significant statements of mine are indeed substantially true" (p. 219). Professor Royce would doubtless also hold that there is a countless multitude of doings and sufferings of Newton about which we cannot now make any intelligible statements. So far as the "substantially true statements" are concerned, does not Professor Royce (and everybody else) fall back upon the procedure of which instrumentalism is simply a generalized description? And as far as the other to us non-existent "truths"[8] are concerned, does the conception (or the Being) of the Absolute help us one bit? Upon the Absolutist theory, what explanation can account for this partiality on the part of the Absolute? Why has it rendered certain events so opaque and silent and others so transparent and communicative? Is there any explanation that does not take us back to the instrumentalist terms – terms of vital doing under conditions of natural and social need, adaptation and success? And so far as our belief in the existence of the Absolute is concerned, why should we adopt a different logical procedure from that which has brought us to believe certain things about Newton? If the continuities, the transmissive bearings of life, of experience, suffice in the case of Newton to enable certain intellectual formulations – reflections – to prosper while dooming others to defeat, why, if the Absolute exists, should we not, *a fortiori*, wait till conditions have made the conception of its existence one that works out under tests? And, lacking these instrumental tests, what right have we to assert the truth of what, by Mr. Royce's own hypothesis, is a purely private, personal idea?[9]

8 Not "truths," but events, on any except a preordained idealistic basis.

9 "Instrumentalism in so far correctly defines the nature which truth possesses in so far as we ever actually verify truth." Ibid., p. 224 (italics mine).

II.

As respects certain truths, some instrumentalists – Professor James particularly – have made much of the significance of vicarious social verification. In Mr. Royce's words: "Since we are social beings, and beings with countless and varied needs, we constantly define and accept as valid very numerous ideas and opinions whose truth we do not hope personally to verify... . If we personally do not verify a given idea, we can still accept it then upon its credit value. We can accept it precisely as paper, which cannot now be cashed, is accepted by one who regards that paper as, for a given purpose, or to a given extent equivalent to cash."[10] This procedure Professor Royce accepts as an actual procedure, while he holds that reliance upon it is inconsistent with the instrumental conception of truth, – that, consistently, instrumentalism must identify the act of giving credit with truth itself, that is to say, anything is true to which we find it expedient to give credence at a given moment. Mr. Royce disclaims being an intellectualist of the rationalistic type, but he employs the good old rationalistic device of rigid alternatives. Either the assertion which I accept on credit *is* already true (truth belongs to the assertion anyway) or else by its truth I mean simply that I give credit to it. The former alternative surrenders instrumentalism; the latter puts it in the position of making truths offhand, while you wait – the sanctioning of caprice, whim, etc.

For reasons which I hope will appear presently, I am particularly interested in the implications of the "credit" notion with respect to its content. Before dealing with this phase of the matter, it seems necessary, however, to devote space to the formal dilemma. Upon close inspection it will be found, I think, to resemble most cases of formal alternatives in philosophic discussion. Two extremes are set up as exhaustive, while as matter of fact multitudes of other alternatives glide freely through wide-open intervening meshes. What *should* it mean upon the instrumental theory to accept some view or idea as true upon social credit? Clearly that such an acceptance itself works. And if the environment, the medium of action, be social could any other method save that of accrediting the results of experience in others be expected to work? There is nothing so licentious about the matter as Professor Royce's abstract logic would make out; the acceptance upon credit is subject to precisely the same sort of tests – of working under conditions – as acceptance on the basis of more direct personal verifications. What is indicated is that the social medium of life is as continuous as we have seen life itself to be. One has verified in innumerable cases that under certain conditions one can trust to the experience and the reports of others; one has found

[10] Ibid., pp. 224–45.

out that the limits between one's own experience and that of another are quite arbitrary and elusive. Besides this general verificational background, there is the specific verification, through working, of *acceptance* of this particular belief upon the credit and authority of some particular group of persons. And besides, there is frequent verification through the experiences of others who have given credit to these assertions – a method which could be made to appear vicious by the logic of abstractionism, but which, in inductive logic, is independently cumulative and hence confirming. In short, one doesn't, as an instrumentalist, accept arbitrarily on credit; he accepts on probation, hypothetically, just as one accepts his own hypotheses when they first occur to him. As this acceptance is confirmed by his works, the acceptance becomes a genuine accrediting; it has received the kind of trying by experimental tests in life that the conditions permit. That this is the way in which sensible men proceed can be shown by an argument *ad hominem*, indicating that even an absolutist must *actually* so proceed. Let us admit with Professor Royce that to the assertion in question truth or falsity already inherently belongs. Now, being unable to verify the matter directly, what shall be my attitude? I cannot, by hypothesis (Professor Royce's own hypothesis), be sure whether it is true or false, although I am sure it is already either one or the other. According to Professor Royce the only recourse possible is to accept or reject, just arbitrarily, by whim, by what seems agreeable at the moment. In short, the dilemma is one which applies only to those who hold Mr. Royce's view, and for them it takes the form of a choice of the two alternatives: Complete scepticism as to what is the truth or falsity of most things in history and nature, or else the loosest go-as-you-please most wayward opinionatedness. Other people employ the cautious testing of the kind and amount of credit to be given to others' ideas and reports that is described in the instrumentalist account.

As I have already stated, I find my significant interest attaching to the conception of social credit, and to the implied analogy of belief with credit in business, for this suggests that my *personal* experience is itself social in origin, matter and outlook. In good business, it is intimated, there is some value behind the *credit*; namely, in the philosophic analogy, truth. In purely speculative business, on the contrary, there is nothing but credit behind the credit: the instrumental theory of truth in the philosophic analogy. Now that business, modern business, is done so largely on credit seems to me a significant fact, and one which is peculiarly important for the instrumental theory. For so far as modern business proceeds upon a credit basis, it does *not* rely upon equating credits to values pre-existing; modern manufacturing and commerce would go into wholesale bankruptcy were such its basis. It proceeds upon the basis of the *potentialities* of what already exists, upon the *future* operation of industry, good faith and consumption to realize these potentialities. Only in times of panic is there a falling back upon the past, upon the already existent store. And the immediate effect of the insistence upon backing *from behind* of already extant values is to restrict business. There must, indeed, be something behind – fields, woods, mines, human labor, human intercourse, mutual trust, desires, etc. But the credit is not measured by them – not by them just as back there, behind. It is measured by an anticipated future use of them. It is not a matter of their being there in a finished state; it is a matter of their expected consequences, when something is done to them and with them. Credit operates for the more effective and varied use of what is there; not to reduplicate it in some parallel series. And it is the outcome, the actual consequence, that confirms or condemns any particular giving of credit.

I have no wish to base conclusions or theories on a possible analogy. I do wish, however, to secure its full suggestive force. Credit exhibits a possible future outcome operating as present factor to guide and enrich the conditions whose possibilities it relies upon. So does intelligence. Both involve a risk, an uncertain speculative element; both involve, therefore, the need of check and test, of responsibility to the achievement of ends, the production of consequences. Both involve something "behind" them, prior existences; but neither of them is a reiteration or reinstatement of the prior; both are concerned with the potentialities of things, and take effect in endeavor to make potentialities real. And as credit is distinctly a social phenomenon, so is the accrediting which marks the life of thought. Social verification is not, taken by and large, a *pis aller*, in default of "personal" verification. It, and it alone, *is* verification; personal verification is but a step on this social road – an encouragement, an authorization to go ahead. Experience, life – just as is that phase of experience called business – *is* social, and it exhibits this sociability nowhere more than in the continuity, the interpenetration, the reciprocal reinforcement of meanings and beliefs. Instead of an Absolute being required to substantiate this social phase of the life of intelligence it is much more probable that the Absolute is a somewhat barren and dry isolation and hypostatizing of the everyday sociality of experience. The accrediting of others' experience is the fact that our personal experience is so much other and more than the narrow personal private matter upon whose "acceptance" Mr. Royce founds his dilemma.

If then, I were to try to gather together the significant strands of instrumentalism in opposition to Professor Royce's welcome of it as a convenient road to absolutism, I should say that as method for philosophy it indicated a more severe intellectual conscience; less free and easy use of the concept of Truth in general and more careful use of truths in particular to designate such conceptions and propositions as have emerged successfully from the test conditions that are practically appropriate. In substance, as distinct from form or method, I should say it meant recognition of intelligence as the way in which future possible consequences became effective in the present – the recognition of real time and real potentiality – and a recognition of the utterly false character of the prevailing notion of the sheer privacy, the egotistic isolation, of experience, of conscious life. The case is immensely understated when we restrict ourselves to the possibility of pragmatic verification of acceptance of beliefs on credit from others – adequate as is the noting of this possibility for the purpose of securing exemption from Professor Royce's dilemma. The fact is that the life, the experience (including the organic acts of ideas, opinions, judgments, etc.) of "individual man" is already saturated, thoroughly interpenetrated, with social inheritances and references. Education, language and other means of communication are infinitely more important categories of knowledge than any of those exploited by absolutists. And as soon as the methodological battle of instrumentalism is won – as it will be, not by instrumentalists, but by the constantly increasing influence of scientific method upon the imagination of the philosopher – the two services that will stand to the credit of instrumentalism will be calling attention first, to the connection of intelligence with a genuine future, and, second, to the social constitution of personal, even of private, experience, above all of any experience that has assumed the knowledge-form.

# REVIEW OF
# *THE PROBLEM OF CHRISTIANITY*

L.P. Jacks, Review of *The Problem of Christianity*, *Hibbert Journal*, vol. 12 (1913).

*The Problem of Christianity. Lectures delivered at the Lowell Institute in Boston and at Manchester College, Oxford.* – By Josiah Royce, D.Sc. (Oxon.), Professor of the History of Philosophy in Harvard University. 2 vols. New York: The Macmillan Company, 1913.

The title of this book – *The Problem of Christianity* – suggests its importance, but scarcely indicates its scope. The problem of Christianity is here so extended that it becomes co-terminous with the combined problems of logic, psychology, epistemology, ethic and metaphysic. It is in the form of a world-problem that the question is raised, and in the form of a world-view that the answer is offered. But if at times we lose sight of questions easily associated with the epithet "Christian," we are always brought back to them by the returning sweep of the author's thought. Every chapter is closely inter-related with its neighbours, and the whole book forms a compact and systematic presentation of a single thesis. I am inclined to think that the book might be summed up as a Christology, though I doubt if the author himself would fully approve of the description. For though he takes some pains to disavow Christology as the term is commonly understood, the very arguments which he uses for that purpose lead him to assert Christology of another type.

One of the most striking and challenging features of the book is the transference to the Holy Spirit in the Church of the functions usually assigned to Christ. We are accustomed to much confusion on this point in the writings of Christian theologians. But there is no doubt as to the meaning of Professor Royce. The active, guiding Power in the Christian Community is the Spirit; and it is only due to a historical accident that this Power has been otherwise distinguished as Christ. This central position, Professor Royce maintains, was assigned to the Spirit by St Paul. "I believe in the Holy Ghost; in the Holy Catholic Church." These are the essential articles of the Christian faith, and, in their deeper meaning, here interpreted as the "Doctrine of Loyalty," they are eternally true. Thus the famous proposal "to do something for the honour of the Holy Ghost" has been carried into effect by Professor Royce with a whole-hearted thoroughness which would have greatly disconcerted the original proposer. In much of this, his work appears to me to fall into line with the thinking of the late Father Tyrrell, though there is no evidence that any of his works have been read by our author. The difference between Tyrrell and Royce involves little more than questions of nomenclature. To these, however, the latter thinker does not attach much importance. "Loyalty to the Spirit of the Beloved Community" is for him the path of salvation for all souls, and it matters little by what names the roads are called so long as they all converge to the one goal. "The Beloved Community" interpreted, be it observed, as a true *Individual*, and the guarantee (if not the substance) of all that is *real*, is the one object of worship, love, service; the fountain of grace and healing; the Atoner and Redeemer: in a word – God. So long as this is recognised in thought and in deed the ultimates are secure, and all differences of opinion within the one great agreement are without peril to the soul.

The word "peril" prompts me to state, at this point, what I have found most welcome and most impressive in this book. It contains a note of solemn warning, addressed primarily, unless I am much mistaken, to Liberal theologians. Thoroughly Catholic in outlook and temperament as the author undoubtedly is, nothing could be further from his way than the indiscriminating optimism into which Liberalism has so often degenerated. To him, as to St Paul, the natural state of man is one of uttermost peril. The isolated individual is "lost." His moral burden is such that in his isolation he is utterly incapable of bearing it. Startling indeed is the paradox that society is continually training its members, not to automatic obedience, but to rebellion; imposing an ever-increasing burden on the individual, and at the same time quickening the spirit of revolt by developing his individual self-consciousness; until at last the cry breaks forth from him, "O wretched man that I am, who shall deliver me from this body of death?" The will of the isolated individual is a traitor, and precisely this knowledge of his treachery, brought to self-consciousness by the education he receives from society, gives birth to the tragic conflict of his soul and awakens within him the felt need of grace, of atonement, salvation. How is salvation possible? He cannot undo his deeds; nor can they be undone by another. He is in the Hell of the Irrevocable. But, thanks be to God, there is a way of escape. For the world is organised as a "Community of Interpretation," and through loyalty to this, through throwing in his lot with the Holy Catholic Church of all loyal souls, a means may be contrived whereby the world shall be better off than if the treacherous deed had not been done. "Quite apart from the judgment of any of the gods, and wholly in accordance with the true rational will of the one who has done the deed of betrayal, the guilt of a free act of betrayal is as enduring as time... . No repentance, no pardoning power can deprive us of the duty and – I repeat – the precious privilege of saying that of our deed." But, on the other hand, "no baseness or cruelty of treason so deep or so tragic shall enter our human world, but that loyal love shall be able, in due time, to oppose to just that deed of treason its fitting deed of atonement. The deed of atonement shall be so wise and so rich in its efficacy, that the spiritual world, after the atoning deed, shall be better, richer, more triumphant amid all its irrevocable tragedies, than it was before that traitor's deed was done."

Observe what is involved in these remarkable statements.

First, there is the implication that a merely individual salvation is impossible. Elsewhere, and continually, Professor Royce reiterates the principle that we are saved *together* if we are saved at all; our salvation being the joint work of a community, in which each of the members is active, in one spirit of loyalty (which is "Christ") to an end to be shared by all. There never was, and according to Royce never can be, a religion of salvation which expresses its aspiration in any other form than this, "*we* shall be caught up *together*." On a recent occasion I heard a number of revivalists in a back settlement of America singing a hymn of which the refrain is

> "When the roll is called up yonder
> I'll be there, I'll be there."

Such a hymn, sung by an isolated individual, would be impossible. Sung *together*, as they were singing it, its true meaning was "*we*'ll be there." So far these revivalists – I believe they are called "the Holy Rollers" – were illustrating the Roycean doctrine of Loyalty.

Secondly, the atoning process has its origin in the very constitution of the universe. "The history of the universe, the whole order of time, is the history, and the order, and the expression of the Universal Community." In the deepest sense the world is the Church, the members whereof are selves, engaged in an endless task of mutual interpretation. Such interpretations are not by word only, but by deed. Here, then, hidden within the very substance of reality, is an endless store of possibilities whereby guilt can be re-interpreted and a means found whereby the world will be made richer than it would have been had the guilty deed never been done. This is Atonement. Its significance is cosmic; its work is everlasting; its necessity is rooted in the laws of being. And its benefits are all for the loyal soul.

From all this the reader will be prepared to find in Professor Royce's work the fullest recognition given to the social aspect of religion. And not of religion alone. "The universe...is a realm which is through and through dominated by social categories. Time, for instance, expresses a system of essentially social relations. The present interprets the past to the future. At each moment of time the results of the whole world's history up to that moment are, so to speak, summed up and passed over to the future for its new deeds of creation and interpretation." The same holds of logic – its functions are determined by social categories; of the theory of knowledge – things are what we perceive them to be in virtue of social interpretation; of self-consciousness – I *am* the interpretation of my past to my future; my being as an individual is a triadic group of a being interpreted, a being interpreting, and a being to whom the interpretation is addressed. Our inner life is "a conscious interior conversation wherein we interpret ourselves." All thinking is social – the work of a community. In thinking I *address* a thinker and I address him on the basis of thoughts which have been addressed to me. Philosophy, too, is thus a conversation of a community of minds. Wherever one turns, therefore, among the many realms that are put under contribution for Professor Royce's great thesis, we find, dimly or clearly outlined, the foundations of the Holy Catholic Church, the ground plan of the City of God. Even when a purely technical question of logic is under discussion, he remains true to the great articles of his faith, "I believe in the Holy Ghost; in the Holy Catholic Church."

Such a work cannot fail to touch the thought of the age at many vital points. It marks a great advance on traditional Hegelianism in that it gives a human or rather a social version of what has long been degenerating into a mere logical formula – "thesis, antithesis, higher synthesis." Those who have parted with Hegelianism will have to consider whether the objections they take to its dry verbalism hold good as against this living and human exposition of its principles. I do not suppose that Professor Royce will satisfy them. For, notwithstanding all the new life he has put into the old bones, he still bears many traces of the hole of the pit from which he was digged. Some of these remainders I have myself found difficult to harmonise with the new message.

Much will depend on our ability to fully understand and accept what Professor Royce advances as to the function he calls "interpretation," for this is the central term of his thesis. It is at this point that I feel least certain of having grasped the full meaning of Professor Royce's thought. If he means what I take him to mean, then it would seem to me that he has propounded one more theory of knowledge which is made to do duty for the knowing process itself, and he would lie open to the criticisms which Bergson and others have brought against this form of "intellectualist" fallacy. It is unlikely, on the face of it, that so cautious and fully equipped a thinker would lay himself open to this criticism. Subtle as this kind of fallacy is, Professor Royce is far too old a hand in these matters to fall readily into the trap. None the less, I will venture to state where the difficulty lies, for I have reason to know that others besides myself do not feel quite sure of their ground in following Professor Royce at this point.

It is easy to agree with Professor Royce that the cognitive process is not exhausted by the dual classification of perception and conception. Such a classification appears to be exhaustive only when mental facts are taken one by one. When they are viewed together, in their contrasts, conflicts, and contrary "leadings," its insufficiency is plain. It does not cover what takes place in a process of comparison; it has nothing to say which throws any light on the reconciliation of discrepant or antagonistic ideas. It does not explain a single scientific discovery. To cover this vacant ground Professor Royce introduces the term "interpretation." Interpretation takes place whenever two conflicting ideas are mediated by a third, so that we "look down as from above" upon the two in unity, and behold their conflict at an end. This third idea is elsewhere described as interpreting one member of the conflicting or contrasted pair to the other; as happens when, by introducing the idea of the sonnet, we are able to express something of Shakespeare's genius in terms of Dante's, thereby comparing the two as poets. The form of interpretation is therefore triadic; there is (1) an idea to be interpreted, (2) another idea to which the interpretation is addressed, (3) and the mediating idea which effects the exchange of the one idea into terms of the other – the interpreter. Science is an endless series of such interpretations, and science, on that account, truly knows the real. The triadic form is not, however, peculiar to knowledge; it characterises the structure of reality. The world is real, and each object in the world is real just so far as, and just because, it manifests the triadic process of interpretation.

Now I can accept all this without serious demur when it is offered as an *ex post facto* description of what *has taken* place when, say, a given scientific discovery has been accomplished. Any attempt to describe that discovery in terms of perception and conception, or the "cashing" of the one into the other, leaves out of account what is most striking in the result of the process, and I can find no objection to the term "interpretation" as supplying what this defective analysis lacks. But if, on the other hand, I am asked to take this account as an adequate rendering from the inside, of what *is taking* place while the mind of the would-be discoverer is engaged in his search, then it seems to me that the essential thing is left out. Professor Royce, unless I misread him, does not observe the distinction between the discovering and the discovery; he does not discriminate between the mind as already possessed of the mediating idea, and the mind while still on the look-out for it. Here are two ideas, A and B, which have to be interpreted one to the other; and C is the mediating idea which will do what is required. I am already in possession of A and B and stand puzzled at their contrast or conflict. I am on the look-out for C. *How do I find it?* A crowd of ideas are offering themselves, in succession or together, as mediators. How from among this throng of candidates do I manage to pick out C as the one which will do the business? By what principle do I reject D, E, F? What are the marks of a genuine mediation? That it mediates? Professor Royce is surely anticipating when he puts "interpretation" into the cognitive *process* itself. Interpretation is what the process lacks, not what it possesses; and it is precisely as still lacking the interpretation sought, and as still *looking* for it, that knowing, as distinct from knowledge, is a cognitive *function* at all. The particular *functioning* in question is all over when the mediating idea appears. We are told that interpretation is the stimulus and inspiration of knowledge. So in a sense it undoubtedly is. But what is it that inspires the knower while the interpretation is still to seek? These questions may suggest why it seems to me that knowing, as a process in being, escapes the analysis of Professor Royce no less completely than it escapes the analysis of those whom he justly criticises for reducing it to perception and conception. He has made a finer net than they; but no net however fine will catch the living waters.

But the task of criticism is repellent. For one statement that I feel tempted to criticise there are a hundred which I am compelled to admire. Seldom have I read a book of modern philosophy so profoundly suggestive, so stimulating, so kindled with fine ethical fire. What matters is that here and there one's private notions get a jostle, if all the time he walks in company with a thinker whose thoughts are stirring the solemn deeps of life? Professor Royce is such a thinker. Whatever he touches he illuminates; his finger-tips are organs of light. All things lovely and of good report are the stronger for his book. Its message of " Loyalty" is needed; it is the answering challenge of a noble mind to all that is most menacing in the disorders of the present age.

# PROFESSOR ROYCE AND THE PROBLEM OF CHRISTIANITY

Rev. John T. Driscoll, "Professor Royce on the Problem of Christianity," *North American Review* (1913).

In a recent work, *The Problem of Christianity*, Professor Royce makes an attempt to set forth a philosophy of Christianity which is based upon human experience and is in essential harmony with the teaching of philosophical idealism developed in his Gifford Lectures, *The World and the Individual*. In the Preface he states that these views have been gradually maturing since 1908, when he published *The Philosophy of Loyalty* and find expression in the Bross Lectures of 1912 on *The Sources of Religious Thought*. A review of his philosophical idealism expounded in *The World and the Individual* is contained in a former treatise on "Christian Philosophy." My purpose now is to criticize his attempt to apply this idealism to the Problem of Christianity wherein he discusses the Christian Doctrine of Life with the avowed purpose of setting forth the Essence of the Christian Religion.

## The Problem of Christianity

To Professor Royce the Problem of Christianity arises from the relation of Christianity to the mind of today. The question he proposes to discuss is "in what way, if in any, can the modern man consistently be, in creed, a Christian?" The two terms of the comparison are clearly stated – viz., Christianity and the modern man. The means of the comparison are twofold: to state in empirical terms certain aspects of Christian Social experience and to defend these aspects in the light of a re-examination of certain fundamental metaphysical ideas. Thus three terms enter into the discussion: the modern man, a metaphysical theory, Christianity.

To Professor Royce the modern man is a postulate and is "one who is supposed to teach what the education of the human race has taught him." "This postulate," he continues, "includes a doctrine that the human race, taken as a whole, has some genuine and significant spiritual unity, so that its life includes a growth in genuine insight," and adds that this doctrine contains "the implication that in light of common insight gradually attained by the whole race, our creed should be tested and, if needs be, revised." The inference drawn from these words is that the teaching of the modern man is true. Yet in fact we inherit the follies as well as the wisdom of the ages. What criterion is here presented to guide me between the truth and error of the past? Or to guide Professor Royce in disagreeing with traditional Christianity? Why should it be taken for granted that a discussion of the Problem of Christianity means the revision of Christianity up to the mental state of the modern man? Does not a suspicion enter the mind that the modern man might be revised up to the teaching of Christianity? The term, modern man, therefore is a fiction. Or it may be a modest way by which Professor Royce designates himself. Yet we are told that the test of a scientific discovery is the consensus of opinion, and that philosophers of today "do not agree regarding any one philosophical opinion." Even Professor Royce explains that these volumes are the exclusive result of his own study, that they contain a new interpretation of Christianity, and is at pains to point out how he differs from Hegel, James, Bergson, Professors MacIntosh and Sanday. May not the claim be made that they have inherited the wisdom of the ages? In truth, Professor Royce's doctrine is based on a postulate or assumption which can be maintained only by one who accepts his system of philosophical idealism.

Professor Royce admits that he faces the study of Christianity from the view-point of metaphysical idealism and that he applies the spirit of this idealism to the problems arising from the study. In this idealism are found no terms as "soul" or "mind." He admits "the self" or person and holds that it is constituted by conscious memory. The active element in the self is the "idea," which is a "volitional process" and is defined as "a plan of action." The ordinary Pragmatist – *i.e.*, Professor James – is concerned with the direct and immediate effect of the "idea-striving." Professor Royce regards the ultimate purpose or "goal" of the idea and terms himself an "absolute Pragmatist."

Professor Royce denies immediate perception of the self or other selves. He deprecates the controversy about "precept" and "concept," calls these "sterile," and bases his whole system on a new and integrating cognitive process which he calls interpretation – that is, the mediating between two ideas or processes by means of a third. Only by interpretation do we know the self, for self is not "a datum," but a life or process containing three elements: past, present, and future. Interpretation sums up past experience into present experience, sets for us our future task, and thus brings us into touch with the real world. The Real World is therefore the interpretation of our present experience, namely, Appearance, and the idea of the goal of experience, namely, Reality. By interpretation only do we know other selves and things. For they are only "appearances" of reality, "embodiments" of the idea, "signs" with a meaning. The reality, the idea, the meaning are attained by interpretation, and our interpretations are "signs" to be further interpreted. Thus experience shows that our life is a realm of signs and is made up of interpretations of signs. Metaphysics generalizes this doctrine and applies it to the world at large. Hence the world is a process of interpretation not in its wholeness at any one moment, but through an infinite series of acts whereby the present progressively interprets the past to the future, thus constituting the temporal order. Thus the universe is one vast cosmic process of humanity moving on to its goal where is attained an all-embracing unity of consciousness. "The absolute, the sole and supreme Reality," is the entire process which is essentially social as made up of many individual selves. The aim and result of the process is the Absolute Self, which Professor Royce calls "the ideal community (common self) of all mankind."

Between the individual self on its way to the goal are various "spiritual communities," that is, common or social selves, through which man has closest relations to the immeasurably vast cosmic process, which is conceived as a process of coherent social evolution. Unity of consciousness constitutes the individual self. In like manner a unity of consciousness – a common consciousness among many individuals – constitutes a community, namely, a common self. This unity of consciousness is based upon a common memory and a common ideal or hope among many individuals. As a social being, man lives in communities. The community has a sort of organic unity, a mind of its own, and behaves like a conscious unit or a "suprasensible being." The notion of the community suggests to Professor Royce a solution of the philosophical problem of the Many and the One, and also gives occasion to unfold his fundamental religious doctrine of the Two Levels, that is, man the individual and man the community.

Assuming the principle that religion is the product of certain human needs, Professor Royce seeks the origin and teaching of Christianity in Christian experience, not in the individual religious experience of Professor James, but in "that form of social religious experience which, in ideal, the Apostle Paul viewed as the experience of the Church." For religion is essentially social, in Professor Royce's view, because of man's essential relation to the social evolutive process of the cosmos. He holds that the human individual Jesus is not the founder of Christianity and denies that the problem of Christianity can be solved by views respecting the person of Jesus. For Christianity preaches salvation and salvation cannot come from an individual, but only from loyalty to a community of ideal purpose. Besides, historical evidence as to Christ's teaching is insufficient. "Humanly speaking," Jesus gave "the impetus" to the movement in preaching the Kingdom of Heaven, and humanly speaking this can be explained by "genius." Hence the modern man can be a Christian without holding any definite views about the person of Christ. Nor can the Apostle Paul be considered the founder, for what he taught he learned from the religious experience of the Christian Church. Professor Royce holds that the Christian community was the human founder of Christianity, but has no hypothesis about the origin of the community through lack of historical evidence. Yet he maintains that we have "priceless information about the essence of Christianity of the Pauline Churches and their actual life." The interpretation of the social religious experience of these churches reveals three ideas most characteristic of primitive Christianity – viz., the Community, the Lost State of the natural man, Atonement and Grace. The discussion of these ideas are Professor Royce's contribution to the Problem of Christianity on the basis of a Social Study of Christian Origins.

### The Christian Doctrine of Life

Professor Royce holds that the problem of Christianity is the Christian Doctrine of Life. He says that this can be considered in a twofold light; as the product of human evolution and the outcome of a long history, and as the product of the social experience of the Pauline Churches. In the former view it is "the problem of humanity"; in the latter "it has features distinctively Christian." Therefore, he maintains that the doctrine should be analyzed in its relation to the whole lesson of human history and in the light of a philosophical study of this history, in order to know what Christianity is and means in the religious history of the race.

The Christian Doctrine of Life is constituted by the Three Ideas. Professor Royce teaches that these ideas have "a basis in human nature," are "the expressions of universal human needs, independent of Christianity," are "the verifiable results of the higher social religious experience of mankind," "can be estimated and put into practice without presupposing any one view of God or of revelation," and are "religious, for they relate to the salvation of mankind." This aspect is their "human and empirical aspect," for they furnish "a purely human philosophy of loyalty" and yet "are based upon metaphysical truths whose significance is more than human" (Lect. VIII).

To Professor Royce the natural condition of man is a state of social chaos. Man is an animal living in communities. These communities exist in human history in countless different forms and grades "of which the visible and historical Church is one instance." From the communities he derives religion, language, civilization, and all his natural powers. Constant tension and conflicts exist between self, his fellows, and the social will, which produce consciousness of self; that is, conscience. The standard of the social will, namely, the *law* of St. Paul, is an attempt to bring about social harmony, but in reality creates new and more complex tensions by the application of social discipline. Through this social training our self-will is developed and ideals arise. The more cultivated the training, the stronger grows the self-will. The evil increases and the burden grows heavier. The individual may obey (conduct), but he inwardly revolts (consciousness of conduct). As culture advances, the revolt (distraction of will) increases; for high social cultivation trains Individualism. Thus the individual is by nature subject to an overwhelming moral burden which springs from the *original sin* of social contentiousness, and is increased by social training and by personal guilt. His natural condition is one of sin, for the sinfulness belongs to the race in its corporate capacity and the social order breeds conscious sinners. No act of his can save him. Escape is not from this type of cultivation – that is, the *law*. Help (salvation, which is winning the true goal of life) must come from a source above his level – that is, the *spirit*, which rescues him and lifts him from his fallen state.

The higher source, whence salvation comes, is, according to Professor Royce, the Community. For communities tend to be organized into more composite communities of still higher grade, of vaster conscious unity. Through the community the individual is most closely related to the world process, shares its spirit and lives its life, a life of ever-increasing conscious unity. Apart from the spirit and life of the community, the individual is viewed as "morally detached" and in "a lost state." Hence we read that the doctrine of the Community is "a doctrine about the being nature, and manifestation of God."

Here is unfolded Professor Royce's doctrine about the two levels of human existence: man, the individual, on the level of *the flesh* and *the law*, and man, the community, on the level of the *spirit*. He holds that they are levels of mental human beings and differ as two grades of human life. The individual regards the community as higher, nobler, more powerful, more enduring than himself, and shows this practical faith by devoted loyalty to its interests. He no longer loves according to the *flesh* – that is, as a mere individual loves a mere individual – but according to the *spirit*, and this love is loyalty. To him loyalty becomes the solution of the problem of personal life. The loyal "are, in ideal, essentially kin," in them all is "a spirit essentially one," and as loyalty begets loyalty, the logical development of the loyal spirit is "the rise of the consciousness of the ideal of a universal community of the loyal." Hence the higher of the two levels is essentially, endlessly, and divinely above the individual level, and to act as a member of such a community is to win what religion calls salvation. This loyalty, namely, thoroughgoing devotion to a cause which unites many selves in one, appeals to the individual by fixing attention on a life incomparably vaster than his own, and belongs to no one time, country, or people. Hence experience shows that salvation for man lies in the purely human philosophy of loyalty and loyalty is a religion, for it creates a new type of consciousness – love for the Community – and thus effects a spiritual transformation in the individual.

The "Lost State" includes not only the "morally detached" individual – that is, one who has not found his ideal community, but also the individual who, having found it, has lost it by proving false to the ideal – a traitor. Is there any reconciliation between him and his community, his moral world? Not on the part of the traitor; his deed cannot be undone and by it he belongs to the "Hell of the Irrevocable." But atonement can be given the community through heroic deeds performed on his behalf by some faithful servant in whom the very spirit of the community is incarnated. Treason's lost causes have proved to be opportunities for humanity's most triumphant loyalty. It is a human triumph of the creative spirit of humanity that could not undo the treason, but, through skill and ingenuity, effected the heroic act which transformed the meaning of the treason and made the world better by a transfiguration of loss into gain. In illustration, Professor Royce cites the story of Joseph and his brethren, where Joseph is the symbol for the spirit of the family and the result of the atoning act is a more perfect family unity. Through atonement the traitor enters into a saving union with the community, for his act of treason, now transfigured, is part of the community life. Hence atonement is the function in which the life of the community culminates. It teaches that in due time loyal love will oppose its atoning deeds to treason's sin. Professor Royce holds that Christianity expressed this teaching in the symbolic form of a report concerning the supernatural work of Christ, and humanity must express it through the devotion, genius, skill, labor of its loyal servants in whom its spirit is incarnated. The teaching and the symbol, he adds, "are two sides of the same life – at once human and divine."

The doctrine of the two levels arising from the study of human experience is, according to Professor Royce, the doctrine out of which the whole of Christianity grows. For Christianity, he tells us, was founded on the idea of a Community, whose spirit or life was the spirit or life of its risen Lord, held as a present possession by an ideal common memory of a past event, "the rising of Jesus to the realm of the spirit," and by an ideal common hope of a future event, when, according to the Apostle, "we should rise with him" to the spirit, with love enlivening and completing both memory and hope. This belief, he says, grew out of the Master's teaching about the Kingdom of Heaven. Professor Royce holds that, historically speaking, Christianity never appeared as the religion taught by the Master, but as an interpretation of his teaching, going beyond it, and this was due to the presence of the founder's spirit. The enlargement of doctrine is shown especially, he says, in the fact that the Master, like other religious leaders in the world's history, emphasized God and our neighbor only. Whereas the Apostle Paul introduced a third being, a corporate Entity, "the Body of Christ," which he claims to be "a new revelation" discovered in his experience of an Apostle as the product of the life of the Christian Community itself and due to "the spirit of his Lord." To Paul the Church was "the very presence of his Lord," at once "a fact of present experience and a divine creation," hence "a mystery," "whose origin was wholly miraculous." Professor Royce holds that this belief "constitutes a new beginning in the evolution of Christianity. The Master had laid stress on the value of individual life, but St. Paul, as also Professor Royce, holds individuality to be the source of all our sin and woe. Only by ceasing to be a mere individual, through love for the Body of Christ, can one be saved. Thus the neighbor is transfigured as a member of the Beloved Community. We love him not as an individual – this the Master taught, but as a member of this Divine Community which, in ideal, is one conscious unity of all mankind. The spirit of the "risen Lord," which is the life of the Body, through love becomes our own. Hence love is loyalty and loyalty is Christian faith and Christian faith is grace and grace is the mystery of the incarnation in another form. Thus salvation comes through loyalty, for loyalty involves "an essentially new type of consciousness" – that is, "the consciousness of one who loves the community as a person."

Professor Royce holds that the Master's teaching concerning the Kingdom of Heaven, which the Apostle presented in a new revelation as the Body of Christ, "developed into the conception which the historic Church formed of its own mission," but says that the true Church is "one endlessly and conscious human spirit, whose life is to be lived on its own level"; hence invisible and still to be created by a process of evolution.

Therefore, according to Professor Royce, an examination into the Christian Doctrine of Life shows (1) how the Spirit, the Community, the process of Salvation, are genuine realities transcending any of their human embodiments; (2) that Christianity is the most effective expression of religious loyalty which the human race has, in its corporate capacity, expressed; (3) that the rock upon which the true and ideal church is built is the doctrine that the Community, wherein dwells the divine redeeming spirit, is, through loyalty, the source of salvation.

## The Essence of Christianity

The aim and result of the work under discussion is to point out what is vital in Christianity, so that the modern man may know what to hold and be a Christian. Professor Royce gives the solution of the problem by way of an illustration. Let us suppose the case of a young, highly educated, Greek Philosopher who became a convert of the Pauline Church and, after living the life of an earnest Christian, at length dies. He comes to life in due time, is carefully instructed in our art, history, philosophy, and then is brought face to face with Christianity as it now exists. How, asks the Professor, can he, astonished and saddened at the essential changes which have taken place, retain his Christian faith? And answers:

> The one thing he must hold fast is the Pauline Doctrine of the presence of the redeeming divine spirit in the living church. This is the essence of Christianity in the Pauline Churches and in all the subsequent ages of Christian development. Thus he will keep in touch with historical Christianity – His church will neither be the official church nor the sect – His test of the church will be simply this, that it actually unifies all mankind and makes them one in the divine spirit. All else in Paul's teaching he may come to regard as symbol or as legend. This is the essence of the faith of the Apostles.

This solution sounds strange coming from such a source. Professor Royce's volumes are a treatise in religious Social Psychology. A fundamental principle of this Psychology is "that religion springs from our conscious needs" and he expressly states that "the religious needs of the modern man are different from any ever before experienced and still greater changes will come in the near future" (I. 387). Why not then give the redivivus young Greek a course in religious Social Psychology and prepare him not only to accept a changed Christianity, but to *look with suspicion* upon a Christianity that has not changed? Again Professor Royce teaches that the "person" or "self" is not "a datum," but a "life" or "a process" and implies the description to the individual self, the social self, and the absolute self, of which the world-process is the expression. The social or common self – that is, the Community – is the basic idea in this treatise and has a marvelous richness of possible expansion without any limitation or interruption so far as the nature of the common self is concerned. Now both experience and science tell that growth or development is a law of life. On this doctrine of the self, I ask why does Professor Royce think that his young friend should be surprised or that he should regard the Pauline community as "a datum" or a fixture and not as "a life" or "a process"? In the emergency the simple and consistent course for the author is, not to forget his own philosophy, but to give a clear exposition of his theory of knowledge and of metaphysical idealism to his perplexed friend. Moreover, Professor Royce holds that interpretation is the ruling category of mental life and of the world-process, and that it is of the nature of interpretation to create something new. Hence our mental life, our code of morality, everything about us, change at each succeeding moment, as also does the conscious time-stream change. He applies this principle to the Pauline community and says that this being, the Body of Christ, first discovered the three ideas constituting the Christian Doctrine of Life in the effort to interpret the Master's teaching, that these ideas were a "new revelation" and "a new beginning in the evolution of Christianity," and that, furthermore the dogmas of the Trinity and of the Incarnation were only symbols whereby the Pauline consciousness attempted to set forth the relation between the Absolute, the Spirit of the Pauline community, and the human founder Jesus. Now the young man should be aware of this. The reader will be forced to conclude that the Greek was totally ignorant both of Professor Royce's philosophy and of the evolutive life of the Pauline Churches as he has described this life.

In presenting a symbolic interpretation of Christianity, Professor Royce is influenced by his theory of knowledge, which exhibits the "idea" as a conscious ideal-striving and by his metaphysical idealism which considers the universe as an ideal evolution of one endlessly creative and conscious human spirit. This evolutive spirit he calls the Universal or the Beloved Community, namely, the whole common consciousness of mankind. This is the one reality; all else are figures or symbols – partial embodiments of the reality. Hence God is a symbol for the community as a whole. The historical Church is a partial embodiment and the ideal Church is another name for the community. The ideas making up the Christian Doctrine of Life, the parables of Jesus, the dogmas of the Church are symbols of the evolution process in whole or in part. The human individual Jesus is the incarnation of the Spirit or life of humanity, just as the Christian Church is the incarnation of the Spirit of Jesus, and as we ourselves are the incarnations of humanity's spirit or life, when, through loyalty, we become one with this life or, through heroic deeds, we atone for humanity's wrongs. Hence Professor Royce questions the historical truth of the Gospels and holds that the life of Jesus was "the object of many legendary reports so framed that they include a symbolism whereby a portion of the *true faith* is expressed."

This explanation is not new. He proposes for our acceptance the mythical theory of Strauss written not as a historian nor as a theologian, but as a disciple of Hegel's Idealism. Strauss viewed the Hegelian process in its subjective aspect, sought the basic truths of Christianity in the early Christian consciousness, regarded Christ of the New Testament as the outcome of this consciousness, and held that legendary reports and embellishments were merely symbols for spiritual ideas. But the theory was too fanciful, could not withstand the comparison of the truthful matter-of-fact character of the New Testament writings with the Apocrypha and was rejected by scholars. In *Old and New Faith* 1870 Strauss confessed to disappointment at the outcome of his labors.

Professor Royce writes that he has "approached this study not as a historian, nor as a theologian, but as a philosopher." Therefore the criticism regards him as a philosopher only.

To him the Community is the fundamental notion in the religious history of the race and in Christianity. The community is the *common* self and, he says, is constituted by a common consciousness. Thus the definition of the community is based upon the definition of the Self. He holds that the Self is constituted by conscious memory. Hence the individual is a self because he possesses a present unity of conscious memory ideally extended to the future. But the teaching that consciousness constitutes the Self is an error in philosophy coming down from Locke and Kant. Conscious memory *makes me aware of* my personal identity and *presupposes* it. Memory or loss of memory does not change *me* or what *I* did. Forgetfulness, aphasia, dementia, delirium, sleep, do not change the person or self, but produce different *states* of the same Self. Hence a distinction should be made between *Self* and the *states* of the Self. Hence the notion of Professor Royce's Community is radically erroneous.

Again, in describing the natural state of man, he adopts the teaching of Hobbes and Spencer. But in fact this teaching is only a *philosophical theory* and *not proved*. Rousseau and his followers hold the peaceful state of the natural man. This opinion is a *philosophical theory* also, and *not proved*. Therefore upon a philosophical theory not proved and not universally accepted by anthropologists he bases his doctrine of the origin of the community. What becomes of his criterion that the consensus of opinion is necessary for a scientific hypothesis?

From the notion of the Community springs Professor Royce's doctrine of the Two Levels, which he claims to be the fundamental principle in religious history and in Christianity. Now in fact the careful reader distinguishes *three* levels – viz., the individual, the community actually existing, and the ideal community, namely, of ideal purpose, He draws on some current Sociological Psychology to show that actual communities have a mental and ethical unity of their own which makes them appear to the individual as "Suprapersonal beings." He leaves the reader to imply that all this applies to *ideal* communities. But this implication is not at all clear. True, actual communities may not be made up of soul-mates or affinities, but they have a moral unity, or, to use the author's thought, a unity constituted by the spirit. Why then could not the individual find "his fulfilment and moral destiny" in devoted loyalty to actual communities? Furthermore, this current Sociological Psychology is based on the definition of the Self, which was shown to be erroneous, and regards man as an animal progressively evolving a human nature – another philosophical theory not by any means proved.

The fundamental error of Professor Royce is his teaching concerning the nature of man and of mental life. In denying immediate perception he falls into phenomenal idealism which develops into a metaphysical idealism where *idea, spirit, humanity* are regarded as the only realities. But as a matter of fact these are only *Personifications*. He does not seem to be aware that notion, judgment, and reasoning are fundamental elements in our mental life. Finally he defines the "idea" in terms of will. But this is contrary to the testimony of consciousness. That intellect and will are different is an elemental fact of conscious experience. The intellect is the cognitive mode or form of our conscious life; whereas the will is the source of motive power. A psychologist would be no more justified in combining intellect and will than would be a physiologist in blending the afferent and efferent nerves in one act. Moreover, these faculties are unequal in the individual. Intellect and will are called modes in which our soul-life is manifested. Hence, though distinct from each other, they are not separated in the sense that they are two entities, but unite in a unity by virtue of the spiritual principle – viz., the soul, whose modes of activity they are.

This is the aim of the present article: to point out that the most noteworthy publication of the year on the Philosophy of Religion, carefully constructed and written in beautiful language with a wealth of illustration, is, in the last analysis, based upon an erroneous definition of the "idea" – the most fundamental and apparently the simplest element in mental life.

# REVIEW OF
# *THE PROBLEM OF CHRISTIANITY*

William Ernest Hocking, Review of *The Problem of Christianity*, *Harvard Theological Review*, vol. 7 (1914).

*The Problem of Christianity*. By Josiah Royce. 2 vols. The Macmillan Company. 1913. Vol. I: The Christian Doctrine of Life, pp. xlvi, 426; Vol. II: The Real World and the Christian Ideas, pp. vi, 442.

Lectures on the Hibbert Foundation, read at Manchester College, Oxford, January to March, 1913. The first series was previously delivered before the Lowell Institute, Boston.

The encounter of the powerful current of Royce's thought with the Christian tradition is an event of the first importance. It was inevitable, in the steady growth of views first announced in *The Philosophy of Loyalty* in 1908, that Royce should come to terms with Christianity simply as the most conspicuous germane fact in contemporary life. It was characteristic of him that he should meet this fact honorably and objectively, "not as the one true faith to be taught, and not as an outworn tradition to be treated with enlightened indifference, but as a central, as an intensely interesting, life-problem of humanity." It could have been foreseen that Christian thought would receive at his hands a radical sifting and restatement – a restatement for which we were partly prepared by the address, "What is vital in Christianity?" printed in this journal in October, 1909. But there is here a freshness of treatment, a vigor and clarity, an accurate sympathy, and a breadth of interpretative power, which has outrun anticipation. Whether or not we agree that Christianity is best conceived as "the religion of loyalty," of loyalty to a "beloved community" which is the invisible Church, Christianity must henceforth mean something greater to all interpreters; and what is more, it must mean something nearer, more vital, and more acceptable to the modern man, "for the strengthening of whose heart" this book, in large measure, was written.

The appeal of the work to the modern mind will be due in part to the angle from which Royce approaches his subject; namely, from experience rather than from metaphysics, and from universal human experience rather than from the peculiar experiences of individuals here and there. Three ideas he distinguishes as essential in Christianity: that of sin, both original and deliberate, from which the individual is powerless to free himself, and whose penalty is endless; that of atonement for sin; and that of the divine community, through which the atonement comes, and in which man must win his salvation. Each of these ideas, Royce insists, is a product of human nature in its moral capacity, quite apart from Christian or other theology. "If there were no Christianity and no Christians in the world, the idea of atonement would have to be invented before the higher levels of our moral existence could be fairly understood... . The problem of atonement daily arises...is daily faced...and in principle and in ideal, daily solved." And as for salvation in the community, "these considerations are based upon human nature. They have to do with interests which all reasonable men, whether Christian or non-Christian, more or less clearly recognize, in proportion as men advance to the higher stages of the art of life." This method has the immense advantage of giving verifiable substance and actuality to these religious conceptions, which the contemporary mind in its joy of recovery from an over-strained inwardness is prone to regard as alien and outworn. On the other hand, the method is apt to carry with it a foregone conclusion which is critical for the problem in hand; for the only content of Christianity that could be reached through such a general appeal to human nature is a content which has no necessary connection with Christianity, and our interpreted Christianity is in some likelihood of becoming a purely "natural" or philosophical religion. The historically unique elements of the religion, if any such are essential, are likely to be excluded by the conditions of the inquiry. I shall recur to this matter later.

As to the actual origin of these ideas in our own tradition, Royce is not inclined to attribute any of them to Jesus. "All three appear to be due to interpretations of the mind of the Master which came into existence only after the earthly period of teaching had ceased." The reflective teaching about Christ, as the spirit of the Church, seems to Royce more definitively Christian than the teachings of the man Jesus; and while it is clearly the Pauline formulation which chiefly impresses him, the true founder of Christianity, in his view, is no one person, but the early Christian community itself. Only through the transformation of the object of devotion in this community from the particular person to the living spirit of the community did the motive of religion find its true centre; which is not in the "love" of the synoptic gospels, undeveloped as this is in its social bearings, but in the "charity" of the epistles – a motive founded in the conception of the community, wherein Christianity becomes the religion of loyalty.

Especially illuminating, in the first volume, are the treatments of moral evil and its penalties. It is not the "sick soul" but the clearly self-judging soul that finds sin and damnation to be its portion on the natural level of moral events. Original guilt is no invention of an artificial theology; it is an expression of the truth that the individual, endowed with self-consciousness by the human community with its laws and standards, is in this process necessarily also endowed with a self-will estranged from the community which has called it forth. Individualism is a by-product of communality, on the human level; so that our "very consciences are tainted by the original sin of social contentiousness." Powerless to deliver himself from the body of this death, salvation must come to the natural man through union with a non-legal community on another level, an essentially lovable community, divine in its spirit; loyalty to such a community, if it can be found, is the "only cure for the natural warfare of the collective and the individual will." But there is a deeper stage of guilt. It is the sin of the man who has known the meaning of adoption, who has received the grace and assumed the obligation of loyalty, and who has become traitor to the cause which was his. This is the sin against the Holy Ghost; unpardonable; not in the sense that an alien Deity has set an arbitrary limit here to his indulgence, but in the sense that the traitorous person cannot forgive himself, and that whatever his further attitude, his deed remains irrevocable, he remains forever one who has been a traitor. The view that such treason is possible and actual is the free, the non-Platonic element in the moral vista of Christianity. It is precisely the man who knows the good who is able to play the traitor; and on this tragic possibility depends the entire worth of our world, as a world of continuous freedom in the re-affirmation of our loyalty. And it is, furthermore, the opportunity for an atoning act, which must come from the spirit of the wronged community itself, an act which apart from the particular deed of treason would not be possible, but which, when it comes, makes the world better than without this treason it could have been.

Atonement, in this view, must be a repeated or continuous process, meeting sin as sin arises. The idea of a single atoning deed which at one stroke anticipates all possible future treasons, can mean no more to this philosophy than a type or symbol. Atonement is, for Royce, a temporal process; but it is not, in the strict sense, historical.

Salvation then depends upon the continuous work of the divine community; and the practical issues of religion turn upon the metaphysical issues, Is there such a divine community? and Where shall it be found? This inquiry is the burden of the second series of lectures; and the argument here is of extreme logical interest, both intrinsically and as a development of Royce's own metaphysical position. With characteristic skill, he singles out an aspect of cognition, which proves in the end to involve certain decisive judgments as to the nature of reality.

This aspect of cognition is interpretation; and Royce, following out suggestions made by Charles Peirce, wishes to set interpretation beside perception and conception, or rather above them, as a third fundamental process of knowledge. Empiricism has sought to know reality primarily by perception, rationalism by conception; Bergson, basing himself upon a Kantian dream, attempts to define a third species of knowledge which he calls intuition, but this Royce regards as merely a species of perception. Interpretation stands in sharp contrast to these operations. Both perception and conception are solitary, implying a simply dyadic relation between the thinker and his object; interpretation is a social cognition, triadic in structure, as when A interprets B to C. The objects of perception are things; the objects of conception are abstractions, universals; the objects of interpretation are minds, or expressions of mind, signs which the mind offers for the reading of an interpreter. And minds can be known only by interpretation; they cannot be perceived, nor can they be known by conception, for they are not abstractions. Perception and conception terminate upon their objects and give rise to no further processes; but an interpretation is itself a mental expression, and so offers material for further interpretation, defining a never-ending task. Thus the life of an individual is a continual reinterpretation of his own past, a perpetual inner conversation in which the present self interprets the past self to the future self.

The self is thus an object of interpretation, no mere datum of perception; and time itself has no other existence than as the object of this interpretative process. Whether within the mind or between minds, the motive of interpretation is to bring about a unity among differing elements, accomplishing mutual understanding without abolishing their distinctions. It creates a social structure which is as different from the indiscriminate merging or Bergsonian "interpenetration" of elements on the one hand as it is from pluralistic independence on the other. It creates, in brief, a community, in which the problem of the one and the many is solved.

Now the real universe is such a community of interpretation – this is Royce's argument. For by "reality" I mean simply the true interpretation of the conflicts and antitheses which experience presents, an interpretation not in my possession, but which I must believe to exist as I believe in reality at all. "Unless both the interpreter and the community are real, there is no real world."

This universal community, a necessary object of my loyal interpretation of life, though not at all of my perception, whether now or at any future time, is the divine community; it is the City whose maker and builder is God. As the ultimate object of devotion and hope on the part of all loyal souls, this community is the invisible Church. The world is the perpetual process of its spirit; and the salvation of the world is the progressive victory over evil through the reconciling and atoning deeds which this spirit makes possible. This is also the supreme object of the Christian faith: I believe in the Holy Ghost, the Holy Catholic Church, the communion of saints.

Of this conception of Christianity as a whole, it is inadequate to say that it is true; one must say that like every great interpretation it enlarges that which it interprets; and if I add that it is not the whole of essential Christianity, I am not forgetting that it must be received primarily as an enhancement of what Christianity may mean to us. I shall not dwell upon the tempting metaphysical discussions, though I must question in passing whether interpretation is a primary cognitive process. Interpretation is concerned with predicates, with the "what" of things; it has no original power over existential propositions. Further, as every interpretation, including a theoretical first one, presumes the existence of the minds addressed by the interpreter, the belief in the existence of minds beyond my present self cannot be a *product* of interpretation. The knowledge of other minds which, as Royce truly shows, cannot be completed without an infinite process of interpretation, must be present in some simpler and more immediate fashion before the interpretative process can begin; the goal in some diminished form must be present from the beginning. I mention this because it is entirely characteristic of Royce's thought; the infinite deferring of the goal is to him incompatible with its realization at any point in time. For this reason the essential can never become the historical, atonement can never be an accomplished fact, and the true Church can never be found as an existent institution. Historical Christianity, for Royce, is the bearer of a true doctrine; it is not the continuator of any final historic deed. The memories of the Church, as an actual human community, go back to definite points of time, and constitute the Church what Royce calls a "community of memory"; these memories animate the particular historic statements of the creed as well as the commemorative acts of the Lord's Supper. But these particular elements disappear from the creed of the modern man who accepts our author's view; nor would he find in that creed a reason for identifying himself with the hopes and labors of any visible Church.

Neither the atoning deed nor the divine community is brought to earth by this doctrine in historically identifiable form, valid for all men as a common object. Christianity is left in the region of the universal; and thereby the foundation for a truly universal community, an historic unity of all particular spirits and their loyal endeavors, is not laid. If this is true, it may be because that one of all the characteristic ideas of Christianity which to many thinkers is most central has retreated into the background and at last eluded our author's grasp – the doctrine of the Incarnation.

# REVIEW OF
# *THE PROBLEM OF CHRISTIANITY*

William Adams Brown, Review of *The Problem of Christianity*, *Journal of Philosophy*, vol. 11 (1914).

*The Problem of Christianity*: Lectures delivered at the Lowell Institute in Boston, and at Manchester College, Oxford. By Josiah Royce. New York: The Macmillan Company. 1913. 2 Vols, pp. xlvi, 425; 442.

Some years ago the present writer chanced to be in Cambridge at the time when Professor Royce was delivering his lectures on the "Essence of Christianity" which were subsequently published in the *Harvard Theological Review* under the title, "What is Vital in Christianity." The lectures were delivered upon the invitation of the Students' Christian Association which, if my memory is not at fault, suggested the topic. Chancing to meet Professor Royce at the time, I expressed my satisfaction that we were to have the benefit of his thought upon so practical a theme. Royce shook his head. "I did it," he said, "because I promised, but I will never take such a subject again; it is too concrete for my taste."

Readers of the two substantial volumes in which Professor Royce has embodied his views upon the problem of Christianity must rejoice that his excursion into the realm of the concrete has not proved so isolated an experience as he anticipated. We are all the richer for sharing his thought on a theme which has proved of perennial interest to humanity, and we feel safe in assuming that he himself has found the hours spent in studying the origins of Christianity, and thinking over again the questions which its existence raises, an enlarging and rewarding experience. Those who, like the present writer, have made it their life-work to study the problems of Christian theology welcome the entrance into this well-cultivated field of an independent thinker who brings the virility of mind, the broad outlook, and at the same time the earnest religious spirit which characterize the distinguished philosopher who so ably carries on the tradition of idealism in the oldest of our American universities.

Yet it must be confessed that the spirit which uttered itself in the remark which was quoted in our opening paragraph is still in evidence in the volumes under review. Like Hegel, whom Professor Royce follows in his attempt to give a philosophic interpretation of the essence of Christianity, the American idealist believes that absolute truth is revealed in history, but he is equally sure that you must not identify it with any particular historical phenomenon, even if that phenomenon be one so august and sacred as the Christian religion itself. To the man who has the insight to see it, truth is present everywhere and always as the inner meaning of that which, looked at from the outside, appears simply as a series of brute facts. What is needed above all things is the formula, and this it is the business of the philosopher to furnish us. How it is to be applied, what bearing it will have upon the special problems of the individual life, he leaves to others as no part of his professional concern.

Yet it would be a great mistake to confuse Royce's conception of the essence of Christianity with Hegel's. In spite of superficial similarities there is a real difference. Between Hegel and Royce there lies a mass of critical research devoted to the investigation of the facts of the Christian religion. Professor Royce disclaims any right to speak at first hand of the questions under controversy in this criticism; yet he writes as an intelligent layman who has studied what the critics have to say and comes to his own problem with an independent understanding of their results. You feel, in reading his pages, that the religion with which he deals is really the Christian religion, not some independent construction of his own brain. Some Christians may feel – many will doubtless feel – that there are aspects of the Christian religion – and these fundamental aspects – which find no place in Royce's book, but what he gives they will recognize as a part at least of the religion they know, and they will feel in him, therefore, a kindred spirit. To take but a single illustration, – it would be difficult to find a more illuminating piece of analysis than the comparison which the author draws between Buddhism and Christianity in the seventh chapter of his first volume, a comparison equally just in its estimate of similarity as in its recognition of difference.

The book falls into two parts, independent yet complementary. The first, entitled the "Christian Doctrine of Life," is a study of the essence of Christianity considered as an objective historical phenomenon. The second, which the author entitles "The Real World and the Christian Ideas," asks the question how far the Christian solution of the problem of life can maintain itself at the bar of metaphysical inquiry. Thus the two parts of Royce's book cover substantially the ground which is discussed by contemporary German apologetics under the titles "Das Wesen" and "Die Wahrheit des Christentums."

The plan has advantages and disadvantages. Its advantage consists in its clear recognition of the fact that the problem of Christianity is one of definition as well as of proof. Before we can tell what Christianity signifies we must know what it is, but this is in dispute not only among non-Christians, but among Christians. It is methodically correct, therefore, to isolate this question for independent discussion as Royce does.

On the other hand, the method has disadvantages, in that it separates matters that belong together. The definition of Christianity involves among other things a description of the beliefs of Christians about ultimate realities, notably about the nature of God. But this question, fundamental for the understanding of every religion, Royce passes over with only incidental reference,[1] reserving his discussion, so far as he gives one, for the second part of his treatise. The result is a description of Christianity which omits altogether what most Christians would regard as the heart of their religion. Royce himself admits this and defends his method on the ground that Christians have believed many things in the past which we all recognize to-day have been outgrown. But whether this can apply to a conception so fundamental as that of God is a question which requires fuller discussion than our author has given it.

To begin with the first problem, that of the essence of Christianity, it may be premised at the outset that Professor Royce believes that the quest of such an essence is legitimate and important. If the world has a meaning, if history is more than a mere succession of events without inner relation and spiritual significance, then a great historical phenomenon like Christianity must have some significance which can be discovered by the sympathetic and reverent student. History, as Royce conceives it, is more than a science. It is a philosophy, a search for the inner unity which connects events and makes them luminous and meaningful to the instructed observer.

There are, however, two possible methods of interpreting an historical phenomenon like Chistianity, each of which has its advocates. You may find your essence revealed at some particular point of time, identifying it either with the teaching of the founder, the content of the Bible, or the dogma of the church, as the case may be. Or you may find it in some spirit which runs through the whole course of history and whose full secret is only gradually apprehended. You may say of Christianity, It is the religion of Christ, meaning the religion that Christ taught, or you may say, It is the religion of Christians, meaning that it is the experience into which Christians have progressively entered as they have tried to understand and interpret Christ. Royce's view is of the latter kind. Like Schleiermacher and Ritschl he takes his stand within the consciousness

[1] E.g., Vol. 1., 202, 205.

of the Christian community, which he regards as the real creator of Christianity. He does not think it possible to press back of this consciousness and to recover some more primitive form of faith which, when recovered, must henceforth be our test of true religion, nor indeed is he greatly interested in the attempt. The church rather than Christ is the constitutive idea of Christianity, and the church is only another name for the ideal community, which is the unifying principle of philosophy and religion alike.

Holding this view, it is not strange to find Professor Royce indifferent to the results of recent critical study of the life of Jesus. Of the founder of Christianity he speaks with great respect and of many of his reported teachings he gives a sympathetic and in many respects an illuminating interpretation (*e.g.*, Jesus's teaching concerning love), but as to his own place in the religion that bears his name he professes himself agnostic. It is not simply that he feels the difficulties raised by modern criticism – that we could well understand – but, that the picture of Jesus as presented in the Gospels, the picture of a particular individual embodying a definite ideal of service and brotherhood and love, finds no natural place in his philosophy. In contrast to Hegel, who insists that the ideal personality who incarnates the principles of his philosophy must at some definite time appear. Royce does not expect "any human and visible triumph of the ideal in history" (Vol II., page 430). All that we can hope for is an approximation toward that ideal, the assurance that somewhere and somehow (not here and now) it is realized in the eternal.

Passing from method to result, we find that our author discovers the essence of Christianity in three controlling ideas: the idea of the church, or the universal community through loyalty to which alone the individual realizes his destiny; the idea of sin, or the moral contradiction in which the individual finds himself necessarily involved because of the conflict between his own will and that of the community, and the idea of atonement, or the saving deed of the community or its chosen representative through which this disharmony is overcome and the individual restored to his true place in the communal life. The ideas which underlie the discussion have already been anticipated in earlier works, notably in *The Philosophy of Loyalty*, and *The Sources of Religious Insight.* But the treatment forms a unity and can be followed without reference to any of the author's previous works.

Fundamental for Royce's thought is the conception of the community as an independent entity having a unity of its own as definite and as empirically verifiable as that of an individual personality. This conception to which Royce had come on independent grounds in his *Philosophy of Loyalty* he holds to be the central reality for the Christian consciousness. The Pauline church, or, as he paraphrases it, the beloved community, is in fact the community of the loyal. This is the body of Christ, the sphere in which his spirit expresses itself, the end in devotion to which every individual finds his true self fulfilled.

This view of the church explains Royce's view of the second of the great Christian conceptions, that of sin. The supreme sin, according to our author, is disloyalty, treachery to the cause of the community. But this he finds to be the inevitable result of the conflict between the individual's wants and desires and the claim of the community of which he is a part. The more highly developed the individual, the more conscious he is of capacities and desires that are inherently worthy, the more he rebels against the restraints which the community puts upon him, the more his experience approximates that of Paul in the seventh chapter of Romans. What is the remedy for this situation? It is the remedy which Paul discovered, namely, the existence of a new and higher social order, in loyalty to which the individual can find his highest desires fulfilled. Such a community is the church of Christ. Through loyalty to it alone salvation is possible. But what of those who have proved false to this new and higher allegiance? Such would seem to have committed the unpardonable sin, a sin for which even if others could forgive, they could never forgive themselves. What has religion to offer to those who have been disloyal to the cause of loyalty? This brings us to the third of the ruling ideas of Christianity which Royce discovers, namely, that of atonement.

Professor Royce finds in the Christian emphasis upon the atonement one of its chief claims to our acceptance. "The human aspect of the Christian idea of atonement," he tells us, "is based upon such motives that if there were no Christianity and no Christians in the world the idea of atonement would have to he invented before the higher levels of our moral existence could be fairly understood (Vol. 1., page 27l). It is quite true that the particular theories of atonement which meet us in the official theology of Christianity are unsatisfactory. But this is because the problem has been conceived in too superficial and external a way. Either, like the penal theory, the deed has been isolated from its consequences and atonement found in some form of legal substitution; or like the moral theories, a moral transformation of character in the individual has been considered sufficient. But what is needed is something more profound than either, such a dealing with the tragedy of sin that the world shall be the better for the fact that it has happened. What if it should appear that the traitor's deed of disloyalty prove the occasion for some corresponding deed of love so wise, so gracious, so winning in the beauty of its unselfish adaptation to the tragic situation that not only others, but even the traitor himself who is responsible for the evil that called it forth must recognize that the world is the better for its having been done. Such a deed, could it be done, would fulfil the conditions of a real atonement, and such, in the opinion of our author, is the remedy which Christianity proposes for the tragedy of sin.

In spite of the abstract form in which it is cast, one must recognize in the analysis a true insight into the genius of historical Christianity. It is the more to be regretted that the author should have passed so lightly over other ideas to which most Christians would attribute equal if not superior importance, namely, that of God, the ultimate object of Christian faith, and Jesus Christ, the historic mediator of his revelation.

Of the reason for the first omission I have already spoken. The explanation of the second appears in the second and metaphysical part of the book. It is here made clear that the reason why Royce gives no independent doctrine of God is that he identifies God with the community, which from a different point of view is only another name for the living Christ or the Holy Spirit of historic Christian theology. This identification is possible because the community which is the object of Christian loyalty is not the empirical society we call the church in any one of its many conflicting forms, but a noumenal reality which as completely transcends present (and for that matter all future possible) experience as the God of Kant himself.

Royce's justification for his identification of the ultimate reality, or God, with the ideal society, has two parts. The first develops the idea of the community as the ultimate metaphysical reality; the second gives reasons for the belief that such a reality actually exists. The former occupies chapters nine and ten, which deal with the Community and the Time Process and the Body and its Members; the latter is discussed in chapters eleven to fourteen, which treat of the significance of interpretation for our knowledge of reality. Two concluding chapters draw certain practical conclusions.

Of the first point I can speak briefly. Royce makes use of Wundt's *Studies in Social Psychology* to defend the thesis that the community is a true unit in that it has a common past and a common future. It has a common past because the same historical event may enter into the consciousness of each of its members who, through this common inheritance, become what Royce calls a community of memory. It has a common future because each of its members may work for the same ideal, and this common purpose constitutes them a community of expectation.

We have no criticism to make of this interesting discussion other than to remark that it opens the way for an interpretation of history far more concrete and vital than that which Royce has given. If the possession of a common past is essential to the existence of a community in the sense in which Royce defines it, then it would seem that the specific historic facts which constitute that past must bulk more largely than they do for our author, and the Christian's backward look to Jesus as the founder of the Christian community can not be dismissed in the summary manner in which he dismisses it.

More interesting, because more original, is Royce's use of the theory of interpretation as a justification of his metaphysical position. For this theory he confesses his indebtedness to Mr. Charles Peirce, that fruitful source of suggestion to American philosophers. But the use which Royce makes of it is his own. According to this view there are not two methods of knowledge as ordinarily supposed, perception and conception, but three, perception, conception, and interpretation. Perception is concerned with that which is immediately given in experience; conception with general ideas reached by a process of abstraction; but interpretation is the process by which we share what we have experienced with other persons for purposes of common action. Both perception and conception admit of being stated in individual terms, but interpretation is essentially social. It takes for granted the existence of a society of persons and would be meaningless without it.

Here again there is much that is interesting in Professor Royce's discussion, over which it would be a pleasure to linger. But we are concerned here primarily with its bearing upon his argument as a whole. If we understand him aright, what he gives us is a new variety of the ontological argument. We must assume, so the argument runs, that the reality which is implied in the very processes of our knowledge has objective existence. As used in the older forms of the ontological argument this reasoning, even if its validity were admitted, could give us at most a highly abstract result such as Kant's "Ens Realissimum." But as used by Royce in the light of his doctrine of interpretation it gives us the most concrete of all results, namely, the beloved community itself. If all our knowledge involves the process of interpretation, and interpretation is meaningless without the existence of the community with whose members insight is shared, then we must believe that the nature of ultimate reality is social, which is the thesis which is to be proved.

A corollary of the doctrine of interpretation is the doctrine of signs. A sign is any object which admits of interpretation, *e.g.*, "a word, a clock-face, a weather vane, or a gesture" (p. 283). Not only art and literature, but science and common sense, are constantly making use of signs. Experience itself may be defined as "a realm of signs" (p. 289), and history is constantly presenting us with objects which through interpretation give us insight into the nature of reality. What we all recognize as valid in particular instances Royce would extend to the world as a whole. "The world is the community. The world contains its own interpreter. Its processes are infinite in their temporal varieties; but their interpreter, the spirit of this universal community – never absorbing varieties or permitting them to blend – compares and through a real life interprets them all" (p. 324).

One must regret that Professor Royce has not followed this clue further and given us a classification of signs with special reference to the signs of which religion makes use, and especially the particular religion which he is studying. This would enable us to test the correctness of his previous analysis and discover why he omits from his catalogue so many of the ideas which have played so large a rôle in historic Christianity. But this would take him back into the realm of the concrete, from which he has so happily escaped. As it is, we must be content with the general principle without application in detail.

In one of his closing chapters Professor Royce, by a use of the creative imagination, not uncommon among philosophers, calls back from the grave a Pauline Christian and, transporting him across the lapse of years into the new world of modern science, presents him with a copy of *The Problem of Christianity*, in order to discover how far he will recognize in it the essence of his own religion. As could hardly be otherwise under the circumstances, the test is successful and the position of the author triumphantly vindicated. For a moment, to be sure, our convert hesitates, but being at heart a gentleman as well as a philosopher, he recognizes in Professor Royce a kindred spirit and soon finds himself at home in his new environment.

If the reviewer might venture upon a like liberty he would suggest a repetition of the experiment. There were more types of Christians in the Pauline community than one, and it may be that a second visitor would look at the matter from a somewhat different angle. He might address this new interpreter of Christianity as follows: "This religion that you call Christianity has much that attracts me. I recognize my own experience in your description of sin and of salvation. I respond with enthusiasm to your plea for loyalty, but there is one thing I miss, and that is a personality fitted to call forth my loyalty. Such a personality I knew in Jesus Christ, the founder of the church to which I gave my allegiance. But in this sublimated community, which I am not at liberty to identify with any existing society. I look in vain for my Master and my Lord. What I need is not the divine in general, but the divine as revealed in the human, and such a revelation I find in the person of Jesus. I rejoice in your protest against reducing Christianity to a mere ethical system. I welcome your re-emphasis upon the universal and metaphysical elements in my faith, but why need the emphasis of the one involve the sacrifice of the other? Christianity to be sure, is religion, not ethics; but it is ethical religion, and the reason why Christ must ever hold the central place in Christian faith is the fact that he embodies to the imagination of men in the picture of a human life principles universally applicable. He is the sign by which we interpret the universe and discover the nature of the social order after which we are to strive. Put back Christ into Christianity and I shall find myself at home in the beloved community whose ideals you have so fascinatingly sketched."

Whether our resuscitated Pauline Christian would speak thus I do not know but I am sure this is a sentiment which will find an echo in the heart of many a modern Christian as he lays down Professor Royce's book.

# REVIEW OF
# *THE PROBLEM OF CHRISTIANITY*

Hastings Rashdall, Review of *The Problem of Christianity*, *Mind*, vol. 23 (1914).

*The Problem of Christianity*. Lectures delivered at the Lowell Institute in Boston, and at Manchester College, Oxford. By Josiah Royce, D. Sc. (University of Oxford), Professor of the History of Philosophy in Harvard University, New York. Macmillan, 1913.

This is a difficult book to review. It discusses a number of subjects and arrives at conclusions in each of them which, though in the author's view they are closely connected, may appear less so to those who are not prepared to accept his system *en bloc*. It will be quite impossible to discuss all of them (or indeed any of them) with the thoroughness which they deserve, and in such an account of them as is possible I shall venture to depart somewhat from the order in which they are treated by Prof. Royce himself.

Prof. Royce finds the "essence of Christianity" in the idea of salvation through love or passionate loyalty to a community – a community of persons who themselves possess this love to the community. The love that saves is, indeed, a love towards all mankind, but the precise good which the possessor of this love desires to promote in the objects of it is to make them members in the body which is united by the tie of mutual love. This idea is, it is admitted, only adumbrated in the teaching of Jesus Himself. Its full realisation is the great discovery of St. Paul and of the Churches which he founded. The distinguishing character of Christianity is that it is the religion in which this idea was for the first time, and is now, appreciated in the fullest degree. Though the community to which the Pauline Christian felt so passionate a loyalty was the actual organised Christian Church, the idea which lay at the bottom of this sentiment is, according to Prof. Royce, capable of being completely detached from any actual visible community. The Church of the philosophical Christian who accepts Prof. Royce's interpretation, is an "invisible Church," and it is never to become visible, or even (it would appear) any more visible than it is at present. And it is through union with this invisible Church that he is to obtain salvation. The following passages will perhaps give a somewhat fuller idea of Prof. Royce's position: –

"First, it is needful for me to point out that, despite certain stubborn and widespread misunderstandings, the Christian doctrine of love, as that doctrine appears in the parables and in the Sermon on the Mount, involves and emphasises a very positive and active and heroic attitude towards life, and is not, as some have supposed, a negative doctrine of passive self-surrender. And, secondly, I must also bring to your attention the fact that the Master's teaching about love leaves unsolved certain practical problems, problems which this very heroism and this positive tendency of the doctrine make by contrast all the more striking" (I., 77–78).

"Critics, as well as mistaken friends of the Master's teachings, have supposed Christian love to be more or less completely identical with self-abnegation – with the amiably negative virtue of one who, as the misleading modern phrase expresses the matter, 'has no thought of self.' Another modern expression, also misleading, is used by some who identify Christian love with so-called 'pure altruism'" (I., 79).

"Now, against such misunderstandings, many of the wiser expounders of Christian doctrine, both in former times and in our own, have taken pains to show that love, as the Jesus of the sayings and of the parables conceived it, does *not* consist in mere self-abnegation, and is not identical with pure altruism, and is both heroic and positive" (I., 79, 80).

"For the Jesus of the sayings not only rejoices in the divine love whereof every man is the object, but also invites every man to rejoice in the consciousness of this very love, and to delight also in all men, since they are God's beloved. The man whom this love of God is to transform into a perfect lover cannot henceforth merely forget or abandon the self" (I., 80).

"Every man, this self included, has just such an unique value, and must be so viewed" (I., 81).

"But now let us return to the relation of love to the services that one is to offer to one's neighbor. What can the lover – in so far as Jesus describes His task – what can he do for his fellow-man?"

"To this question it is, indeed, possible to give one answer which clearly defines a duty to the neighbor; and this duty is emphasized throughout the teaching of Jesus. This duty is the requirement to use all fitting means – example, precept, kindliness, non-resistance, heroism, patience, courage, strenuousness – all means that tend to make the neighbour himself one of the lovers" (I., 85).

"Buddhism fully knows, and truly teaches, where the root of

bitterness is to be found – not in the outward deed but in the inmost heart of the individual self. But what, so far as I know, the original Southern Buddhism *never* clearly made a positive part of its own plan of the salvation of mankind, is a transformation of the self, *not* through the *mere* destruction of the narrow and corrupt flesh which alienates it from the true life, *but by the simple and yet intensely positive* DEVOTION *of the self to a new task – to its creative office as a loyal member of a beloved community*" (I., 344, 345).

"It is of course also true that Jesus during His life had, as an individual man, taught a doctrine, and done a work, which made this first Christian community possible. In this sense it is correct to say that the man Jesus, in so far as He was merely an individual man, is the founder of Christianity. But when we say this, we must add that, so far as we know of the teachings of the man Jesus, they did not make explicit what proved to be precisely the most characteristic feature of Christianity – namely, the mission and the doctrine of the Christian community itself. The doctrine of Christian love, as the Master taught it, is not yet, in explicit form, the whole Christian doctrine of life. For the Christian doctrine of life is a doctrine which is unintelligible apart from the ideal of the universal community" (I., 416–17).

"We are saved through and in the community. There is the victory which overcomes the world. There is the interpretation which reconciles. There is the doctrine which we teach. This, so far as we have had time, in these brief lectures, to state our case, is our philosophy, and this doctrine, as we assert, is in agreement with what is vital in Christianity" (II., 390).

These passages will by themselves fail to do justice to the force and freshness with which Prof. Royce develops this thesis. I have been obliged to leave out much of what he says about the nature of communities in general and the relation of the individual to his own community. The ideas are perhaps at bottom not quite so original as the author himself seems disposed to think. But there is abundant need for their emphatic assertion, and Prof. Royce's enforcement of them constitutes a very valuable protest against many of the misrepresentations of Christianity which are current both among theologians and among philosophers. Prof. Royce tells us that the extent of his Hegelianism has been exaggerated, and that he is now less of a Hegelian than he used to be. The protest is particularly important as coming from one who will at least command respect among philosophers of a Hegelianising tendency. In making the idea of community and of love to the community into *the* essence of Christianity, we certainly have a new and notable departure. For it is remarkable that, in spite of Hegel's insistence upon the community as the source of the individual's morality and spiritual life –

in spite of his pushing (some of us will say exaggerating) the idea of the social character of Morality to such a point that (as has been said) there is no moral Philosophy at all in Hegel, but only political Philosophy – both the Master himself and most Hegelianising writers on the Philosophy of Religion make singularly little of the idea of the Church. This is no doubt largely due to the extreme individualism of Lutheranism – as compared with Romanism, Calvinism, and all the religious bodies which have originated in England. German Philosophers and Theologians alike hardly ever seem able to shake themselves free from the Lutheran tradition. To most German Protestants the Church is little more than "the society for maintaining public worship," while to insist much on the importance of this one function of worship which is allowed to the Church is to many liberal Protestants a note of defective "spirituality." The extreme subordination of the Church to the State in Protestant Germany finds expression in such sayings as "The State is masculine; the Church is feminine." And it is chiefly among Germans and Germanising Anglo-Saxons that there has been any serious treatment of religious Philosophy or philosophical Theology. The idea that Religion is a little private transaction between "a man and his Maker" has sunk deep into the popular Protestant consciousness. Ritschlianism (in spite of Ritschl's own idea that the Church rather than the individual Christian is the object of salvation) is an extreme exaggeration of this tendency. It bases the whole evidence of Religion upon the impression made upon the individual believer by the picture of Christ's personality, and makes almost its whole content to consist in the personal relation thus established. Harnack, as Dr. Sanday has remarked, seldom uses the term "Church" without some note of disparagement, and the same may be said of most German Theologians before Troeltsch, a writer to whom Prof. Royce acknowledges his indebtedness. The Mysticism which is now becoming fashionable in England – at the opposite pole of thought from Ritschlianism in other respects – agrees with it in this individualising tendency. The individual is supposed to discover God by his unaided reflection, and to enjoy an immediate vision of God which owes nothing to his religious community and its tradition. And idealistic Philosophers have strengthened the tendency by habitually speaking as if, in flagrant defiance of historical fact, the "mystical" type of "religious experience" were the only one.

Against these tendencies Prof. Royce's theory is at least a very welcome and much-needed protest. Whether you look at the matter historically or psychologically, Prof. Royce is to my mind wholly right. If we study the lives of the mystics themselves, we find abundant evidence of the large extent to which their environment explains the experiences which they themselves – or at least rather their undiscriminating admirers – are disposed to regard as direct communications from on high. And if we look at the particular history of Christianity, the latest research is making it more than ever plain that (however strongly we may assert that it was the personality of Jesus which created the Church) it is simply impossible to discriminate (when you come to details) between the sayings which are genuine utterances of Jesus and those which are due to the working of His spirit and influence in the Church. Indeed, in this matter I believe that Prof. Royce is even more right than he knows. He is, I venture to think, disposed to attribute a greater importance in the evolution of Christianity to the personal thought of St. Paul than is warranted by the facts. Theologians have too often written as if the ideas of Christians had simply stood still between the taking away of their Lord and the appearance upon the scene of St. Paul. Many of the ideas which are often associated with the teaching of St. Paul are much more probably due to the common consciousness of the primitive Church, though St. Paul doubtless gave them their classical expression in religious literature. To deny or ignore all this does not really add to the personal supremacy of Jesus; for Loisy is not far wrong in saying that the greatest thing that Jesus did was to found the Church. That this little body of little-educated Jews should have been able to originate such great ideas is the best testimony to the greatness of their Master.

So far I can follow Prof. Royce's central idea, and I would wish to speak with the utmost respect of the brilliancy and the deep ethical and religious feeling with which that idea is developed. His paper contains the best exposition that I know of the deepest essence of Christian morality, and the best reply that I know to the current misrepresentations of it as an essentially "other worldly" or "world-renouncing" doctrine – misrepresentations from which even Troeltsch is not altogether free. And yet I cannot but feel that there is considerable exaggeration in making this *the* essential idea of Christianity, whether we examine the matter historically or from the point of view of the present religious consciousness. If he had confined himself to saying that the idea of universal love – understood as he explains it – was the central idea of Christian Ethics, and that in the teaching of Jesus – not so clearly in that of St. Paul and the later Christian community – the right state of the soul was made to consist in this universal love, he would have been saying what was undeniably true. Prof. Royce has no doubt admirably expressed the difference between Christian love and the Buddhistic negation of self on the one hand or mere Utilitarianism on the other. It would, indeed, throw considerable suspicion upon Prof. Royce's claims to express what has always been the essence of Christian Morality if we were to suppose that such an interpretation of it was absolutely new. This it certainly is not. I would refer for instance to certain chapters of Seeley's *Ecce Homo* as containing substantially the same interpretation of Christian morality, if we put aside Seeley's assumptions about the actual meaning of the Kingdom of Heaven to Jesus Himself which could not now be defended. Nor indeed is what Prof. Royce says about the essentiality of the Christian Society to a true conception of Christianity any great advance upon Seeley's exposition of it, except that Prof. Royce has formulated it in the language of technical Philosophy and connected it with philosophical views about the nature of human society in general in a way which Seeley of course did not attempt to do. But to make the idea of the Community into the *whole* essence of Christianity seems to me seriously defective.

In the first place when thus isolated from everything else in Religion and Ethics the idea of the Community tends to lose most of the characteristics which would attach any one to it. It is not, be it remarked, the idea of universal love but the idea of an actual community of people who practise this love towards each other which Prof. Royce regards as the essential element in Christianity. But why should there be this passionate attachment to a community which is not the community of the human race, and why this passionate desire to get other people into it? If the Christian Church had been nothing but a community attached to the idea of a community the attachment to it could hardly have been accounted for. Historically the bond of union between religious communities has invariably been attachment to a common body of ideas. No doubt this very idea that Salvation to be sought by loyal service to a community which is potentially co-extensive with mankind is itself one of the ideas which the Society possessed and was anxious to communicate to its members, and perhaps it is the most important of them. But it was not all. Religions invariably involve a theory of the Universe – a Metaphysic as well as an Ethic. Of course Prof. Royce may say that he happens not to believe in the particular theory of the Universe which the early Christians professed, and that he does believe in the ethical idea just described. He is no doubt entitled to dream of a society which has shaken off the early Christian Metaphysic but retains its fundamental ethical idea. But it may be doubted whether any society could inspire this passionate loyalty if attachment to this idea were its whole *raison d'être*. Even if it were, this ethical idea would be logically prior to the idea of the Community. In the history of Religion what we see everywhere is that the idea comes first, the community next. It is true that from the nature of the Christian idea the Community is more necessary to the realisation of it than in the case of other Religions. A Buddhist might be saved in solitude. A Christian cannot, if the Christian doctrine of salvation (as Prof. Royce interprets it) be true. But historically the ardour of Christians for their community was explained by their holding in common a number of other beliefs besides this belief in the Community. And historically the belief in a God of love and a supreme revelation of Himself through a human Personality and the doctrine of a blessed Immortality to be attained through loyalty to that truth were the strongest forces which attracted men to the community. In particular it is rather surprising that a thinker who grasps so clearly the importance of that new idea of Christianity which converted Morality into Loyalty to a visible and concrete community should seem to be so blind to the value of the equally new idea which identified it with loyalty to an ideal Being who was also an historical person. Loyalty to the personal Christ has been (and surely is) even a more vital element in Christianity than loyalty to the community.

At this point Prof. Royce will probably protest that I am taking too seriously his language about the "beloved community." He admits that the community does not exist in any outward and visible form. It is not any branch of the actual Christian Church or all of them put together. It has no outward and visible existence, and never will have. Now of course we all know what an ideal is, and it is the nature of the real world or, as Philosophers say, of the phenomenal world to fall short of the ideal, and some of us may even be disposed to recognise a profound meaning in Plato's further doctrine that after all it is the ideal that is the most truly real. But what I am disposed to complain of in Prof. Royce's treatment of the subject is that there is simply no relation in his theory between the actual and the ideal. His ideal community is a χωριστὸν εἶδος – a universal which does not reside, to any extent or in any degree, in its particulars. When he comes to actual or even to possible Christian societies, he has nothing but rather contemptuous expressions for them which we expect to meet with in those very writers whose view of the nature of Religion he justly regards as over-individualistic, and who do not understand the social character of the religion, the religious consciousness, religious experience, religious ethics. All the things that Prof. Royce tells us about human society – the reality of its common life, its being a "person" and the like would simply be untrue if the society of which he speaks were merely an ideal, a city in the heavens. Much of Prof. Royce's language about the real and "personal" existence of societies seems to me somewhat exaggerated and misleading; but I am quite in sympathy with what at bottom I take him to mean, and I will assume for the moment that it is all true and accurately expressed. And the truer it is, the more it compels us to recognise that it can be true only of some actual human society or societies. No doubt the ideal is not and never will be *perfectly* realised by any actual, organised society, or by all of them put together. But Prof. Royce's practical teaching can only be applied to actual life by the existence of societies which *attempt* to realise the idea, and by individuals who attach themselves to whatever society seems to them the best adapted here, now, for them – to represent or symbolise this great idea of the community of the redeemed. And if that is so, actual Churches and organisations ought not to be spoken of in the rather patronising tone which Prof. Royce usually adopts towards them. In recommending to the individual – at least to the philosophic individual – an attitude of complete detachment from all existing religious organisations, all traditional creeds and systems, all signs and symbols and incarnations of the spiritual reality, Prof. Royce is, as it seems to me, practically unsaying and contradicting all the valuable teaching in the earlier part of his work about the essentially social character of Religion and of all the higher moral and spiritual life of man. He would be quite justified in insisting strongly – more strongly even than he has done – upon the gulf which yawns between the magnificent ideal of the Churches and their actual practice, upon the necessity for reform, for adapting their teaching to the ideas of the age and so on. But to suggest to the individual that he should practically be content with a Church which exists only "in the heavens" is in effect to tell him to give up that article of belief in the Church to which Prof. Royce attaches so much importance. A Universal must have particulars. A Church which existed only in the heavens would not be a Church at all. The inconsistency would be patent to every one if we transferred this way of thinking to the State. Undoubtedly no actual State is more than an inadequate attempt to realise the true ideal of the State as it presented itself to a Plato, an Aristotle, or a Hegel; but, so far as I am aware, no one who has treated the State in the spirit of any of these philosophers has ever combined such an exalted view of the ideal State with such contempt for the actual State as is practically expressed by Prof. Royce for the actual or even for every possibly actual Church or Churches. A man who should profess sympathy with the Hegelian idea of the State and recommend Anarchism, or at least Stoic "autonomy" and detachment, in practice would have very inadequately learned the true lessons of Hegel's political thought.

But at this point I may be again reminded that at bottom the "beloved community" of which Prof. Royce tells us is only a name for humanity at large. At times Prof. Royce tells us so in so many words. But this only makes the inconsistency the more glaring. Doubtless mankind does form in some sense a community. But nobody knows better than Prof. Royce that a community of all mankind – at least so long as that community has no outward and visible social and political organisation or expression – cannot be to the individual all that a community ought to be. It must be in lesser communities than this that the true idea of a community must be realised; and these communities must be actual, concrete, more or less organised. Does not Prof. Royce tell us that it must be the supreme effort of the members of the "beloved community" to turn other men into members of it? How can he do this if they are already members as fully as they ought to be? If it be suggested that to make them members of an ideal community is only another way of saying to produce a moral or spiritual change in them such as might be constituted by entrance into an actual community – to behave towards every other as if one were trying to make them members of a community, I would submit that this is to idealise the conception of a community to a point at which it ceases to be a community at all or to have anything in common with the Christian Church or any other of the actual religious communities of history. And yet to say this would be to ignore the lesson which Prof. Royce's own study of Christianity so vigorously teaches.

This account of Prof. Royce's view of the Church is not complete without some reference to his theory of Atonement. In a chapter on "Time and Guilt" he insists upon the irrevocable character and consequences of moral choice. There is, in Prof. Royce's view, a certain "actual and deliberate sin against the light" – a "sin against the Holy Ghost," the consequences of which are irrevocable. The Hell to which by such a sin the individual is doomed, or rather to which he dooms himself, is self-chosen. The individual who has been guilty of it will feel (or does Prof. Royce mean that he ought to feel? – the distinction does not seem to be recognised): "It is my precious privilege to assert my own reasonable will, by freely accepting my place in the hell of the irrevocable, and by never forgiving myself for this sin against the light. If any new deed can assign to just that one traitorous deed of mine any essentially novel and reconciling meaning – that new deed will in any case certainly *not* be mine. I can do good deeds in future; but I cannot revoke my individual past deed" (I., 266–67). The only way in which the sin can be atoned for is that something should be done "which gives to my very treason itself a new value; so that I can say, not 'It is undone'; but 'I am henceforth in some measure, in some genuine fashion, morally reconciled to the fact that I did this evil'" (I., 281).

The author insists on the inadequacy of the idea of substitution or of modern "moral" theories of Atonement, like that of M. Auguste Sabatier, based on the actual effects upon the heart of self-sacrificing love. We want an *objective* atonement. The "triumph over treason" which is required "can only be accomplished by the community, or on behalf of the community, through some steadfastly loyal servant who acts, so to speak, as the incarnation of the very spirit of the community itself." This faithful and suffering servant of the community may answer and confound treason by a work whose type I shall next venture to describe, in my own way, thus: First, this creative work shall include a deed, or various deeds, for which only just this treason furnishes the opportunity. Not treason in general, but just this individual treason shall give the occasion, and supply the condition of the creative deed which I am in ideal describing. Without just that treason, this new deed (so I am supposing) could not have been done at all. And hereupon the new deed, as I suppose, is so ingeniously devised, so concretely practical in the good which it accomplishes, that, when you look down upon the human world after the new creative deed has been done in it, you say, first, "This deed was made possible by that treason; and, secondly, *The world, as transformed by this creative deed, is better than it would have been had all else remained the same, but had that deed of treason not been done at all.* That is, the new creative deed has made the new world better than it was before the blow of treason fell" (I., pp. 307–8).

Prof. Royce does not pretend that the death of the historical Christ is much more than a symbol of this idea. And yet he contends that this is something very like "the form which, as I believe, the Christian idea of atonement has always possessed when the interests of the religious consciousness (or, if I may use the now favourite word, the subconsciousness) of the Church, rather than the theological formulations of the theory of atonement, have been in question. Christian feeling, Christian art, Christian worship, have been full of the sense that *somehow* (and *how* has remained indeed a mystery) there was something so precious about the work of Christ, something so divinely wise (so skilful and divinely beautiful?) about the plan of salvation – that, as a result of all this, after Christ's work was done, the world as a whole was a nobler and richer and worthier creation than it would have been if Adam had not sinned" (I., pp. 318–19).

To the orthodox Christian who accepts premisses which Prof. Royce could not accept, the work of Christ might perhaps be considered to have this supreme value. But why has the work of Christ any such value unless a "satisfaction for sin" be required such as only a sinless and divine Being could offer, or unless we accept any of the numerous orthodox theories which profess to demonstrate the necessity of such a death? If the answer be found in the teaching, the life, the character, the self-sacrificing love of Jesus as illustrated or supremely expressed by His death, can these seriously be said to have a value outweighing the negative value of the sins of the whole world, apart from the effects which they have produced upon human souls and lives? And if we do say that it is the consequence upon the actual moral condition of human beings that gives it this supreme value, are we not back again at a "subjective" theory of Atonement? If its value may be said to be objective in the sense in which all values are objective for those who believe in values at all, this might be equally alleged by the partisans of the "subjective" or "moral" theories which Prof. Royce regards as so inadequate: the objective value lies in a subjective effect. Or, if Prof. Royce replies that he is only thinking of what Christians in the past have felt, and that for himself the objective atonement is constituted by the supremely noble deeds of all history which have been made possible by all the "sins against the Holy Ghost," I should ask whether there is really any sense or any utility in speaking of these deeds as "atoning" for guilt? If Prof. Royce were to plead that they have actually made possible for all these sinners a repentance, a renewal, an amendment of life which was not possible without them, there might be some meaning in saying that they are atoned by the good deeds; but this Prof. Royce cannot contend, for he admits that repentance, amendment, forgiveness by the community might all be possible without any such "atoning deeds." Does he say that only by virtue of these can the individual "forgive himself"? If a man really says to himself: "My sin has produced so much good in the world that I need not now mourn over my bad deed any longer," this does not seem to me a particularly edifying state of mind. Even if it be the fact that the quantity of good which has been introduced into the world by the atoning deeds made possible by all the sins against the light exceeds the good that would have been possible without them, I doubt the expediency of calling this an "atonement." If the man really persuades himself that because of these deeds his sinful act is "undone" (that is Prof. Royce's view), he surely deceives himself. The value of these "atoning deeds" may be important from the point of view of theodicy, but it seems to me to have no religious or moral value for the individual soul seeking "reconciliation." His deed cannot be made less bad than it was, nor his present spiritual position improved, by any such good consequences which may have flowed from his sin. He can only be restored, renewed, forgiven by that repentance which according to the teaching of Jesus was the one thing needful for "justification," but which Prof. Royce disparages. To put my criticism in the technical language of the old Theology, Prof. Royce's doctrine of the Atonement is quite unconnected with any theory of justification, or, if there is any theory of justification, it is an intelligible and immoral theory. He does not show how Atonement of this kind can be any real value to the sinner.

And here I cannot help expressing my regret that philosophers who undertake to develop the inner meaning of the historical doctrines of the Christian or any other historical religion do not take the trouble to read a little more about their origin and history. Prof. Royce very modestly disclaims for himself any competency to deal with critical or historical questions. And yet after all the historical origin of a belief has some bearing upon its philosophical interpretation. If religious philosophers would study the origin of the Atonement doctrine, they would perhaps come to the conclusion that that origin is to be sought simply and solely in the authority of Isaiah liii., and other prophecies of the Old Testament, messianically interpreted. If the notion of an "objective" Atonement owes its origin simply to a mistaken interpretation of documents believed to be authoritative, he will perhaps feel dispensed from finding an explanation of it either in "Christian experience" or universal religious experience. No doubt the doctrine did appeal to very real needs and cravings of the human spirit; but, unless we are Pragmatists, we are not bound to accept doctrines as true because they are comforting – still less because they were comforting to people whose intellectual envisagement of the Universe was not the same as our own. The fact that the Atonement doctrine originated neither in the teaching of Jesus nor in "Christian experience" may not prevent its having in it an element of eternal truth, but perhaps this element may be adequately expressed by something like the subjective view which commends itself to mere "Theologians," like M. Sabatier, who know something about the origin of the doctrines which they attempt to interpret, and whose theories Prof. Royce treats rather scornfully. If the "objective" theory was really imposed by authority, if those who attempted to explain the theory either fell into grossly immoral views or ended by substituting for it a theory which was not really objective, the philosopher is surely not bound to find an equivalent for an objective Atonement in terms of philosophical thought. That this equivalence is on Prof. Royce's own theory very problematical, is so evident that I can hardly think it will meet with much acceptance either from really orthodox thinkers or from those who very properly want to reinterpret the truth implied in traditional Theology in terms of more modern thought.

I have been obliged to pass over much that Prof. Royce tells us about the nature of communities in general – much which he tells us that most philosophers do not understand. But there is one portion of his doctrine which is too original to be ignored. Prof. Royce has been much impressed by Prof. Peirce's purely logical conception of "interpretation." He has remarked truly that neither those who exalt perception at the expense of conception nor those who exalt conception at the expense of perception can adequately explain the nature of our knowledge of other people's minds. My neighbour's mind is not an object of which I can have any direct perception, nor is it "a *general* or *abstract character* a *type*, a *quality* or some complex object based upon such universals" (II., p. 127). Here is Prof. Royce's own solution of the problem: –

"If, then, there be any cognitive process whose proper object is your neighbour's mind, this process is neither a mere conception nor yet a mere perception. Is it, then, some synthesis or combination of perceptions and conceptions? Or is it, finally, some third form of cognitive process, which is neither perception nor conception, and which cannot be completely describable in terms of combined perceptions and conceptions? Now it appears that the word 'interpretation' is a convenient name for a process which at least aims to be cognitive. And the proper object of an interpretation, as we usually employ the name, is either something of the nature of a mind, or else is a process which goes on in a mind, or, finally, is a sign or expression whereby some mind manifests its existence and its processes" (II., 128–29).

It is quite impossible for me adequately to expound Prof. Peirce's original theory or Prof. Royce's attempt to bring out by its aid the inmost nature of the ideal community adumbrated in the historical Christian Church as a "community of interpretation." I must be content with indicating that there is this important side of Prof. Royce's teaching which I have not been able to examine. I confess that I do not find it either very intelligible or very satisfactory.

My general view of this remarkable work is that it contributes a most valuable element to that philosophical interpretation of Christianity which our age needs but that it is in one way redundant, in another incomplete. It is redundant because it is mixed up with certain highly technical notions about communities and the nature of our knowledge of one another which will seem to many of more questionable value in themselves and not so closely connected as Prof. Royce supposes with the ethical and religious ideas which he is studying; it is incomplete since it ignores many elements in Christianity which are of equal value with the elements which impresses Prof. Royce. The magnificent exposition and vindication of the Christian doctrine of Love and the idea of the Christian community seem to me one of the most valuable contributions to the Philosophy of Religion which have been made by any thinker of our time. This is a most important element in Christianity, but I cannot think that it contains a full solution of "the problem of Christianity." After all this would be too much to expect in any one work of any one writer, however eminent.

# REVIEW OF
# *THE PROBLEM OF CHRISTIANITY*

A.C. Armstrong, Review of *The Problem of Christianity*, *Philosophical Review*, vol. 23 (1914).

*The Problem of Christianity*. By Josiah Royce. New York, The Macmillan Company, 1913. 2 vols. pp. xlvi, 425; vi, 442.

These notable volumes reproduce lectures delivered in 1912–13 at the Lowell Institute in Boston and Manchester College, Oxford. Their original form conditions certain features of the discussion. The vivacity, even eloquence of the oral presentation enlivens the printed argument. But the professional reader misses at times the uninterrupted precision of technical exposition. In one point, however, the gain outweighs any loss. Professor Royce's discussion of Christianity is born of experience. Its source is to be found in the experience of a philosopher and a convinced Idealist. But, as the preface suggests, it is no discussion of the closet, framed by the application of *a priori* categories to assumed religious facts. If any one so misconceives the author's method, the study of a single chapter will suffice to correct the error: he need but read in Lecture VI the profoundly moving account of the Christian principle of atonement in relation to human experience and to the modern mind.

The first volume deals with Christianity as a doctrine of life, the second with Christianity and its metaphysical basis. One problem is common to both, the problem of essential Christianity – what is it in the first place? and how is it to fare amid the vicissitudes of later culture? Recent philosophers of religion have often neglected this problem, but from their position Professor Royce emphatically dissents. For him Christianity is the form of faith which so far in the evolution of the world best fulfills the function of religion in the changing life of man. For the principal ideas of Christianity he also cherishes respect: sin and grace and atonement, these are not to be minimized but interpreted. For they are grounded in the spiritual experience of the race. And so they possess objective reality, a fact which confutes the advocates of "liberal" doctrine, as well as the dogmatists who petrified them into literal abstractions. The solution of the problem is to be found in the idea of the spiritual community. As loyalty forms the keynote of the author's ethics, so the studies of his later years have led him to an Idealistic religion of loyalty. The Pauline doctrine of the body and the members re-appears in the idea of the "Beloved Community." It is to this that devotion is due, and disloyalty to it constitutes the irrevocable sin of the spiritual traitor. In communion with the spiritual body grace is to be found; salvation is redemption from disloyalty through union with the spirit of the whole. Even the irrevocable sin can be atoned for: the deed can never be wiped out, but through the work of a redemptive agent it may be made the occasion for common spiritual gain which had otherwise been impossible. So even the traitor may realize the good that his evil, his irrevocable evil, has brought forth.

The method of the argument varies with the phases of the problem. The fundamental Christian ideas are considered from the standpoint of spiritual experience. Together they constitute the Christian doctrine of life, whose truth and value are attested by their conformity to this experience. But experience has metaphysical implications. Therefore the inquiry proceeds from the discussion of the Christian ideas to the discussion of their basis in reality. This implies primarily the reality of the community, a reality which, as the author holds, has been underestimated by the great majority, even of the best writers hitherto. As the individual consciousness, so the social mind develops its characteristic life. This is other and richer than the consciousness of the detached individual. And as it is richer in itself, so it has characteristic manifestations in language, in institutions, above all as the center of the ethical and spiritual ideal. Professor Royce stops short, indeed, of the personification of the community, although isolated expressions in his earlier argument appear to favor such a conclusion. But short of this, and short of ignoring the individual personalities which compose the common body, he exalts the community to the highest place. To the community devotion is due, as to it in fact devotion is given beyond that which is bestowed on any individual. The Christian ideal is true, because it is congruous with the truth of the community idea. The Beloved Community as a constantly realizing, but never fully realized ideal – is the Kingdom of God for which mankind are summoned to labor and to pray.

The metaphysics of the community once more links Christianity with the reality of the world at large. The community itself is the type-form which best solves the old problem of the many and the one. And through a study of knowledge it leads to a new development of Idealistic doctrine. Traditional theories from Plato to Bergson have recognized two modes of knowledge, perception and conception. The Platonists have emphasized the latter, the empiricists, down to James and Bergson, with equal partiality have magnified the perceptual form of thought. To neither school, nor to the many who now discern the constant fusing of perception and conception, has it been given to note a third and more important form. This is "interpretation." Self-consciousness is the interpretation of the individual's present and his future to himself. History is the interpretation of the past in lessons for the present and the time to come. Science proceeds by the verification of hypotheses, and verification is interpretation of the individual's discovery into established doctrine accepted by the common mind. Following Charles Peirce, from whom he derived the germ of his own theory, Professor Royce defines interpretation as a triadic mode of cognition. There is that which is to be interpreted, there is the mind to which it is to be interpreted, there is the interpreter to mediate the two. More abstractly, interpretation is illustrated by comparison. Terms do not agree or differ – merely. They agree – or differ – through the mediation of a third, which interprets their likeness or difference. But this interpreter, this third, involves fresh problems. Whence come new mediations and new interpreters – to infinity.

Finally, this highest form of knowing supplies the clue to universal metaphysics. The time-order is of the nature of interpretation. The evolution of the world is the manifestation in time of the one ideal-reality through successive partial syntheses of interpretation. The spirit of the world is the infinite interpreter, as the spirit of the community is the mediator of all its individual members. So the metaphysics of the community and the metaphysics of the world are one. And essential Christianity, summed up in the idea of the Beloved Community, articulates into the final truth about the world.

That his philosophy of religion suggests manifold questions is recognized by the author, who also frankly considers the issues raised. Two classes of these only can be noted here. In the field of religion proper, and of Christianity, his conclusions most directly challenge current views in regard to a class of questions which may be termed questions of personality. The influence of the Founder of Christianity on the primitive Christian community; the relation of the individual to the community in any religious body; the personal character of religious devotion and of its objects – these are conceived differently by Professor Royce and many later thinkers. As already noted, he avoids the conclusion that the community is a person, and rightly; but what of the Spirit of the Community, and what of the Infinite Interpreter? In philosophy, most interest will be aroused by the new doctrine of knowledge. Is 'interpretation' specifically different from that fused synthesis of perception and conception which is justly recognized as the common form, or is it a phase of the same essential process? Is comparison the type of interpretation, or must not other forms of synthetic thinking be correlated with it? In either case, does the noëtic ground compel the inference to the metaphysical conclusion? And if so, does the new Idealism free us from the ultimate difficulties which were involved in the religious philosophy of the old?

# INSTITUTIONALISM AND MYSTICISM

W.R. Inge, "Institutionalism and Mysticism," *Hibbert Journal*, vol. 13 (1914).

A lecture by the Very Rev. W. R. Inge, Dean of St. Paul's, delivered at the Memorial Hall, Farringdon Street, 5th March 1914.

It happens sometimes that two opposite tendencies flourish together, deriving strength from a sense of the danger with which each is threatened by the popularity of the other. Where the antagonism is not absolute, each may gain by being compelled to recognise the strong points in the rival position. In a serious controversy the right is seldom or never all on one side; and in the normal course of events both theories undergo some modification through the influence of their opponents, until a compromise, not always logically defensible, brings to an end the acute stage of the controversy. Such a tension of rival movements is very apparent in the religious thought of our day. The quickening of spiritual life in our generation has taken two forms, which appear to be, and to a large extent are, sharply opposed to each other. On the one side, there has been a great revival of mysticism. Mysticism means an immediate communion, real or supposed, between the human soul and the Soul of the World or the Divine Spirit. The hypothesis on which it rests is that there is a real affinity between the individual soul and the great immanent Spirit, who in Christian theology is identified with the Logos-Christ. He was the instrument in creation, and through the Incarnation and the gift of the Holy Spirit, in which the Incarnation is continued, has entered into the most intimate relation with the inner life of the believer. This revived belief in the inspiration of the individual has immensely strengthened the position of Christian apologists, who find their old fortifications no longer tenable against the assaults of natural science and historical criticism. It has given to faith a new independence, and has vindicated for the spiritual life the right to stand on its own feet and rest on its own evidence. Spiritual things, we now realise, are spiritually discerned. The enlightened soul can see the invisible, and live its true life in the suprasensible sphere. The primary evidence for the truth of religion is religious experience, which in persons of religious genius – those whom the Church calls saints and prophets – includes a clear perception of an eternal world of truth, beauty, and goodness, surrounding us and penetrating us at every point. It is the unanimous testimony of these favoured spirits that the obstacles in the way of realising this transcendental world are purely subjective, and to a large extent removable by the appropriate training and discipline. Nor is there any serious discrepancy among them either as to the nature of the vision which is the highest reward of human effort, or as to the course of preparation which makes us able to receive it. The Christian mystic must begin with the punctual and conscientious discharge of his duties to society; he must next purify his desires from all worldly and carnal lusts, for only the pure in heart can see God; and he may thus fit himself for "illumination" – the stage in which the glory and beauty of the spiritual life, now clearly discerned, are themselves the motive of action and the incentive to contemplation; while the possibility of a yet more immediate and ineffable vision of the Godhead is not denied, even in this life. There is reason to think that this conception of religion appeals more and more strongly to the younger generation today. It brings an intense feeling of relief to many who have been distressed by being told that religion is bound up with certain events in antiquity, the historicity of which it is in some cases difficult to establish; with a cosmology which has been definitely disproved; and with a philosophy which they cannot make their own. It allows us what George Meredith calls "the rapture of the forward view." It brings home to us the meaning of the promise made by the Johannine Christ that there are many things as yet hid from humanity which will in the future be revealed by the Spirit of Truth. It encourages us to hope that for each individual who is trying to live the right life the venture of faith will be progressively justified in experience. It breaks down the denominational barriers which divide men and women who worship the Father in spirit and in truth – barriers which become more senseless in each generation, since they no longer correspond even approximately with real differences of belief or of religious temperament. It makes the whole world kin by offering a pure religion which is substantially the same in all climates and in all ages – a religion too divine to be fettered by any man-made formulas, too nobly human to be readily acceptable to men in whom the ape and tiger are still alive, but which finds a congenial home in the purified spirit which is the "throne of the Godhead." Such is the type of faith which is astir among us. It makes no imposing show in Church conferences; it does not fill our churches and chapels; it has no organisation, no propaganda; it is for the most part passively loyal, without much enthusiasm, to the institutions among which it finds itself. But in reality it has overleapt all barriers; it knows its true spiritual kin;

and amid the strifes and perplexities of a sad and troublous time it can always recover its hope and confidence by ascending in heart and mind to the heaven which is closer to it than breathing, and nearer than hands and feet.

But on the other side we see a tendency, even more manifest if we look for external signs, to emphasise the institutional side of religion, that which prompts men and women to combine in sacred societies, to cherish enthusiastic loyalties for the Church of their early education or of their later choice, to find their chief satisfaction in acts of corporate worship, and to subordinate their individual tastes and beliefs to the common tradition and discipline of a historical body. It is now about eighty years since this tendency began to manifest itself as a new phenomenon in the Anglican Church. Since then, it has spread to other organisations. It has prompted a new degree of denominational loyalty in several Protestant bodies on the Continent, in America, and in our own country; and it has arrested the decline of the Roman Catholic Church in countries where the outlook seemed least hopeful from the ecclesiastical point of view. Such a movement, so widespread and so powerful in its results, is clearly a thing to be reckoned with by all who desire to estimate rightly the signs of the times. It is a current running in the opposite direction to the mystical tendency, which regards unity as a spiritual, not a political ideal. Fortunately, the theory of institutionalism has lately been defended and expounded by several able writers belonging to different denominations; so that we may hope, by comparing their utterances, to understand the attractions of the theory and its meaning for those who so highly value it.

Aubrey Moore, writing in 1889, connected the Catholic revival with the abandonment of atomism in natural philosophy and of Baconian metaphysics. These were, he thought, the counterpart of individualism in politics and Calvinism in religion. The adherents of mid-Victorian science and philosophy were bewildered by the phenomenon of "men in the nineteenth century actually expressing a belief in a divine society and a supernatural presence in our midst, a brotherhood in which men become members of an organic whole by sharing in a common life, a service of man which is the natural and spontaneous outcome of the service of God."[1] In the view of this learned and acute thinker, Catholicism, or institutionalism, is destined to supplant Protestantism, as the organic theory is destined to displace the atomic.

More recently Troeltsch, writing as a Protestant, has emphasised the institutional side of religion in the most uncompromising way. "One of the clearest results of all religious history and religious psychology is

[1] Moore, *Science and the Faith*, Introduction.

that the essence of all religion is not dogma and idea, but cultus and communion, the living intercourse with the Deity – an intercourse of the entire community, having its vital roots in religion and deriving its ultimate power of thus uniting individuals, from its faith in God." "Whatever the future may bring us, we cannot expect a certainty and force of the knowledge of God and of His redemptive power to subsist without communion and cultus. And so long as a Christianity of any kind shall subsist at all, it will be united with a cultus, and with Christ holding a central position in the cultus."[2]

From America, that last refuge of individualism, there has come a pronouncement not less drastic. Professor Royce, the author of the admirable metaphysical treatise entitled *The World and the Individual*, has recently published a double series of Hibbert Lectures on "The Problem of Christianity," in which he affirms the institutionalist theory with a surprising absence of qualification. The whole book is dominated by one idea, advocated with a *naïveté* which would hardly have been possible to a theologian – the idea that churchmanship is the essential part of the Christian religion. "The salvation of the individual man is determined by some sort of membership in a certain spiritual community – a religious community, and in its inmost nature a divine community, in whose life the Christian virtues are to reach their highest expression and the spirit of the Master is to obtain its earthly fulfilment. In other words, there is a certain universal and divine spiritual community. Membership in that community is necessary to the salvation of man... . Such a community exists, is needed, and is an indispensable means of salvation for the individual man, and is the fitting realm wherein alone the kingdom of heaven which the Master preached can find its expression, and wherein alone the Christian virtues can be effectively preached."[3] These statements, which in vigour and rigour would satisfy the most extreme curialist in the Society of Jesus, are not a little startling in an American philosopher, who, as far as the present writer knows, does not belong to any "Catholic" Church. The thesis thus enunciated is the argument of the whole book, in which "loyalty to the beloved community" is declared to be the characteristic Christian virtue. It is true that the satisfaction of Professor Royce's Catholic readers is destined to be damped in the second volume, where he forbids us to look for the ideal divine community in any existing Church, and expresses his conviction that great changes must come over the dogmatic teaching of Christianity. But for our purpose the significant fact is that throughout the book he insists that Christianity is essentially an institu-

[2] Troeltsch, *Die Bedeutung der Geschichtlichkeit Jesu für den Glauben*, pp. 25 sq.

[3] Royce, *The Problem of Christianity*, vol. i. p. 39.

tional religion, the most completely institutional of all religions. For Professor Royce, to be a Christian is to be a Churchman.

Our last witness shall be the learned Roman Catholic layman, Baron Friedrich von Hügel, the deepest thinker, perhaps, of all living theologians in this country. "It is now ever increasingly clear to all deep impartial students, that religion has ever primarily expressed and formed itself in cultus, in social organisation, social worship, intercourse between soul and soul and between soul and God; and in symbols and sacraments, in contacts between spirit and matter." He proceeds to discuss the strength and weakness of institutionalism in a perfectly candid spirit, but with too particular reference to the present conditions within the Roman Church to help us much in our more general survey. He mentions the drawbacks of an official philosophy, prescribed by authority; "only in 1835 did the Congregation of the Index withdraw heliocentric books from its list." He emphasises the necessity of historical dogmas, but admits that orthodoxy cherishes, along with them, "fact-like historical pictures" which "cannot be taken as directly, simply factual." He vindicates the orthodoxy of religious toleration, and refuses to consign all non-Catholics to perdition, lamenting the tendency to identify absolutely the visible and invisible Church, which prevails among "some of the (now dominant) Italian and German Jesuit Canonists." Lastly, he boldly recommends the frank abandonment of the Papal claim to exercise temporal power in Italy. This is not so much a critique of institutionalism as the plea of a Liberal Catholic that the logic of institutionalism should not be allowed to override all other considerations. The Baron is, indeed, himself a mystic, though also a strong believer in the necessity of institutional religion.

We have then a considerable body of very competent opinion, that a man cannot be a Christian unless he is a Churchman. To the mystic pure and simple, such a statement seems monstrous. Did not even Augustine say, "I want to know God and my own soul; these two things, and no third whatever"? What intermediary can there be, he will ask, between the soul and God? What sacredness is there in an organisation? Is it not a matter of common experience that the morality of an institution, a society, a state, is inferior to that of the individuals who compose it? And is organised Catholicism an exception to this rule? And yet we must admit the glamour of the idea of a divine society. It arouses that *esprit de corps* which is the strongest appeal that can be made to some noble minds. It calls for self-sacrifice and devoted labour in a cause which is higher than private interest. It demands discipline and co-operation, through which alone great things can be done on the field of history. It holds out a prospect of really influencing the course of events. And if there has been a historical Incarnation, it follows that God has actually intervened on the stage of history, and that it is His will to carry out some great and divine purpose in and by means of the course of history. With this object, as the Catholic believes, He established an institutional Church, pledged to the highest of all causes; and what greater privilege can there be than to take part in this work, as a soldier in the army of God in His long campaign against the spiritual powers of evil? The Christian institutionalist is the servant of a grand idea.

There are, however, a few questions which we are bound to ask him. First, Is his idea of the Church Christian? Did the Founder of Christianity contemplate or even implicitly sanction the establishment of a semi-political international society, such as the Catholic Church has actually been? Orthodox Catholicism maintains that He did. Modernism admits that He did not, but adds that if He had known that the Messianic expectation was illusory, and that the existing world-order was to continue for thousands of years, He would certainly have wished that a Catholic Church should exist. And, argues the Modernist, if it is a good thing that a Catholic Church should exist, it is useless to quarrel with the conditions under which alone it can maintain its existence. The philosophical historian must admit that all the changes which the Catholic Church has undergone – its concessions to Pagan superstition, its secular power, its ruthless extirpation of rebels against its authority, its steadily growing centralisation and autocracy – were forced upon it in the struggle for existence. Those who wish that Church history had been different are wishing the impossible, or wishing that the Church had perished. But this argument is not valid as a defence of a divine institution. It is rather a merciless exposure of what happens, and must happen, to a great idea when it is enslaved by an institution of its own creation. The political organisation which has grown up round the idea ends by strangling it, and continues to fight for its own preservation by the methods which govern the policy of all other political organisations – force, fraud, and accommodation. There is nothing in the political history of Catholicism which suggests in the slightest degree that the spirit of Christ has been the guiding principle in its councils. Its methods have, on the contrary, been more cruel, more fraudulent, more unscrupulous, than those of most secular powers. If the Founder of Christianity had appeared again on earth during the so-called ages of faith, it is hardly possible to doubt that He would have been burnt alive or crucified again. What the Latin Church preserved was not the religion of Christ, which lived on by its inherent indestructibility, but parts of the Aristotelian and Platonic philosophies, distorted and petrified by Scholasticism, a vast quantity of purely Pagan superstitions, and the *arcana imperii* of Roman Cæsarism. The normal end of Scholasticism is a mummified philosophy of authority, in which there are no problems to solve, but a great many dead pundits to consult. The normal end of a policy which exploits the superstitions of the peasant is a desperate warfare against education. The normal end of Roman Imperialism is a sultanate like that of Diocletian. It is difficult to find a proof of infallible and supernatural wisdom in the evolution of which these are the last terms. We read with the utmost sympathy and admiration Baron von Hügel's loyal and reverent appeals to the authorities of his Church, that they may draw out the strong and beneficent powers of institutionalism, and avoid its insidious dangers. But it may be doubted whether such a policy is possible. The future of Roman Catholicism is, I fear, with the Ultramontanes. They, and not the Modernists, are in the line of development which Catholicism as an institution has consistently followed, and must continue to follow to the end. I can see no other fate in store for the *soma* of Catholicism; the germ-cells of true Christianity live their own life within it, and are transmitted without taint to those who are born of the Spirit.

We must further ask the institutionalist what are his grounds for identifying the Church of God with the particular institution to which he belongs. On the institutionalist hypothesis, it might have been expected either that there would have been no divisions in Christendom, or that all seceding bodies would have shown such manifest inferiority in wisdom, morality, and sanctity, that the exclusive claims of the Great Church would have been ratified at the bar of history. This is, in fact, the claim which Roman Catholics make. But it can only be upheld by writing history in the spirit of an advocate, or by giving a preference, not in accordance with modern ethical views, to certain types of character which are produced by the monastic life of the Catholic "religious." It is increasingly difficult to find, in the lives of those who belong to any one denomination, proofs of marked superiority over other Christians. Of course, we know little of the real character of our neighbours as they appear in the eyes of God; but in considering a theory which lays so much stress on history as Catholic institutionalism does, we are bound to make use of such evidence as we have. And the evidence does not support the theory that we cannot be Christians unless we are Catholics. Nor does it even countenance the view that we cannot be Christians unless we are enthusiastic members of *some* religious corporation. Professor Royce seems to have been carried away by the idea which prompted him to write his book; but a little thought about the characters of his acquaintances might have given him pause.

The mechanical theory of devolution which assumes so much importance in some fashionable Anglican teaching about the Church need not detain us long. The logical choice must ultimately be between the great international Catholic Church and what Auguste Sabatier called the religion of the Spirit. The religion of all Protestants, when it is not secularised, as it too often is, belongs to this latter type, even when they lay most stress on the idea of brotherhood and corporate action. For with them institutions are never much more than associations for mutual help and edification. The Protestant always hopes to be saved *qua* Christian, not *qua* Churchman.

A third question which must be asked is whether institutionalism in practice makes for unity among Christians, or for division. Too often the chief visible sign of the "corporate idea" of which so much is said, is the rigidity of the spikes which it erects round its own particular fold. The obstacles to acts of reunion (which in no way carry with them the necessity of formal amalgamation) are raised almost exclusively by stiff institutionalists The much-discussed Kikuyu case has brought this home to everybody. But for these uncompromising Churchmen, Christians of all denominations would be glad enough to meet together at the Lord's table on special occasions like the service which gave rise to this controversy. Anglicans are well aware that the differences of opinion within their body are far greater than those which separate some of them from Protestant Nonconformity, and others of them from Rome. Allegiance to this or that denomination is generally an accident of early surroundings. To make these external classifications into barriers which cannot be crossed is either an absurdity or a confession that a Church is a political aggregate. A Roman Monsignor explained, à *propos* of the Kikuyu service, that no Roman Catholic could ever communicate in a Protestant church, because in so doing he would be guilty of an act of apostasy, and would be no longer a Roman Catholic. This attitude is consistent with the Roman claim to universal jurisdiction; for any other body it would be absurd. The stiff institutionalist is debarred by his theory from fraternising with many who should be his friends, while he is bound to others with whom he has no sympathy. His theory is once more found to conflict with the facts.

Lastly, we must ask whether institutionalism is really a spiritual and moral force. Of the advantages of *esprit de corps* I have spoken already. No one can doubt that unity is strength, or that Catholicism has an immense advantage over its rivals in the efficiency of its organisation. But is not this advantage dearly purchased? Party loyalty is notoriously unscrupulous. The idealised institution becomes itself the object of worship, and it is entirely forgotten that a Christian Church ought to have no "interests" except the highest welfare of humanity. The substitution of military for civil ethics has worked disastrously on the conduct of Churchmen. Theoretically it is admitted by Roman casuists that an immoral order ought not to be obeyed; but it is not for a layman to pronounce immoral any order received from a priest; if the order is really immoral, "obedience" exonerates him who executes it; in all other cases disobedience is a deadly sin. The result of this submission of private judgment is that the voice of conscience is often stifled, and unscrupulous policies are carried through by Churchmen, which secular public opinion would have condemned decisively and rejected. The persecution of Dreyfus is a recent and strong instance. If all France had been Catholic, the victim of this shocking injustice would certainly have died in prison. It is extremely doubtful whether the presence of a highly organised Church is conducive to moral and social reform in a country. The temptation to play a political game seems to be always too strong. In Ireland, the priesthood has probably helped to maintain a comparatively high standard of sexual morality, but it cannot be said that the Irish Catholic population is in other respects a model of civilisation and good citizenship. In education especially the influence of ecclesiasticism has been almost uniformly pernicious, so that it seems impossible for any country where the children are left under priestly influence to rise above a certain rather low level of civilisation.

The strongest claim of institutionalism to our respect is probably the beneficial restraint which it exercises upon many persons who need moral and intellectual guidance. It is the fashion to disparage the scholastic theology, and it has certainly suffered by being congealed, like everything else that Rome touches, into a hard system; but it is immeasurably superior to the theosophies and fancy religions which run riot in the superficially cultivated classes of Protestant countries. The undisciplined mystic, in his reliance on the inner light, may fall into various kinds of *Schwärmerei* and superstition. In some cases he may even lose his sanity for want of a wise restraining influence. It is not an accident that America, where institutionalism is weakest, is the happy hunting-ground of religious quacks and cranks. But also an institution has the power of setting everyone to work for it. In unorganised Christianity a great deal of spiritual energy runs to waste, which a great Church would know how to utilise. Lastly, we must not undervalue the steadying influence of ancient and consecrated tradition, which is kept up mainly by ecclesiastical institutions. These probably prevent many rash experiments from being tried, especially in the field of morals. Even writers like Dr. Frazer insist on the immense services which consecrated tradition still renders to humanity. These claims may be admitted; but they come very far short of the glorification of institutionalism which we found in the authors quoted a few pages back.

The institutionalist, however, may reply that he by no means admits the validity of Sabatier's antithesis between religions of authority and the religion of the Spirit. His own religion, he believes, is quite as spiritual as that of the Protestant individualist. He may quote the fine saying of a medieval mystic that he who can see the inward in the outward is more spiritual than he who can only see the inward in the inward. We may, indeed, be thankful that we have not to choose between two mutually exclusive types of religion. The Quaker, whom we may take as the type of anti-institutional mysticism, has a brotherhood to which he is proud to belong, and for which he feels loyalty and affection. And Catholicism has been rich in contemplative saints who have lived in the light of the Divine presence. The question raised in this paper is rather of the relative importance of these two elements in the religious life, than of choosing one and rejecting the other. I will conclude by saying that our preference of one of these types to the other will be largely determined by our attitude towards history. I am glad to see that Professor Bosanquet, in his fine Gifford Lectures, has the courage to expose the limitations of the "historical method," now so popular. He protests against Professor Ward's dictum that "the actual is wholly historical," as a view little better than naïve realism. History, he says, is a hybrid form of experiences, incapable of any considerable degree of being or trueness. It is a fragmentary diorama of finite life-processes seen from the outside, and very imperfectly known. It consists largely of assigning parts in some great world-experience to particular actors – a highly speculative enterprise. To set these contingent and dubious constructions above the operations of pure thought and pure insight is indeed a return to the philosophy of the man in the street. "Social morality, art, philosophy, and religion take us far beyond the spatio-temporal externality of history; these are concrete and necessary living worlds, and in them the finite mind begins to experience something of what individuality must ultimately mean." Our inquiry has thus led us to the threshold of one of the fundamental problems of philosophy – the value and reality of time. For the institutionalist happenings in time have a meaning and importance far greater than the mystic is willing to allow to them. Like most other great philosophical problems, this question is largely one of temperament. Christianity has found room for both types. I have only argued that the aberrations or exaggerations of institutionalism have been, and are, more dangerous, and further removed from the spirit of Christianity, than those of mysticism.

# ROYCE'S PHILOSOPHY OF RELIGION

Edwin S. Carr, "Royce's Philosophy of Religion," *Bibliotheca Sacra* (1914).

Popular interest has recently been aroused by the writings and lectures of Professor Royce. He has not heretofore been conspicuous as a champion of orthodoxy. His lectures, however, at Beloit College, before the Lowell Institute, and at Manchester College, Oxford, since published under the title, *The Problem of Christianity*, have attracted much attention in religious circles. In a recent communication to the *Advance* (Nov. 13, 1913), an Iowa Congregational minister declares that Royce has established the truth of the old-fashioned Calvinistic doctrines of Sin, Penalty, Divine Grace and Atonement "with an inexorable logic from which there is no escape." And he adds the remark, from which surely there can be no dissent, "When these doctrines come from the leading philosophical thinker of America, and from an institution popularly regarded as liberal, the event is even more noteworthy." This noteworthy achievement so impresses the *Advance* editor that he prints the letter of the Iowa minister under the caption, "Royce, Defender of the Faith."

In a recent number of *Faith and Doubt*, a magazine established for the defense of orthodoxy, appears a review of Royce's "Sources of Religious Insight." The writer is in nothing critical but in all things commendatory. Professor Royce is hailed as the Moses who shall lead our doubting and troubled age into the promised land of faith and freedom. And his final exhortation runs, "By all means read the book."

It should be an interesting and profitable study to trace the development of Dr. Royce's philosophical opinions and religious experience.

Josiah Royce was born in Grass Valley, California, in 1855. He received the degree of A.B. from the University of California in 1875, and a Ph.D., from Johns Hopkins in 1878. He was instructor in English Literature and Logic in the University of California from 1878 to 1882, instructor and assistant professor of Philosophy from 1882 to 1892, and since 1892 has held the chair of History of Philosophy at Harvard University.

Note that he began his academic career as instructor in English Literature. This is where he belongs; the line for which his mental gifts fit him. He is a rhetorician and an expositor of other men's opinions rather than a thoroughgoing and consistent thinker. He first gained public recognition and notoriety by attacking the prevalent conceptions of God and immortality. Later, as he attempted to construct some sort of philosophy, he was driven more and more to accept the essential principles of the only permanently satisfactory philosophical system our race has produced – the Christian.

Royce's general philosophical position is the modified Hegelianism represented during the last generation by Professor T. H. Green in England, and by Professor Otto Pfleiderer in Germany. From Kant's "transcendental unity of apperception" has been developed an all-embracing World-Consciousness, in which the finite mind knows the external object, and the knowledge of which is religion. Finite beings and things are thoughts of the Infinite Consciousness, and the history of the universe is the progressive unfolding of the Absolute Thought. The transcendental unity of apperception has thus been made the source of all truth and life; it is the Hegelian God, deified and enthroned, and universal humanity is summoned to bow and worship. What is Kant's transcendental unity of apperception? It is simply the unity of the finite consciousness – the sense of oneness, selfhood, which abides through all changing mental states, and makes possible the union of subject and object in the act of knowledge. One of the most extraordinary achievements of Kant's idealistic successors was to take this unpretentious principle of our inner life, disguise it in the garb of an unintelligible terminology, quote Scripture about it, and so metamorphose it into the Divine Being. The result is that we "see all things in God," "in the transcendental unity of apperception we live and move and have our being." This theory has manifest advantages in dealing with ultimate philosophical and religious questions. God has two or three distinct meanings, and the philosopher can use the one which suits his convenience; so that there is little difficulty in refuting the common-sense objector, or reducing him to speechless astonishment. God may mean (1) the unity of the finite consciousness; (2) the general principle of unity in the universe [(1) and (2) may fall together for the pantheistic idealist]; (3) the popular notion of Christian theism. It is very easy, on this theory, to prove the existence of God. Do you know the book or the table before you [in the unity of your inner consciousness (1)]? Then you know God [which means (3) to the hearer], for He is the principle of unity in this knowledge.

Hegelian thought has in general two characteristics: (1) It is difficult to preserve the independence and freedom of the individual over against the Absolute; (2) In the philosophy of religion the old Christian terminology is retained, but with new and revolutionary meanings. The new meaning, however, is nowhere clearly stated, nor its relation to the traditional beliefs clearly defined.

In this last point we find the explanation of the Iowa minister's enthusiasm for Royce and also of the review of Royce's book in *Faith and Doubt*. These good men are among the many orthodox writers who have been deceived by the ambiguities of the Hegelians.

While in Chicago recently I met a prominent London clergyman who is about to publish a book on current religious topics. He asked me to look over the proof sheets. He has a chapter on "Immortality," in which he repudiates modern substitutes for the traditional belief in continued personal existence after death, especially opposing the ambiguities of the Hegelians. Then proceeding to his positive argument for the traditional view, the keystone of his argument is a quotation from T. H. Green, the distinguished Oxford professor, whom he eulogizes in the strongest terms as a defender of the orthodox position. The quotation is essentially the oracle of Hegel: "It is a principal element of religion that the soul is immortal; as the object of the interest of God it is elevated above the finite."

The obscurity of the Hegelian doctrine of immortality is cleared up somewhat by an interesting little fragment in the posthumous works of Professor T. H. Green: "The immortality of the soul, as = the eternity of thought, as = the being of God, is the absolute first and the absolute whole. As a determination of thought everything is eternal. What are we to say then of the extinct races of animals, the past formations of the earth? They are eternal, as stages in an eternal process. Relatively to our temporal consciousness, they have perished; relatively to the thought, which, as eternal, holds past, present, and future together, they are permanent; their very transitoriness is eternal. The living agent, man, like everything else, is eternal as a determination of thought." And so the Christian doctrine of personal immortality becomes the pale abstraction that the life of man is a transient incident in universal history, but known forever in the thought of God. When we inquire if we shall know God in a future life, we are told that we shall be known through eternity by the Absolute Thought, as having existed at a certain point of time, soon to vanish forever, so far as conscious, personal existence is concerned, in the abyss of the infinite ages!

Royce's first important book was *The Religious Aspect of Philosophy*. All theistic systems, which make God a first cause, are involved in an infinity of contradictions and finally impaled on one or the other of the horns of the old dilemma, "In this bad world the Creator is either not omnipotent or not good." The way out is to substitute for the Christian personal God the Absolute Thought of the later Hegelians – an all-embracing pantheism which makes finite persons and things thoughts of the Absolute. In the constructive section the Infinite Thought becomes a "Judge of our ideals" and an "infinite Seer of the Good as well as of the Evil," though it cannot be said to be good and to exert itself for the realization of the good, for it is to possess no causal power lest it become responsible for this bad world. At the end the moral aim set up is "the realization of the eternal life of an Infinite Spirit." This moral aim is in no way justified by his argument, for "Life" and "Spirit" mean much more than Thought.

Immortality as conscious continuous existence is discarded. Immortality for a finite being is inconceivable, and the expectation of it is immoral, because selfish. "You love the ideal for its own sake. It is not your triumph you seek, but the triumph of the Highest." It is well to contrast this clear-cut repudiation of the traditional belief with the ambiguous verbiage of his Ingersoll lectures on Immortality.

Here is Royce's philosophy of religion in its original form. His attitude of supercilious patronage toward the popular creed is suggested in the preface: "As the author has no present connection with any visible religious body, and no sort of desire for any such connection, he cannot be expected to write an apology for a popular creed. It is his aim not to arouse fruitless quarrels, but to come to some peaceful understanding with his fellows touching the ultimate meaning and value and foundation of this noteworthy custom, so widely prevalent among us, the custom of having a religion." It is a far cry from this philosophcal Colonel Ingersoll of 1885 to the defender of the faith in 1912.

It is not difficult to classify Royce at this period. The type is very common. A young man with some knowledge of current science and philosophy, but with no thorough or sympathetic understanding of Christian theology – regarding theology as a compound of imbecility and superstition. But having the pen of a ready writer and a head quick in jumping at conclusions, he discovers an easy opportunity to make a stir in the world by knocking out the foundation of the prevalent religious system. As he is driven, however, by criticism and more mature reflection to modify his views, in the long years of repentance for having hastily given to the world the youthful "reconciliation," he draws nearer and nearer to the standpoint of Christian theism. It would be greatly to the advantage of philosophy if it were made a requirement for all philosophical degrees that the student should have taken a course of lectures in theology in some respectable divinity school. Professor George S. Fullerton, of Columbia, who took Professor George P. Fisher's course in History of Doctrine at Yale, has never made such a "break" as that of Royce in *The Religious Aspect*.

Royce claims one original feature in this book – the proof of the system of monistic idealism from the possibility of error. For some reason Royce has grown lukewarm on this argument, and it has disappeared from his later writings and discussions. When I was a student at Harvard in 1893–94 I wrote a paper on this argument, in which, to my own satisfaction and to that of a philosophical expert to whom I submitted it, I showed the argument to be unsound. As the problem interested me and I was ready to be shown where I was wrong, I called on Professor Toy of Harvard Divinity School, and proposed to submit my paper to him. He declined with thanks, saying he had never made a careful examination of Professor Royce's argument. I then called on Professor Bowne, the distinguished philosopher of Boston University. He said he had never paid much attention to Royce's argument, but he would read my paper if I would pay him for it.

I state this item of personal experience to show how deep an impression was made on the Boston scholars by Royce's Hegelian dialectic. To some it did not appeal at all; the professional philosopher was willing to give a few hours or day[1] to it at so much per.

A long step, or one might safely say a tremendous leap, in the direction of Christian theism is apparent in Royce's next book, *The Conception of God*. The Absolute Thought of *The Religious Aspect* has experienced a remarkable transformation. "The attribute of Omniscience, if it were one regarded as expressing the nature of a real being would involve the presence of other attributes, – Omnipotence, Self-consciousness, Self-possession, – yes, I would uhesitatingly add, of Goodness, Perfection, and Peace." Evidently a reasonably satisfactory presentation of the Christian personal God. No attempt is made to reconcile the antagonistic conclusions of the two books: "Consistency is the bugbear of small minds"; "It is the death of your philosophizing if you come to believe anything merely because you have once maintained it." In the ten years between the two books Royce's religion has had opportunity to grow, and has made excellent use of the time.

Having reached a satisfactory conception of God, the next Hegelian problem is that of the individual. It is commonly asserted that Hegelianism is a pantheism which makes impossible any real independence and freedom for the individual over against the Absolute. This is the theme of the next book, "The World and the Individual."

That his result here is not very satisfactory will be most readily and clearly evident from a study of Royce's little book, *The Conception of Immortality*. Some good people named Ingersoll, possessed by the idea that the traditional belief in immortality should be defended against the assaults of modern skepticism, left a legacy to Harvard University to provide for an annual course of lectures on that subject. How can you

[1] Vol. LXXI,. No. 282. 8.

expect an up-to-date Harvard professor to hold the old fogy notion of conscious existence beyond the grave, when Dr. Hugo Münsterberg, the great psychologist of the philosophical faculty, declares it incredible that the human personality should continue when the sense-organs have disintegrated in death? And yet here is the income of $5,000 offered each year to some distinguished gentleman who can speak for a few hours on something he can call immortality. The temptation is evident for the man who has literary wares to sell. As Congregationalists we have no call to sling mud at our Unitarian brethren in this connection. It is the same temptation with which the Andover professors have been wrestling for a generation and to which at last they have gracefully and permanently succumbed.

It is needless to say Royce does not hold the traditional view of immortality. His position on this matter, set forth in *The Religious Aspect*, is about the one point in the book from which he has not "progressed." How then can he give the Ingersoll lectures on Immortality? His treatment of this problem compels that recognition of the originality of his genius which the "argument from error" could not extort.

Royce's idea, briefly stated in popular terms, is this. A thoroughgoing philosophical examination of the alleged human individual discloses the fact that there is nothing to him of a really worthy and self-subsistent sort. What may happen to this incomprehensible "it" when he falls into the Hegelian Nirvana no human wit can surmise, and why should the Ingersoll family be concerned about it? It is a hard guess what may happen "when this mortal shall have put on individuality."

The conspicuous institution in the work and the saving agent for the individual and society is the "Beloved Community." "The spirit of loyalty to the Beloved Community is able to supply us not only with a philosophy of life, but with a religion which is free from superstition and which is in harmony with a genuinely rational view of the world" (Preface). Royce's notion of the "Beloved Community" is simply the old conception of the invisible church universal. The old religious and doctrinal terms are largely retained: the Divine Spirit, sin, the law, atonement.

Royce's church, however, has certain peculiarities. (1) The ideal of the Beloved Community first found expression in Paul's epistles. "We possess, in the Pauline epistles, information which is priceless, and which reveals to us the religion of loyalty in its classic and universal form." (2) This church has no living connection with, and no interest whatever in, any alleged individual founder. In the Preface the objection of a distinguished authority on Christology is considered. "You speak of this early Christian community as if it were its own creator. How could the church have existed without its founder? Does not your theory hang in the air?" The author replies: "This book has no hypothesis whatever to offer as to how the Christian community originated." This distinguished authority on Christology should investigate the Hegelian theory of origins, using as concrete illustrations Topsy, who "jest growed," and Alice's experience in Wonderland when she saw "a grin without a cat." It may seem surprising that the author did not take Masonry as the type of the Beloved Community. This order is animated by the "Spirit" of fraternity and philanthropy, and goes on just the same whether or not it was founded by Solomon and George Washington.

Royce asserts emphatically and a little peevishly in the Preface that he has never been an Hegelian, and that if he has been he has reformed. It is a little hard to make this square with his attitude towards the individual founder of the church. The cavalier treatment accorded the individual over against the community seems in exact harmony with the general Hegelian theory, where the individual is always getting lost in the void of the pantheistic Absolute.

Nineteen years ago, while a candidate at Harvard for an A.M. degree, I wrote a thesis on "The Development of Modern Religious Thought, Especially in Germany." From this I quote: "In the view of Hegel, Spirit is 'the idea turning back upon itself and beholding itself as soul, as society and as God.' One needs to have in mind this Hegelian conception of spirit, rather than the ordinary Christian doctrine of the Holy Spirit, as he approaches the study of Hegel's 'kingdom of the Spirit' – the Church. Christ did not rise from the dead in bodily form; he 'arose in the spirit of the Christian community.' This 'spirit' has no relation to the historic Jesus, no relation to an assumed third person of the Divine Trinity – at least in the sense of the traditional orthodoxy. It is rather to be compared to the *esprit de corps* of a social club or an army."

Royce seems to claim that the suggestion for his theory of the Beloved Community came from twentieth-century facts, belonging to our; common ethical and religious experience. However that may be, it is quite apparent that in essential features his "church" and Hegel's exactly correspond, and that Hegel has the advantage by about a century in point of time.

As in the "church" notion, so in the use of other Christian terms, we find the same ambiguous and illusory humbug. "Sin" is so completely atoned for that the "sinfulness of sin" disappears, and the theory falls under the heresy of those who taught that the fall was a fall upward. Under his discussion of "penal" atonement, where he speaks of appeasing an "angry God," the inadequacy of his theological knowledge and his subjection to vulgar prejudice are ludicrously apparent. In developing his own atonement theory, why does he not speak of angry

Beloved Community that must be appeased? Why does not the Community freely forgive the sinner without demanding atonement? In his own exposition of the atonement, substitute Heavenly Father for Beloved Community, and we have a reasonably satisfactory statement of our modern theory of the atonement. If Royce had heard a communion sermon during the last thirty or forty years, he would not have cherished the illusion that his atonement theory was something new.

It is certainly depressing that this sort of stuff, the sweepings of the metaphysical workshops of Germany where Hegelianism has been dead for a generation, can be successfully worked off on our gullible American people.

What shall we do about it? This, at least, can he said: –

1. Christian theology must become independent and self-respecting. Are we satisfied that our American Christianity should continue so lacking in intelligence or in self-respect or in both, as to be so extremely delighted to receive even the left-handed patronage of a man like Royce? A Harvard professor of theology, Professor C. C. Everett, has well said: "Religion must be recognized as one of the essential and fundamental facts of life. It is a fact that does not ask either of philosophy or science leave to be. Religion represents the fullness of the nature; each system of philosophy represents only a part of the nature. Theology should maintain her old position as queen of philosophy as well as of science."

2. Our general public must cultivate a greater interest in the truth, and less in intellectual dainties and novelties.

It was the custom at Harvard Divinity School years ago to have a weekly conference of professors and students on themes of interest to ministers. On one occasion one of the students, a somewhat "raw person" from the rural districts, suggested that the Apostle Paul preached justification by faith as the cure for the social ills of his time. Comment was made on this by Professor Thayer, the distinguished authority on New Testament Greek.

"Yes; but we must remember that the idea of justification by faith was fresher in Paul's time than now."

"Fresher?" Yes, but is it now any the less true and vital? That two and two make four is not fresh; but modern mathematics has never improved upon nor found a substitute for it.

# PROFESSOR ROYCE ON CHRISTIAN THOUGHT

John W. Buckham, "The Contribution of Professor Royce to Christian Thought," *Harvard Theological Review*, vol. 8 (1915).

Theology is constantly recognizing, more fully and more freely, the closeness of its relation to philosophy. Starting though they do from different impulses – theology attempting to interpret experience and philosophy to attain knowledge – they converge upon a common field. No great theologian but influences philosophy, no great philosopher but affects theology.

Of American philosophers since Edwards, no one has made so rich, profound, and extensive a contribution to religious thought as Josiah Royce.

I.

It is impossible to understand Professor Royce's philosophy without realizing its close relation, from the very start, to the problems of *religion* or rather of theology. It is not without significance that the title of his earliest volume is *The Religious Aspect of Philosophy* and that of his latest, *The Problem of Christianity*. That the religious interest was uppermost in the awakening of his puissant mind is left without a shadow of doubt by an equivalent statement in the preface of the first volume, as follows: "The religious problems have been chosen for the present study because they drove the author of philosophy, and because they, of all human interests, deserve our best efforts and our utmost loyalty."[1]

The note of loyalty, as well as that of religious interest, thus early struck, emerges later as the keynote of his ethical teaching.

One does not read far in this first fresh and vigorous volume, written at the age of thirty, before realizing that it came from the reaction of a deeply reverent penetrative mind, trained in a home of piety and a church of power, against the religious conceptions then prevalent in practically all, even the freest and broadest, American churches. The

[1] *The Religious Aspect of Philosophy*, p. v.

author sees that religion cannot be true to itself without asking "how the highest thought of man stands related to our highest needs what in things answers to our best ideals."

> Here are questions of tremendous importance to us and to world. We are sluggards or cowards if, pretending to be philosophic students and genuine seekers of truth, we do not attempt to do something with these questions. We are worse than cowards if, attempting to consider them, we do so otherwise than reverently, fearlessly, and honestly.[2]

In particular, it was the limitation of *the idea of God* then prevalent in both orthodox and liberal churches which aroused his concern, and it is with this doctrine that the book is mainly occupied. Very clear and imperative rings his challenge to those who are content with "their own little contemptible private notion and dim feeling of a God." "Take heed," he writes, "lest your object of worship be only your own little pet infinite, that is sublime to you mainly because yours."[3]

The Being whose existence depends upon the traditional arguments "aptly compared to medieval artillery on a modern battle-field," the God "who is constantly producing noteworthy effects and so getting himself into the newspapers," is, in his unfettered, critical judgment worse than none. In place of such a god the author prefers to conceive of God as "Universal Thought," and as such he essays to interpret Him.

The pathway by which he reaches the certainty that there is such a Being is the study of the nature of error. The argument drawn from the possibility of error is, in brief, as follows:

> That there is error is indubitable. What is, however, an error? The substance of our whole reasoning about the nature of error amounted to the result that in and of itself alone, no single judgment is or can be an error. Only as actually included in a higher thought, that gives to the first its completed object, and compares it herewith, is the first thought an error.[4]

This "Inclusive Thought" is none other than God. Everything else may be doubted except this.

> They reckon ill that leave me out;
> When me they fly, I am the wings;
> I am the doubter and the doubt.[5]

[2] Ibid., p. 5.

[3] Ibid., p. 13. The quotations are from the First Edition.

[4] Ibid., p. 431.

[5] Ibid., p. 484.

The All-Thinker is also the All-Enfolder, the Infinite Spirit, Universal Will. Yet His inmost essence is Thought.

> "Nor heart nor love, though these also are in it and of it. Thought it is, and all things are for Thought, and in it we live and move."

II.

In Professor Royce's next book, a fascinating and penetrative review of modern philosophy, entitled *The Spirit of Modern Philosophy*, published in 1892, he moves forward toward a fuller conception of the Divine Being as containing not only Thought but Worth – the values of the "world of appreciation." This advance in his interpretation of God came to complete and signal expression in the philosophical discussion at the University of California in 1895 – perhaps the most noteworthy that has occurred in America. The chief contributions to this discussion were published in the volume, *The Conception of God*. In the brilliant address with which Professor Royce opened the discussion, he presented the conception of God as embodied in attribute of Omniscience. God is the Absolute, Organized Experience, "related to our experience as an organic whole to its fragments."[6] The existence of such an Absolute Experience is proved – and here we have the proof from the nature of error in another form – by the fact that the very denial of it is an appeal to it as vindicator of the denial; for nothing can be true or false except it be such to an Inclusive Experience. "The very effort to deny an absolute experience involves, then, the actual assertion of such an absolute experience."[7]

Without lingering upon this subtle form of proof – a stronghold of philosophical argument which the forces of scepticism find it easier to go around than to demolish – is it impertinent to ask: What is gained by proving that there is a Universal Experience? That is easily granted without proof. The thing needing proof is that this Universal Experience is God.

Professor Royce claimed for this conception of God that it was "distinctly theistic and not pantheistic."[8]

> For my own part, then, while I wish to be no slave of any tradition, I am certainly disposed to insist that what the faith of our fathers has genuinely meant by God, is, despite all the blindness and all the unessential accidents of religious tradition, identical with the inevitable outcome of a reflective philosophy.[9]

6 *The Conception of God*, p. 44.

7 Ibid., p. 43.

8 Ibid., p. 49.

9 Ibid., p. 50.

Against this assumption Professor Howison, who represented the distinctly personalistic point of view in the discussion, protested, declaring that such a representation of God "is not the conception of a Being that we can adore at all. The fault of it at the bar of the religious reason is, that by force of the argument leading all the contradictions and tragic discords belonging to experience must be taken up directly into the life of the Absolute; they are His experiences as well as ours, and must be left in Him at once both dissolved and undissolved, unharmonized as well as harmonized, stilled and yet raging, atoned for and yet unatoned."[10]

Under the searching criticism of Professor Howison, who insisted that the conception of the Divine Being as Absolute Experience is not only unworshipful but inimical to God's ethical nature and also that it contradicts the freedom of the individual, Professor Royce wrote a supplementary essay upon *The Absolute and the Individual*, which is included in the same volume. In this he lays stress upon the process of individuation which takes place in the Absolute, endeavoring to show that the Absolute "has room for ethical individuality without detriment to its true unity."[11]

In seeking to accomplish this end, Professor Royce – whether consistently or not we will not here pause to discuss – defines God both as a self-conscious individual and as "the only ultimately real because the only absolutely whole individual."[12] This Whole Individual embraces every individual ego, each individual's plan being "identically a part of God's own attentively selected and universal plan."[13] The language reminds one of a certain Protestant theologian not now in so high repute as formerly.

III.

The Absolutism thus outlined reaches its full expression and defence in Professor Royce's greatest and most profound work – on the whole probably the most thorough and sustained work of American philosophy – the Gifford Lectures, *The World and the Individual.* If I venture not only to characterize but to criticise this masterpiece of philosophical thought, it is not without a reverent sense of the original power and imperishable worth of this burning bush of high and holy thinking which so few turn aside to see.

[10] Ibid., p. 123.

[11] Ibid., p. 137.

[12] Ibid., p. 272.

[13] Ibid., p. 292.

Just as "Universal Thought," becoming suffused with feeling and reality, gave place in Professor Royce's conception of God to "Universal Experience," so "Universal Experience" has here become purified and uplifted into Universal Selfhood. Will has become more central than Thought, and Moral Purpose than Experience. In a word, the conception of God has advanced in the Gifford Lectures distinctly toward that of a Person.

Nowhere perhaps, unless it be in Fichte's works, has the nature of personality and its relation to God been so richly and sympathetically unfolded as in these volumes – *The World and the Individual.* And yet task so splendidly assailed is in itself more than a labor of Hercules, and the want of success in establishing the main thesis cannot but be felt by the reader. To show how the One can be the One and yet the many, the Self a Self and yet the selves – this is indeed a "stickit" problem even for a mind possessed of all the subtlety as well as the sincerity, the power as well the persuasiveness, of the author of these extraordinary volumes.

These lectures, however, constitute a rich mine of philosophic theory. Several truths essential to our understanding of the interpretation of personality and of knowledge, stand out in them with a definiteness and completeness of statement seldom reached in the literature of philosophy. Such, for instance, is the remarkable exposition of the distinctness and yet the relatedness of "World of Description" and the "World of Appreciation." Professor Royce has, in these volumes, together with his analyses of consciousness in *Studies in Good and Evil*, given us an insight into the nature and meaning of the self which constitutes a most valuable contribution to the understanding of personality, and thus of Christianity as the religion of personality.

Sensitive as he is to the inner autonomy and worth of the finite selves, Professor Royce nevertheless does them an essential injustice. He endeavors to conserve their selfhood while encompassing them all within both the purview and the activity of an All-Inclusive Self. With extraordinary resourcefulness and patience he pursues the task of the adjustment of these contrasted selves, seeking to guarantee to the finite selves a freedom that will save them from the paralysis of determinism, and to the Inclusive Self a transcendence that will save him from the responsibility of the evil committed by the finite selves.

These antinomies of selfhood are, indeed, by no means peculiar to the philosophical premises of Professor Royce. Snares and pitfalls beset every theory that tries to explain with accuracy the relationship of God and man. And yet Professor Royce's monism serves to aggravate the difficulties to the highest degree. The personal God of theism is at least free from complicity with the materialities and imperfections and misdeeds of the finite selves. He may indeed seem too separate remote from the finite selves to enable us to say with so much realism as does Professor Royce of his Absolute, "In whom we live and move and have our being." Nevertheless, the immanence which a Perfect Person may have in imperfect, finite persons through the operation of sympathy – "grace," as the old theologians called it, – may be a truer immanence than this all-inclusive absorptionism.

At all events Professor Royce's discussion of the relations of the Self to the selves concludes with an unresolved problem. In the end, all the participants suffer from this universal Absolutism. The individual finite self suffers because he is so nearly swallowed in the Whole. To sure, each of us possesses, according to Professor Royce, a "uniqueness of meaning" which gives him a certain worth and significance to the Universal Self; but *for himself* and *to himself* he is a zero. The conception of God suffers too in this monism, because He is, after all, not a true Person, but only the Aggregate of persons. It is in vain – is it not? – that Professor Royce assigns personality to such a Being, though defining it in comprehensive words:

> Now from our point of view, God is a Person. Temporally viewed, His life is that of the entire realm of consciousness in so far as, in its temporal efforts toward perfection, this consciousness of the universe passes from instant to instant of the temporal order, from act to act, from experience to experience, from stage to stage. Eternally viewed, however, God's life is the infinite whole that includes this endless temporal process, and that consciously surveys it as one life. God is thus a Person, because, for our view, He is self-conscious, and because the Self of which He is conscious is a self whose eternal perfection is attained through the totality of these ethically significant temporal strivings, these processes of evolution, these linked activities of finite selves.[14]

This conception of God as eternally and consciously surveying his life as one, rescues Professor Royce's Deity from being a mere symbol for the evolutionary process, or the mere totality of the striving selves. Yet can He be both the perfection and the process, both the strivings and their beholder?

## IV.

The Gifford Lectures were published in 1901. Between this time and the publication of his remaining books a marked change of direction, or at least of emphasis, appears in Professor Royce's thought. It is a change

[14] Vol. II, p. 418.

away from the speculative and abstract toward the ethical, the practical, and the social. A more deeply human interest pervades his later work, a closer touch with the immediate needs of his fellow-men and of his time.

How far this was due to the stirring crusade of Pragmatism which began about this time, especially to the acute and telling thrusts at Absolutism made by Professor James, how far to the general change in the temper and interest of the age, and how far to the natural development of his own ever vital and progressive thought, it is hard to say. A rare and beautiful catholicity of mind is one of Professor Royce's finest traits. Whatever pains he may have felt from the stings and arrows of his outrageous pragmatic foes, he has manifested no resentment, made no efforts to defend Absolutism – doubtless thinking that it is able to defend itself – and without deflecting from his own course – only pausing at Professor James' death to pay him such tribute as only a great thinker can give to a comrade – he has quietly appropriated whatever was relevant in the criticism aimed against Absolutism and moved steadily on his way in the development of his own philosophy.

Now emerges in the symphony of his teaching that ethical and spiritual note destined to take its place as the recognized and resonant refrain of his whole teaching, the principle of *Loyalty*. Here at length appeared in clear radiance a truth fundamental in the structure and quality of his thinking which all the world could grasp. It is as the "philosopher of loyalty" that Professor Royce will be most widely known. The volumes which embody this new attitude are, *The Philosophy of Loyalty* (1908); *William James and Other Essays* (1911); *The Sources of Religious Insight* (1912); and *The Problem of Christianity* (1913).

In his *Philosophy of Loyalty*, with all its noble idealism and ethical realism, a self-refuting note was incidentally struck which it remained for the author himself tacitly to correct in his later work. I refer to the possibly unethical and irrational implication of the principle of loyalty which is there put forth, *i.e.*, insufficient discrimination as to the cause to which loyalty devotes itself. "Loyalty to loyalty" means, when carried to its logical conclusion, that the loyalty of the criminal to the gang, of an obstinate man to an opinion, of the patriot to his country "right or wrong," are all covered by the aegis of a virtue that may thus be distorted into a sanction of the most selfish and disastrous ills. Loyalty to a worthy cause, unselfish, pure, rational – as course the author intended – alone is good and great. Professor Royce fastened upon such a cause, incomparable in its worth and beneficence, when, in his latest philosophical book, he took up again definitely the subject out of which his thinking had originally sprung about which it had ever been revolving – Christianity. The Manchester College Lectures upon *The Problem of Christianity*, delivered at Oxford in the spring of 1913, touch the problem to the quick.

"The Problem of Christianity." Ever to the philosopher Christianity is too much a problem and too little a solution. And yet it could never be an adequate solution, did it not also offer an ever insistent problem. Professor Royce solves the problem in terms of Loyalty. The terms are true – though perhaps Love comes even nearer than Loyalty to the heart of Christianity[15] but is his object of loyalty the real one? The Beloved Community is the *loyal* community. Yes, but to what is it loyal? To itself, says Professor Royce, and no one would wish to contradict him. But what is the secret of its loyalty? Who created the Community? Loyalty does not spring objectless and motiveless from the void. The Community is loyal to itself because loyal first to one who created it and holds it together.

It is difficult to understand how Professor Royce could have so far failed to recognize the potency of the Christ personality as the cohesive centre of the Church. It is true he makes a place for the Indwelling Christ – the Spirit of the Community – but not for the incarnation of the Spirit in Jesus. It was the incarnate Word who gave origin and impetus, concreteness and unity, to the early church. Nor has the personality, thus vital at the outset, however obscured, ever been lost in the subsequent life of the Church. In answer to the question. Who was the founder of Christianity? Professor Royce replies, Not Jesus, nor Paul: we first find the essence of it in the Pauline churches. In other words, he leaves question of its founder unanswered. To leave it unanswered is to leave the problem of Christianity unanswered.

## V.

What is the conception of God in the Oxford Lectures? The answer cannot be a definite one, for there is no distinct and clearly apprehensible teaching upon this topic, either in the Bross Lectures upon *The Sources of Religious Insight* or in *The Problem of Christianity*. The very term "God," so frequent and so pregnant with meaning in earlier volumes, is rarely found in the later. Not that the author has rejected his former point of view. Indeed, in the lecture on the *Doctrine of Signs*, the theory of "Absolute Voluntarism" is strongly reaffirmed. Yet the emphasis has changed. Manifestly the conception of God has passed into a new stage of development. Is it a more potent conception, or not?

Throughout *The Problem of Christianity* a distinction is made

[15] Loyalty represents the will side of love; love includes both spontaneous and volitional elements.

between the Community and the Spirit of Community, and at one point at least a third distinction is suggested – namely, that of "Charity itself, the love of the Community by all its members, and of the members by the Community."[16] Definitively or inferentially, the reader is led to associate God with each and all of these – the Community, the Spirit of the Community, and the Love of the Community. Here is a striking correspondence – though Professor Royce does not himself point it out, and possibly does not himself recognize it – with the threefold trinitarian distinction, God the Father, Son, and Holy Spirit.

In the Community there is thus always, even when viewed as the Universal Community, or Humanity, something spiritual and ideal. This it is which sets Professor Royce's Community-loyalty far apart from and above Positivism and every other form of the worship of Humanity. It is never the Community in its empirical nature or its mass aspect, that Professor Royce presents to us as divine and worthy of devoted loyalty, but always the Community as an *Ideal* in process of realization. This Ideal Community, we are led to infer, is practically what we have all along been ignorantly worshipping. Whom therefore we have ignorantly worshipped, He, or It, is declared unto us.

The actual Community corresponding to this burning inner ideal, Professor Royce admits, nowhere exists. The Community, though a Community of memory, is still more a Community of hope, of expectation.[17] The Church is an invisible ideal rather than an actual institution.

> For the true Church is still a sort of ideal challenge to the faithful, rather than an already finished institution – a call upon men for a bravely quest, rather than a present possession of humanity. "Create me" – this is one word that the Church, viewed as an idea, address to mankind.[18]

Thus does this "institutionalist," as he is amusingly termed by Canon Inge in the *Hibbert Journal*,[19] describe the Church. Institutionalist he is only in the sense of one who cries, "Ring in the *Church* that is to be."

It is impossible not to feel that this divinity of the Community is, in effect, a form of the doctrine of Divine Immanence, and that it only lacks the supplementary truth of transcendence to become a fresh and illuminating expression of Christian Theism. And yet true and complete transcendence is never predicated of God by Professor Royce. The

[16] Op. cit., p. 192.

[17] II, p. 51.

[18] I, p. 54.

[19] July 1914.

Community has indeed a kind *immanent* transcendence, so to speak. It transcends itself, holding within itself ever the seed of its own perfection. But this possibility of perfection is never conceived as coming from Above, from the Father of lights. If, instead of being simply the Spirit *of* the Community, this Spirit were only conceived as the Spirit *in* the Community, having its source *above* the Community, we should be able to recognize at once the Holy Spirit, the Indwelling Christ of Christian experience; but this distinction Professor Royce does not permit us to make.

Very closely does this untrammelled thinker approximate to the theistic conception, especially in the fascinating lecture on *The Realm of Grace*. But always he stops just short of it and retreats to his stronghold of a society of individuals, a community which he prefers to call *super-personal* – although he is willing call it a person, "if by person you mean a live unity of will, of love, and of deed."[20] No one surely would object to that definition of person, if only again that unity is in and of and for itself as well as in and for others. In other words, to be a person the Divine Person must, like the human, be an entelechy – an end in Himself. That is, according to Christian theology, God is not only immanent but transcendent.[21] According to this conception a society having a composite consciousness cannot be in the full sense a person, nor a person a society.

Universal Thought, Universal Experience, Universal Selfhood – this, roughly speaking, is Professor Royce's ladder to perfection. Manifestly it is a progressive approach to that which for Christian theology is most essential in Deity – Personality. And yet the goal is never reached. For this Universal Person is not only an incomplete Person but worse, since there is limitation and evil in Him – the limitation and evil of all the selves composing Him.

In *The Problem of Christianity* Professor Royce partly overcomes this objection by identifying God, not with universal humanity but with those groups, or that inclusive Group, which includes the best in the human persons – the "Universal Community." But even so, not one of these groups alone, nor all together, can be regarded as having perfect or fulfilled personality. Limitation and evil exist in even the highest, the Christian Community.

There is no such thing, then, in fine, as Fulfilled Personality, the Perfect Person, according to Professor Royce – except in idea. If one is

[20] I, p. 332.

[21] It is unfortunate that, as Professor George F. Moore has pointed out to the writer, the term immanence, in its exact derivative sense, precludes transcendence. That which remains in a thing obviosly cannot transcend it. Yet what can the theologian do in such a case but assert that meanings transcend terms?

content with this conclusion, as satisfying either the intellect or the heart, he has here the highest formulation of his creed. But let him not infer that this is the only God rationally defensible. For out of the intuitive insight of the soul, out of the deeper implications of the moral nature, out of the teleology of the universe, natural and spiritual, there arises a conviction of the reality of a Perfect Person, lifted up, yet whose Presence fills the temple of humanity. This conviction of God has possessed the major mind of humanity in all the thinking ages, including our own. It has appealed more strongly than any other to reason as well as to faith.

VI.

In the second series of the Manchester Lectures, dealing with the metaphysical aspect of Christianity, Professor Royce brings forward a conception in which Philosophy and Christianity throw light upon each other and to whose elucidation he has been giving further attention in a recent course of lectures at the University of California – namely, the principle of *interpretation*, involved in what he has termed the *Triadic Theory of Knowledge*.

The Community is a community of interpretation. Its most useful member is the interpreter. Knowledge of self and of others is interpretative knowledge. The most serviceable function in the life of the Community is that of interpretation or mediation. Christianity is a religion of interpretation. It is a "Doctrine of Signs."

This is no new principle, to be sure, in Royce's thinking. It runs through all his work. Its deepest and most searching application to Christianity had already been made in the last of three addresses upon *What is Vital in Christianity*, given at the Phillips Brooks House at Harvard University in the spring of 1909, and published in *The Harvard Theological Review* and later in the volume, *William James and Other Essays*. In the last of these addresses, having shown the shallowness of that conception of Christianity which regards it as a culmination of cosmic evolutionism and leaves on one side its ministry of reconciliation, in words that touch the deeps of human experience the speaker concluded thus, concerning the meaning of comradeship in sorrow:

> God wins perfection through expressing Himself in a finite life and triumphing over and through its finitude. And our sorrow is God's sorrow. God means to express Himself by winning us through the very triumph over evil to unity with the perfect life, and therefore our fulfilment, like our existence, is due to the sorrow and the triumph of God Himself. These two theses express, I believe, what is vital in Christianity.

This truth finds still ampler expression in the lectures on Time and Guilt and Atonement in the first series of the Oxford lectures.

It has thus been given to Professor Royce to recall to the mind of our time, from the vantage-ground of philosophy, one of the great realities of Christian faith, too far overlooked in the hasty superficialism of present-day theology – the doctrine of Atonement.

Yet here once more Professor Royce pauses upon the hither side of a great truth as Christian theology has, in its larger insights, conceived it. Not merely from within the community but from above comes interpretation. Incarnation, according to Christianity, means, not simply that the Spirit of the Community incarnates itself, but that the Spirit that created the Community is also its Savior, entering into a lower order of spiritual life than its own to inform and redeem it.

"As individuals we are lost," says Professor Royce, and we assent. We are saved, he affirms, by coming into right relation with the Community. Yes, we answer, but by coming into right relationship not primarily with the Community, but with the Spirit of the Community, with God, and through Him into relation with the Community. In other words, the primary and fundamental redemptive relationship is that between the soul and God – mediated by the Community. In this conception the only dyadic relation which is "dangerous" is, as a friend of mine has remarked, not that between a pair of persons as such, but that which has not become "triadic" through the presence of the Universal Interpreter who was in Christ – yes, and in every loving member of the Community in the degree of his sacrificial spirit – reconciling the world unto Himself, and thus to itself. It is such a God: "above all and through all and in you all" who alone satisfies our need,

> That we may lift from out of dust
> A voice as unto Him that hears,
> A cry above the conquer'd years
> To One that with us works, and trust.

## VII.

In all too rapid and inadequate way we have endeavored to follow the course of Professor Royce's thought as it relates to Christianity, from the clear cold springs of its earlier critical and speculative beginnings along the deepening and broadening channel of its profound study of the nature of God and the relationship of the One and the Many, to the later period of its calm and fertilizing flow into the fields of great social interests, where it encircles the broad meadows of human fellowship, waters the roots of loyalty, and interprets some of the deeper truths of Christianity.

It is quite too cheap and professional for the philosopher to dispose of this original and resourceful contribution to philosophy as a form of Hegelianism. It will not stay within these limitations. Or for the theologian to set it down as an insidious form of scepticism or pantheism. It is far too genuinely informed with the spirit of the article, "I believe in the Holy Ghost; the holy Catholic Church; the Communion of Saints." Throughout the later volumes indeed, barring the philosophical phraseology, the very spirit of Christianity, as Paul interprets it, is reflected. In the entire literature concerning Paul, it may be said in passing, few have interpreted his mind with so keen and sympathetic a discernment as has this unconventionalized Christian.

Whatever further amplification or modification this fertile and inexhaustible mind may give to his philosophy, it stands before us as a noble and impressive whole, demanding to be evaluated and put to usury. It would be a grave loss not to honor with criticism as well as with application to life, a philosophy of so large and vital significance. It is ripe for interpretation, for testing, and for food – food for the many as well as the few.

It is somewhat strange in view of the position which Professor Royce holds in the philosophical world, the deep and extensive influence he has exercised as a teacher, the originality and scope of his contribution to the literature of philosophy, that so few attempts have made either to expound or to estimate his philosophy as a whole – especially from the view-point of theology. Eucken and Bergson have in Royce a worthy American compeer in the great task of spiritualizing life. His philosophy, like theirs, makes for the regnancy of the Ideal. It is a deeply religious philosophy. As time throws it into perspective it will be seen how truly great a philosophy it is – great in its success, greater still in unfulfilled endeavor. For it may well be that we have Royceanism the last and most splendid – yet futile – effort to construct an enduring temple of Monism. The structure as such is not only incomplete but insecure – not so much from assault from without as from a general abandonment of the monistic position and from self-criticism. For the very dialectic of the philosophy itself, the inner strife of its contending principles, refusing to submit to a foreordained synthesis, has adjudged itself and led to that extraordinary self-expansion in Professor Royce's system which has brought his thought ever closer to the throbbing human interests and problems of our time and made him so great an "interpreter." In other words, Professor Royce has tacitly passed judgment upon his own system by constantly surpassing it. It is true that his whole work has a marked unity of purpose and movement, but it is the unity of a development that is too large to be self-fulfilled.

It is this very self-transcendence, therefore, this constant advance, that gives us the assurance that in this philosophy we have that which no closed system can rival – a philosophy full of fructifying ideas, bound together by a constantly enlarging conception of the world, the self, and God. We of the theological guild, who are too easily content with conventional ideas, have much to learn from the philosophy of Professor Royce, and, whatever the degree of our dissent, should be eager to acknowledge our large indebtedness to him.

# THE DOCTRINE OF EVOLUTION AND THE CONCEPTION OF GOD

Ukichi Kawaguchi, "The Doctrine of Evolution and the Conception of God," *American Journal of Theology* (1915).

The one far-reaching contribution of the nineteenth century is the inductively formulated concept of evolution. The researchers made by Darwin and other biologists were so convincing that not only the fact of evolution but also its methodological and theoretical implications have become fundamental in all organic social sciences. Theology for a time stubbornly resisted the theory of evolution in its field. But so empirically convincing is the theory and so universally is it applied in other fields of investigation that theology cannot remain immune from its influence. The theological application of the doctrine, however, has been limited to the history of theology. It has not yet been made to its basal object, God. The purpose of this paper is to ascertain the significance of the doctrine of evolution for certain elementary problems connected with the conception of God.

The method employed in this study is as follows: First, we shall indicate the problems due to the attempt to relate the traditional conception of God to the doctrine of evolution. Secondly, we shall make a brief criticism of the solutions of the problems given in Royce's absolute idealism and Eucken's philosophy of life. This will be followed by a statement of the results and the theological implications of our study.

## I. Problems Involved in the Relation of the Evolutionary Theory and the Traditional Conception of God

One of the essential evolutionary ideas is that of change. The static view of the world was characteristic of the prevailing philosophies and theologies prior to the dawn of modern science; the satisfactions of life were found in absolutes, finalities, immutabilities, eternities, fixities. With the growth of biological science the view of reality as changing has been gaining ground and has come to dominate the very thought and life of the modem world. Bergson, indeed, universalizes the idea of change, making it the very essence of life.[1]

Another element of the evolutionary theory is the notion of growth in the being of reality. Previous to the full sway of organic science, evolution meant an unfoldment of something already given. Reality was held to be ready-made; hence it was not subject to the process of growth. Over against this closed view world, the modern theories of evolution stand for an actual growth in the being of things; for organic beings are not merely evolving what were their latent potentialities, but they are growing in the content of their being. It is particularly one of the radical contentions of Bergson that there is a *real* growth in things. Reality, for him, is not ready-made; but it is constantly creating, becoming, growing, adding to itself new worlds.[2]

The theories of evolution, moreover, hold to the view of the continuity and solidarity of organic beings. Lamarck constructed a phylogenetic tree showing the oneness of organic forms. The enormous amount of inductive data accumulated by Darwin in his works, *The Origin of Species* and *The Descent of Man*, is intended to establish the organic relation of all living beings, man included. This belief is shared by all biological scientists. Bergson apparently differs from them in his view of the evolution of life as taking place in divergent lines; yet he is fundamentally one with them in his recognition of the unity of all living forms by virtue of the original impetus of life.[3]

What now are the factors of this process of change, growth, and continuity? Here, as to the philosophy of evolution, opinion differs. According to Lamarck and Darwin, the actual forces of evolution are natural, although the agency of God is admitted in their deistic view of him as the first cause.[4] In opposition to their view, Bergson maintains the *élan vital* as the fundamental cause of the evolutionary process.[5] But however various their views as to the ontological nature of the factors of evolution, they all agree in the idea that these factors are immanent in the organisms and in their environment.

[1] See *Creative Evolution*, pp. 1 ff.

[2] Op. cit., pp. 251 ff.

[3] Op. cit., chap. ii; cf. pp. 251 ff.

[4] Lamarck, op. cit., I, 113; Darwin, *The Origin of Species*, pp. 424 f.

[5] For views on this matter, see Jordan and Kellogg, *Evolution and Animal Life*, pp. 9 f., 468 f.; Kellogg, *Darwinism Today*, p. 378; Henderson, *The Fitness of the Environment*, pp. 305 ff.; Wallace, *Darwinism*, chap. v; Simpson, *The Spiritual Interpretation of Nature*, pp. 254 ff.; Schmucker, *The Meaning of Evolution*, chap. xix.

This leads, finally, to the question of teleology in the process of evolution. This is another mooted problem. Lamarck believed that forms of life were tending from less perfect to more perfect forms.[6] Darwin considered that the organic evolution has reached its summit in man; but he refused to commit himself to any definite view as to the ultimate destiny of human life.[7] Bergson repudiates radical mechanism and radical finalism alike, but does deny all purpose in the evolutionary process.[8] That there is some purpose in the process is not denied by these evolutionists. The purpose they would admit, in view of their conception of the organic world as involved in the process of change and growth, marked by accidents, setbacks, and the like, is bound to be a changing, growing and therefore finite purpose.

We may, then, summarize the meaning of the evolutionary theory in the statement that, according to it, all forms of life are characterized by the process of change, growth, and organic continuity, which is effected by the forces immanent in the organisms and in their environment in accordance with a limited, growing purpose.

Turning now to the traditional conception of God, we note that it embodies the two essential ideas, namely, God as the transcendent supernatural personality and as the absolute being. The conception of God as the transcendent supernatural personality underlies all systems of orthodoxy.[9] The worldview underlying this conception of God is a philosophy which divides reality into two realms: a natural and a supernatural. The connection between the two is effected by means of supernatural acts of God. Accordingly, the emphasis in this view of God is placed upon his specifically supernatural deeds in his relation to the world of nature and of man.[10] Now, it is this insistence on the supernaturalness of God in his relation to the world that leads orthodox theologians to oppose the modern doctrine of evolution. To hold that the world and man have come to be what they are by the process of a slow and gradual evolution means atheism.[11] It should here be noted that their antagonism to the evolutionary theory is due mainly to the desire to maintain intact the finality of their system deducible from the infal-

6 See Packard, *Lamarck the Founder of Evolution*, pp. 323, 345 f.

7 *The Descent of Man*, pp. 702 ff.

8 Op. cit., pp. 265 ff.

9 See, e.g., Greene, "The Supernatural," *Princeton Biblical and Theological Studies*, pp. 142 ff.

10 See, e.g., Hodge, *Systematic Theology*, I, 535 ff., 550 ff., 151 ff.; II, 378 ff.; Shedd, *Dogmatic Theology*, I, 393 ff., 61 ff.; Strong, *Systematic Theology*, I, 353 ff.; II, 371 ff., 669 ff., etc.

11 See, e.g., Hodge, op. cit., II, 11 ff.; Shedd, op. cit., I, 449 ff.

lible scripture given by the transcendent, supernatural God, and to furnish a positive basis of assurance to men that he is powerful to perform even miraculous deeds, if necessary, for their ultimate victory.

The other essential element in the traditional conception of God is the idea of him as the absolute being. This is the philosophic view of God which orthodoxy endeavors to combine with the conception of the supernatural and individualistic God of popular Christianity. Philosophically conceived, God is the ultimate reality, the source and ground of all existence. God so viewed possesses such attributes as spirituality, infinity, perfection, personality, immutability, and the like.[12] God as such is beyond all the limitations of time and history. He is absolutely immutable in his essence, attributes, and purpose.[13] With this insistence of traditional theology on the absoluteness of God goes also its effort to retain the finality of its system. The absoluteness of the divine revelation, the uniqueness of Christ, the completeness of Christianity, all stand or fall with the doctrine of the absoluteness of God. Hence he must by all means be conceived of as the absolute being free from time and historical change.[14]

In brief, these two elements – God as the supernatural personality and as the absolute being – constitute the basic ideas in the traditional conception of God. They represent the practical ethico-religious and philosophical interests of man in his attempt to interpret the world and human life. But it is this very view of God as the supernatural personality and the absolute being and the presuppositions which it implies that are opposed to the theological implications of the evolutionary theory. Hence there arise many problems in the attempt to bring the traditional conception of God into relation with the doctrine of evolution. Some of these problems we may now state.

The problem of method comes to our first notice. The method followed by science in the formulation of the evolutionary theory is antithetical to that employed by traditional theology in the construction of its conception of God. The former employs the inductive, empirical method; the latter, the a priori appeal to revelation. The one outstanding feature of evolutionary theories is that they are formulated as result of more or less careful empirical investigations of the processes in the organic world.[15] It is quite otherwise with traditional theology. It

[12] See Strong, op. cit., I, 248.

[13] See Hodge, op. cit., I, 390 f.; Shedd, op. cit., I, 351 f.

[14] The absoluteness of God, from the standpoint of orthodoxy, does not, however, signify that he embraces the whole of reality (sec Hodge, op. cit., I, 382 f.).

[15] One may question this statement with respect to Bergson. It should be replied, however, that he, too, set forth his theory of evolution after years of study in field of organic evolution.

maintains that God has made his final revelation of himself in the Scripture. Its conception of God, therefore, is obtained by a systematic analysis of the content of this infallible revelation.[16] Which method should, then, be used in the formulation of the conception of God? This is a critical problem, for on its solution depends largely the character of any conception of God.

The problem of method is closely connected with the other problem: that of the relation between theology and science. This involves a metaphysical problem, viz., Can the affirmations of science be held final on the ontological realities with which theology deals or must theology maintain that there is more to reality than is revealed by science? Traditional theology, having an infallible source for its affirmations, does not make any real use of the results of scientific investigation. This dogmatism of traditional orthodoxy has been polemically transferred to what Perry calls naïve, uncritical naturalism[17] which assumes that it has the last word on the matter of reality. Manifestly here we have a conflict between the two dogmatisms. What then shall be done with the conflict?[18]

Another problem is that of God as the supernatural personality. Traditional theology, as we have seen, holds the view of God as the sovereign person who has determined the course of the world and who expresses his relation to it in specific supernatural acts. The evolutionary theories know only this world where the forces that carry on the evolutionary process are immanent in the organisms and in their environment. These theories know no such supernatural interventions from an unknown realm of reality as is assumed by traditional theology. Thus is raised the problem of the transcendence and immanence of God. Is God organically related with the life-process or is he to be identified primarily in miraculous interventions? This question is closely bound up with the next problem, namely, that of God as the absolute being.

The traditional conception of God tenaciously maintains his freedom from the exigencies of time and history; evolution is wholly foreign to the character of God. But in the evolutionary theory change and growth are held as characteristic of all the forms of life. Accordingly, absolutes, finalities, eternities, perfections are not found anywhere in the realms open to scientific investigation. But is God free from change and growth? All admit that our ideas of God have changed from the days of primitive man. But do change and growth hold true only of our concep-

[16] See, e.g., Hodge, op. cit., I, 182 f., 364.

[17] *Present Philosophical Tendencies*, chap. iv.

[18] See, on this point, Perry, op. cit., chap. v, "Religion and the Limits of Science."

tions of God and not of the object of these conceptions? Is God absolute or is he in any sense finite? This is the most critical problem that calls for a careful consideration.

And there is yet another problem to be mentioned, namely, that of God's relation to the world and man. The traditional conception of God assumes the distinct creation and absolute control of The world by the divine will. The theories of evolution, however, reduce existing things to so small beginnings that the creation of them seems scarcely worthy of the supreme being. The evils involved in the process of natural and human evolution also cast a serious doubt upon the assumed absolute control of the world by God. What, then, is the real nature of God's relation to the world and man?

The foregoing may be said to constitute the essential problems involved in the effort to effect a tenable relation between the evolutionary theory and the traditional conception of God. We shall now turn to certain typical recent attempts at their solution.

## II. A Criticism of Certain Typical Recent Solutions of the Problems

Here we shall take certain aspects of the discussions in Royce's absolute idealism and Eucken's philosophy of life in order to illustrate the problem we have in mind. For these philosophers of religion, more than any of the professional theologians of our time, recognize the inadequacy of the traditional conception of God and are fully conscious of the problems raised by modern, scientific concepts, including the evolutionary theory.

In general it can be said that Royce works out his conception of God from the standpoint of his absolute idealism. He analyzes human temporary and fragmentary experiences and absolutizes them into an all-inclusive, absolute experience.[19] Or he analyzes human ideas or thoughts and reaches his theory of being and considers this theory as the basis of his system.[20] Thus he makes the Absolute Experience or Being the ultimate basis of our finite experience and thought. It is from the standpoint of such an Experience or Thought that Royce finds the criterion of his evaluation of the world and man. Accordingly, the method of Royce is opposed to that of the empirical theories of evolution. The intellectualism and apriorism of his method are in full accord with his general system of thought.[21]

But it should not be overlooked in this connection that there are

[19] *The World and the Individual*, II, lecture iii.

[20] Op. cit., I, 339 f.

[21] See *The Sources of Religious Insight*, pp. 84 ff., 109 ff.

numerous statements in Royce's works, which are not in agreement with his dialectic method. In the work, for example, which is distinctly devoted to the problem of religious knowledge, Royce speaks much of individual and social experiences as sources of religious insight and appeals to the actual experiences of those who practice religion as guides for us to the truth.[22] These and other assertions of Royce[23] show that one real interest of the author is to ascertain the data of our common individual and social experiences and to construct his theory of the world and human life on precisely such experiences. Hence just so far as he deals with our experience in its varied aspects, Royce is not in line with his absolutist method; one must pass by a metaphysical leap from the method of experience to an all-inclusive experience or thought.[24] But on the other hand, just to the extent that Royce makes use of the data of our experience he is in agreement with the inductive method of the evolutionary theory; and to that degree he has worked out the bearing of the theory in the formulation of his conception of God.

To speak next of his attitude toward science, it is not difficult, in view of the fact that philosophically Royce does not employ the empirical method, to ascertain what it would be. He is not satisfied with the interpretation of the world given by science and offers his idealistic theory as the final view of the universe.[25] There is much truth in his statement: "The modern naturalistic and mechanistic views of reality are not, indeed, false within their own proper range, but they are inadequate to tell us the whole truth."[26] But to maintain that the theory of being, as Royce holds, must determine all the interpretation of nature and of man[27] is against the empirical temper of our age. But on the other hand, the very fact that Royce affirms even the temporal reality of our experience of the world and assigns this temporal order to the work of science shows that he is interested in viewing the facts of life from an empirical point of view; and so to this extent he must modify absolutist philosophical theory. But to the degree that Royce takes such an empirical attitude he illustrates the bearing of the evolutionary theory on the problem of God.

[22] Ibid., pp. 26 ff., 37 ff., 166 ff.; Cf. *The Problem of Christianity*, I, 12 ff.; The World and the Individual, I, pp. 55, 401; II, 362.

[23] See, *The Problem of Christianity*, I, 387 f.; II, 5.

[24] *The World and the Individual*, II, 11 ff.; cf. *The Sources of Religious Experience*, pp. 109 f., 137, 144 f.

[25] *The World and the Individual*, II, 207 ff.; *William James and Other Essays*, pp. 6o ff.

[26] *William James and Other Essays*, p. 72.

[27] *The World and the Individual*, II, 8 f.

To come now to the nature of God, we find that Royce conceives of him as the Absolute Being, Thought or Experience, Will or Purpose.[28] It is evident that such a conception of God is fundamentally different from that logically growing out of the evolutionary view. This demands that if there be a God, he must not only be immanent in the world but must himself be actually involved in the process of change and growth. The God of Royce is, it is true, immanent in the world of thought – engaged in the work of interpreting the world. He is not such a static absolute as that of Spinoza. But he is eternally what he is – there is no change and increase in his being.

Yet it is worthy of note in this connection that this conception of the eternal absoluteness of God needs modification in the light of many of Royce's statements which indicate finite aspects of this God. To cite a few, we note the following:

> The only way to give our view of Being rationality is to see that we long for the Absolute only in so far as in us the Absolute also longs, and seeks, through our very temporal striving, the peace that is nowhere in Time, but only, and yet absolutely, in eternity. Were there no longing in Time, there would be no peace in eternity... . The right eternally triumphs, yet not without temporal warfare. This warfare occurs, indeed, *within the divine life itself*... . I sorrow. But the sorrow is not only mine. This same sorrow, just as it is for me, is God's sorrow.[29]

These and similar expressions of Royce indicate clearly a God striving to attain the goal of his perfection. But in the last analysis Royce would maintain that this impression of God's finitude is due to our finite temporal point of view. From the point of view of the Absolute, his will is completely expressed, his tasks perfectly done, his moral life absolutely finished.[30] If God is thus eternally complete in himself, why does he suffer, struggle, and long to be perfect at all? Is his suffering and struggle only apparent and his eternal perfection an actual fact? In other words, Royce, to be consistent, has to affirm either the suffering of God as real and so his God as finite or his sufferings as an illusion and hence his God as eternally complete. Royce does not wish to do either. He feels too keenly the realities of our life to pronounce his God all-

[28] See *The World and the Individual*, I, 339, 341, 394 ff.; II, 335, Lectures iii, vi; cf. *The Conception of God*, pp. 1 ff.; *The Problem of Christianity*, II, 296, 324, 373 ff.

[29] *The World and the Individual*, II, 386, 398, 409; cf. *William James and Other Essays*, pp. 183, 296.

[30] See *The Religious Aspect of Philosophy*, pp. 442 ff.; *The Conception of God*, pp. 8 ff.; *The World and the Individual*, II, 302.

complete and perfect, untouched by our finite experiences. Yet impelled by his absolute idealism, Royce maintains that the all-inclusive perfect being is at the heart of the universe.[31] But just in so far as he interprets God in terms of our evolutionary experience, Royce departs from his absolutist philosophical position and approaches the conception of God necessitated by the evolutionary theory.

These two aspects – those that are in agreement with his absolute idealism and those that are in accord with the evolutionary theory – we may note finally in connection with his conception of God's relation to the world and to man.

It is maintained by Royce that God is morally perfect.[32] This moral perfection of God is not a result of struggle on his part.[33] Royce, moreover, declares that God is not merely immanent in the world but is identical with the totality of the universe in all its expressions.[34] This being the case, the world of nature and of man must be absolutely good.[35] But the theories of evolution indicate to us that there are connected with the evolutionary process of the world merciless struggles, miseries, wastes, anomalies, sufferings. These forms of evil we cannot deny, nor can they be explained away. Yet Royce holds that the world is good when it is viewed in its entirety.[36] An empirical evolutionist would, however, scarcely consider the processes of nature so idealistically as does Royce.[37] The actual process of nature suggests either that the God immanent in it is impotent to carry out his plans without evil consequences, or that there are evil forces which are counteracting activities. But Royce admits neither hypothesis. He must contend for the view that the world considered *sub specie aeternitatis* is perfect. Yet he does not deny all reality to the evils in the world; he admits their temporal reality and seeks to give significance to their existence.[38] Here again we see a deviation from absolute idealism and a tendency on his part toward the standpoint of the evolutionary theory.

To speak now of Royce's view of God's relation to man, we need to observe that since God is the all-inclusive Individual of the world,

[31] *The Religious Aspect of Philosophy*, pp. 436 ff.

[32] *The Religious Aspect of Philosophy*, pp. 441 ff.; *The Conception of God*, p. 8.

[33] *The Religious Aspect of Philosophy*, p. 448.

[34] *William James and Other Essays*, pp. 168 f., 285 f.

[35] *The Religious Aspect of Philosophy*, p. 444.

[36] *The World and the Individual,* II, 379.

[37] *The World and the Individual*, pp. 219 ff.

[38] Ibid., I, 380 ff., II, 388 ff.; *The Sources of Religious Insight*, pp. 215 ff.

embracing all finite beings and since the latter have no existence apart from the former, a logical consequence would be that finite beings possess no real freedom and individuality. Yet he distinctly attempts to show that finite spirits possess their own individuality and freedom.[39] In view of the fact that each finite being expresses in his unique manner the will of the Absolute, he holds that he possesses freedom and individuality. Hence there are provided all the possibilities for a genuine moral life.[40] And in the temporal order of the world there are real moral deeds done and real achievements toward a better world.

But this insistence of Royce upon moral activity leads us to ask: Why should we struggle against the apparent forces of evil to create a better world, when the world in its essence is all complete and finished? Why must we struggle through the evils of life to obtain perfection, as is held by Royce,[41] when there are no real evils in the world, and we stand before our God all complete.[42] Unless there are possibilities for change and growth in the world we cannot see how there could be real moral life for us finite beings. If the world is finished in reality, even now, as Royce holds, so that we cannot change its course, the only course open to us is to deny the reality of movement and progress in the world of our experience and engage in mystic contemplation of an "eternal" world. Moreover, as God is not ultimately found in the world where actual evolution is taking place, we can find him only in escaping from such a world. What other course than this can we follow when we are told that the real world is perfect, but that this perfection is not to be found in time, and that our comfort lies in the knowledge of the Eternal?[43] But Royce would not tolerate such a life. His interests lie in the actual experiences of the social realm.[44] A consistent absolute idealism would give up all real interest in our evolutionary experience and urge a life of speculation as to the eternal perfection of the world. Royce declines, however, to accept this path. The moral and religious appeals of our world are so great that he must accept and deal earnestly with them. In following this course he deviates from the standpoint of his absolute idealism and comes to the position of the evolutionary theory that stands for the reality of the time-process in which God and man are actually engaged for the creation of a better world.

[39] *The World and the Individual*, II, lecture vii.

[40] Ibid., pp. 343 ff.

[41] *William James and Other Essays*, pp. 171 ff., 287 ff.

[42] *The World and the Individual*, II, 150.

[43] Ibid., pp. 379, 411.

[44] *The Problem of Christianity*, lectures ii ff.

With the criticism of Royce's solution of the problems raised by the evolutionary theory, we may now pass to another typical solution, that given in Eucken's philosophy of life.

The central thought of Eucken is his conception of a world-transcendent spiritual life, a whole of reality, which he identifies with God. This God, the cosmic spiritual life, furnishes the solution to all the problems of human life. A pertinent question is: How does Eucken come to his conception of such a God? He repudiates the intellectualism of idealistic philosophy, the subjectivism of Romanticism, and such voluntarism as that of Schopenhauer.[45] In place of these methods Eucken uses what he calls the noölogical method. "To explain noölogically," writes Eucken, "means to arrange the whole of the Spiritual Life as a special activity, to ascertain its position and problem, and through such an adaptation to illumine the whole and raise its potencies."[46] It is through the use of such a method that Eucken arrives at his conception of an independent spiritual life and views all things from the standpoint of such a life.[47] And this a priori procedure of Eucken is in full accord with his philosophical position. Nevertheless, in spite of his interest in an absolutist metaphysics, Eucken, like Royce, is constantly concerned with the actual struggles and conflicts of our experience; he is incessantly engaged in setting forth the life-process in its progressive development. It is not something beyond human experience with which Eucken deals; but he investigates the living interests of the life-process itself. Yet believing that we cannot discover a stable basis of life in the empirically ascertained facts of life, Eucken distrusts this method and falls back on his a priori procedure. Thus we see in Eucken, as we saw in Royce, a double tendency: a tendency to deal with the facts of life empirically, and a tendency to view them from the standpoint of an a priori assumption.

This double tendency appears also in his attitude toward science. Eucken fully appreciates the worth of science as it enables us to control the forces of nature.[48] This appreciation of science is made manifest in his repudiation of the naïve supernaturalism of traditional Christianity,[49] and in his acceptance of the fact of evolution.[50] He holds

[45] *The Truth of Religion*, pp. 73 ff.

[46] *The Truth of Religion*, p. 178; cf. pp. 453 ff.; *Life's Basis and Life's Ideal*, pp. 154, 242 f., 351 f.

[47] *Main Currents of Modern Thought*, pp. 129 ff.

[48] *Life's Basis and Life's Ideal*, pp. 345 f.

[49] Ibid., pp. 6 ff.; *The Truth of Religion*, pp. 521 ff., 549 ff.

[50] *Main Currents of Modern Thought*, pp. 257, 262 f., 278.

that it is not natural science that creates trouble for us, but our weakness in spiritual convictions.[51] But a question here is: Can he really appreciate and do justice to scientific concepts, the evolutionary theory included, without accepting the method by which these concepts are formulated? The method and theory of evolution seem so closely bound up with each other that one will find it very difficult to accept the one and reject the other with any consistency. Eucken is willing to view man as a product of nature, provided he is allowed to maintain that in man there appears in the course of his evolution an independent life.[52] This insistence upon the superempirical factor in the evolutionary process is, indeed, in line with his absolutist position. But the very fact that Eucken views so much of reality from the standpoint of the evolutionary theory is significant.

Now in regard to the traditional conception of God as the transcendent supernatural personality we find that Eucken has set aside its supernaturalistic features and retains what he regards as its eternal element.[53] It is this retention of an eternal element – an Absolute Spiritual Life in union with man – that at once opens up the problem of God as the Absolute Being.

Eucken conceives of God as the Absolute Spiritual Life above the limitations of time and history.[54] Such a God, for Eucken, is the very foundation of all time-order. Man cannot find satisfaction in history, if there is not disclosed in it to him "an overhistorical nature."[55] We seek for a basis of life. But we cannot find it in our immediate experience, thought, or activity; for in the whole life of immediate existence all is change and uncertainty. We must seek it beyond our psychic state – in a whole of life which is not subject to time.[56] Moreover, to conceive of God in terms of history and evolution means to surrender the absoluteness of all truth.[57] There are, however, many elements in his philosophy which would naturally lead him to conceive of God in terms of the evolutionary theory. For example, his emphasis on activity rather than on thought as an essential means of appropriating reality:[58] his

[51] *The Problem of Human Life*, pp. 541 f.

[52] *The Life of the Spirit*, p. 271.

[53] See *The Truth of Religion*, pp. 576 ff., 544 ff.

[54] Ibid., pp. 208 f., 214.

[55] Ibid., p. 175.

[56] *Life's Basis*, etc., p. 154, cf. pp. 275 ff.

[57] See *The Truth of Religion*, pp. 379 f.; cf. pp. 537 ff.; *Christianity and the New Idealism*, p. 41.

[58] *Life's Basis*, etc., pp. 220 ff., 255 ff.

recognition of movement and history as characteristic of the modern age:[59] his view of God as immanent in the world of man, helping him to be one with himself[60] – all these and the other like elements call for the view of God as a changing being. But instead of carrying out the logic of these elements, Eucken would insist upon the view of God as the Absolute Spiritual Life above the changes of time.

This affirmation of God's unchangeability, however, can be consistently maintained by Eucken only as he views the ultimate meaning of the world of experience in static terms and conceives of God's relation to the world and man somewhat after the fashion of traditional supernaturalism. But his activistic faith does not permit him to accept the traditional supernaturalism of Christianity. He conceives of God as involved in a vital relation with the movements of history.[61] If Eucken consistently followed out this conception of God's relation to a growing world and humanity in dynamic terms, it would be exceedingly difficult to maintain his absoluteness. For how can a God who is in dynamic relation to the world and who is involved in the processes of change and growth remain unaffected by such processes? We have sufficiently indicated many features in his philosophy that are irreconcilable with his contention for the unchangeability of God. And these very elements show clearly that he has not been able to escape the bearing of the evolutionary theory on his conception of God.

This influence of the theory appears also in his view of God's relation to the world and man. Eucken ultimately conceives of God's relation to the world in terms of immanent idealism.[62] This conception, however, conflicts with his opposition to immanent idealism seen in his indictment of the evil processes of the natural world.[63] The irrationality of the world and its oppositions to the values and aims of human life force Eucken to acknowledge that evils present to us an insoluble enigma of life.[64] Eucken's admission of the reality of evil in the world and its consequent irrationality suggests either that his God is impotent to control the evil forces in the world, or that they are due to some non-divine factors. In either case God would be finite in power. But Eucken, impelled by his avowed philosophical position, maintains that the

[59] *The Life of the Spirit*, pp. 104 ff.

[60] *The Truth of Religion*, pp. 221 ff.

[61] See *Christianity and the New Idealism*, pp. 45 ff.; Life's Basis, etc., pp. 188ff; *Main Currents of Modern Thought*, pp. 318 ff.

[62] See *The Truth of Religion*, pp. 220 f., 165 ff.; *Main Currents*, etc., p. 459; *Life's Basis*, etc., pp. 270 f.

[63] *Life's Basis*, etc., p. 20; cf. *The Truth of Religion*, pp. 290 ff.

[64] *Life's Basis*, etc., pp. 280 f.; *The Truth of Religion*, pp. 490 ff.

world, despite its insoluble evils, is due to the immanent activity of God.[65]

To come now to Eucken's view of the relation of God and man, we observe that he considers this relation from the standpoint of the practical interests of human life. God as the Absolute Spiritual Life is absolutely necessary to give content and subsistence to the life of man; without such a God man would be bound by the evil forces of the natural world and so could not attain to his destiny. It is through struggles, sufferings, conflicts, that we come to the sense of our union with God; we must fight with all our might against the forces of evil if we are to possess the life of God in our soul, for in the hardest fight we gain the clearest vision of God.[66]

A question arises at this point: What is God's relation to us in our struggle? Is he implicated in our conflicts with the antagonistic forces of the world? Eucken flatly denies that God participates in such depressing aspects of our experience. All that we need to know, according to him, is that God does help us out of the apparent defeats of our life.[67] This is because Eucken desires to preserve the freedom of God from the changes and experiences of time. But we should particularly note that he gives very little space to an exposition of his contention that God is above the changes and sufferings of our existence. On the other hand, abundant space is given to his exposition of the life-process of man in its historical development. Moreover, the very phrase most used by Eucken to represent God, namely, "spiritual life," stands for a reality which is derivable in and through our changing experience.

### III. Results and Implications of the Foregoing Discussion

First, as regards the methodological problem, the result of our study of Royce and Eucken may be stated as follows:

Royce, whose method is fundamentally based on an Absolute Experience or Thought, or an All-inclusive Insight, which he assumes a priori, nevertheless gives much space to the examination of the facts of changing, growing, temporal social experience. He is fully aware of the movements of empiricism, especially since the days of Kant, and so is unable to ignore inductive investigation in matters of philosophy and religion.[68] In very marked degree, the same attitude toward empiricism in method characterizes Eucken. He has given up the power of thought relied upon by all intellectualistic systems of philosophy, for he finds it

[65] *Life's Basis*, etc., pp. 270 ff.

[66] Ibid., pp. 246 f., 255 ff.

[67] *The Truth of Religion*, pp. 432 ff.

[68] See his article, "The Eternal and the Practical," *Philos. Rev.*, XIII, 113 f., 142.

incapable of giving us the true insight into the problems of human life. True, philosophically Eucken undertakes to view the problems of life from the standpoint of an independent spiritual life. But in reality he is constantly dealing with the actual experiences of the life-process in its struggles, conflicts, oppositions, tasks.

This methodological tendency suggests that if theology is to keep in line with the inductive, evolutionary method of contemporary sciences, it cannot follow the method hitherto employed. The traditional method of expounding and systematizing a given quantity of supernatural revelation located in an infallible church or scripture[69] is becoming more and more untenable; for the investigations in biblical science are constantly bringing to light the differences between the content of biblical revelation and that of modern religion.

An increasing number of theological thinkers, who have felt the power of scientific investigations, especially in the field of religion, can no longer follow the traditional method. These men feel that theology, in order to take its place among the sciences of our age and to accomplish its work for the furtherance of religious life, should employ the method demanded by the evolutionary theory. In adopting such a method of experimentation and verification theology will indeed lose its claim to finality in content, but it will find a vaster field for its investigation and gain scientific worth for what it discovers through the medium of the new procedure.[70] Theology, then, in following the inductive method of the evolutionary theory will seek for the sources of its doctrines in the common religious experiences of people as these experiences are critically expounded in investigations dealing, particularly, with the history of religions and the psychology of religious experience. Christian theology will, of course, study its religious inheritance in the records, especially of the Hebrew and Christian peoples, in order to gain suggestive contributions toward the solution of its religious problems. Significant personalities, notably the prophets and Jesus and his apostles, will constitute a specially valuable source of religious insight. Yet theology will not be limited to their contributions. It will, in accordance with its empirical, evolutionary method, deal with contributions on matters of religion coming from any other worthy source. It is thus the great field of human religious experience in the largest sense with which theology would empirically deal.[71]

Secondly, what is the relation between theology and science? Royce, in

[69] See, e.g., Hodge, op. cit., I, 182 ff.; Shedd, op. cit., I, 70 ff.

[70] See Ames, *The Psychology of Religious Experience*, p. 320; "Theology from the Standpoint of Functional Psychology," *American Journal of Theology*, X, 232.

[71] Cf. Johnson, *God in Evolution*, chap. ii, "Concerning Method."

accordance with his absolute idealism, maintains that philosophy has the last word on the subject of reality. Yet he recognizes the truths of science as inductive descriptions of the temporal order. Moreover, he gives a high value to the deeds and events of our temporal experience.[72] What he opposes in science (natural science) is its uncritical affirmation that all reality consists of physical elements and that all forms of existence are explicable in terms of such elements. Eucken likewise appreciates the place and worth of science in modern life. But he cannot tolerate the scientific naturalism which reduces all reality to the plane of physical mechanism. Thus these philosophers of religion hold that the discoveries of natural science do not constitute the whole of reality; and that, accordingly, theological or religious affirmations must be given their due validity; and yet they tend to ground these affirmations on the facts of evolutionary experience. This implies that both science and theology are called upon to face the facts of life and of existence in a thoroughly empirical fashion, and to consider themselves as co-operating means of furthering the ongoing evolution of life. This implication of our study calls for a brief comment.

It is fully manifest that such theories of evolution as those of Lamarck and Darwin are based on a more or less thoroughgoing empiricism; and that they assume an undogmatic attitude toward their theories. Bergson, too, does not claim finality for his system.[73] This undogmatic attitude of the evolutionists is characteristic of the best of our contemporary scientists. Pearson, for example, points out the incompleteness of science and considers its concepts or laws as mental shorthand, useful to the work of man.[74] This thoroughly empirical attitude of the evolutionists is not what we find in the case of traditional theologians; their theological declarations are marked by some dogmatic absolutism. They maintain that they have absolute truth in some form, and they contend for the immunity of their theological doctrines from the encroachments of science; for them the findings of empirical study cannot form the foundation of their theological affirmations – they must be grounded on some a priori principle underivable in and through human experience.

It is quite clear, then, that such a theological position does not seem to be in agreement with the implications of the evolutionary theory. It is quite apparent that the best way, in so far as our present age of culture and civilization is concerned, is adopt the hints given both by the historians of religion and by the men of science and conceive of the doctrines

[72] See, e.g., "The Reality of the Temporal," *International Journal of Ethics*, XX, 296 ff.

[73] See op. cit., pp. 44 ff., 265 ff.

[74] See *The Grammar of Science*, pp. 23, 86 f.; cf. Ostwald, *Natural Philosophy*, pp. 28, 31; Poincaré, *The Foundations of Science*, pp. 340 f.

both of science and of theology as working hypotheses, which we acquire through the process of experimentation, for the achievement of the higher values of life.[75] In thus conceiving the work of science and theology in relation to the interests of human life there is suggested a tentative relation between them, namely, the relation of co-operative activity in the interest of promoting the development of man in his struggle for existence. The whole realm of existence, then, will be open to science for investigation,[76] so that it may go on with its work of observation, description, classification, explanation of the processes of nature, of human society, and of our psychological phenomena in order to have control over them in the behalf of man; while theology is to proceed with its task, aided by the results of scientific investigation in various fields, of interpreting particularly religious phenomena and of formulating concepts, doctrines, hypotheses of the objects of religion which will best further, in a given age, its ideal ends. Such a theory of the relation of theology and science seems to be the implication of the result of our study in so far as this relation is concerned.

Thirdly, let us look at the problem of God as the supernatural personality. Royce, as has been observed, has completely abandoned the Kantian things-in-themselves and conceives of God in terms of immanent idealism. For him there is no other world than the world of thought and will, and God is organically bound up with such a world. Eucken cannot indorse the view of God as belonging to a supernatural world and as coming to us by means of miraculous donation. God is considered by him to be the very basis of all existence, in spite of the appearances to the contrary.

The significance of this result for theology may be stated as follows: that, to be in line with and represent helpfully the evolutionary view of the world, theology must abandon its traditional way of conceiving God in terms of dualistic supernaturalism and must think of him as immanently active in the world of nature and of man. But orthodox theologians generally decline to carry out this implication; they refuse to view God in terms of dynamic immanence; and they are not wholly willing to surrender the supernatural transcendence of God in the traditional sense of the word. The underlying reason for the disinclination to conceive God completely in dynamic relations with the world is twofold: theologians have not, on the one hand, acquired scientific confidence in the normal evolutionary activities of the immanent forces in the world;

[75] See Ames, "Theology from the Standpoint of Functional Psychology," *American Journal of Theology*, X, 219–32; *The Psychology of Religious Experience*, chap. xvi; I. King, *The Development of Religion*, chap. xiii.

[76] Pearson, op. cit., p. 24.

and, on the other hand, they desire to preserve the supernatural character of their religion. This attitude is expressed by orthodoxy in its affirmation of the Scripture as the supernatural revelation of God, of the incarnation of Jesus as the miraculous intervention into the course of history, of salvation as the supernatural act of the Holy Spirit – in fact, the whole system of orthodoxy is based upon specific supernatural acts of God interposed into the course of nature and of human history.[77]

A suggestion toward an immanent conception of God's relation to the world is given by G. A. Gordon in his book *Religion and Miracles*, where he points out that religion does not stand or fall with the fate of miracles.[78] Thus to conceive of God in terms of dynamic immanence and to have confidence in his normal activities in the world would, indeed, be in accord with the evolutionary theory which eliminates the miraculous from the organic realm[79] and would be also working out the implication of the result of our study on the problem of God as the supernatural personality.

Fourthly, we come to the problem of God as the absolute being. This is the most critical problem of our investigation. For it immediately opens up the question of absoluteness and finality versus finitude and relativity in matters of religion and ethics. The evolutionary theory stands for the relative and finite view of all reality. God, from this evolutionary view of the world, is to be conceived in terms of change and growth, the essential characteristics of the living world with which he is vitally related. Traditional theology, on the contrary, contends for the system of absoluteness and finality in religion and ethics. This contention of traditional theology is a direct consequence of its view of God as the eternally complete and perfect being of the world. With respect to the problem which arises in view of the antithesis involved in the two systems, Royce presents God as the All-inclusive, Absolute Being of the universe, free from the temporal aspects of our experience. Yet we found that Royce attributes to God such characteristics of our evolutionary experience as suffering, striving, satisfaction. Hence God, at least when viewed from our finite point of view, is involved in the process of change and growth, so is a finite being, although he is held to

[77] See William and Scannell, *A Manual of Catholic Theology*, Vols. I, II; Hodge, op. cit., I, 151 ff., 617 ff.; II, 378 ff., 675 ff., Shedd, op. cit., I, 61 ff., 533 ff.; II, 261 ff., 353 ff.; etc.; cf. W. B. Greene, "The Supernatural," *Princeton Biblical and Theological Studies*, pp. 143 ff.; C. W. Hodge, "The Finality of the Christian Religion," ibid., pp. 452 ff.

[78] See especially pp. 7, 33, 82, 130, 165 ff.; and for a very suggestive contribution on this subject of God's relation to the world, see G. B. Smith, *Social Idealism and the Changing Theology*, especially chap. v.

[79] Weismann, op. cit., I, 6; cf. Pfleiderer, *Evolution and Theology*, p. 9.

be the Absolute Being, when viewed from an eternal point of view.[80] God, for Eucken, is the Absolute Spiritual Life, the independent basis of all temporal order. But from the standpoint of actual experience, we must view God in terms of our conflict, struggle, and activity. Thus God, according to Eucken, would be involved in the evolutionary features of human experience. Thus we may say that Royce and Eucken tend, in spite of their absolutistic positions, toward the conception of God in terms of evolutionary experience.

The implications of this tendency would be a full cognizance of the evolutionary and finite characteristics of the conception of God, which appear in Royce and Eucken and which are hard to unify with their absolutistic position. Theology should conceive God in terms of those qualities that are in accord with the results of empirical investigation of the world and particularly of human religious experience. In assuming this attitude toward the facts of the world and life, we should be led to a theory of reality positively involved in the processes of change, movement, development. In fact, one of the clearest indications of our immediate experience is the consciousness of the time-process, of history, of something done. Höffding points out that in view of the fact that our empirical world is not finished but that it always presents new experiences and riddles, we are unable to have a complete knowledge. He suggests the idea that this unfinishedness of our knowledge "may perhaps be connected with the fact that Being itself is not ready-made, but is still incomplete, and rather to be conceived as a continual becoming, like individual personality and like knowledge."[81] So far, then, as our scientific studies and our empirical experiences show, we ourselves and the realities with which we are related are characterized by change, incompleteness, unfinishedness, growth, development.[82]

Now a critical question is whether God can be conceived to be free from the process of evolution. We have observed that from the standpoint of our actual empirical experience, the philosophers of religion above consulted attribute to God in some measure the evolutionary features of human experience. This experiential mode of conceiving God, it would seem, should be made dominant, for it is not in accord with the empirical temper of our age to find reality outside of evolutionary experience and to define it other than in terms of such experience.[83] There may be a realm or realms in the universe where

[80] *The World and the Individual*, II, 133 ff.; "The Reality of the Temporal," *International Journal of Ethics*, XX, 270 f.; *The Philosophy of Loyalty*, pp. 394 f.

[81] *The Problems of Philosophy*, p. 120; cf. p. 136.

[82] See Schiller, *Studies in Humanism*, essay xix; cf. Moore, op. cit., pp. 37 f.

[83] See Ames, *The Psychology of Religious Experience*, pp. 26, 317 f.

change, unfinishedness, development are not found and where God may be exempt from time and history; but the world of our empirical science and experience and God as he is known in the experiences of the race are all marked by temporal features. Consequently, God should be conceived under the category, not of completeness and of immutability, but of becoming and of development.

This conception of God in terms of evolutionary experience, rather than under the category of some metaphysical absolute, is demanded by our religion and ethics. If by religion we mean pietistic contemplation, philosophic knowledge, or passive receptivity, then the conception of God as the absolute being, free from the finite aspects of our world and experience, may be satisfactory. But if religion means not merely faith in the conservation of values,[84] but also an effort of life to attain to its highest values in the world, then we must conceive of God, not only in terms of immanence, but primarily as vitally and actively related with us in the achievement of the values of religion.[85] The God demanded by practical religion must be a being who really shares in our struggles, conflicts, failures, successes, victories. Such a God, as James suggests, has really been the God of the Hebrew and Christian religions. Practical religion demands, not the Absolute who includes all beings by his all-embracing knowledge, nor the Absolute who is completely independent of the world of his creation, but a God who really hears our prayers and who is actually co-operating with us to realize the aims and values of human life. Moreover, from the point of view of our ethics, we need such a conception of God. The futility of the traditional view of God as the absolute being who has determined the course of the world and of human history in accordance with his eternal plan becomes self-evident when we see that our moral life demands that it ought to and really can change the character of our moral universe. Höffding remarks thus on this point: "If Being were finished, harmoniously and unchangeably, Ethics would be impossible. All Ethics demands that there be effort. But there would be no room for effort, if everything were in eternal and actual completeness."[86] Thus both religion and ethics call for a view of God, not as an absolute, but as a relative being, actually interrelated with us in our religious and moral life.

But thus to bring relativity and becoming into the very being of God means, of course, that we must abandon that absolute ground of religious and ethical assurance which is believed to be given to us by

[84] Höffding, *The Philosophy of Religion*, pp. 9 ff., 215 ff.

[85] Cf. G. B. Foster, *The Function of Religion*, pp. 173–83.

[86] *The Problems of Philosophy*, p. 151; cf. pp. 158 ff.; Schiller, op. cit., essay xviii on "Freedom."

traditional conceptions of God as the absolute controller of the world and human life. An evolving God does not guarantee beforehand the ultimate success of our moral universe.[87] But as a matter of fact the most staunch believers in the traditional view of God must admit that the absolute certainty as to their salvation is not a question of fact but of faith; they are to be religious and ethical in the hope that they may be saved. This uncertainty as to final victory will not necessarily lead us to pessimism and inactivity. For we are so constituted that even when we are thus uncertain of our ultimate success, we work so much the harder, hoping that we may, with God's help, bring the world to a happy issue. God, then, from the standpoint of practical religion and ethics, may be conceived of as that great environing reality of the growing universe, who is ever responsive to the calls of our need, who represents our highest ethico-religious ideals and values, and who is constantly working with us for the achievement of these ideals and values. At any rate, such seems to be the theological implication of our study as to the problem of God as the absolute being.

And, fifthly, the problem of God's relation to man and the world calls for a brief comment. It has been partly discussed in the consideration of the preceding two problems. To begin with the problem of the relation of God and man, we observe that the philosophers, whom we have considered, differ on this point from the standpoint of their philosophies, yet in the main agree from that of empiricism. Royce's absolute idealism would reduce man to the plane of complete dependence on an all-inclusive being of the world, yet Royce, moved by his moral experience, contends for the ethical selfhood of man. Eucken is not interested in finding out the exact ontological relation of God and man; his interest is primarily a practical one: How can man be saved from the forces of this antagonistic world? His answer is that it is God who is the fundamental presupposition of man's salvation. Yet this salvation is not a matter of donation; man must achieve it through struggle and work. Thus Eucken assumes the dignity and power of man.

This suggests that the primary concern of theology should be to conceive the relation between God and man on the basis of the facts disclosed by experience. Theology, working from this standpoint, will be aided by such sciences as anthropology, biology, sociology, psychology, the history of religions, and the like. In studying the results of such sciences and in consulting the experiences of actual men and women, we discover their sense of dependence on, and independence of, the environing world. Man as we find him is conscious of his dependence on his social as well as his physical environment. But this consciousness of

[87] Cf. McTaggart, *Some Dogmas of Religion*, pp. 259 f.

man's dependence on his environment is not all of his experience; he often finds himself superior to his natural environment, and while he feels himself closely bound up with his social environment, he refuses to surrender the sense of his own initiative and responsibility. Theology must take account, not merely of the consciousness of man's dependence on, but of his independence of, his environment, so that it may not define his relation to God wholly in terms of receptivity but perhaps primarily in terms of co-operative activity directed toward the establishment of a society of love and righteousness. In thus conceiving the relation of God and man, we are enabled to meet the view demanded by the evolutionary theory which, as we have seen, holds that the forces making the evolution of life possible are resident in the organisms and in their environment.

To speak now of the problem of God's relation to the world, we must frankly admit that we cannot, so far as we know, give answer either to the question concerning the beginnings of the world or to that concerning its present ontological relation to God. The theory of cosmic evolution traces the development of our world to small beginnings, and the doctrine of organic evolution conceives life as arising from some protoplasmic germs; but we do not know, as James says, the whence and how of the world – they are matters, as yet, of speculation. Meanwhile, what religion wishes to ascertain is whether God is now in some way related with the process of the world. This raises at once the question of teleology and of evil.

With regard to these questions, Royce, as we have seen, considers the world of nature as embodying, though in a partial manner, the will of God; and affirms, at least, the temporal reality of the evils in the world. Eucken could not tolerate the idea that nature as such is the cause of human evolution; for him God must be working in the process of nature for the production of man. As to the problem of evil, he admits its reality, but confesses its insolubility. Thus, the tendency of thought is to hold that there is some purpose discoverable in the evolutionary process of the world and to assume a practical attitude toward the problem of evil.

That there is some limited purpose in the world-process is admitted by many evolutionists. Lamarck, Darwin, Bergson would hold that higher forms of life are produced through the evolutionary process.[88]

Moreover, that there are evils in the world is admitted by all the evolutionists, though opinions differ as to the explanation of evil. One may conjecture that God is a limited being and hence he is unable to

[88] Cf. Baldwin, *Darwin and the Humanities*, pp. 81 ff.; Moore, *Pragmatism and Its Critics*, pp. 257 ff.; Hobhouse, *Development and Purpose*, pp. xxvi ff., 367, 371 f.

control the world without involving it in evils. Or one may say that the elements in the world are not yet harmonized, hence the presence of evil.[89] This is indeed a dark problem. Theology must deal with it wisely and critically. But from the standpoint of practical religion and ethics, it seems sufficient to say, in view of our inability as yet to give a satisfactory explanation of God's relation to the evils in the world, that what is demanded of us is to recognize their existence and to struggle and work with God in opposition to the evils in us and in the world in order to create a world of love and righteousness.

We have been concerned in this study to show that men like Royce and Eucken who do not profess to stand philosophically for empirical evolutionary method and theory nevertheless employ many elements derivable in and through experience and make certain affirmations concerning God on the basis of these empirical elements. The theological implication of our study is that in order to be in harmony with the empirical temper of our age, theology is called upon to follow the inductive method demanded by the evolutionary theory and to formulate its conception of God on the basis of the facts ascertainable, particularly, in the field of religion and ethics. This, in short, seems to be the bearing of evolutionary theory on the conception of God; and the typical recent philosophies of religion which we have examined give fruitful suggestions for the theologian who desires to grapple seriously with the problems raised by the doctrine of evolution and to construct a tenable conception of God in an age of evolutionary science.

[89] So Hobhouse, op. cit., p. 368; cf. Höffding, *The Problems of Philosophy*, pp. 136, 150, 158 ff., 173 f.

# JOSIAH ROYCE – A PERSONAL IMPRESSION

This essay was read at a meeting in commemoration of Josiah Royce held at the University of Chicago, November 22, 1916 and later published in George Herbert Mead, "Josiah Royce – A Personal Impression," *International Journal of Ethics*, vol. 28 (1917).

My own response to Professor Royce in 1887–88 may, I think, be regarded as fairly typical of his appeal to many of the young men and women who found themselves caught in the speculative problem of the time. That problem had been fashioned in theology. Even those who were outside the churches had in the back of their minds the fundamental assumptions of the philosophy of the church: that the world was ordered by some personal purpose whose result was assured, while the successful results of the lives of individual men and women depended largely upon their willingness to fit into this rational moral purpose – that this purpose was bound in some way to realize the fullest development of their individual thought, culture, and character. The problems that intrigued us were still largely speculative. The social questions had not as yet become insistent, nor were we caught as yet in scientific implications of these later years. We wished to be free to follow our individual thinking and feeling into an intelligent and sympathetic world without having to bow before incomprehensible dogma or to anticipate the shipwreck of our individual ends and values. We wanted full intellectual freedom and yet the conservation of the values for which had stood Church, State, Science, and Art. We came out of a narrow Scottish intuitional philosophy, that crystalized problems into dogmas, and paralysed thought; out of a puritan conception of life that standardized conduct by self-denials both passional and economic, and yet found in the business and social success which the community approved a sort of guarantee of rightness with God and His universe. Emerson had represented for us a mood rather than a method, and only irritated our thirst for a doctrine which would let us think without barriers and still do God's service in a world of moral order.

We had the docile attitude of those who had received their culture and science from abroad, and out of whose democratic achievements had arisen no thought or act that could measure up to those of Europe. Politically we might think ourselves the leaders of the world. Those who thought and read and travelled made no pretensions of our having expressed the meaning of life either in lasting aesthetic or philosophic forms. To youths of such minds and attitudes Professor Royce opened up the realm of romantic idealism. What had been barriers of thought became but hazards in the game. Contradictions, instead of marking the no thoroughfares of reflection, became the guide posts toward higher levels of reality. To have achieved the dialectic was to have won a liberty that not only needed no eternal vigilance to insure its security, but even found in any threatened restraint only wider fields within which to range. And yet this intoxicating doctrine proved the reality of God by the very notion of error. Out of it blossomed a forever waxing individuality, higher spiritual orders of church and state, and a true infinity that was the heritage of anyone who could think – *à la* Hegel.

And then this came not only in the form of philosophy; it was embalmed also in culture – and puritan America took over in the form of culture what it would never have tolerated in life and conduct, much as one delights in the insects which have been incased in yellow amber. There should be a special edition of the *Spirit of Modern Philosophy* bound in tooled morocco with illuminated borders and initialed paragraphs and illustrated with preRaphaelite art – to symbolize what it meant to young men when Royce first taught in Cambridge.

The predominant impression he left upon me was of clear ideas and luminous vistas, of subtle athleticism of thought, and an inexhaustible universe of explication and illustration. Philosophy was no longer the handmaid of theology nor the textbook for a formal logic and a puritan ethics. The bodily reality of the world was of the texture of thought – and if anywhere this idealistic doctrine has been achieved it was in the audience of Josiah Royce.

He was no jealous occupant of the platform. He delighted in the thinking and expression of others. The generosity of his appreciation left a warmth behind that inevitably grew into an affection that went with the admiration which the operation of his powerful brain always inspired, while the keenness of his questions detected inaccuracies and pricked the bubbles of spurious conceptions.

I could follow his courses, unfortunately, only through one term and part of another, for a physical breakdown took him away during the winter. But I received an impression from him of freedom of mind, and of dominance of thought in the universe, of a clear unclouded landscape of spiritual reality where we sat like gods together – but not careless of mankind – and it was a vision that followed me for many years.

# INDEX